Creative Instructional Methods for
- **Family & Consumer Sciences**
- **Nutrition & Wellness**

Valerie M. Chamberlain, Ph.D.
University of Vermont

Merrilyn N. Cummings, Ph.D., CFCS
New Mexico State University

Glencoe McGraw-Hill

New York, New York   Columbus, Ohio   Chicago, Illinois   Peoria, Illinois   Woodland Hills, California

The authors wish to express special appreciation to:

Adela Castro, New Mexico State University, for keyboarding manuscript.

The staff at the Career Center of the University of Vermont for their help with career and employment information.

Dr. Carolyn Douglas Henderson for the Student Assumption of Responsibility Scale.

New Mexico State University for a sabbatical leave that provided Merrilyn Cummings time to work on this book.

Glencoe/McGraw-Hill

A Division of The McGraw·Hill Companies

Send all inquiries to:
Glencoe/McGraw-Hill
3008 W. Willow Knolls Drive
Peoria, IL 61615-1083

ISBN 0-07-822616-3

Printed in the United States of America

3 4 5 6 7 009 12 11 10 09 08

Valerie M. Chamberlain is a Professor of Family and Consumer Sciences Education and Nutrition Education at the University of Vermont. She has taught at both the high school and university levels, including 6 years at Florida State University and 15 years at Texas Tech University before returning to the University of Vermont where she earned her Bachelor's degree. She earned both her Masters and Doctorate degrees at Florida State University.

Dr. Chamberlain's teaching expertise and service to the profession have been recognized with many honors and awards. She was named Author of the Year in 1985 by the American Home Economics Association and given a Leader Award by the Association in 1990. She was named an honorary member of the Family, Community and Career Leaders of America (FCCLA) in 2000.

In addition to her teaching excellence, Dr. Chamberlain is a prolific writer. She has been an author on 10 textbook programs and has written over 135 articles for scholarly and professional publications. She has given presentations, workshops, and classes in many states and been involved in professional research. She is known for her dedication to improving teaching skills.

Merrilyn N. Cummings is a Professor of Family and Consumer Sciences Education at New Mexico State University where she has taught for 18 years, serving as Department Head for three of those years. Prior to that, she taught 10 years at Texas Tech University.

After earning her Bachelor of Science degree in Home Economics Education at the University of Connecticut, Dr. Cummings taught middle school Home Economics. She then earned her Masters and Doctoral degrees in Home Economics Education at Cornell University.

Dr. Cummings has received several Outstanding Teaching Awards. She was named an American Home Economics Association Leader in 1988 and New Mexico Home Economist of the Year in 1992. She has held many local, state, and national leadership roles, including a term on the National Board of Directors of Family, Career and Community Leaders of America (FCCLA). In 1995 she was inducted into the New Mexico FHA/HERO Hall of Fame.

One of Dr. Cummings' key roles has been mentoring new professionals in the field. In addition to her teaching, she conducts research, has published extensively, and consults with school districts to improve teaching effectiveness.

CONTRIBUTING AUTHORS

Paul Buzzell, M.S.
Information Systems Specialist
Nutrition and Food Sciences
University of Vermont

Ginny Felstehausen, Ph.D.
Professor
Family & Consumer Sciences Education
Texas Tech University

Mary Helen Mays, Ph.D. MPH, MBA, RD/LD
Interim Director
Program and Grants Administration
Community Voices, El Paso, Texas

Sandra W. Miller, Ph.D.
Professor Emeritus,
Family & Consumer Sciences Education
University of Kentucky

Susan D. McLaughlin, M.P.A., CPP-R
Program Coordinator,
The Connecticut Council on Problem Gambling

Stephen J. Pintauro, Ph.D.
Associate Professor
Nutrition and Food Sciences
University of Vermont

Marilyn Swierk, CFCS, CFLE
President, MS Innovations
AAFCS Chair, Elementary, Secondary, and
  Adult Education
Wickford, Rhode Island

Ruth G. Thomas, Ph.D.
Professor
Family Education
University of Minnesota

Deborah Tippett, Ph.D., CFCS
Head and Professor
Human Environmental Sciences
Meredith College

Charlotte Tulloch, Ed.D.
Teacher Educator
Special Populations
University of Kentucky

Helen M. Ballard, M.S., CFCS
Special Programs Coordinator
Child Nutrition Programs
Vermont Department of
  Education

Mary Ann Block, Ph.D.
Professor
Human Sciences
Tarleton State University

Weslyn Browning, M.S., CFCS
Culinary Arts Instructor
Lovington High School
Lovington, NM

Sue Couch, Ed.D.
Professor
Family and Consumer Sciences
  Education
Texas Tech University

Kathy C. Croxall, Ph.D.
Assistant Professor
Family and Consumer Sciences
Southern Utah University

Roberta Larson Duyff, M.S., RD, CFCS
Food and Nutrition Consultant
President, Duyff Associates
St. Louis, MO

Lillie Beasley Glover, Ph.D., CFCS
Professor
Family and Consumer Sciences
South Carolina State University

Lela G. Goar, M.S.
New Mexico FCCLA State Adviser
Eastern New Mexico University

Martina Green, M.Ed.
Curriculum Developer
College of Medicine
University of Vermont

Bonnie Greenwood, Ph.D., CFCS
Associate Dean for Academic
  Affairs
Associate Professor, Family and
  Consumer Sciences Education
Florida State University

Mary Harlan, Ed.D.
Professor and Chair
Dept. of Family and Consumer
  Sciences
University of Central Arkansas

Barbara A. Holt, Ph.D.
Clark County Agent, Family and
  Consumer Science
Cooperative Extension Services
University of Arkansas

Sonja D. Koukel, M.S.
Curriculum Specialist
Curriculum Center for FCS
Texas Tech University

Cathleen T. Love, Ph.D.
Associate Vice Provost
Penn State University

Brenda Barrington Mendiola, M.S.
Curriculum Director
Irion County I.S.D.
Mertzon, Texas

Cheryl A. Mimbs, Ph.D.
Assistant Professor
Family and Consumer Sciences
  Education
Southwest Missouri State
  University

Teresa Muskopf, M.S., M.Ed., C.H.E.S.
Professor
Family and Consumer Sciences
Framingham State College

Lora Ann Neill, Ph.D., CFCS
Assistant Professor
Department of Family Sciences
Texas Women's University

Elizabeth A. Odell, M.F.T.
Associate Consultant
Family and Consumer Sciences
Connecticut Dept. of Education

Ruth Pestle, Ph.D.
Emerita Professor
Family and Consumer Sciences
  Education
Florida State University

Bonnie Rader, Ed.D.
Professor
Family and Consumer Sciences
California State University,
  Long Beach

Marianna Y. Rasco, Ph.D., CFLE
Professor and Chair
Dept. of Family and Consumer
  Sciences
Abilene Christian University

Sue Reichelt, Ph.D.
Assistant Professor
Family and Consumer Sciences
  Education
Texas Tech University

Virginia Richards, Ed.D., CFCS
Assistant Dean
College of Health and
  Professional Studies
Georgia Southern University

Marilyn Swierk, CFCS, CFLE
President, MS Innovations
AAFCS Chair, Elementary,
  Secondary, and Adult
  Education
Wickford, Rhode Island

Deborah Tippett, Ph.D., CFCS
Professor and Head
Dept. of Human Environmental
  Sciences
Meredith College

Margaret Torrie, Ed.D., CFCS
Associate Professor
College of Family and
  Consumer Sciences
Iowa State University

Janis B. Van Buren, Ph.D., CFCS
Professor and Human Sciences
  Chair
Texas A&M University—
  Kingsville

Janice R. Wissman, Ed.D., CFCS
Associate Dean
College of Education
Kansas State University

TABLE OF CONTENTS

Chapter 1

You as an Educator

You plan to be an educator in the future. Have you stopped to think that you are one now? On an informal basis, you probably already provide information to others about many topics, including those related to your course of study. People may seek your advice about a popular diet, the value of a certain type of exercise, child health concerns, managing resources, balancing work and family, or other topics.

Parents, too, are continuously educating their children. These usually aren't planned teaching sessions, but they occur and are important nonetheless. That's the distinction in informal education. The teaching and learning are unplanned. Often, the teaching is also unintentional. Think about the way teens' attitudes and behavior are influenced by those they try to emulate. As an educator, you, too, will be a role model, even when you aren't in your teaching role.

While almost everyone is an informal teacher, your career will involve educating others in a more planned way. This teaching may occur in a great variety of settings, from a traditional classroom, to a distance education course, or even through a social service agency.

This chapter sets the stage for the rest of the book. In the remaining chapters, you will learn more about teaching opportunities in Family and Consumer Sciences, Nutrition, Health and Wellness, and other fields. You will also explore the varied work settings for educators, personal traits of effective teachers, and what it means to be a professional.

Formal vs. Nonformal Education

When you think about formal education, you probably think of schools, yet formal education may not be "formal" in the usual sense of the word. It doesn't have to be lecture-based or teacher-oriented. It does not follow one form, structure, or model, nor is it stiff and rigid. Instead, *formal education* refers to teaching and learning found in educational institutions like schools, universities, technical centers, and early childhood programs. In formal education, you usually progress from one grade, course, or school to another in a planned sequence. Upon completion of a planned program, you may be rewarded with a certificate, diploma, license, or degree.

Nonformal education programs are often facilitated by professionals, but the learners tend to come and go. There is less likely to be a definite ending point than in formal education programs. For example, self-help seminars, in-service training, and nutrition counseling programs are usually nonformal.

While you probably have a specific career goal in mind, during your professional life, you may well teach in both formal and non-formal settings. The chapters that follow present information that's applicable to both types, and examples of both are included. Throughout, you will be adapting knowledge, skills, and ideas to fit your intended career. That's important, but also use this opportunity to implement them in other situations as well.

 # Family and Consumer Sciences

Family and Consumer Sciences (FCS or FACS) is the umbrella discipline for programs with a similar foundation. At the middle school level, courses might be called "Life Skills." At the university level, programs have many titles. Graduates of family and consumer sciences programs have many career opportunities that range from the well known to the uncommon. Some take Family and Consumer Sciences Education (FCSE) programs to prepare for a teaching career. Others become specialists in specific content areas and work for business, industry, government, or as entrepreneurs. However, professionals in both groups are typically involved in teaching, whether in formal or nonformal situations. These range from being a preschool teacher to working as a credit counselor, a culinary arts instructor, with teen parents, or as an interior design professor at a university. In spite of this diversity, all areas in FCS are connected by their unique focus on improving the lives of individuals, families, and communities.

Family and consumer sciences professionals use their interdisciplinary background to teach resource management and problem solving. Whenever possible, their approaches are proactive, helping people live as fully and as well as possible. This proactive approach is less expensive than the personal, social, and financial costs of crisis intervention and remediation of serious problems. However, FCS professionals help in these areas as well, dealing with problems such as child abuse, malnutrition, and bankruptcy.

✳ Formal Family and Consumer Sciences Education

Family and Consumer Sciences is taught formally as a discipline in elementary schools, middle schools, high schools, technical centers, community colleges, and universities. States require teachers in elementary through secondary schools to have educational certification. This usually requires completion of a course of study in education and passing a competency test. Institutions above the secondary level set their own requirements.

Decisions about what is taught in FCS-related classes for grades K-12 are generally made at the state or local level. However, the National Association of State Administrators for Family & Consumer Sciences (NASAFACS) initiated a project to develop a national standards document to help those making curriculum decisions. The *National Standards for Family and Consumer Sciences Education* were published in 1998. The standards emphasize process skills—particularly higher-level thinking, communication, leadership, and management—that lead learners to various types of action.

The document divides Family and Consumer Sciences into sixteen areas of study. Content standards were developed for each area, along with corresponding competencies, academic proficiencies, and process questions. The sixteen areas are:

- Career, Community, and Family Connections
- Consumer and Family Resources
- Consumer Services
- Early Childhood, Education, and Services
- Facilities Management and Maintenance
- Family
- Family and Community Services

- Food Production and Services
- Food Science, Dietetics, and Nutrition
- Hospitality, Tourism, and Recreation
- Housing, Interiors, and Furnishings
- Human Development
- Interpersonal Relationships
- Nutrition and Wellness
- Parenting
- Textiles and Apparel

The national standards provide a resource and coherent vision for FCS programs, but don't dictate what will be taught. Some content areas within Family and Consumer Sciences, such as early childhood education, have developed their own standards leading to official certification. The national standards supplement these.

✳ Nonformal Family and Consumer Sciences Education

The flexibility inherent in Family and Consumer Sciences Education (FCSE) can open doors to many more careers than traditional teaching in a school. It may also lead to positions with Cooperative Extension or with a state Dairy and Food Council program, textbook company, trade association, curriculum center, or producer of teaching media. FCSE graduates work in management training programs, develop teaching and promotional materials for companies, and conduct cooking schools. Others participate in service programs in this country and overseas. State Departments of Education employ FCSE graduates in supervisory and consulting roles and to oversee nutrition education programs. Newspapers and magazines provide opportunities for FCSE majors with writing expertise. Graduates are sometimes employed as professionals in programs such as scouting and Big Brothers/Big Sisters.

Some nonformal education programs, such as Cooperative Extension, service organizations, and community-based outreach programs, also hire college graduates who have majored in noneducation areas of Family and Consumer Sciences. Whether you are in an education program or not, this book can help you prepare for a role as an educator in nontraditional settings.

 # Nutrition

Nutrition is often taught in schools as part of Family and Consumer Sciences education. However, nutrition education is also widely taught outside of school classrooms. Its importance stems from nutrition's vital role in promoting good health and alleviating many health conditions.

Some people who convey nutrition information are called *nutritionists*. However, that term has no standardized definition. A person who uses that title might work in a health food store or counsel clients in a fitness center. The individual may or may not have earned a degree with a major in nutrition. There is no specific credential identified with being a nutritionist.

In contrast, a *registered dietitian* (RD) is certified as a specialist in the science of nutrition. An RD has completed at least the minimum of a bachelor's degree in a program approved by the Commission on Accreditation for Dietetics Education of the American Dietetics Association. A supervised work experience or an internship is required, along with passing a national registry examination.

Registered dietitians work in hospitals and other health care facilities educating patients about nutrition and administering medical nutrition therapy. RDs may also manage food service operations in these settings, as well as in other facilities. In that capacity, they may supervise everything from purchasing to food preparation to paraprofessional staff. (*Paraprofessionals* are aides trained to work with professionals.) Registered dietitians are also employed in sports nutrition and corporate wellness programs, product development, nursing homes, and food-and-nutrition-related businesses. Some are in private practice, while others are engaged in community nutrition education programs. Whatever the setting, the goal of registered dietitians is to improve the public's quality of life through healthful eating habits.

Health and Wellness Education

Quality of life is closely tied to health. That's why health and wellness educators are needed in so many settings, both formal and nonformal. As with Family and Consumer Sciences, national standards have been developed for school health education. Content is divided into these areas:

- Community Health
- Consumer Health
- Environmental Health
- Family Life
- Mental and Emotional Health
- Injury Prevention and Safety
- Nutrition
- Personal Health
- Prevention and Control of Disease
- Substance Use and Abuse

These content areas also indicate some of the arenas in which nonformal education takes place. For example, a health professional might work for the American Red Cross teaching disaster preparedness. Another, with additional counseling training, might be part of a smoking prevention program aimed at teens. What additional possible positions related to nonformal health and wellness education can you identify?

Cooperative Extension System

Every state has a Cooperative Extension System that provides a two-way link between its land grant university and the people of that state. Research-based information from these universities, the United States Department of Agriculture (USDA), national research institutions, and industry is brought to citizens in practical forms. Based on their work with state residents, Extension employees bring people's real-life concerns and questions to the university for possible research.

Educational strategies used in Extension include community-based programs, workshops, seminars, demonstrations, TV and radio programs, newsletters, newspaper articles, and other publications. Information is also provided through hotlines, toll-free numbers, websites, and interactive television networks.

These approaches are implemented by state specialists with expertise in areas as diverse as family wellness and resource management, as well as topics related to agriculture. Specialists coordinate and implement programs at state and regional levels and keep county Extension agents updated in their content areas. Generalists are also employed at local, county, and/or regional levels to coordinate programs on topics such as parenting, food safety, wellness, and youth development. Extension professionals also train volunteers who take on active roles in educational programs.

✳ 4-H

The youth leadership development component of the Cooperative Extension System is called 4-H. It is the largest out-of-school, nonformal, youth education program in the world. Members are ages 9 to 19. At local, county, or regional levels, Extension agents coordinate volunteers who organize local 4-H clubs. The goal is to help people improve their lives through educational processes that use scientific knowledge focused on contemporary issues and identified needs. Programs provide opportunities for goal setting, decision making, and group building.

✳ Expanded Food and Nutrition Education Program

Cooperative Extension agencies run the Expanded Food and Nutrition Education Program (EFNEP). Its objectives are to assist families and youth with limited resources in acquiring the knowledge, skills, attitudes, and behavior changes necessary for nutritionally sound diets. Extension professionals train and supervise paraprofessionals and volunteers who teach food and nutrition information and skills to clients in their homes and in small groups.

EFNEP shapes its program to meet individual families' needs. Choosing more nutritious foods and stretching food dollars are examples of EFNEP lessons.

✳ WIC

The Special Supplemental Food Program for Women, Infants, and Children, known as WIC, is a federally funded program. It provides nutrition education, health and nutrition screening, breastfeeding information, and an individually prescribed package of nutritious foods to a targeted population. The program began when Congress determined that many pregnant, postpartum, and breastfeeding women plus infants and young children from families with inadequate income are at special risk.

The USDA works with state health departments and Indian tribal councils to deliver WIC assistance. Women, babies, and young children enter the program only if certified by a health care worker as having a nutrition-related problem.

WIC vouchers are not food stamps. (Many WIC participants are working mothers.) Rather, they are like a prescription for foods that increase iron, calcium, protein, and vitamins A and C in the diet. These "prescriptions" are based on the participant's individual nutritional needs. Extensive nutrition education takes place at WIC clinics. Women and children attend classes and receive educational materials when they pick up their vouchers.

 ## Service Programs

Although there are challenging aspects to working in a service program, the rewards are usually great. Every volunteer's experience is different, but most get enormous satisfaction from making a difference in the lives of people in need. Volunteers help people in poverty stricken areas of the U.S. and abroad. They teach how to grow and prepare healthful foods, ways to improve sanitation practices, procedures to eliminate diseases, and in general, to improve the quality of life for individuals and families.

✳ Peace Corps

The Peace Corps offers opportunities for volunteers in countries around the world. These volunteers provide help ranging from health education to community development projects. Peace Corps assignments are for two years, plus three months of training in the country of service. Peace Corps volunteers must meet certain education and work experience requirements. In addition, high priority is placed on flexibility, resourcefulness, work ethic, and commitment to service. Peace Corps volunteers aren't paid a salary, but they do receive a stipend to cover basic necessities, such as food, housing, and local transportation.

Returned Peace Corps volunteers may choose to put their foreign experience to work in the U.S. Skills developed overseas, such as cultural sensitivity and adaptability, are assets in this country, too. The Peace Corps Fellows Program involves a two-year commitment to work in a community while pursuing a master's degree. There are numerous university partnership programs in education that may be compatible with your career goals.

✳ AmeriCorps

AmeriCorps is a national service program that provides education awards in exchange for community service. The work that AmeriCorps members do is as varied as the members themselves. The following are some of their projects.

- Working with high school and middle school youth in community service activities
- Renovating low-income housing
- Assisting elders or people with disabilities
- Developing community-based health care programs

AmeriCorps members receive a modest living allowance and health coverage while participating in the program. After completing a year of service, they receive an education award that can be used to help pay off student loans or to finance college, graduate school, or vocational training.

The two primary AmeriCorps programs are Volunteers in Service to America (VISTA) and the National Civilian

Community Corps (NCCC). VISTA places individuals in disadvantaged communities to help residents become more self-sufficient. VISTA workers create programs that can continue after they complete their service. The top priority for AmeriCorps NCCC members is improving the environment.

✳ Teach for America

Teach for America is a program in which college graduates commit to teach two years in under-resourced urban and rural schools. Leadership ability, previous achievements, the ability to communicate in Spanish, and a commitment to educational excellence and equity are qualities desired in candidates.

Teach for America is designed to impact the lives of some of the nation's most disadvantaged youth. Consequently, corps members are placed in school districts with the greatest needs. College graduates who were not education majors are placed in communities that have alternate routes into teaching. As a result, districts hire corps members to teach students in grades K-12, paying them beginning teacher salaries and making assignments just as they would for any certified teacher. There is a strenuous summer education program for corps members before they begin teaching.

 ## Community Education Opportunities

The following ads appeared on the same day in a newspaper. The portions of the ads shown here illustrate the wide variety of opportunities that may be available when you have a background in education, as well as subject-matter expertise. Community education programs are usually nonformal in format. These ads show just a few of the types of educational positions available in business, industry, and government agencies.

Figure 1-1
EMPLOYMENT ADS CHART

WELLNESS CENTER COORDINATOR

If you can plan educational programs for a variety of ages and ability levels, supervise an employee child development center, and can manage schedules effectively, we have just the position for you. Classes for company employees include topics such as weight management, nutrition, fitness, parenting, and caring for aging parents. Responsibilities include scheduling classes, developing curriculum for adult and young child programs, and hiring child care workers.

EMPLOYEE DEVELOPMENT COORDINATOR

Company is seeking someone to oversee the implementation of employee development and training programs. The person we are seeking will report to the Vice President—Administrative Services. Must have excellent organizational, human resources, and communication skills, along with a solid understanding of education and training principles.

HEALTH PROGRAMS OUTREACH SPECIALIST

The Department of Health is seeking Health Programs Outreach Specialists for full/part-time positions in district offices statewide. Work entails outreach duties in conjunction with the delivery of community health promotion activities for Ladies First, Comprehensive Breast and Cervical Cancer Screening, and other health programs. Delivery of outreach activities may involve individual and group work in a variety of settings. Reliable, personal transportation is a must. Some evenings and weekends. Minimum Qualifications: Bachelor's degree, preferably in a health, education, or human services field.

Traits of Effective Educators

What makes an effective educator? You could make a quick list based on your own experiences. Successful educators have many of the same characteristics desired in parents, siblings, business people, service providers, health professionals, and human service employees.

Good communication skills are essential when interacting with learners, parents, clients, patients, coworkers, supervisors, and administrators. Educators use organizational skills daily to manage human and material resources, such as finances, facilities, time, and energy. Flexibility and a willingness to accept and try new ways of doing things are assets. Using helpful suggestions to improve competence, setting goals and being willing to work hard to achieve them, and good interpersonal relationships contribute to success in education, as well as all other fields.

Effective educators develop a philosophy congruent with their values. Most teachers value diversity, willingness to look at differing points of view, and concern for the dignity of their learners.

Strong educators know their subject matter well. When teachers feel secure in their knowledge of the subject matter, they are able to say, "I don't know" when stumped by a question. Those who are unsure of themselves sometimes bluff with an answer. That's the wrong thing to do. The solution is to be well prepared and knowledgeable about your content.

It's helpful to consider the question of traits from several points of view. When learners are asked what characteristics they most value in educators, responses like these are given:

caring	flexible
cheerful	good disposition
competent	kind
considerate	good listener
consistent	organized
cooperative	patient
creative	sense of humor
fair and impartial	well prepared

When professionals are asked what competencies an entry-level educator should have, they list many of the same characteristics mentioned by learners. In addition, professionals are likely to identify these characteristics:

- Dependable
- Self-directed
- Participates in continuing education
- Keeps up–to-date in the field
- Functions in the context of the big picture
- Fosters interdisciplinary approaches
- Uses language, oral and written, correctly
- Is culturally aware
- Communicates effectively with diverse learners
- Is accurate in presenting reliable, valid, and current research-based information
- Uses analytical and critical-thinking skills
- Uses available technology
- Encourages positive human relations
- Works as a team member
- Displays pride in identifying as an educator
- Makes decisions in a timely manner
- Meets deadlines
- Acts for the common good of the profession and the community
- Maintains a professional demeanor
- Practices ethical behaviors

A third way to look at effective educators is to identify the classroom behaviors that they exhibit. This approach is particularly helpful for new educators. "Behaviors Contributing to Teaching Effectiveness," *Figure 1-2* on page 13, gives an example. You could develop similar charts based on behaviors that exemplify other key traits.

Professionalism

Selling ability is a key to success in most professions, but true professionals emphasize the services they have to offer. Family and consumer sciences, Extension, and health and nutrition educators are all salespeople in a sense, but they serve in a primarily advisory capacity. Reference is often made to the bedside manner of the physician and the courtroom finesse of the lawyer. Educators' abilities to make consulting,

Figure 1-2

BEHAVIORS CONTRIBUTING TO TEACHING EFFECTIVENESS

BEHAVIORS	EVIDENCES
Helps build learners' self-esteem.	• Treats questions and imaginative ideas with respect by praising and building on learners' comments. • Shows learners their ideas have value by using them on bulletin boards, displays, and verbally in class. • Helps learners find answers to their own questions. • Teaches learners to praise themselves and others sincerely. • Has learners do things occasionally without concern about evaluation or grading. • Guides learners in setting goals and evaluating realistically. • Ties evaluation to causes and consequences. (What might happen if . . . ?)
Provides time and an environment for learning.	• Gives learners time to think. • Teaches at a pace appropriate to the content and learners. • Provides sufficient time for practice and laboratory activities. • Begins and ends class with consistent routines that provide security. • Starts with activities that create interest and motivate without threatening. • Ascertains level of understanding by asking appropriate questions. • Gives students hints and suggestions for how to remember material. • Repeats subject matter as needed using different approaches.
Provides examples and explanations.	• Gives examples that show how to solve problems and do classwork and homework. • Illustrates with examples that are relevant and meaningful. • Uses the chalkboard and transparencies to emphasize major points. • Describes work to be done and how to do it.
Organizes and reviews.	• Makes sure learners know what to do and how to do it. • Relates subject matter to material covered previously. • Helps learners understand how content will be useful to them now and/or in the future. • Prepares learners well for what they'll be doing next.

writing, educating, and/or advising relevant, exciting, and challenging are equally important to their success as professionals. Professionals contribute to their fields by developing new ideas, strategies, and materials to keep pace with changes in society and by sharing these with others.

✳ Professional Commitment

Have you heard someone refer to an individual's "professional attitude" or "professional commitment"? It isn't easy to explain professional commitment because it encompasses involvement and integration of certain goals and attitudes into an individual's total personality. However, there are a dozen identifiable characteristics that are associated with professionalism and professional conduct.

1. **Professionals render service and show concern for people.** As a professional, you really want to help and to serve others. You are concerned with what you can do for others and how you can do it best.

2. **Professionals don't require close supervision.** You direct yourself and can be depended upon to finish tasks. Self-discipline is a key factor in your success.

The professional doesn't have to be prodded by others. Although you can work independently, you don't hesitate to seek advice and help from others or to work cooperatively with them.

3. **Professionals assume responsibility for their behavior.** You are accountable for your mistakes and errors in judgment. You may seek counsel from others, but you don't transfer your responsibilities to them. You don't make excuses for yourself or get defensive. As a professional, you make your grievances known through the proper channels. You discuss them directly and privately with those in authority. Professionals don't take supplies for their own use or spend working hours on personal e-mail. Teaching materials bought or made with school or agency money are the property of the funding organization and should be left there if you leave. Many educators buy some of their own materials. These remain their personal property.

4. **Professionals don't expect to be paid by the hour.** You work to get the job done well without regard to the standard workweek or compensation for overtime. In fact, you may not regard yourself as an employee at all. You probably consider your administrators and supervisors as professional associates who have objectives and goals very similar to your own. Professional service can't be measured in hours. It is a fact, though, that professionals who demonstrate this principle are often those who advance to positions with the highest salaries.

5. **Professionals maintain good physical, emotional, and mental health.** This requires keeping a sense of humor and managing time efficiently. Professionals need to achieve a sense of balance between their family, personal, and professional lives. Many professionals lack this essential balance. They work so much that their family and social lives and own personal business affairs may be neglected. Sometimes it's better for an educator to get a good night's sleep than to stay up until 3:00 a.m. to refine a presentation. Use time on the job as productively as possible to minimize the need to take work home.

6. **Professionals continually look for ways to improve.** You take advantage of opportunities to increase your knowledge and understanding of your field and to keep informed about recent developments and legislation affecting the profession. A professional seeks and accepts advice and criticism objectively. Self-assessment is also an important aspect of improving your professional competency. To evaluate yourself, you might list your strengths and weaknesses as objectively as possible. You can then establish priorities and develop a plan of action for self-improvement.

7. **Professionals are loyal to colleagues and their employer.** You avoid rumor and refrain from gossiping about fellow workers or the people you serve. You ignore information heard through the grapevine. When necessary, you secure the facts by going directly to those who are authorized to release them. As an educator, you respect confidentiality. The welfare of your learners often requires that personal information remains private. However, there also may be instances when you will have to use great tact and delicate persuasiveness in convincing someone to share problems with others. For instance, if a student confides that she is pregnant, you may help her decide how to tell her parents or encourage her to see a doctor. Keep in mind that the services of another professional may be needed. Never attempt to assume responsibilities for which you aren't qualified.

8. **Professionals don't attempt to advance at the expense of others.** You strive for merit raises, promotions, and advancement on the basis of outstanding performance. However, you don't tear others down to build yourself up. If you hear students' derogatory comments about a coworker, you realize that nothing positive can be gained by listening to unfounded complaints. To engage in similar behavior yourself is highly unethical. The professional is considerate of the welfare of others.

9. **Professionals possess good communication and public relations skills.** This requires expressing ideas objectively, clearly, and concisely. When professionals have to say "no," they explain why. If educators have to say "no" to specific learning experiences or covering certain subjects suggested by the learners, they give reasons for their decisions. See Chapter 24 for additional information about public relations techniques.

10. **Professionals give others credit for their ideas and work.** You mention in an oral presentation the sources of your information and ideas. In written work, the source of information is acknowledged.

11. **Professionals meet commitments fully and on time.** You fulfill all agreements entered into with coworkers and those you serve, whether they're legal contracts or not. You also meet your obligation to use constructive criticism and helpful suggestions offered by supervisors and administrators.

12. **Professionals are proud of their work.** You reflect your pride and satisfaction in your profession to others. This may involve teaching people about your field and the subject matter it encompasses. Educators often have to work consistently, politely, and nondefensively with their administrators and legislators to explain their programs. Advisory councils, at both the local and state levels, offer unparalleled opportunities to publicize your program. Community members can also be involved through committee work and helping to plan and evaluate programs. Asking parents and community leaders to serve as resource people and guest speakers helps keep them informed.

 ## Creating a Positive Professional Image

The place to begin a positive image of your profession is with you. As an educator, you need to have a commitment to your profession. You may have to make a special effort to present a professional image to the public. This means not only knowing your subject matter, but presenting it with a professional demeanor. Personal appearance and actions are two means of interpreting the values of your educational program to others. Your grooming and attire convey to others that you take pride in yourself and your profession. Smiling and conversing sincerely and enthusiastically communicate a different self-concept than frowning, slouching, or being defensive.

When your professional image is in order, it is easier to gain community support. Getting involved in the community, professional organizations, and legislative matters helps others to get to know you. As people become acquainted with you, they will learn more about your profession.

There are a variety of ways to interpret your program to others. Consider a weekly or monthly newsletter containing information about different aspects of your profession, as well as items of local interest. It might be distributed to supervisors, administrators, business personnel, civic clubs, and other interested groups. Other possibilities are programs for community organizations that emphasize various aspects of your profession or a newspaper column with questions and answers about social issues that relate to your program. Teachers have additional channels of communication available: library displays, bulletin boards, showcases, assemblies, programs for parent-teacher associations, websites, radio and TV, and newspapers. The task of expanding and improving the image of your program needs to be a responsibility assumed by each individual in the profession.

Building Your Professional Portfolio

Career Opportunities. For Family and Consumer Sciences, Nutrition, or Health and Wellness, identify at least 10 possible work situations in which a professional would also be an educator. For each situation, identify the learners.

Interviews with Educators. Interview a professional in Family and Consumer Sciences, Nutrition, and/or Health and Wellness, each of whom is an educator in some way. Did the person initially plan to be an educator? What type of educational training does he or she have? What additional information or skills would have been helpful? Write a summary of your interview.

Job Shadowing. Spend parts of several days with a Cooperative Extension professional to experience the variety of activities and responsibilities involved. Write a summary of your experience. Which parts of this position would you feel confident handling? For those you would not, identify what you would need to do to develop the necessary skills.

Professionalism in Action. Write a one- to two-page description of someone you consider to be a true professional according to the criteria identified in this chapter. Include specific examples of this person's attitudes, behaviors, and work that show professionalism.

Chapter **2**

The Learners We Teach

Deborah Tippett, Ph.D. CFCS
Head and Professor, Human Environmental Sciences
Meredith College

Effective educators are dedicated to advancing the learning and well-being of all students. These accomplished professionals personalize their instruction by applying knowledge about human development to understand and meet their students' needs, interests, and abilities.

When you are preparing to teach, it is important to consider not only the needs, interests, and abilities of the learners, but also their preferences, learning styles, and the cultural and community influences on them. You can approach this critical task in a variety of ways, including learning about the developmental characteristics of various age groups, observation, and gathering information.

The purpose of this chapter is to describe the characteristics of various types of learners whom professionals in Family and Consumer Sciences, Nutrition, and Health/Wellness education are likely to teach and to recommend ways to use this information for teaching different age groups. Implications for curriculum and teaching strategies that are responsive to the developmental needs of the learners are included. This chapter focuses on the two most common age groups for educators in these subject areas—adolescent and adult learners. If you plan to work with other ages, use this chapter as a model for gathering similar information.

Adolescent Learners

Adolescence is a time when profound changes occur in physical, cognitive, socio-emotional, moral, and vocational development. Students must make critical life choices, including those related to topics such as drug use, sexual attraction, and the possibility of serious academic failure. Reports from task groups have called for programs that help early adolescents develop personal living skills to function effectively at home, at school, and in the community. Many of these reports also advocate the need for students to develop thinking skills that will help them cope in a rapidly changing, complex society.

Family and consumer sciences programs, in both formal and nonformal settings, can help adolescents develop personal living skills. Opportunities to teach early adolescents will typically be in middle schools, while those with older adolescents will be in high schools. Adolescence can be classified into early adolescence (ages 10-15) and older adolescence (ages 15-18).

We know that human development generally occurs in the same sequence, but timing varies according to the individual. A brief overview of the developmental characteristics of adolescents follows. Then suggestions are made regarding implications for content, environment, and developmentally appropriate practice. In planning curriculum for any age group, it is important to first understand the unique developmental needs of the learners and then to design curriculum and learning experiences that are responsive to their development.

❋ Physical Development

Early adolescence is marked by tremendous growth and physical variability among students. The growth rate in this period of life is second only to the first year of life. In the middle school classroom, you might see a great deal of variability in physical differences among students. On average, girls reach their growth spurt at age 12 and boys at age 14. Girls are more likely to be taller, heavier, and more physically mature than boys during this age period. Girls typically reach their physical and sexual maturity in high school, while boys may continue their physical development until age 20.

During this stage, many physical and hormonal changes occur. This may cause the adolescent to experience a great burst of energy, while at the same time school routine dictates that the student must sit quietly at a desk. Bones grow faster than muscles and students may go through stages of uncoordinated and awkward movements. As bones ossify, students may experience "growing pains," which make sitting still difficult. Many students feel embarrassed and overwhelmed by these dramatic physical changes.

Nutritional needs change for early adolescents. Their appetites increase due to their body growth and, consequently, their stomachs become larger. During growth spurts, adolescents may need more calories as their metabolism increases. Many adolescents have inadequate diets. Some don't get the proper nutrients; others become obese.

This is a time when adolescents are preoccupied with their appearance. Many adolescents spend much time worrying about their appearance and physical differences.

See *Figure 2-1* for the implications of the physical development of adolescents on curriculum development and teaching practices.

Figure 2-1

Adolescents' Physical Development: Educational Implications

- Give learners opportunities to move during the lesson. Encourage physical activity in selecting learning activities.
- Acknowledge the rapid rate and variability of adolescent growth in content areas such as nutrition, health, child development, and clothing. Discuss the influence of nutrition on health and appearance.

❋ Socio-Emotional Development

As early adolescents seem obsessed with their appearance and physical changes, they are also described as egocentric about their thoughts and feelings. They are intensely concerned about their own needs. Elkind (1967) labeled two emotional changes that influence this egocentric behavior as "imaginary audience" and "personal fable of uniqueness." Because many early adolescents are overly concerned with their appearance, they feel that everyone is looking at them and that they always have an audience. They will spend a great deal of time and energy on their appearance. The "personal fable of uniqueness" gives early adolescents the perception of possessing unique problems and feelings. Because they feel unique, they may feel invincible. This sometimes leads to risk-taking behaviors, such as drinking and unprotected sex. Young teens also may feel that common advisory information, such as nutritional guidelines, don't apply to them.

Adolescence is a time when students are seeking independence from their parents. However, families still have a great deal of influence on adolescents' values, future goals, and education. Peers influence decisions regarding social activities.

In early adolescence, same-sex friendships dominate. As learners mature, they become more comfortable with friends of both sexes. Young adolescents are apt to experience crushes on the opposite sex that can change quite frequently. They may be loyal and devoted one day to their new "love" and indifferent the next.

A major developmental task of the early adolescent is seeking identity. Self-concept drops during adolescence as students experience tremendous changes in their lives. They become less certain of who they are and how they view themselves. Older adolescents establish autonomy from their parents. They also evaluate the judgment of authority figures. Learners are seeking ways to know who they are and who they can become in the midst of the profound changes in their lives.

See *Figure* 2-2 for the implications of the socio-emotional development of adolescents on curriculum development and teaching practices.

Figure 2-2
Adolescents' Socio-Emotional Development: Educational Implications

- Plan activities that build on the antecedents of healthy self-esteem, such as competence and a sense of identity. Help students discover who they are and can become.

- Involve families in the learning experience. Acknowledge that different students have different family forms. Invite family members to participate in various activities, such as field trips, receptions, and projects.

- Treat all learners as capable and able by having high expectations. Set up experiences where learners can experience success. Recognize quality work and the accomplishments of students.

- Help students learn to get along with their families and peers. Plan lessons on making friends, communicating effectively, and resolving conflicts.

- Be responsive to diverse student groups. Learners will come from a variety of family structures and socioeconomic, racial, and ethnic groups.

❊ Cognitive Development

Just as there are great variations in physical and emotional development, there are group and individual differences in cognitive development. Piaget (1972) theorized that children ages 7-12 are in the concrete operations stage. They can form mental operations instead of having to physically manipulate objects. In early adolescence, learners are moving to formal operations where they shift from concrete thinking to abstract reasoning. In formal operations, the adolescent increases hypothetical reasoning skills, analytical abilities, and the capability to reason on the basis of symbols and principles.

Since most middle school learners are primarily concrete thinkers, it is important for educators to provide concrete learning experiences. Using active learning and promoting skills that solve real-life problems enhance the learning experiences for this age group. *Authentic learning* is a term that is used to describe learning utilizing real-life problems. As adolescents reach high school, teachers should give them additional opportunities to learn and use abstract reasoning skills.

If the shift from concrete to formal operations occurs, it generally happens in early adolescence, although not all people make this shift in cognitive development. This change allows adolescents to reflect on their own thinking process. Students may become more self-conscious as they grow more introspective. This contributes to the students' egocentric behavior, as well as to their ability to outgrow egocentrism. This cognitive shift also allows adolescents to consciously examine their values. Older adolescents are more likely to move toward critical consciousness where they not only reflect on their own thinking, but also ponder "Why do I think that?"

See *Figure* 2-3 on page 20 for the implications of the cognitive development of adolescents on curriculum development and teaching practices.

Figure 2-3
Adolescents' Cognitive Development: Educational Implications

- Incorporate hands-on learning where early adolescents can be actively engaged in the learning process.
- Use a variety of teaching techniques to accommodate different learning styles and abilities.
- Be responsive to diversity among learners. Help all individuals experience success.
- Give learners opportunities to develop critical-thinking skills to examine the alternatives of any type of action.

Figure 2-4
Adolescents' Moral Development: Educational Implications

- Utilize service learning projects through groups such as Future Career and Community Leaders of America (FCCLA) and 4-H to help students use course content to provide community service.
- Encourage students to improve their homes, schools, and communities. Assist learners in creating meaningful projects.
- Ask students to think about the consequences of their actions and the moral guidelines that influence those choices.

❊ Moral Development

Tied closely to cognitive development, Hillman (1991) has suggested that moral development shifts from the desire to do something good for someone else when there is a reward, to the desire to do good in order to maintain good relations. As thinking expands for adolescents, they see many solutions to complex problems in idealistic terms. Middle school learners are often intensely idealistic because they see all the possibilities and none of the obstacles. This age group is genuinely interested in helping others through service learning projects. Adolescents become more concerned for what is "right" and demonstrate concern for those less fortunate.

See *Figure 2-4* for the implications of the moral development of adolescents on curriculum development and teaching practices.

❊ Vocational Development

Adolescents become aware of their career potential, develop job skills, experience employment opportunities, and develop a career plan for their future. In middle grades, students explore career opportunities and begin to identify their skills, interests, aptitudes, and abilities. High school students formulate realistic career plans for their future. They make decisions about postsecondary education and career paths. It is important for adolescents to learn about careers from a variety of sources. Their knowledge of the breadth of career options is generally limited. Many only consider career choices identified by family members, neighbors, and the media. Educators can help learners explore the variety of options available to them.

See *Figure 2-5* on page 21 for the implications of the vocational development of adolescents on curriculum development and teaching practices.

As you can see from the suggestions given in *Figures 2-1* through *2-5*, there are many ways in which family and consumer sciences, nutrition, and health education professionals can be responsive to the developmental needs of adolescents. In 2000, the Search Institute completed a review of literature on healthy development of adolescents from the sixth to the twelfth grades. As a result of this work, the Search Institute developed "40 Building Blocks of Healthy Development" that can help young people grow up to be healthy, caring, and responsible. These 40 building blocks are identified and explained in *Figure 2-6* on pages 22-25. Suggestions have been added to illustrate ways in which you, as an educator, can assist adolescents in developing these assets.

Some of the content suggested by the Search Institute is part of the family and consumer sciences and health curricula, such as family and interpersonal relationships, goal setting, and decision making. Other assets can be met through extracurricular activities in programs sponsored through FCCLA, 4-H, and other organizations. Educators in Family and Consumer Sciences have many opportunities to help learners make healthier life choices; to develop personal living skills for effectively functioning at home, at school, and in the community; and to promote the thinking skills essential in today's world.

Adult Learners

Lifelong learning is a function of our changing society. More adults are seeking both formal and nonformal education programs. Some of the societal reasons for the increase of adult learners include:

- **Increased life expectancy.** More people are living longer. Therefore, adults have more leisure time during retirement and increased opportunities to take classes and seminars.
- **Increased concern with health and wellness.** Adults are interested in learning about the roles of nutrition and fitness in the quality of life.
- **Increased immigration.** As people from different countries and cultures immigrate to the United States, there is a need for more education for adults from other countries.
- **Increased information and expanding knowledge in all areas of life.** With technological advances, adults have greater access to information through the Internet, distance learning (via computer), and cable TV.
- **Increased use of technology.** Adults are seeking educational opportunities to update job skills, change jobs, and to more fully utilize available technology. For example, many adults want to use the Internet to keep in touch with family and friends and to research various topics.
- **Increased complexity of life.** As knowledge grows with an expanding information base, adults will seek ways to solve new and existing problems of daily living.

As an educator, you may work with adults in a variety of settings to facilitate learning, including teaching classes, seminars, or workshops for adults. For example, you might provide on-site job training on conflict resolution or provide nutrition counseling for individuals or small groups of adults.

Figure 2-6

FORTY DEVELOPMENTAL ASSETS

The Search Institute (2000) identified the following building blocks of healthy development that can help adolescents in grades 6-12 grow up to be healthy, caring, and responsible. Suggestions have been added to include ways in which educators can assist adolescents in achieving these assets.

ASSET TYPE	ASSET NAME	DEFINITION	SUGGESTIONS FOR EDUCATORS
Support	Family Support	Family life provides high levels of love and support.	Include content that encourages supportive family relationships.
	Positive Family Communication	Young people and their parents communicate positively, and young people are willing to seek advice and counsel from parents.	Work on strategies to improve communication skills between parents and teens. Give assignments that encourage teens to communicate with parents.
	Other Adult Relationships	Young people receive support from three or more nonparent adults.	Work with teens as FCCLA advisor, 4-H leader, or community volunteer.
	Caring Neighborhood	Young people experience caring neighbors.	Plan activities that focus on what makes a good neighbor.
	Caring School Climate	School provides a caring, encouraging environment.	Create an environment that is supportive, inviting, and encouraging to all learners.
	Parent Involvement in Schooling	Parents are actively involved in helping young people succeed in school.	Encourage parent participation in school functions. For example, invite parents to be guest speakers, chaperones on school trips, and school volunteers. Invite parents to special functions such as receptions and banquets.
Empowerment	Community Values Youth	Young people perceive that adults in the community value youth.	Involve community in FCCLA activities and 4-H programs. Invite community to participate in school programs.
	Youth as Resources	Young people are given useful roles in the community.	Encourage youth to participate in service learning projects in the community.
	Service to Others	Young people serve in the community one hour or more per week.	Plan service learning projects in which learners use program content to provide community service.

Figure 2-6 (cont'd)

FORTY DEVELOPMENTAL ASSETS

ASSET TYPE	ASSET NAME	DEFINITION	SUGGESTIONS FOR EDUCATORS
Empowerment (cont'd)	Safety	Young person feels safe at home, at school, and in the neighborhood.	Discuss ways to make homes more secure. In the classroom, establish clear rules and procedures. Invite community leaders to speak on making the neighborhood a safe place to live.
Boundaries and Expectations	Family Boundaries	Families have clear rules and consequences and monitor the young people's whereabouts.	Emphasize in parenting education the importance of establishing family rules.
	School Boundaries	School provides clear rules and consequences.	Establish procedures and policies that are clearly communicated to the learners.
	Neighborhood Boundaries	Neighbors take responsibility for monitoring young people's behavior.	Discuss importance of neighbors in the community.
	Adult Role Models	Parents and other adults model positive, responsible behavior.	Model positive, responsible behavior. In parenting classes, talk about importance of modeling this type of behavior.
	Positive Peer Influence	Young people's close friends model positive, responsible behavior.	Discuss the importance of having positive, responsible friends.
	High Expectations	Both parents and teachers encourage young people to do well.	Have high expectations in the classroom.
Constructive Use of Time	Creative Activities	Young person spends three or more hours per week in lessons or practice in music, theater, or other arts.	Demonstrate creative activities that students can do outside of school.
	Youth Programs	Young person spends three or more hours per week in sports, clubs, or organizations at school and/or in community organizations.	Work with youth through FCCLA or 4-H activities.

Figure 2-6 (cont'd)

FORTY DEVELOPMENTAL ASSETS

ASSET TYPE	ASSET NAME	DEFINITION	SUGGESTIONS FOR EDUCATORS
Constructive Use of Time (cont'd)	Religious Community	Young person spends one hour or more per week in activities in a religious institution.	Discuss the role of religion in developing values and making decisions.
	Time at Home	Young person is out with friends "with nothing to do" two or fewer nights per week.	Encourage youth to spend time at home with family. Discuss importance of downtime at home.
Internal Assets Commitment to Learning	Achievement Motivation	Young people are motivated to do well at school.	Have high expectations of learners.
	School Engagement	Young people are actively engaged in learning.	Make content relevant to the lives of learners.
	Homework	Young people report doing at least one hour of homework every school day.	Give students meaningful homework assignments.
	Bonding to School	Young people care about their school.	Use learning strategies that promote a feeling of community within classroom. Work on school pride projects.
	Reading for Pleasure	Young people read for pleasure three or more hours per week.	Bring in current books and magazines that relate to content. Have a reading corner as a reward when learners finish their work early.
Positive Values	Caring	Young people place high value on helping other people.	Plan service learning projects in FCCLA and 4-H.
	Equality and Social Justice	Young people place high value on promoting equality and reducing hunger and poverty.	Encourage participation in service learning projects, such as planning nutritional meals for a homeless shelter.
	Integrity	Young people act on convictions and stand up for their own beliefs.	Use ethical dilemmas in case studies to give youth opportunities to practice moral reasoning.
	Honesty	Young people tell the truth even when it is not easy.	Discuss the importance of honesty in relationships.

Figure 2-6 (cont'd)
FORTY DEVELOPMENTAL ASSETS

ASSET TYPE	ASSET NAME	DEFINITION	SUGGESTIONS FOR EDUCATORS
Positive Values (cont'd)	Honesty (cont'd)		Encourage youth to be honest and compassionate.
	Responsibility	Young people accept and take personal responsibility.	Give youth leadership positions where they have to exhibit responsibility.
	Restraint	Young people believe it is important not to be sexually active or to use alcohol or other drugs.	Discuss the importance of taking responsibility for personal actions and the consequences of not practicing restraint.
Social Competencies	Planning and Decision Making	Young people know how to plan ahead and make choices.	Include planning and decision making in the curriculum.
	Interpersonal Competence	Young people have empathy, sensitivity, and friendship skills.	Teach lessons on positive characteristics of friends.
	Cultural Competence	Young people have knowledge of and comfort with people of different cultural, racial, and ethnic backgrounds.	Explore the influences of various cultures on families, foods, values, and health practices.
	Resistance Skills	Young people are able to resist negative peer pressure and dangerous situations.	Discuss the importance of developing resistance skills. Promote projects such as "Stop the Violence" with FCCLA.
	Peaceful Conflict Resolution	Young people seek to resolve conflict nonviolently.	Plan lessons that deal with conflict resolution.
Positive Identity	Personal Power	Young people feel they have control over things that happen to them.	Teach concepts such as planning, decision making, goal setting, and problem solving.
	Self-Esteem	Young people report having high self-esteem.	Work to build the antecedents of self-esteem, such as competence and a sense of identity.
	Sense of Purpose	Young people report that their lives have purpose.	Help youth develop goals and dreams for the future.
	Positive View of the Future	Young people are optimistic about their personal futures.	Assist learners in developing a realistic career plan.

✳ Principles of Working with Adult Learners

Malcolm Knowles, considered to be the father of adult education, developed six core principles for working with adult learners. These principles, according to Knowles, Holton, and Swanson (1998), "enable those designing and conducting adult learning to build more effective learning processes for adults." (p. 2) The authors presented a conceptual outline, shown in *Figure 2-7* below, to illustrate the six principles.

Figure 2-7

The Adult Learner

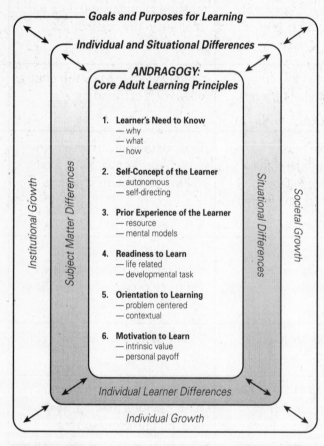

From *The Adult Learner: The Definitive Classic in Adult Education and Human Resource Development*, by M.S. Knowles, E.F. Holton and R.A. Swanson. Copyright © 1998 by Gulf Publishing Company, Huston, TX. Reprinted by permission.

✳ *Principle 1: Learner's Need to Know*

Adults seek educational opportunities on a need-to-know basis. The educator must set the stage for learning so that adult learners will see the relevance of the topic in their lives. How will this topic enhance their quality of life at home, in the workplace, in their community? Raising awareness of the need for the educational experience is critical in working with adults.

There are a variety of ways to assess the learners' needs and their expectations. At the beginning of a multipart class, you could ask learners to list their goals and expectations for the experience. You could use this as an opening activity. If it's possible to contact the participants prior to the program, ask for this information, then use the feedback to refine your planning. Strategies for gathering information from learners will be discussed later in this chapter.

✳ *Principle 2: Self-Concept of the Learner*

The definition of an adult is one who is responsible for his or her own life. This implies that as learners they have a need to be seen by other people and treated by others as being capable of self-direction (Knowles, Holton, & Swanson, 1998). The role of the educator of adults moves from being a teacher to a facilitator of the learning experience. Adults often feel anxious about being in an educational setting. They may bring negative previous experiences from their earlier education. Understanding and reducing anxiety are keys to working with adults (Lawler, 1991). It is important to create an emotional climate where adults feel comfortable and secure. Avoid activities that would put adults on the spot. For example, the author of this chapter once conducted a workshop for middle school teachers. She modeled for the teachers activities that would be appropriate for middle school students. The teachers felt uncomfortable with the learning activities that required competitiveness and physical activity. While middle school students may welcome this type of activity, many adults are fearful of being embarrassed in front of others.

❊ Principle 3: Prior Experiences of Learner

One of the advantages of teaching adults is that they bring richer experiences to the program. Knowles, Holton, and Swanson (1998) warned that adults also bring mental habits and biases that sometimes inhibit learning. For example, if you are leading a workshop for child care providers on positive discipline techniques, there may be adults who have spanked their own children. Helping these adults understand research findings that suggest spanking often has long-term negative effects will require sensitivity on the part of the facilitator.

Using learning strategies that encourage active participation of learners, such as small group discussions and case studies, gives adults opportunities to bring their prior experiences to the classroom. Give learners an opportunity to ask questions and participate in the learning experience. For example, one trainer who was giving an in-service session for teachers gave each participant a set of sticky notes in the shape of a school bus. At the front of the room, the trainer placed a large piece of poster board with a parking lot drawn on it. She invited participants to "park their questions" there as the session progressed. At appropriate times during the daylong workshop, she led the group in addressing the questions. This provided an opportunity for all the participants to ask and answer questions without one or two individuals dominating the discussion.

❊ Principle 4: Readiness to Learn

Adults often seek educational opportunities when they are faced with developmental changes in their lives, such as becoming a parent or facing the challenges of health problems. For example, an adult recently diagnosed with high cholesterol and heart disease may be much more likely than before to be ready to learn about the influence of diet and exercise on health and wellness.

❊ Principle 5: Orientation to Learning

The motivation to learn is directly proportional to how learners view that the subject matter covered will help them in their personal or professional lives. Real-life situations provide the context for learning. For example, if you wanted to teach a personal finance seminar for the Cooperative Extension Service, you would more likely reach motivated learners with more specific sessions with titles such as "Financing Your First Home," "Improving Your Credit Rating," or "Planning for Retirement" rather than simply "Budgeting." Adults could select one or more seminars based on their personal needs and interests.

Case studies are beneficial in providing real-life situations. You can write realistic scenarios by asking participants to identify issues or problems they would like to see addressed. One college teacher uses this technique to develop case studies to teach decision-making models. She asks students to identify difficult decisions that either they or someone they know has had to make. The educator then uses these situations to write case studies, changing names and any personal identifiers. Chapter 11 gives more information on using case studies and other simulated experiences.

❊ Principle 6: Motivation to Learn

Adults tend to be more internally motivated to learn than younger learners. They often seek opportunities to learn, whereas younger learners are required to be in school. For example, employees are more likely to select a continuing education course if they believe it will help them perform better at work. Adults will be more interested in attending a weight management program if they are internally motivated to look and feel better through improved health, as opposed to being advised to attend by a family member. Lawler (1991) advised educators to help participants write action plans at the end of an educational experience to incorporate ways that this educational experience will help them in the future. Some presenters ask participants to write letters to themselves, identifying what they have learned and how they will change as a result of the seminar. The presenters collect the letters and mail them to the participants at a later date.

Teaching adults can be both rewarding and challenging. There are opportunities for professionals in Family and Consumer Sciences, Nutrition, and Health/Wellness education to teach adults in both formal and nonformal settings. Using the six core principles will assist educators of adults to plan and implement educational experiences for them.

 ## Getting Acquainted with Learners

Much of this chapter has presented an overview of the characteristics and needs of learners. There are strategies that you can use to directly collect information about your audience. Depending on the time you have with the learners, various approaches can be used. For example, in a formal school setting you could invite students to write you about themselves, telling you what they think you should know about them to teach them effectively. Students might include information about their families, pets, hobbies, interests, and preferred learning activities. It is also important to research information about their culture and community to understand these influences. Chapter 3 gives additional suggestions.

To introduce a topic at a workshop or seminar, you might ask learners a series of questions that will give you a brief snapshot of them. For example, if you are preparing a nutrition education session for teen mothers, you might begin the session by asking the following questions:

- Raise your right hand if you have brothers or sisters.
- Rock your arms, like a cradle, if your child is under six months of age.
- Pat your head if you ate breakfast this morning.
- Swing your arms like a jogger if you exercise each day.
- Circle your eyes if you watch TV every day.
- Raise both hands if you cook meals in your home.
- Check an imaginary list if you shop for the groceries for your family.

- Make a triangle with your fingers if you know the categories of the Food Guide Pyramid.
- Put your head on the table if you would like more sleep at night.
- Stand up if you would like more information on how to provide the nutritional needs of your child.

This type of exercise can vary according to the audience you are trying to reach. It allows the leader to take a quick survey on habits, characteristics, and interests. Writing questions that fit your group and topic make this an enjoyable and beneficial introductory activity. The questions can be adapted to fit all age groups. Even senior citizens enjoy the movement that this type of activity involves.

If you have contact information for those who will be attending a presentation you are giving, you might contact them ahead of time. That way, you can assess their needs and interests prior to the learning experience. For example, you could ask the following:

- What is your reason for attending this seminar?
- What experience have you had with this topic?
- What would you like to accomplish at the end of this seminar?

The responses to these questions give insight into the learners' needs and expectations of their time with you. You can also use their input in planning the content.

 ## A Key to Effective Teaching

A critical task of educators is to understand their learners. Being aware of the developmental needs of learners can help you plan a curriculum that is responsive to their needs and interests. Educators work with adolescent and adult learners in a variety of settings. Following the principles for working with adults can help you teach them more effectively. Intentionally gathering information about specific audiences will assist you in learning more about the individuals you teach, thereby facilitating planning educational experiences that are meaningful to them.

References

Elkind, D. (1967). Egocentrism in adolescence. <u>Child Development</u>, <u>38</u>, 1025-1034.

Hillman, S. (1991). What developmental psychology has to say about early adolescence. <u>Middle School Journal</u>, <u>23</u>, 3-8.

Knowles, M.S., Holton, E.F., Swanson, R.A. (1998). <u>The adult learner: The definitive classic in adult education and human resource development</u>. Houston, TX: Gulf Publishing Company.

Lawler, P.A. (1991). <u>The keys to adult learning: Theories and practical strategies.</u> Philadelphia, PA: Research for Better Schools.

Piaget, J. (1972). Intellectual evolution from adolescence to adulthood. <u>Human Development</u>, <u>15</u>, 1-12.

Search Institute (2000). <u>Forty developmental assets</u>. Minneapolis, MN: Search Institute.

Building Your Professional Portfolio

Adolescent Development and Education. This chapter includes five charts linking the developmental characteristics of adolescents with implications for curriculum development and teaching strategies. Add to each list, basing your recommendations on your knowledge and research of adolescent development.

Developmental Assets. Choose 15 of the 40 Developmental Assets from Figure 2-6. For each, plan one specific and concrete activity that would appeal to adolescents. Specify the age level and course or learning situation for which each would be appropriate.

Adapting for Different Learners. Plan a lesson for young adolescents on a nutrition or health topic that also affects other ages. Show how you would adapt this lesson for adult learners.

Learning About Learners. Plan five specific strategies, other than those suggested in this chapter, for getting to know your learners. Specify the age level and course or learning situation for which each would be appropriate.

Chapter 3

Curriculum Development and Concept Organization

"The whole art of teaching is . . . the art of awakening the natural curiosity of . . . minds."
Anatole France

No matter what the setting or the age group, effective teaching is systematic and organized. That requires planning. The planning process will come alive and be more meaningful if you think of yourself in your teaching role as a needs analyst, decision maker, hypothesis tester, and experimenter. Teaching is a continual learning process for you, the educator, as you develop hypotheses about what might work, experiment, and then shape your future teaching based on past results. The successes of last year, last week, or last session—as well as your shortcomings—will inspire new approaches that will make you a better educator. Your decisions, hypotheses, and experiments are based on data that you continually collect and process in terms of your educational setting. Effective planning enhances your strengths as a teacher.

The Curriculum Development Process

Curriculum planning and development encompass much more than what is written on paper. They are the sum total of all the processes that are thought through, written down, implemented, and evaluated to achieve desired ends with a given audience. Curriculum development is ongoing. "Steps in the Curriculum Process," *Figure 3-1* on page 31, depicts this process. Most planning starts at a broad level of outlining concepts. These are then blocked out into time frames. Major learning experiences and terminal, or end, objectives are then added

for each block of time. After that, more specific planning is done. The educator works from the broad overall plan to the more specific plan.

✳ Gathering Data from Input Factors

So where do you begin? As an educator, you are faced with an enormous responsibility in deciding what to teach and how to teach it. Your learners have many needs, and you have so much to share with them. As in any good decision-making process, the first step is to gather input data on which to base decisions. These teaching decisions include subject-matter content, learner objectives, learning experiences,

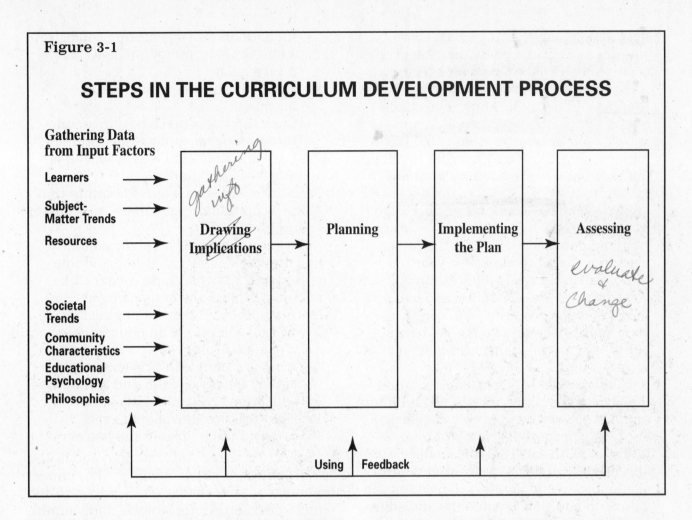

Figure 3-1

STEPS IN THE CURRICULUM DEVELOPMENT PROCESS

Gathering Data from Input Factors

Learners →
Subject-Matter Trends →
Resources →

Societal Trends →
Community Characteristics →
Educational Psychology →
Philosophies →

Drawing Implications *(gathering info)* → **Planning** → **Implementing the Plan** → **Assessing** *(evaluate & change)*

Using | Feedback

resources, and assessment. Teaching decisions based on a solid foundation of accurate and current information will ensure relevance in your curriculum. This, in turn, will generate interest among your learners.

An effective educator, therefore, starts by gathering data for a set of input factors. The question then becomes "What do I need to know to make the best teaching decisions?" A good database will consist, at a minimum, of information about the learners, the latest developments in the subject area(s), available resources, societal trends, community characteristics, and basic principles of educational psychology. It will also identify the philosophies of the people and institutions with whom you work.

- **The learners.** As educators seek to know their audiences, they must learn about the learners' demographics and backgrounds, as well as their needs, interests, and goals. To accomplish this, you need to understand where learners have been and where they want to go. Information on their family and life experiences, pre-

vious contact with the subject matter, and future plans of the learners need to be assessed. You will also want to gather data on learners' ability levels, gender, ages, and socioeconomic and ethnic backgrounds. The size of the group will also impact your planning. Gathering this information about the learners enables you to boost the relevance of the curriculum, the efficiency of your planning, and the effectiveness of your instruction. Such data are often gathered through the use of needs assessment strategies. Learners or their parents or guardians can provide information through interviews and/or questionnaires. However, it's essential to respect privacy and never *require* learners to divulge personal or family information. Needs assessments allow you to target your audience needs, interests, and goals.

- **Subject-matter trends.** Effective educators stay informed about the latest developments in the many facets of their disciplines. That's a challenge, but essential for keeping curriculum up to date.

- **Available resources.** As you assess resources, look at the personal assets you bring to the situation, as well as the material, financial, and other human resources available. In addition, analyze available community resources, such as agencies, people, and businesses, that could facilitate learning. Tight budgets that result in limited supplies are a reality for many teachers. Today's educators need to be creative in making limited resources go as far as possible. Start to scan your environment and save items that might be useful for teaching. Consider your personal energy as a valuable resource. Plan your days, weeks, and months to balance the demands on yourself and conserve your energy whenever possible. Remember to tap into the unharnessed energy of your learners.

- **Societal trends.** Trends in society, from the local community to national and international scenes, need to be considered as educators prepare learners for their future in all these arenas. Keeping abreast of political, social, cultural, and economic developments is a must for educators. In addition, community and state policies, mandates, standards, and attitudes affect educational decisions. These must be continually assessed by educators for potential impact on the curriculum.

- **Community characteristics.** Each community setting offers unique resources, philosophies, and trends. Get to know the community by assessing attitudes, values, and even the rural/suburban/urban nature of the community and its size. All will impact curriculum decisions. In some towns or families, ethnicity and its traditions are a significant influence. You will want your curriculum to fit in to the "flavor" of the community.

- **Educational psychology.** Much research has been conducted that shows certain teacher behaviors are more likely to facilitate learning. Educators need to analyze their teaching and incorporate principles of educational psychology. Examples of basic principles of educational psychology include:
  - Active learner involvement increases retention.

- Individuals learn best what seems relevant to their immediate lives and future goals.
- Positive reinforcement speeds learning.
- Learning takes place best in a non-threatening, accepting environment.
- Learning that can be generalized is more readily used.

And the list goes on. Planning that's based on such principles will foster success.

- **Relevant philosophies.** The first philosophy that needs to be analyzed and integrated into your planning is your own personal philosophy of teaching and learning. Reflect on questions such as:
  - What is the role of an educator?
  - What is learning?
  - What is Family and Consumer Sciences? What is Health and Wellness education? Nutrition education?
  - What relationship should exist between the educator and learners?

Educators need information about the philosophies of other people who impact their teaching decisions. Depending on the educational setting, this may include administrators, supervisors, coworkers, parents, and the learners. The philosophies of these individuals may not always match your own, but an understanding of their points of view will make you a more effective decision maker as you build curriculum.

Gathering information can take place in many ways, including talking with or interviewing people, observing, reading, surveying, and listening. Keep in mind that adding to and updating your information base is an ongoing and daily process. This makes teaching an exciting challenge!

✳ Drawing Implications

Once you have gathered information about your situation, the next step is to reflect on and carefully analyze this information. This is the step identified in *Figure 3-1*, "Steps in the Curriculum Development Process" on page 31, as drawing implications. Based on your analysis, you will begin to make some teaching decisions for your specific situation. In this process, you, as an educator, are using an "If . . . then . . ." mode of thinking. Some examples that illustrate this approach follow:

- If I know that most of my learners are from economically disadvantaged homes, then I need to limit my expectations regarding money spent for projects.
- If weight loss is of interest to the participants, then I need to demonstrate how to prepare low-fat vegetable soups rather than chowders or cream soups.
- If my session lasts 90 minutes, then I need to utilize a wide variety of activities to keep the learners focused for this length of time.

Analyzing information is an ongoing process. For each bit of information you collect, you start to draw implications in your mind. Along the way, your implication-drawing process will continue to pull various pieces of information together.

❋ Planning

The next step in curriculum development is the actual planning process. Your plans are like road maps. They help you move your learners forward toward important goals that should improve the quality of their lives. These goals will be derived from the input factors. Your ability to facilitate learning is directly related to how carefully you have developed a solid base of information and correctly drawn implications. Unfortunately, some educators try to start at this planning point in the curriculum development process. If the educator begins planning without first taking time to gather input data and draw implications, the resulting curriculum is likely to be shallow and out of touch with the learners.

Sometimes, instead of starting from scratch, you may select portions of other available curricula, add new material, rework portions, and shape a new, up-to-date curriculum appropriate for your unique situation. Planning involves many different levels. Block plans for an entire year, a long-term program, or a conference enable you to allocate reasonable amounts of time to each topic. Then unit plans are developed for the respective topics. Finally, you will make daily lesson, session, or workshop plans.

The various types of plans consist of different components, including concepts, generalizations, objectives, learning experiences, resources, and assessment techniques. You will learn about the different types of plans and each of these components in more depth in this book. Some topics are addressed in this chapter and others in subsequent ones. For now, assume that planning is complete and move on to the next step in the curriculum development process: implementation.

❋ Implementing the Plan

Once written plans have been completed, you are ready to implement them. In other words, you are ready to teach. As will be emphasized throughout this book, utilizing a variety of teaching strategies and learner involvement are critical for effective implementation. Carrying out learning experiences and teaching methods involves using a number of specific teaching skills. Chapters 5 and 8 provide guidelines for designing appropriate learning experiences and developing the core teaching skills they depend upon.

❋ Assessing

Next comes the assessment component in which you gather information to determine your success, the success of your learners, and the success of your curriculum plan. This assessment process involves an honest appraisal of both the strengths and weaknesses of your program, your progress as an educator, and your product—that is, your learners' knowledge.

In some situations, assessment feedback comes from testing procedures. However, a great deal of feedback will come from informal, or nontesting, means of evaluation. Conversations with and/or written input from advisory council members, parents, administrators, supervisors, former students, current learners, employers, business leaders, and other educators can provide valuable information to help you refine your curriculum.

✳ Using Feedback

But you are not finished! The curriculum process has only just begun. Once you have determined what went well and what needs improvement, you are ready to feed that information back into the curriculum development process.

Educating is a process of continual change. Educators may realize that input data were incomplete or inaccurate, the implications drawn weren't on target, or the plans weren't as complete as they might have been. They may feel that a skill wasn't as polished or a method as well orchestrated as it might have been. This is simply the reality of teaching. No educator is perfect; however, a growing, dedicated teacher continually strives to improve. This is possible when you put feedback to work. You make new decisions, try new teaching experiments, and test new hypotheses the next time you teach.

Imagine how stagnant and boring educating would become if you neglected to use feedback (as indicated by the arrows at the bottom of *Figure 3-1*) to improve your program. You would repeat your weaknesses instead of using them as stepping stones for growth, revision, and revitalization. You would be "stuck in a rut"!

Commit to becoming a dynamic, growing, exciting educator who uses the process and continually modifies, changes, and grows. You can make each teaching opportunity richer and more rewarding for both you and your learners. Information that forms the basis for teaching decisions is changing so rapidly that you must be flexible to stay ahead of the curve with a relevant curriculum that truly meets learners' needs.

 ## Selecting and Organizing Content

Planning curriculum is like going on a guided tour. You have various options about how to reach your destination (or broad program goals), but by planning your itinerary in advance, you save time and confusion. Planning, though, doesn't rule out the possibility of taking a side trip at some point. You might stop en route, choose different transportation at the last minute, or be detained by an unexpected event. It's easiest to reach your goals by planning how to attain them, yet staying flexible as you work to achieve them.

Having laid the critical groundwork through a complete analysis of input data and the drawing of implications, you are ready to forge ahead with the first level of planning. This broadest level involves selecting and structuring the subject matter you will teach to reach your broad program goals. The biggest frustration that educators face is realizing there is much more content to be taught than there is allotted time. You will use your analysis of input data, and the implications drawn will be used to help prioritize the subject matter. Sift out the most important and relevant concepts for your audience, based on your needs assessments, other input data, and the implications drawn. These concepts must then be organized into a meaningful structure.

One of the primary goals of educators is to help learners analyze and verbalize relationships among concepts. When learners can do so, they are prepared to formulate their own generalizations that tie together various concepts. Having pulled together their own generalizations, learners are ready to apply these ideas to other problems and decisions in their lives. Learning becomes the development of a series of connections among concepts that hold real meaning and relevance for the learner.

✳ Concepts Defined and Characterized

A *concept* is a key idea, topic, or main thought. It is what a person thinks about a particular subject or topic. A concept consists of a core of abstract meanings that an individual attaches to something. As shown in "A Depiction of a Concept," *Figure 3-2* on page 35, this core of meanings is enmeshed in feelings and emotions that the person associates with it. Finally, words or symbols are used to communicate ideas or concepts.

Because background experiences vary, respective learners will attach various meanings to a particular idea or concept.

Figure 3-2

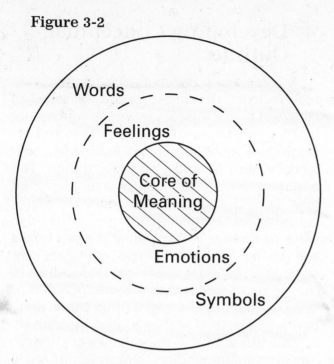

A Depiction of a Concept

Thus, each of your learners may have a different concept or core of meaning for any given idea. The meaning attached to a concept may be simple or complex, depending on the frequency and types of experiences each learner has had with it. For example, when the question "What do you think of when I say food?" is asked of four-year-olds, their response might be: hot dogs, ice cream, cookies, and lunch. Children will identify favorite foods and simple concepts for which they have a frame of reference. If middle or high school students were asked the same question, their responses may also include favorite foods. However, because their concepts of food are broader and more complex, some might mention nutrition, the Food Guide Pyramid, health, calories, or a vegetarian diet. If registered dieticians talk about food, they might discuss specific nutrients, dietary allowances, enzymes, and quality control. The individuals described think of food differently because their cumulative experiences relating to it have been so varied.

One of your first tasks as an educator is to assess where your learners are in terms of their concepts about the topics to be cov-

ered. You need to acknowledge that everyone won't enter or exit your learning environment with identical concepts. You can't teach someone your concept. Your goal is to build upon, embellish, and expand each learner's core of meaning through a series of well-planned learning experiences. In addition, you need to help learners clarify the feelings they attach to their concepts. There is no way to truly separate the cognitive and affective components of concepts.

In addition to recognizing that concepts vary from one individual to another, remember that these ideas are constantly changing because of new experiences. Concepts are seldom fixed or final, but they usually develop slowly through additional experiences in a variety of situations. Your teaching is one of these vital experiences.

Concepts change and grow not only for an individual, but also within a society. Therefore, as noted in the section on input factors, an analysis of societal trends needs to precede concept selection for a curriculum. For example, for a long time the American family was thought of as a husband, a wife, and children. Today, many other family forms are recognized.

✻ Determining Concepts to Teach

So how do you decide what concepts to teach? The following are some factors you will want to consider in gleaning the concepts that are most relevant to the needs, interests, goals, and abilities of your learners.

✻ Using Input Data

Refer back to *Figure 3-1* and to the material about input factors on pages 31-32. Focus on your learners to determine which ideas, from all the concepts you might teach, would be most helpful to them. Review any needs assessments done or input obtained from the learners themselves. Then look at societal trends. Select the concepts that will best prepare your learners to function fully in society at the community, national, and global levels. You need to keep up to date on the latest developments in your discipline as well and provide learners with new concepts and skills to keep them on the cutting edge. Sometimes the philosophies of community members or supervisors will place parameters on concepts you can cover. Be sure you know what those are.

❋ *Local and State Mandates and Competencies*

Philosophies about what should be taught are sometimes formalized into local, state, or licensing mandates that must be followed. These mandates may clearly indicate what topics or concepts may and may not or must be covered in programs offered by your agency, program, or school. Incorporating these into your plan will reflect your political savvy and avoid unnecessary conflicts.

For those teaching in schools, there may be state competencies in your subject matter area that have been developed for instructors to follow. Some state administrators expect much closer adherence to these than is the case in other geographic areas. Find out if there are state competencies in your discipline and then determine if these are seen as guidelines for teachers or if strict adherence is expected. Select the concepts you teach accordingly.

❋ *National Program Standards*

To provide more consistency across states, many program areas have developed national program standards, such as the National Health Education Standards for use by teachers. The National Standards for Family and Consumer Sciences document clearly identifies subject matter that falls within the field of Family and Consumer Sciences.

Usage of national program standards varies from state to state. Personnel in some states use the national program standards, and others expect teachers to follow the state competencies. In other states, you will be encouraged to use the national standards as a guide from which to pick and choose concepts that best meet the needs of learners in your setting. However they are used, national standards provide a guide for your concept selection—in school situations, as well as less formal settings.

❋ Developing Conceptual Outlines

A *conceptual outline* is the product that results from the organization of selected concepts into a logical system. A conceptual outline may be developed for an entire curriculum, a specific course, workshop, conference, unit of study, or presentation. The major, main, or key topics are identified first. Then the subconcepts under the major concepts are delineated. "Scope" is the term used to denote what subject-matter topics are to be covered. These concepts are organized in a sequence corresponding to the order in which they will be included in the curriculum. Concepts often build upon one another; thus sequence may be critical.

Educators new to the process of curriculum development often simply write out a conceptual outline and assume that it's satisfactory. Typically, this process of developing a conceptual outline takes more work and refinement than that. The following steps are suggested in order to develop a conceptual outline:

- Brainstorm to generate a list of all possible concepts you might cover in your program, class, or workshop. This brainstorming may be done individually or with others, such as people who represent the target audience. Nouns are the primary part of speech used in writing concepts. Verbs and articles aren't needed.
- Base your list on input factors and accompanying implications you have drawn regarding learners and their needs; society and community; resources; subject-matter trends; educational psychology; and philosophies, mandates, competencies, and standards.
- Look at your time frame and determine how much can realistically be covered in the time you have.
- Ask other professionals in your field and adult learners to provide input on your brainstormed list to help you decide which concepts are most and least important. Ask their help in identifying concepts you don't have listed that might be included and any that might be deleted.

- Eliminate concepts seen as least important. Add others proposed by your colleagues or learners. You have now developed the scope of your program.
- Take the concepts remaining and organize them into a logical sequence of concepts and subconcepts for your program. As you develop the sequence of concepts, keep in mind the following principles of curriculum organization:
  - Use an outline format.
  - State concepts clearly and concisely.
  - Be sure all subconcepts listed below a concept relate to, or are aspects of, the concept they are under.
  - Provide enough detail for any person familiar with the subject matter to know what is to be covered.
  - Work from what your learners already know, introducing them to new material at a pace appropriate to their learning abilities. Build on their prior knowledge.
  - Present simple concepts first.
  - Present concrete concepts before presenting more abstract ones.
  - Take advantage of opportunities to repeat concepts in various aspects of the curriculum. Reinforcement of concepts enhances learning.
  - Reassess and adjust your conceptual outline as needed.

Conceptual outlines show at a glance the development of concepts throughout an entire curriculum. Three examples are included here to illustrate various aspects. On page 38, *Figure 3-3*, "Conceptual Outline for Three Courses or Workshops on Consumer Education," illustrates how concepts relating to consumer education could evolve throughout three levels of courses or a series of workshops.

Figure 3-4, "Conceptual Outline on Promoting and Maintaining Health for a Portion of a Senior High Course or Series of Adult Workshops," on page 39 could be used in teaching the promotion and maintenance of health. The major concepts are an overview of health, individual health, family health, factors contributing to health problems, strategies for prevention/alleviation of health problems, and adjusting to health problems. Look at the logic behind the order of the concepts and subconcepts. Presenting the overview first helps assure everyone has a basic understanding of health as a foundation for the other concepts. Individual health affects family health so they are sequenced next. If you see how various factors contribute to health problems, then you are ready to work on strategies for prevention/alleviation and adjustment.

Teaching the material in this conceptual outline might take as little as several days or as long as several weeks, depending on the background experiences, interests, and needs of the learners. For some audiences, such as a group of people affected by diabetes, it might be important to cover many of the subconcepts in depth and, perhaps, to add others. For other students, it might be meaningless to do more than touch on the main points. The scope of a conceptual outline will vary with the learners. For example, much of a senior high conceptual outline would be irrelevant for middle school learners. *Figure 3-5*, "Conceptual Outline for Middle School Youth on Promoting and Maintaining Health," on page 39 would be more appropriate for younger students. While the scope has been altered, you will see that appropriate sequencing has been maintained.

we do

❋ Creating Block Plans

Once you have outlined the topics to be covered in a course or other setting, you are ready to block out the conceptual outline by weeks, days, or hours. This indicates which concepts will be covered in specific periods of time. When you put the concepts from your outline into designated time frames you are building what is known as *a block plan*. You are determining the amount of time you will devote to various concepts and subconcepts.

Many educators begin with a calendar or day-planner format, blocking out the number of hours, days, or weeks they have to teach the course and writing down the major topic areas to be covered in each time frame on this block. For instance, in an eighteen-week comprehensive course the teacher

Figure 3-3 — CONCEPTUAL OUTLINE FOR THREE COURSES OR WORKSHOPS ON CONSUMER EDUCATION

A. CONSUMER EDUCATION	B. CONSUMER EDUCATION	C. CONSUMER EDUCATION
Workshop I	Workshop II	Workshop III

1. **Values**
  a. How acquired
    1. Family
    2. Friends
    3. Community
    4. School
    5. Religious group
    6. Mass media
  b. Identification
  c. Changes
  d. Effects on consumer decisions
 	
2. **Goals**
  a. Short-term
  b. Long-term
  c. Changes
  d. Effects on consumer decisions
 	
3. **Needs and wants**
  a. Differences
  b. Examples
  c. Effects on consumer decisions
 	
4. **Managing resources**
  a. Money
  b. Time
  c. Energy
  d. Skills
	1. **Types of marketplaces**
	
	2. **Sources of consumer information**
	
	3. **Advertising**
	
	4. **Labels: Clothing and Food**
	  a. Care
	  b. Use
	  c. Nutrition
	  d. Unit pricing
	  e. Open and pull dates
	
	5. **Buying guidelines**
	  a. Clothing
	  b. Food
	
	6. **Warranties and guarantees**
	
	7. **Checking accounts**
	
	8. **Credit**
	  a. Open-end
	    1. Credit cards
	    2. Line of credit
	  b. Closed-end loans
	    1. Installment
	    2. Single-payment
		1. **Economic systems**
		
		2. **Types of income**
		
		3. **Taxes**
		
		4. **Spending plans**
		
		5. **Buying**
		  a. Appliances
		  b. Furnishings
		  c. Housing
		  d. Transportation
		  e. Insurance
		
		6. **Renting**
		  a. Housing
		  b. Equipment
		
		7. **Savings and lending institutions**
		  a. Commercial banks
		  b. Savings associations
		  c. Credit unions
		  d. Finance companies
		
		8. **Consumer agencies**
		  a. Government
		  b. Private
		
		9. **Legislation**
		
		10. **Careers**

might block out four weeks for personal development and family living, two weeks for child development, four for foods and nutrition, three for clothing and grooming, one for housing, two for career skills, and two for consumer education. The instructor would write in these major content areas by weeks on the block for the course. Then the teacher would go back and fill in the concepts within each major topic area that would be covered each day. For example, the concepts included in the conceptual outline for child development would be distributed across the ten days allocated to that content area. This process would be repeated for each subsequent major topic area.

To plan a workshop, you would block out the concepts and subconcepts for each session. Block plans may be simple or complex, depending on whether just major concepts or both major concepts and subconcepts are included. The "Block Plan for Senior High Class or Series of Adult Workshops on Promoting and Maintaining Health," *Figure 3-6* on page 40, shows one way in which the health concepts identified in *Figure 3-4* on the next page could be covered in nine classes or workshop sessions. In this case, major concepts and subconcepts are included in the block plan.

Once you have blocked out the concepts from the conceptual outline onto a block

Figure 3-4
Conceptual Outline for Part of a Senior High Course or Series of Adult Workshops on Promoting and Maintaining Health

I. **Health: An Overview**
   A. Definition
   B. Types
   C. Reasons to maintain
II. **Individual Health**
   A. Characteristics of a healthy person
   B. Habits that promote health
   C. Impacts of individual health on family health
   D. Resources available for maintaining individual health
III. **Family Health**
   A. Characteristics of a healthy family
   B. Physical health needs across the life span
   C. Emotional health needs across the life span
   D. Mental health needs across the life span
   E. Resources available for maintaining family health
IV. **Factors Contributing to Health Problems**
   A. Genetics
   B. Life cycle
   C. Diet
   D. Obesity
   E. Lack of exercise
   F. Smoking
   G. Alcohol
   H. Drugs
V. **Strategies for Prevention/Alleviation of Health Problems**
   A. Know risks
   B. Change lifestyle
   C. Reduce stress
   D. Eat healthfully
   E. Maintain appropriate weight
   F. Exercise
   G. Avoid smoking and drugs
   H. Limit alcohol use
   I. Consider alternative medicine
   J. Investigate interrelationships of physical, emotional, and mental health problems
VI. **Adjusting to Health Problems**
   A. Diabetes
   B. Hypertension
   C. Heart disease
   D. Osteoporosis
   E. Terminal illnesses

Figure 3-5
Conceptual Outline for Middle School on Promoting and Maintaining Health

I. **Health: An Overview**
   A. Defined
   B. Reasons to maintain
II. **Individual Health**
   A. Characteristics of a healthy person
   B. Habits that promote health
III. **Family Health**
   A. Characteristics of a healthy family
   B. Ways to help your family stay healthy
IV. **Factors Contributing to Health Problems**
   A. Genetics
   B. Poor diet
   C. Lack of exercise
   D. Smoking
   E. Alcohol use
   F. Drug use
V. **Strategies for Prevention of Health Problems**
   A. Eat healthfully
   B. Exercise
   C. Avoid smoking
   D. Avoid alcohol
   E. Avoid drug use

plan, you are ready to add additional components, such as terminal objectives and major learning experiences, to this skeletal plan. When these additional components are added to the block to give it more detail, the result is known as a *unit plan*. On pages 72-73 in Chapter 6 you will find an example of a unit plan with terminal objectives and learning experiences included.

Lesson plans are more detailed and include even more information, such as enabling objectives, content notes needed by the educator when presenting the material, key questions to be discussed in class, specific student activities, and assignments. See pages 79-81 in Chapter 6 for an example of how a lesson plan is developed from a unit plan.

Figure 3-6

BLOCK PLAN FOR SENIOR HIGH CLASS OR SERIES OF ADULT WORKSHOPS PROMOTING AND MAINTAINING HEALTH

MONDAY OR SESSION 1	TUESDAY OR SESSION 2	WEDNESDAY OR SESSION 3
I. Health: An Overview A. Definition B. Types C. Reasons to maintain	**II. Individual Health** A. Characteristics of a healthy person B. Habits that promote health C. Resources available for maintaining individual health D. Impacts of individals' health on family health	**III. Family Health** A. Characteristics of a healthy family B. Physical health needs across the life span

THURSDAY OR SESSION 4	FRIDAY OR SESSION 5	MONDAY OR SESSION 6
III. Family Health (cont.) C. Emotional health needs across the life span D. Mental health needs across the life span E. Resources available for maintaining family health	**IV. Factors Contributing to Health Problems** A. Genetics B. Lifestyle C. Stress D. Diet E. Obesity F. Lack of exercise G. Smoking H. Alcohol I. Drugs	**V. Strategies for Prevention** A. Know risks B. Change lifestyle C. Reduce stress D. Eat healthfully

TUESDAY OR SESSION 7	WEDNESDAY OR SESSION 8	THURSDAY OR SESSION 9
V. Strategies (cont.) E. Lose weight F. Exercise G. Avoid smoking and drugs H. Limit alcohol use I. Consider alternative medicine J. Investigate inter-relationships of physical, emotional, and mental health	**VI. Adjusting to Health Problems** A. Diabetes B. Hypertension C. Heart problems	**VI. Adjusting (cont.)** D. Osteoporosis E. Terminal illnesses

✳ Generalizations

Generalizations unify various aspects of a subject by showing the relationships among concepts. A generalization is a statement that expresses a complete thought and underlying truth and also has an element of universality. This means that a generalization can be applied in a wide number of situations worldwide. Generalizations are the basic principles and understanding that describe or explain phenomena.

There are three levels of generalizations. The first level may be a simple statement of fact, definition, description, analogy, identification, or classification. A second-level generalization shows relationships among ideas or makes comparisons. It may include more ideas than a first-level generalization and involves greater depth and scope of subject matter. A third-level generalization explains, justifies, interprets, or predicts. It may be more remote in time and space than a first- or second-level generalization. Examples of the three levels of generalizations follow:

Level 1: Milk is a food.

Level 2: Your health is affected by the food you eat.

Level 3: Your body size is partially determined by the kinds and quantity of food you consume.

The first example is a simple statement expressing a universal truth. The second shows that there is a relationship between health and food intake. The third example makes a subtle prediction by pointing out that the food that people eat has an effect on their growth and physical maturation.

The level of generalization that learners can be expected to formulate depends upon their previous personal and educational experiences, their innate intelligence, and the learning activities they take part in. Some learners may seldom go beyond the first level, while others easily formulate third-level generalizations. On the other hand, learners may reach only the first level in some subject areas and the third level in others. The level achieved depends in part on the depth with which the content is treated in the educational setting. When planning lessons, however, it is generally advisable for educators to try to help learners form generalizations above the first level. At the first level, generalizations are often shallow statements of fact. Such facts may be forgotten or become irrelevant in students' lives outside the classroom.

✳ *Formulating Generalizations*

A generalization expresses only one idea; therefore, it's inappropriate to use a colon or semicolons in writing one. Generalizations should normally be limited to about twenty words. That will keep them from being too complex or having no real meaning. Value judgments are also inappropriate. Consequently, words and phrases like the following are *not* used: it is *vital* that . . . ; it is *important* to remember . . . ; one *must* . . . ; *a person should* . . . ; and this *ought* to be done so that. . . .

The following phrases may be helpful in writing generalizations because they minimize the likelihood of making value judgments and facilitate making statements that show relationships:

is affected by	*is subject to*
is dependent on	*may be associated with*
is limited by	*may be developed by*
is promoted by	*may be enhanced by*
is related to	*may be identified by*
is the result of	*may be necessary for*
is a product of	*may be modified by*
is an integral part of	*constitutes a pattern for*
is influenced by	*contributes to*

Instead of being provided with generalizations, learners should be led to formulate their own. When given generalizations, learners are denied the challenge and opportunity to think for themselves and to use higher-level thought processes. Educators who write out generalizations in advance can guide learners in developing appropriate generalizations more effectively. This can be done when developing the conceptual outline or in the unit or conference planning process. This preplanning necessitates that educators clarify where they intend to lead their learners. As an educator, it's your responsibility to plan learning experiences and activities that help learners arrive at generalizations that are meaningful to them and are stated in their own words. Most learners won't state generalizations exactly as their leaders would, but through the skillful use of appropriate and probing questions, educators can encourage learners to formulate, clarify, and refine their own generalizations. Initially, learners may be helped to generalize by being asked to respond to questions like these:

- What have you learned from the lesson today?
- How can our discussion be summarized in a few sentences?
- What are the main ideas we have been talking about?
- How are the main ideas we discussed related?
- How does today's discussion relate to what we studied yesterday?
- How can these ideas be applied to new or different situations that you face or might face in the future?

Answering questions like these not only helps learners summarize the material that has been covered but also aids instructors in evaluating the effectiveness of their teaching and student achievement. Learners quickly forget most disconnected facts they study. Generalizations that are formulated have a longer life because they can be used as guidelines in the present, as well as in the future. When learners are able to develop generalizations showing the interrelationships among concepts, they are better prepared to transfer learning from one situation to another.

 # Continuing the Planning Process

After curriculum concepts are identified and developed into a conceptual framework and generalizations are formulated that link the major concepts, you are ready for the next step. It involves developing the behavioral objectives indicating expected achievement. Learning experiences are planned to enable learners to meet these established objectives. Resources that are available and needed to implement the learning experiences must be planned concurrently with the learning experiences. Evaluating learner achievement of the objectives is usually an ongoing and continuous process throughout the unit of study and may culminate at the end of the term in a final assessment or project. Each of these processes is discussed in the next few chapters.

Building Your Professional Portfolio

Input Factors. Describe possible input factors that impact curriculum development in your educational setting or one in which you anticipate working. For each input factor, draw an implication for your teaching.

Curriculum Change. Interview someone who has been an educator at least five years. Ask the person to describe ways in which he or she has changed the curriculum to adapt to evolving input factors.

Developing a Conceptual Outline. Develop a conceptual outline for teaching a family and consumer sciences, nutrition, or health/wellness topic that has been in the news recently. Write a description of the audience for which the outline is intended.

Block Plan. Prepare a block plan for a unit you will teach. Adapt it to two different identified audiences.

Chapter 4

Objectives and Competencies

In the past, many educators formulated their goals in broad, general terms with lots of loopholes. For example, educators may have wanted their learners to "gain a greater appreciation of a healthful lifestyle." However, "appreciation" is a difficult factor to measure objectively. Furthermore, if learners are to be evaluated on their "greater appreciation of healthy living," surely many are astute enough to give at least lip service to their "appreciation." How, then, can educators appraise and assess the learners' sincerity? Certainly all educators want to work constantly and diligently to help learners develop positive attitudes toward their subject matter, but one has to question if this can be done objectively. This example shows the inherent weakness in nebulous and vaguely stated objectives.

The current practice is to emphasize objectives that specify the ultimate behavior expected of learners. The terms *behavioral*, *performance*, and *instructional objectives* are often used synonymously. Behavior can be measured objectively because there is concrete evidence of achievement. In other words, the objectives describe or identify what the learners have to do to demonstrate their attainment of the objectives. Because the anticipated results of instruction are clear, there is measurable evidence of the outcome of the educational process. Behavioral objectives are applicable to learners of all ages and backgrounds in a wide variety of situations: classroom students, on-the-job trainees, 4-H members, athletes, student pilots, management trainees, or anyone else for whom there is an expected level of performance.

Domains of Learning

Objectives are divided into three categories of learning called:

- Cognitive domain
- Affective domain
- Psychomotor domain

The cognitive domain is concerned with rational learning—knowing and thinking. Knowledge, use of the mind, and intellectual abilities are emphasized. The affective domain deals with emotional learning—caring and feeling. Attitudes, appreciations, interests, values, and adjustments are all considered to be in this domain. The psychomotor domain relates to physical learning—doing and manipulating. Speed, accuracy, and dexterity are concerns in developing physical skills in this domain.

No subject matter pertains exclusively to one domain, but various content areas are more closely linked with one domain than another. For example, the subject areas of nutrition or textiles are most closely associated with *cognitive* learning. Family relationships, parenting, and work ethics are more concerned with the *affective* domain. Examples of development in the *psychomotor* domain are transferring someone from a car to wheelchair and hanging wallpaper.

All three domains should be considered when planning strategies for teaching, although for each content area one domain may be emphasized more than others. In the study of nutrition, for example, remembering, understanding, relating, analyzing, synthesizing, and assessing nutritional knowledge aren't enough. Learners also need to develop an interest in, appreciation for, and positive attitude toward using their knowledge. In addition, students have to be able to prepare food so it's nutritious. Certainly, one of the major purposes of teaching how to make a splint is to help individuals develop physical skill and expertise. They also have to develop a desire to perform these skills quickly, safely, and accurately plus know when a splint is needed.

❋ Levels of Objectives

Each of the three domains is divided into a hierarchy of levels—from the simplest to the most complex. *Figure 4-1*, "Domains of Learning" on page 45 shows the levels of each domain from lowest to highest. This chart also shows the abbreviations you will use to identify domains and levels in your teaching plans.

Typically, learners have to achieve objectives at lower levels before they can accomplish those at higher levels. To attain objectives at each level, people generally have had to master the skills of the levels below in consecutive order. Sometimes they skip a level by intuitively grasping the subject matter, but usually only one level. Therefore, behavioral objectives relating to one concept are planned and written to conform to the hierarchies of the domains. Educators

may plan for learners to achieve below the highest possible level. In fact, objectives formulated for some content areas may specify achievement that reaches only the first, second, or third step in the hierarchy.

This isn't meant to imply that younger learners or those of lower ability can't use higher-level thinking processes. Students in the primary grades analyze, synthesize, and evaluate in relation to simple concepts. Low-ability students may need to be encouraged to use higher-level thought processes. Teachers may select less complicated content for them to study than what is presented to other students. The levels of learning are applicable to all learners regardless of age, innate intelligence, or environmental background.

❋ Cognitive Domain

For proof of learners' achievement, there is a need for concrete, objective, and measurable evidence in all three domains of learning. In the cognitive domain, educators can gather this evidence by having learners identify facts, give examples, apply principles, analyze situations, plan solutions to problems, and evaluate results, According to Bloom in the *Taxonomy of Educational Objectives, Handbook l, Cognitive Domain,* there are six levels of learning in the cognitive domain. These six levels range from simple to complex mental behaviors. They include knowledge, comprehension, application, analysis, synthesis, and evaluation.

❋ *Knowledge: Recalling and Remembering*

This level emphasizes facts, information, and specifics. It serves as the foundation upon which the others are built. The knowledge level involves remembering material in a form very close to that in which it was originally encountered. It depends on memorizing or identifying facts. You may think of it as the learner's "file" of information that can be recalled or brought to mind later. Examples of behaviors at this level include reiterating the names of the muscles that have been studied, reciting the Dietary Guidelines for Americans, or identifying the colors in a color wheel.

Objectives at the knowledge level include the ability to:

cite   label   recite
define   list   reproduce
identify   name   state as given

❋ Comprehension: Understanding and Explaining

This level is concerned with grasping the meaning and intent of material. It deals with content and involves the ability to understand what is being communicated. One example is a reading comprehension test in which students read a section and then explain what it means. Another example would be 4-H members telling what the 4-H motto means in their own words.

Objectives at the comprehension level include the ability to:

convert   give examples   paraphrase
describe   illustrate   summarize
explain   interpret   tell in one's
                                       own words

❋ Application: Using Ideas

Application involves using what is remembered and comprehended. Thinking at this level allows application of what is learned to one's life in new or concrete situations. It includes the ability to use knowledge and learned material in meaningful ways. It may involve applying principles and rules, choosing appropriate procedures, or selecting solutions to problems that are similar to those presented previously. The role of application in the cognitive domain should not be confused with that of developing manipulative and purely physical skills in the psychomotor domain. Selecting foods high in animal sources of protein is an application level of activity. So is categorizing exercises into aerobic, flexibility, and strength-building activities. Making a chart showing soluble and insoluble fiber foods is also a cognitive process at the application level.

Objectives at the application level include the ability to:

apply   demonstrate   show
compute   estimate   solve
depict   relate   use

❋ Analysis: Reasoning

Analyzing involves breaking material into its constituent parts and determining the relationship of these parts to each other and to the whole. It may include identifying components, analyzing relationships among them, and looking at the principles involved in organization. It is taking one step, portion, or piece at a time to clarify the overall idea. Analyzing includes separating relevant material from trivia, distinguishing facts from hypotheses, and differentiating between objective data and value judgments. One example is analyzing a floor plan for features such as possible furniture arrangements, traffic flow, placement of rooms to minimize noise and maximize privacy, and building costs.

Objectives at the analysis level include the ability to:

analyze   determine   outline
associate   discriminate   point out
differentiate   distinguish

❋ Synthesis: Creating

Synthesis is the ability to put parts and elements together into new forms. Ideas are organized into new patterns; materials are put together in a structure that wasn't there before. Creativity and originality are

Figure 4-1	DOMAINS OF LEARNING	
COGNITIVE	**AFFECTIVE**	**PSYCHOMOTOR**
Knowledge (C-K)	Receiving (A-Rec)	Perception (P-P)
Comprehension (C-C)	Responding (A-Res)	Set (P-Set)
Application (C-Ap)	Valuing (A-V)	Guided response (P-GR)
Analysis (C-An)	Organizing (A-O)	Mechanism (P-M)
Synthesis (C-S)	Characterization (A-C)	Complex overt (P-COR)
Evaluation (C-E)		response

emphasized. In planning a unit of study for kindergartners, for example, an individual would consider everything he or she had learned about child development, the subject matter to be taught, teaching methods, media and materials, and ways of getting young children interested and motivated. Similarly, someone designing a toy would synthesize knowledge concerning developmental levels of children, possible materials that would be safe for children, and marketing techniques and procedures.

Objectives at the synthesis level include the ability to:

combine	devise	rearrange
compile	integrate	reorganize
compose	modify	revise
create	organize	rewrite
design	plan	write
develop	propose	

❋ Evaluation: Making a Judgment

Evaluation is concerned with learners' abilities to judge the value of ideas, methods, materials, procedures, and solutions by developing or using appropriate criteria. The criteria are the yardsticks used in making a judgment. Examples include comparing and contrasting styles of parenting, assessing the facilities and services offered at an assisted living facility for seniors, and weighing the pros and cons, in given situations, of buying clothes versus making them.

It should be noted that some educators disagree about whether evaluation actually involves the most complex level of cognitive thinking. Some put it just below synthesis, making synthesis the highest step in the cognitive domain. In either case, educators should build learning experiences that necessitate synthesizing and evaluating into their programs.

Objectives at the evaluation level include the ability to:

appraise	conclude	judge
assess	contrast	weigh
compare	evaluate	

Unfortunately, too often only the knowledge level in the cognitive domain is emphasized and evaluated. Learners are taught facts and specifics and are then asked to repeat them in various ways. What purpose does the information serve if learners don't understand it and can't use it? Most facts, per se, will be forgotten within a short time. Every educator has an obligation to incorporate higher levels of thinking and to build on the knowledge that learners attain.

In most cases it's not enough for learners to acquire only a basic knowledge of facts. Consider someone who learns the names of various tools but doesn't recognize their intended purpose, much less how to use them. The individual would be lost attempting a simple building or repair project.

❋ Cautions for Writing Cognitive Objectives

It's important to note that an objective can be at a level different from what its lead verb suggests. If an objective states, "Compile a list of . . . ," this activity may be at the synthesis level or the knowledge level, depending upon how the rest of the behavioral objective is worded and how the subject matter is presented. "State in your own words . . . " denotes the comprehension level because it involves explaining, which learners can do only if they understand the material. However, "state" is more frequently used at the knowledge level in the sense of reiterating or repeating a fact, such as "State the principal rule of storage." "Identify the solution . . . " implies solving an application problem, even though the word "identify" is generally associated with the knowledge level. These examples illustrate that the behavioral words indicated for each level in the cognitive domain should serve as guidelines only. Sample objectives from the cognitive domain are given on the next page.

Sample Objectives in the Cognitive Domain

The following six behavioral objectives relating to types of housing provide examples at the sequential levels in the cognitive domain.

Level 1: Knowledge. *List* types of housing available in the community.

Level 2: Comprehension. *Explain* the characteristics, advantages, and disadvantages of various types of housing available locally.

Level 3: Application. *Compute* the cost of living in various types of housing in the community.

Level 4: Analysis. *Analyze* given situations to determine types of housing desirable for meeting the needs and lifestyles of various individuals, families, and groups.

Level 5: Synthesis. *Plan* a new housing development to meet the needs of different people and kinds of families.

Level 6: Evaluation. *Evaluate* available housing for the various types of individuals, families, and groups that live in the community.

Obviously, learners have to identify types of housing, such as manufactured homes, duplexes, town houses, apartments, and condominiums, before they can describe the homes' characteristics or summarize their advantages and disadvantages. Likewise, students must understand the provisions of living in various types of housing before they can estimate costs and savings related to maintenance, utilities, insurance, and income tax deductions. Similarly, these factors need to be applied when determining types of housing that best meet the needs of specific individuals or groups. In the example, each succeeding level is dependent upon achieving the lower levels satisfactorily. Occasionally, a level can be bypassed, but this should be done with caution. In the previous example, learners could be asked to evaluate available housing without having planned a housing development.

Remember that plans for education programs don't necessarily have to include behavioral objectives that reach the highest level. In a comprehensive survey course, for

✳ Affective Domain

It is much easier to formulate objectives and evaluate accomplishments in the cognitive and psychomotor domains than in the affective domain because it involves emotions. A learner's interest, attitude, or appreciation must be measured through observable action. This action, or evidence of learning, needs to be clearly specified as it is in this behavioral objective: "Show interest in child development by voluntarily participating in a community service project for children, by relating babysitting experiences, or by reading extra material on this topic."

According to the *Taxonomy of Educational Objectives*, five levels of the affective domain deal with emotional learning. These range from being aware of a particular phenomenon to developing a total philosophy. As learners proceed through the affective levels, they internalize emotions that affect behavior and actions. The organizing principle in this domain is internalization.

✳ *Receiving: Attending and Becoming Aware*

At this level, learners merely become aware of a situation, idea, or process. They notice and are willing to receive certain stimuli. Awareness is developed through the sensory organs. This level includes developing sensitivity, tolerance, and alertness related to a particular issue. Educators are concerned with getting, holding, and directing learners' attention so they'll be willing to try certain behaviors. An example of the receiving level would be Jennifer, a young woman who is becoming aware that some people purposely incorporate soy-based foods in their diet.

Some behavioral tasks associated with receiving are to:

accept	*perceive*
acknowledge	*show awareness*
notice	*show alertness*
pay attention	*tolerate*

✳ Responding: Doing Something About It

In addition to perceiving a particular situation, idea, or process, in responding the learners do something with or about it. They may make the first overt responses in order to comply, but later make them willingly and with satisfaction. Responding involves developing a low level of commitment. At this level, learners follow through with directions, comply with their instructor's request, and respond voluntarily when given alternatives. They are actively involved in the learning process. At this level, Jennifer is reading about the benefits of soy products and signs up for an evening seminar on the topic.

Some words and phrases used to indicate responding are:

accept responsibility	consent
agree to	cooperate
answer freely	contribute
assist	follow
be interested	obey
be willing	participate willingly
care for	respond
communicate	show interest
comply	visit
conform	

✳ Valuing: Taking Action on Your Own

Behavior change

Valuing means that learners are developing attitudes and accepting the worth of objects, ideas, beliefs, or behaviors and also showing preferences for them. They are consistent in responses concerning a particular issue and express opinions about it with conviction, whether they meet with approval or not. There is individual commitment to an underlying value that guides behavior. In other words, the person begins to prize and cherish the position chosen in relation to certain ideas and issues. In addition, at this level, the individual's behavior and actions are consistent and stable enough to make the learner's values identifiable to others. At the valuing level, Jennifer is telling friends about her new interest in soy. She buys soymilk and tofu at the supermarket and regularly tries new recipes at home.

Because valuing relates to developing attitudes, some of the following words can be used to formulate objectives at this level:

adopt	initiate
assume responsibility	prefer
behave according to	seek
choose	show concern
commit	show continuing
desire	desire to
exhibit loyalty	use resources to
express	

✳ Organizing: Arranging Values Systematically

This level includes organizing values, determining the interrelationships among them, and establishing a hierarchy of the dominant ones. Personal ethical standards that learners know about, read about, and watch impact their value systems. Learners analyze evidence and form judgments about social responsibilities. This illustrates how the affective and cognitive domains are interrelated. Value systems drive learners' behavior. Convinced about the value of adding soy to her diet, Jennifer adapts her daily eating plan around a goal of consuming at least 25 grams of soy every day.

Because organizing means to arrange values in priority order according to a system, some words that can be used to establish behavioral objectives at this level are:

adapt	classify	rank
adjust	disclose	reveal
arrange	group	select
consistently		

✳ Characterization: Internalizing a Set of Values

At the highest level of achievement in the affective domain, beliefs, ideas, and attitudes are integrated into a total philosophy of life, or world view. Characterization may be expressed as devotion to a cause. Values are internalized to such a degree that there are persistent and consistent responses in similar situations. Internalized values show up in many facets of a person's life. At this top level, Jennifer is telling friends about the advantages of substituting soy protein for meat protein. She invites them for a meal of vegetarian chili made with soybeans, salad, and pumpkin pie made with tofu.

While Jennifer's actions show her values clearly, it can be extremely difficult to measure achievement objectively at this level. However, these are some behaviors that may be associated with characterization:

act upon	exhibit
advocate	influence
defend	maintain
devote	serve
display	show consistent devotion to
exemplify	support

✳ Cautions for Writing Affective Objectives

There can be a problem with objectives in this domain because evaluating them may become highly subjective. That's why measures of attainment and evidences of achievement should be preestablished and clearly specified. Evidence of achievement in the affective domain is sometimes measured by cognitive behavior. Here are some examples:

- Show interest in children's clothing by *pointing out* self-help features.
- Express concern about the depletion of energy resources by *writing* an article or *preparing* an oral report about how to get better gas mileage when driving.
- Exhibit loyalty to the school chapter of FCCLA by *organizing* an open house for prospective members, by *writing* a code of ethics for officers, or by *proposing* a new installation ceremony.

These affective objectives show that there may be alternative ways designated for measuring affective achievement. When attendance at a certain event is compulsory or when an assignment is required, there is no behavioral evidence of affective achievement, change, or growth.

At the receiving and responding levels, learners see if they are comfortable with perceived values. However, affective objectives at these levels are very often indistinguishable from learning experiences—the actual tasks and activities that enable learners to achieve planned objectives. Notice that it's difficult to differentiate between the following as behavioral objectives or learning experiences:

- to *pay attention to* a demonstration
- to *care for* the organic garden
- to *contribute to* a discussion

Objectives at the knowledge and comprehension levels in the cognitive domain are often more appropriate than objectives at the receiving and responding levels in the affective domain. This is true because the intent of objectives at the receiving and responding levels is usually cognitive in nature. For example, learners pay attention to a videotape in order to cite, identify, or list certain facts or to repeat some cognitive information. When voluntarily answering questions, learners are often giving examples, explaining, or summarizing in their own words. Therefore, cognitive objectives at the knowledge and comprehension levels might be more appropriate to precede affective objectives at the valuing level than affective objectives at the receiving and responding levels.

✳ Sample Objectives in the Affective Domain

There are two primary reasons for the difficulty in measuring achievement in the affective domain: the variables are intangible and evidences of attainment need to be predetermined. These evidences may be specified by using phrases like these in the objectives:

as proved through	by listing
as shown by	by volunteering to
by deciding to	when doing
by giving examples	when participating in
by going to	

Sample objectives in the affective domain follow. They are examples of objectives relating to the guidance of children that would be appropriate for students enrolled in an occupational course in child care services.

These examples illustrate the increased complexity of objectives as higher levels are achieved. At the lower levels, educators do more structuring than at the higher levels, where learners become more self-directive.

✳ Psychomotor Domain

Psychomotor learning is concerned with developing physical skills. Proficiency is sought in performing motor tasks. Speed, accuracy, manual dexterity, and economy of effort are important. The organizing principle is increasing complexity. Simpson, in the *Classification of Educational Objectives, Psychomotor Domain*, has identified five levels in this domain.

✳ *Perception: Recognizing and Detecting Sensory Cues*

Learners become aware, through the five senses, of objects, qualities, and procedures. In other words, sensory stimulation provides the basis for becoming aware of the action to be performed. Learners observe so that they can recognize appropriate behavior and will be able to act accordingly. For example, a demonstrator may show how to knead bread dough and allow learners to touch the dough so they can feel how the texture changes when it has been kneaded sufficiently.

Words that describe behaviors at this level include:

detect	perceive	taste
feel	recognize	view
hear	see	watch
listen	sense	
observe	smell	

✳ *Set: Becoming Ready to Act*

Set is a mental, physical, or emotional readiness for a particular kind of action or experience and the willingness to respond to it. Being physically set involves assuming a body stance appropriate for doing a particular task. In learning how to pick up a heavy object, for example, learners bend their knees and keep their backs straight to achieve the correct posture to perform the action.

Some words that describe behavior at this level are:

achieve a posture	sit
assume a body stance	stand
establish a body position	station
place hands, arms, feet	
position the body	

✳ *Guided Response: Imitating and Practicing*

This involves practicing the action under supervision through imitation or trial and error. Learners repeat one phase of a complex skill by doing it as it was demonstrated. In child development, learners may repeat a finger play exercise as they were shown. In culinary training, the learners may practice measuring accurately on a balance scale.

Here are some of the words that describe behavior at this level:

copy	operate under
duplicate	supervision
imitate	practice
manipulate with	repeat
guidance	try

✳ Mechanism: Increasing Efficiency

At this level, a learned response becomes habitual and is performed with some degree of skill and confidence. There is improved efficiency in performing the action. A student in a health services occupational program may make a bed quickly, smoothly, and with a minimal expenditure of time and energy, using the "once-around" method.

Behavioral tasks include the ability to:

complete with confidence	*increase speed*
conduct	*make*
demonstrate	*pace*
execute	*produce*
improve efficiency	*show dexterity*

✳ Complex Overt Response: Performing Automatically

Learners perform more complicated acts automatically, without hesitation, efficiently, and with a high degree of skill and self-sufficiency. They proceed with assurance, ease, and muscular control. Students may skillfully select and lay out pattern pieces, cut them out, transfer marks to the fabric, pin pieces together, and then stitch them into a new shirt.

Some terms that describe behavior at this level are:

act habitually	*master*
advance with assurance	*organize*
control	*perfect*
direct	*perform*
excel	*automatically*
guide	*proceed*
manage	

✳ Cautions for Writing Psychomotor Objectives

Sometimes the application level in the cognitive domain is confused with psychomotor learning. Making a chart to show the characteristics of natural and synthetic fibers and their primary uses is a cognitive activity because it involves remembering, understanding, and selecting the information to include on the chart. The *only* physical skill involved is in drawing straight lines for the chart.

Psychomotor objectives at the *perception* level are often indistinguishable from learning experiences. For example, learning experiences may consist of activities such as *feeling* the textures of different fabrics, *tasting* vegetables prepared a variety of ways, and *viewing* a video showing prenatal development. This situation is similar to the one that exists in attempting to write objectives at the receiving and responding levels in the affective domain. Low-level cognitive objectives may precede *set* in the psychomotor domain so that perception-level objectives aren't needed in all situations.

The chart below provides sample objectives in the psychomotor domain. They are examples of objectives relating to a person who wants to transform plain bedroom walls with a decorative painting technique such as sponging or ragging. They illustrate progression through the levels of learning in the psychomotor domain.

Sample Objectives in the Psychomotor Domain

Level 1: Perception. *Look at* and *feel* samples of various painting finishes.
Level 2: Set. *Stand* in front of the work surface with paint and paintbrush, sponge, or muslin, using a step stool or ladder if necessary.
Level 3: Guided Response. *Practice* the painting techniques shown in a how-to book or brochure on several sheets of poster board.
Level 4: Mechanism. *Show dexterity* in applying the paint to the actual wall, creating a decorative, textured look.
Level 5: Complex Overt Response. *Maintain efficiency* and *proceed* to complete the entire project with confidence.

Guidelines for Writing Behavioral Objectives

The words and phrases suggested for establishing behavioral objectives in all the domains are intended to serve only as guidelines. The context in which a verb is used can change the meaning and intent so that, in actuality, another level is indicated. For example, at the mechanism level of the psychomotor domain, learners could prepare a convenience food product with skill and efficiency. In contrast, at the highest psychomotor level, complex overt response, they might use a complicated recipe to prepare an elaborate dessert or meal, confidently using appropriate procedures and efficient management techniques.

The context in which a behavioral term is used may indicate a domain that isn't what you might associate it with. To illustrate this, learners could use rules in the cognitive sense of applying them, or they could use their resources to initiate policies they believe in strongly and are committed to, or they could use acquired physical skills to perform a specified task.

Although some educators advocate writing objectives beginning with "The learner should be able to . . . ," the authors of this book believe that such wording is contradictory to the basic premise of using the behavioral approach. How do educators know if learners are able to do something unless they actually do it? Consequently, it's more logical to begin objectives this way: *The learners will:*

Identify . . .

Summarize . . .

Apply . . .

Using this format eliminates the need to precede every objective with "The learners (or "students," "club members," "clients," or "participants") will . . . " Instead, each objective can be worded concisely, starting with a behavioral verb that indicates exactly what learners are expected to do.

Write behavioral objectives to include only one verb and only one idea or variable. It is better to write separate statements for each objective than to try to include too much in one. For instance, if an objective is stated "Identify and analyze . . . ," learners may be able to do the first part but not the second. Consequently, use only one verb in stating each objective; never use behavioral terms indicating different levels in formulating one objective.

An example of a poorly written objective is: "Develop menus for nine consecutive days for children attending a camp for diabetics and for their nondiabetic counselors who need to lose at least ten pounds."

Because there are two ideas expressed here, there should be two objectives. One objective should pertain to diabetic diets and the other to weight-loss diets. In addition, behavioral objectives should be written without qualifying numbers. In this case, the number of days and pounds should be omitted. Instead, these specifics may be included in the learning experiences that are planned to enable learners to meet particular objectives. The poor behavioral objective might be restated: "Plan appropriate menus for diabetic children" and "Develop a dietary plan for losing weight." Menu planning for diabetics shouldn't be limited to camp situations and there is no reason to restrict dietary planning for losing weight to camp counselors. Behavioral objectives should be written in broader and more general terms.

Figure 4-2

VERBS TO AVOID IN BEHAVIORAL OBJECTIVES

Objectives beginning with "to discuss" are extremely difficult, if not impossible, to measure objectively unless educators have previously established the exact criteria by which the discussion will be evaluated. Even when this has been done, learners often bring up valid points that have not been anticipated. When this happens and learners do not include factors expected in the answers, educators are faced with the problem of measuring responses fairly.

The following terms are sometimes used erroneously in formulating behavioral objectives. *These are not measurable behaviors unless they are qualified.*

AVOID USING	
Appreciate	Have faith in
Appreciate fully	Know
Ascribe to	Learn
Become familiar with	Realize
Believe in	Recall
Develop a feeling for	Recognize
Discuss	Recognize the importance of
Enjoy	See the need for
Enthuse	Truly believe
Grasp the significance of	Understand
Have an awareness of	Value

No time frame is specified because it may take several days, weeks, months, or more to attain them.

Figure 4-2 on page 52, "Verbs to Avoid in Behavioral Objectives," will help you distinguish between observable and nonobservable objectives.

✳ Terminal and Enabling Objectives

Higher-level objectives are used when planning a unit, course of study, or conference. In the cognitive domain, these are usually at the analysis level or higher. Occasionally, however, a unit objective at the application level is used. These higher-level objectives may be called *broad*, *overall*, or *terminal objectives*. (The label "terminal objective" or the abbreviation "TO" is used to refer to these higher-level objectives in later chapters.)

Objectives for lessons or small units of subject matter are called *specific*, *daily*, or *enabling objectives*. Their levels lead sequentially to the level of the broad, overall, or terminal objective. For example, the broad unit objective, which relates to the major concept, may be at the synthesis level. Daily objectives, or those relating to the subconcepts, may be at the knowledge, comprehension, application, and analysis levels. Occasionally, the concluding daily objective is at the same level as the broad objective. This is most likely to happen the last day of a unit. An enabling objective, however, does not exceed the level of the terminal objective. If it did, the terminal objective would be inappropriate. Enabling objectives planned for the beginning of a unit or series may stop several levels below the terminal objective. In the example of the menu-planning unit described on page 52, the broad objective is at the synthesis level. The seven specific objectives for the unit might be developed so there are three at the knowledge level, two at the comprehension level, and two at the application level.

✳ Sharing Objectives with Learners

There are advantages in sharing behavioral objectives with learners. Objectives provide guidance for studying. As they review for a test or prepare an assignment, learners know what is expected of them. Some educators write the objectives for the day on the board or provide handouts of both the broad, terminal objective and the specific or enabling objectives. In some situations, the learners help plan the objectives. These may not be expressed in exact, pedagogical terms, but the learners are participating in the teaching-learning process. Their contributions should prove worthwhile because learners often have accurate and strong feelings about what they need to learn and know.

Evaluation is facilitated when behavioral objectives have been formulated carefully and in advance because the objectives predict the type of evaluation that is appropriate and the level at which achievement should be measured. Behavioral objectives also serve as the basis for selecting and planning meaningful learning experiences.

Competency-Based Education

The competency-based approach to education emerged more than thirty years ago because of the growing emphasis society placed on accountability. There was dissatisfaction with existing educational programs as it became evident that many students were leaving school without the basic skills needed to function effectively in the workplace and in society. Taxpayers became concerned about the quality of education programs and the professional abilities of college graduates planning to teach. *Accountability*, as it relates to educators, encompasses relevancy, adequacy, effectiveness, and efficiency.

For learners, competency-based education can be thought of as criterion-referenced education in which the desired outcomes relating to cognitive, affective, and psychomotor behaviors are stated as objectives. Learners are made aware that certain specified *competencies*, or measurable and observable behaviors, are expected of them and that they must demonstrate attainment of these competencies in order to pass. This system takes the use of behavioral objectives beyond their usual application. That is, competencies are ordinarily a measure of *how well* a learner has mastered the material, not just *whether* it has been mastered.

The similarities between the use of behavioral objectives and competency-based education can be illustrated by examining the characteristics of competency-based education.

1. Competencies to be demonstrated, or objectives, are stated in behavioral terms and sequenced according to the needs and abilities of the learners.
2. Achievement is measured by determining if preestablished levels of competence, or performance, have been met.
3. Learners are informed of the levels of competence, or objectives, they are expected to achieve, as well as how they will be evaluated. The criteria for evaluation are shared.
4. The instructional program provides a variety of learning experiences that use different teaching methods and media to enable learners to reach the specified competency levels or to achieve the stated objectives.
5. Because attainment of specified competencies, or achievement of objectives, is the purpose of the educational program, time is not a factor. Some learners may need little time to reach specified competency levels, while others require much more time.
6. Assessment of competency performance, or achievement of objectives, is the primary source of evidence used in the evaluation process. Therefore, the learner must assume a large degree of responsibility for meeting these preestablished

levels of performance. Thus, the learner and educator share responsibility for accountability.

 # Knowledge, Attitudes, and Behavior

Dietitians are the most frequent users of a knowledge-attitude-behavior model because their main focus is to improve clients' nutritional status. In that model, "knowledge" refers to cognitive learning in a broad sense, not just to the first level in that domain. In this context, knowledge is meant to be interpreted as multifaceted and also to include comprehension, application, analysis, synthesis, and evaluation.

The relationship between cognitive attainment and motivational factors is not completely clear. What may be motivating information for one group of learners may not be the least bit motivating for another group. For example, older people are more likely to be motivated by programs focusing on prevention of cancer and osteoporosis than most teens would be.

What is the relationship between cognitive achievement and attitudes? Many studies have failed to substantiate a link between these two variables. Other studies have revealed only a slight relationship between cognitive attainment and attitudes. It's very difficult to draw a cause-and-effect relationship between the two.

✳ Behavioral Change

Well then, is knowledge related to behavior? Probably some knowledge, in the sense of cognitive achievement at various levels, is related to changing behavior, but knowledge is not a strong predictive factor.

Is there a relationship between attitudes and behaviors? There is little evidence to substantiate one. Some scholars theorize that you have to change behavior to change attitudes, rather than the other way around. For example, you might encourage people to adopt energy-saving behaviors. When these consumers see how much lower their own utility bill could be, their attitudes toward energy conservation might be more positive.

How, then, do you assess behavior change as one of your objectives? Changing both attitudes and behavior is a very slow process. Sometimes measuring change takes many years. Recently, health educators have noted lower rates in smoking among the general population, but they have been working on this problem for many years. Education programs about the dangers of being overweight abound, and yet obesity rates continue to increase. Perhaps the objective of the numerous weight-loss and weight-maintenance programs will be realized in years to come. In educational settings where the length of the teaching-learning process is limited, it may not be possible to measure changes in behavior.

Here is one model that outlines six stages for behavior change. It is built on the individual's current behavior and gives a time frame for achievement.

1. **Precontemplation:** The person is either unaware of or not interested in making a change.
2. **Contemplation:** The individual is thinking about changing, usually within the next six months.
3. **Preparation:** The individual actively decides to change and plans a change, usually within one month. Sometimes the person has tried to change previously.
4. **Action:** The person attempts to make the change, but has been doing so for less than six months.
5. **Maintenance:** The change is sustained for six months or longer.
6. **Termination:** The behavior has become so integrated and is so habitual that the person is no longer in the stage cycle.

Behavior change objectives are assessed quantitatively in numbers or in frequencies. In other words, "How many people?" "Compared to twenty years ago, how much . . . ?" An example of an objective in nutrition education focusing on changing behavior might be "Modify dietary habits to eat more healthfully." Attainment of this objective might be measured by the following:

- Number of times healthy dietary changes are made
- Frequency with which dietary modifications are made

In addition, standard dietary intake measures could also be employed to assess dietary changes and modifications such as:

- 24-hour recalls
- Four-day dietary records
- Food frequency questionnaires
- Diet habits questionnaires

Of course there is the ever-present problem of respondents telling what they think you want to hear, what they think they should be doing, and/or repeating what the educator told them. Unfortunately, interventions planned to increase knowledge and to improve attitudes usually haven't resulted in major positive behavior changes. Furthermore, programs focusing on the knowledge-attitude-behavior paradigm provide an ineffective model for planning objectives designed to bring about changes in behavior.

To build a winning football team, a coach wouldn't have players only watch games on TV, memorize the play book, and read stories about football greats' lives, and then test them on this material. Players might do some of these activities, but they certainly would play "real" football—practicing the actions they had viewed and read about. Coaches' half-time pep talks are notorious for trying to build positive attitudes.

Likewise, a chef's achievement isn't evaluated by his or her ability to explain how to prepare light and flaky piecrusts. Similarly, a student can't be asked to read about how to clean teeth, take a written test on the material, and then be called a dental hygienist. Competence is measured by doing—by demonstrating certain techniques or behaviors.

The Language of Objectives and Competencies

As you have seen in this and previous chapters, the educational community uses specific terminology to describe the planning process. Here are terms related to the context of this chapter:

Affective domain—A classification of behaviors consisting of attitudes, interests, appreciations, values, and other aspects of emotional learning measured through observable action. These behaviors are organized in terms of increasing internalization.

Attitude—A feeling or emotion, a mental position assumed toward a person or statement of fact.

Behavior—Anything done that involves action, what a person or people do.

Behavioral objective—A statement specifying what is expected of learners that can be measured objectively because there is concrete evidence of achievement. Sometimes called instructional or performance objectives.

Cognitive domain—Behaviors having to do with intellectual pursuits, thinking, using the mind, rational learning. These behaviors are organized from simple to more complex mental processes.

Competency—The ability to perform a specific set of related tasks successfully to meet a specified standard. May include cognitive, affective, and/or psychomotor skills.

Domain—A logical grouping or classification of thought processes, emotions and attitudes, and skills with common attributes and a hierarchy of levels.

Enabling objectives—Lower level behavioral objectives that lead to achievement of higher level, terminal objectives. Sometimes called specific or daily objectives.

Instructional objective—Another term for *behavioral objective* or *performance objective*.

Performance objective—Another term for *behavioral objective* or *instructional objective*.

Psychomotor domain—Physical learnings in which dexterity, agility, speed, accuracy, and motor-skill efficiency are organized from simple to complex.

Terminal performance objectives—Higher level objectives attained only after a planned series of enabling objectives have been achieved. Sometimes called broad or overall objectives.

Planning for Accountability

The push for accountability in education is unlikely to wane. In school districts, administrators, teachers, and learners all must show that they are well prepared and that appropriate learning has taken place. Many states and districts use standardized or state tests to verify learning—at least in key academic areas. Often, outside funding is tied to a course of study that is planned with clear, behaviorally-based objectives, and success is measured by how well students can demonstrate attainment of those objectives.

If you plan to be in a service-related profession or will work in a business setting, accountability is always required. But regardless of the "stakes," you have seen that the process of carefully planning observable objectives, devising learning experiences that allow learners to meet them, and evaluating mastery really is the essence of teaching.

Building Your Professional Portfolio

Analyzing objectives. View a videotape of a teaching situation. Write out the objectives you believe the educator had planned for the learners to achieve. Explain how the teacher clarified them or why they remained unclear.

Linking concepts and objectives. Select two of the following concepts. For each concept, write objectives labeling domains and levels. Use at least two domains of learning for each concept selected.

- Kitchen safety
- Understanding nutrition facts labels
- Selecting children's toys
- Care of wounds
- Personal characteristics of persons with eating disorders

Building learning. Select any concept and write at least three objectives in each domain for this topic. Label the domains and levels.

Terminal objectives. Write a terminal objective for a topic of your choice. Identify the enabling objectives that would lead to attainment of the terminal objective. Label the levels of all the objectives.

Changing behavior. Outline a plan for changing a nutritional practice using the six steps enumerated in this chapter for changing behavior.

Chapter 5

Designing Learning Experiences

Everyone has had the experience of performing well on a test only to have little or no recall of the material a week later. As an educator, you want your learners not only to remember what you teach them, but also to be able to apply it to their lives. You will be ready to develop successful, meaningful learning experiences once you lay the groundwork detailed in Chapters 3 and 4—identifying concepts to be covered, formulating objectives, and determining the generalizations that learners will be guided to make.

Developing a learning experience, or learning activity, involves choosing an appropriate teaching method and designing the experience itself. Learning activities may be primarily physical, as in using a commercial mixer; social, such as planning an event for nursing home residents; emotional, as in portraying roles in a work-based conflict; or intellectual, such as computing insurance costs. Activities are planned to help learners meet the predetermined objectives. These may be in the cognitive, affective, and/or psychomotor domains.

Various teaching methods can be used to implement the learning experiences. Skits, labs, discussions, debates, and field trips are just some of the methods available. This chapter discusses the many factors an educator must consider in choosing appropriate learning experiences.

 ## Considerations in Selecting Learning Experiences

Learning experiences describe what learners will do and how they are to do it. Like objectives, learning experiences begin with behavioral verbs. Usually they're written so that the verb indicates what the learners, rather than the educator, will be doing. Wording learning activities from the students' point of view helps you become aware of the variety, number of senses, and changes of pace involved. Either approach is acceptable, but consistency is important to avoid confusion about who is to do what. Learning experiences that are planned for an entire unit of study, workshop, or conference may be described in general terms. Learning experiences that are part of a daily lesson plan, seminar, or short program are usually given in more detail. As you develop a learning experience, note any necessary media, materials, and resources that will be needed.

Depending on the plans, learning experiences may be carried out by individuals, by a small group, or by an entire class. They may be part of classroom work, FCCLA activities, or a wellness program. Many variables affect the learning experiences, teaching methods, and media used. However, the most important are the concepts to be covered and the objectives that have been established. Other variables to consider when developing learning experiences are also discussed in this chapter.

✳ Concepts

Concepts are the subject matter or topics that will be the focus of the program or lesson. In designing a learning activity for a given situation, ask yourself, "What's the best way to help my learners clarify these concepts and attain the objectives?" Preparing a meal in the microwave oven, for instance, would most likely be covered using a demonstration, videotape, and/or laboratory experience. Improving family communication might be approached with skits or discussion. Transparencies with overlays, a fabric board with pictures of foods, or a flip chart that builds food groups sequentially could be used equally well to teach the Food Guide Pyramid. When there are several strategies that would be effective, choose the one you are most comfortable with, that hasn't been used frequently or recently, or is the least time consuming to prepare. What method might you choose for teaching teens about guidance techniques appropriate for toddlers? Would you use the same method if the learners were parents?

✳ Basing Learning Experiences on Objectives

A learning experience must reach the level of learning indicated by the corresponding objective but shouldn't exceed that level. Although a learning experience often begins with components at a lower level of learning than that of the objective, ultimately it should reach and match the objective level to enable your learners to attain the objective. In the following example, the objective is at the application level and the accompanying cumulative learning experience begins at the knowledge level and proceeds to the application level.

Behavioral Objective
Use nutrition facts labels to select foods. (Application)
Learning Experience
Look at the information found on nutrition facts labels. Explain how consumers can use this information in selecting foods to eat. Use a variety of nutrition facts labels to pick out the foods highest and lowest in calories, saturated fat, protein, and other specific nutrients. Use information on nutrition facts labels to choose foods that are the best selections for people who are diabetic, are overweight, and/or have heart disease.

An objective at the knowledge level, such as "List information found on a nutrition facts label," might have been used here, but it isn't necessary. If it were included, the learning experience would be restated in two parts. Every stated objective has at least one separate and parallel learning experience planned to enable the learners to achieve it.

An entire class often completes the same learning experience, but sometimes the students are offered choices. Several learners may be able to achieve an objective after participating in a single activity, whereas other classmates may need to complete several learning experiences before they achieve the same objective. Providing several activity options for meeting an objective also allows learners to choose the one they find most useful and effective. Some people learn best by reading, some by discussing the material, and some by working alone to complete a project. Learning styles and multiple intelligences are discussed later in this chapter.

Figure 5-1 on page 60 illustrates how learning experiences can be planned to help learners attain behavioral objectives from the lowest to the highest level in the cognitive domain. Although every cognitive level

Figure 5-1
MATCHING LEARNING EXPERIENCES TO OBJECTIVES

BEHAVIORAL OBJECTIVES	LEARNING EXPERIENCES
Knowledge: List the different types of maturity.	• Read about types of maturity in a selected textbook. • Match the names of the types of maturity written on a chalkboard, poster, flip chart, or transparency with each definition, as it is given.
Comprehension: Give examples to illustrate the various types of maturity.	• Divide into groups of three to five students. Act out situations depicting the ways in which mature and immature behavior are illustrated by the characters in the dramatizations. • Draw cartoons illustrating various types of maturity. • Describe individuals (anonymously) who are mature in some respects and immature in others.
Application: Demonstrate the possible effects of mature and immature behavior.	• Make up and present miniskits showing mature and immature behavior. Then show how the situations could be handled differently to obtain more positive reactions from others.
Valuing: Show a continuing desire to learn more about maturity by completing an extra-credit project.	• Give an oral report relating a situation from literature in which immature behavior had detrimental effects. Tell about an instance in which a literary character showed greater maturity than expected from a person that age. Discuss the effect this had on others. • Read a biography or autobiography about a person having many mature characteristics. Prepare a written or oral report showing how this person expressed his or her maturity.
Analysis: Analyze given situations to determine types and levels of maturity.	• Read case studies. Point out various types and levels of maturity depicted by the people in the stories. • Watch a television show or part of a movie in which the characters demonstrate various types and levels of maturity.
Synthesis: Propose ways to cope with immature behavior.	• Project the future consequences of the mature and immature behaviors of characters by completing a story. • Formulate answers to the letters in advice columns that reveal immature behavior. • Develop a set of guidelines for those who work with preschoolers to use in directing the children's immature behavior into more mature actions.
Evaluation: Evaluate one's own level of maturity.	• Judge one's own maturity using a scorecard, checklist, rating scale, or questionnaire. • Evaluate progress after making and using a plan for self-improvement.

is used here for illustrative purposes, a level is sometimes omitted if it appears that learners can continue up the hierarchy without it. Note that the "valuing" objective is included at a point corresponding to its parallel position in the affective domain. The concepts to be clarified are the types of maturity: chronological, physical, mental, emotional, social, and philosophical.

✳ Variety

It's important to select a variety of teaching methods and media, both from one day to the next and within the same class period or program session. It's not motivating for learners to do the same thing every time you meet. Ideally, seek to have approximately three different types of learning experiences within each class period or session, unless a long laboratory experience is planned. You could need more than three if you teach in a school with longer periods, such as a block schedule. Don't change pace just because it's written in your plan, however. If participants are stimulated by a particular learning experience, capitalize on the teachable moment and continue while interest is keen and learning is still taking place.

✳ The Learners

Effective learning activities are based on knowledge and understanding of the learners who will use them. The length of the learners' attention spans affects the number of different learning experiences needed. Their preferences for certain types of activities need to be considered. The makeup and personality of the group are other influences. If you have a group of active sixth graders, include experiences that involve physical participation. The ways in which participants learn best also must be determined. Some learn most from reading or other visual stimuli, some from discussion, and still others from group projects. Multiple intelligences and how to accommodate them are discussed on pages 64 to 68.

It's essential that all learners become involved in the teaching-learning process. For some, participation may be passive, whereas for others it may be active. Some

individuals might be researching and writing about color theory while others are doing something physical, such as experimenting with the effects of light on colors. The vehicle for participation can reflect individual preferences. The important thing is that each person be involved in some appropriate way.

✳ Number of Senses Involved

Generally, there is greater retention of subject matter when learners use several senses in carrying out a learning activity. Whenever feasible, the participants should not only hear about the topic under consideration, but also see pertinent materials relating to it. Seeing may include reading or viewing appropriate visuals. Many of the topics you may teach will lend themselves to sensory learning. For example, in studying types of fabrics, students can handle samples to learn about fiber content, weave, and various finishes. Actually preparing low-fat versions of favorite foods will leave a more lasting impression than only reading about them because touch, smell, and taste are involved. See "How People Learn—Sensory Modes," *Figure* 5-2 on page 62, to see how sensory data affect people's ability to retain information.

Retention of subject matter is about the same when learners are told about or read about the material. However, if both senses—hearing and seeing—are involved, retention after a time lapse of several days is more than four times greater. Consequently, you should make every effort to involve as many senses as possible in a learning experience without becoming repetitious, boring, or insulting to the participants. Repeating material exactly as it was covered previously can be interpreted as talking down to people.

In a classic study conducted by the Sacony Oil Company in its management training program, it was found that retention improved significantly when the trainees both heard and read about the subject matter. The most impressive finding is shown in *Figure* 5-2 where recall was 65 percent after three days without intervention

Figure 5-2
HOW PEOPLE LEARN—SENSORY MODES

Taste	1.0%
Touch	1.5%
Smell	3.5%
Hearing	11.0%
Sight	83.0%

LEARNER'S ABILITY TO RETAIN INFORMATION STUDIED

10%	of what is read
20%	of what is heard
30%	of what is seen and heard
70%	of what the learner says as he/she talks
90%	of what the learner says as he/she demonstrates

LEARNER'S ABILITY TO RETAIN INFORMATION OVER TIME

	3 HOURS	3 DAYS
Telling alone (Lecture)	70%	10%
Showing alone (Visual aid)	72%	20%
Combination of showing & telling	85%	65%
Teaching others	90%	85%

when both lecture and reading were used. This is compared to 10 percent and 20 percent, respectively, when lecture and reading were each used alone.

❋ Time of Day and Year

When will you be teaching a specific group of learners? Groups that meet early in the morning, just after lunch, or at the end of the day often react to the same learning experiences very differently. Experienced educators also consider the time of year. Very warm weather may rule out some options. In schools, there are learning experiences that wouldn't be well accepted at the beginning of a term because the students and teacher don't know each other very well. For example, students may be reluctant to participate in sociodramas before rapport has been established within the class. Near the end of the school term, students may be restless. Educators often need to plan activities that are especially stimulating and interesting then and just before holiday vacations.

❋ Physical Facilities

The physical facilities, including the amount and availability of space and equipment, affect the learning activities that can be planned and carried out. For example, a room you have reserved in a community center for an adult program may not have any presentation equipment. If you have a small or crowded classroom, it would be difficult to have an activity for children. Sometimes you may be able to borrow or exchange a room temporarily, but this isn't always possible. You may have to adapt the activity to the limitations of your physical facility.

❋ Administrators' Attitudes

The attitudes and philosophies of your supervisors and administrators have a bearing on the methods of teaching you select. If your community is very traditional or slow to accept new ideas, this will influence the learning experiences you use. On the other hand, if you are in a situation where most of the professionals have creative and interesting teaching strategies, it will be easier for you to be innovative, too.

❋ The Educator

Naturally, you will favor some methods of teaching and types of learning experiences more than others because you feel comfortable and secure using them. When something has worked well in the past, it's logical and practical to use it again. However, don't rely strictly on activities that have proven successful. Be open to new teaching methods or learning experiences. Your learners may suggest ideas. If you decide something wasn't successful after several tries, there are always alternatives. Unless you try a method, you don't know how successful it might be.

Learning Styles

A successful educator must acknowledge that students learn in various ways and teach accordingly. The possible variations in learning styles are almost as great as the individual differences among learners. Learning styles describe the circumstances under which students learn best. Auditory learners benefit by listening and visual learners prefer to see what they are learning. A hands-on approach is favored by tactual learners. Some people retain what they learn best after working as part of a group, and others by active, *experiential learning* situations. Experiential learning is a process whereby learners are given an experience, reflect on it, form generalizations from the experience, and then relate it to real-life applications. The learners are participants rather than spectators. Lab experiences and simulations are two examples of experiential learning. You will learn more about this type of active learning in Chapter 13.

Saying students differ in learning styles means that certain teaching strategies, such as visual media, auditory approaches, or hands-on experiences, are more effective with some individuals than others. Older learners are likely to have more than one learning style because their life experiences have helped make them more adaptable. Learning styles include not only preferred ways of learning, but also descriptions of personality characteristics that relate to learning, such as flexibility, cooperation, and introversion. Several theories pertaining to learning styles are discussed in this chapter.

✳ Visual, Auditory, and Tactual Learners

Do you know someone who needs to see something in order to learn it? Perhaps you fall into this category. If so, you are a visual learner. It's possible that you are artistic and have a good sense of color. You may sometimes find it difficult to follow oral directions and to pay attention during lectures. Visual learners benefit from written directions, organizing notes by color coding, and the use of graphics to reinforce learning. These learners can visualize how words are spelled and where information appears on a page.

Auditory learners are just the opposite. They may have difficulty with reading and written directions, preferring to hear the information instead. Such individuals learn by listening to an instructor or tapes, participating in discussions, and interviewing. Reviewing notes aloud or even summarizing material on tape helps auditory learners.

The tactual learner has a knack for putting things together without reading directions. This learner may have trouble sitting still and does best in lessons when there is hands-on physical activity. Tactual learners are often good athletes because they are well coordinated. They require frequent breaks and may be most successful with memorization if they work on it while walking or exercising. Working on a computer helps to reinforce learning for tactual learners because of touching the keyboard.

✳ Concrete vs. Abstract Learners

Two dimensions of how people learn have been identified by David Kolb. He determined that learners perceive material along a continuum from concrete to abstract. Some people, those who tend to be concrete learners, sense and feel their way. They become involved in the learning experience. These individuals jump in to see if something will work. They learn best by doing.

Abstract learners, on the other hand, examine the situation from the outside. They think about it. They process information by observing and reflecting. The two methods are equally "good." They merely represent how learners first approach a problem.

When the concrete and abstract dimensions are juxtaposed, four learning styles emerge:

1. Type One learners perceive *concretely* with their senses and feelings, and process *reflectively* by watching. They are reflective sensor-feelers.

2. Type Two learners perceive with their *intellect* and process *reflectively*, by watching. They are reflective thinkers.
3. Type Three learners perceive with their *intellect* and process by *doing*. They are thinking doers.
4. Type Four learners perceive *concretely* with their senses and feelings, and process actively by *doing*. They are doing sensor-feelers.

❋ Right Brain vs. Left Brain

Work by Bernice McCarthy combined research on learning styles with right-brain/left-brain processing research. The two halves of the brain, the right and the left hemispheres, process information differently. The left hemisphere deals with intellectual, analytical, verbal, logical, and sequential processing, while the right mode involves intuitive, visio-spatial, subjective, unstructured, and random processing. Research indicates that both kinds of processing are equally valuable. However, education concentrates heavily on the left brain, while minimizing the development of the right hemisphere.

❋ Accommodating Learning Styles

You, as an educator, not only have to be sensitive to your students' learning styles, but you also have to decide how much to adapt to them. If you believe individual students' learning styles are constant and unchanging, you may want to match your teaching style to their learning style. On the other hand, you may want to alter students' learning styles by using greater variety in methods, materials, and media. For example, in working with visual learners, you have to decide whether to use only visual strategies because it's efficient, or whether to use other approaches as well because that broadens the learners' scope. By varying your methods and media, you accommodate every student's learning style some of the time. It's also appropriate to offer alternatives to learners. Just be sure that all the options enable students to achieve the lesson, unit, or program objectives equally well.

Multiple Intelligences

The idea that learners have a single, fixed intelligence was dispelled in the 1980s by Howard Gardner's Multiple Intelligence theory. It challenged the view that people are born with a certain amount of intelligence. According to Gardner, "We all have different intellectual strengths or 'intelligences' and we use them all to varying degrees to acquire knowledge, understand the world, engage in problem solving, create, and to meet the challenges in our daily lives."

❋ Multiple Intelligence Areas

Gardner's research suggests that there are at least eight intelligence areas. They are verbal/linguistic, intrapersonal, interpersonal, visual/spatial, body/kinesthetic, logical/mathematical, musical/rhythmic, and naturalist. Everyone has all of these intelligences but not in equal amounts. "Just as we look different from one another and have different kinds of personalities, we also have different kinds of minds," Gardner explains. In all people, one or two intelligences are probably stronger and more fully developed than the others. The challenge for educators is to avoid treating learners the same by catering to just one intelligence. Gardner's philosophy asks "How are you smart?" *not* "How smart are you?"

❋ *Verbal/Linguistic = Word Smarts*

Verbal/linguistic intelligence pertains to words and language. You use this intelligence in listening, speaking, reading, and writing. Favored learning activities include reports, library research, explanations, debate, poetry, feelings, humor, jokes, and biographies. Other activities might be journal, creative, and autobiographical writing.

People high in verbal/linguistic intelligence like seeing, saying, and hearing words, as well as playing with sounds in language. They enjoy reading and usually have highly developed auditory skills as well. Educators, journalists, authors, attorneys, radio and TV commentators, and translators are likely to have these characteristics.

❋ Interpersonal = People Smarts

Interpersonal intelligence is used in relationships. It includes the ability to communicate effectively with others, to have empathy for their feelings and beliefs, and to work cooperatively in a group. It entails mediating conflicts, participating in and leading discussions, and providing feedback. Other activities enjoyed are interviewing, and organizing peers or group project work.

Individuals with interpersonal intelligence tend to be leaders, have many friends, and seem to have an intuitive ability to sense the feelings and intentions of others. They are often counselors, teachers, salespeople, community leaders, and politicians.

❋ Intrapersonal = Self Smarts

Intrapersonal intelligence is based on self-knowledge and self-reflection. People who demonstrate this intelligence are keenly aware of their own inner feelings, strengths, and weaknesses. They are inclined to set goals. They are also reflective and analytical because they use higher-level thinking skills, such as reasoning. They tend to shy away from group and team activities, while enjoying their private time and space.

People with intrapersonal intelligence are often self-employed. Careers vary but include researchers, theorists, and philosophers.

❋ Visual/Spatial = Picture Smarts

This area of intelligence includes being able to visualize objects and to create mental pictures and images. People with visual/spatial intelligence know the location of items; they can picture where an image is on a page. People with this intelligence enjoy drawing, building, making posters and collages, and mapping.

People high in visual/spatial intelligence often enjoy games such as checkers and chess. Depending on whether they are oriented toward the arts or sciences, these individuals may gravitate toward art or sculpture, architecture, engineering, or sciences that emphasize spatial intelligence.

❋ Body/Kinesthetic = Body Smarts

This intelligence is related to psychomotor skills and knowledge of the body and how it functions. It includes using the body to express emotions, play games, and use and interpret body language appropriately. People with body/kinesthetic intelligence enjoy acting, dancing, exercising, and demonstrating. They are hands-on thinkers who need to be physically active. They tend to have excellent large- and fine-motor coordination.

People with body/kinesthetic intelligence use physical gestures, experiment, and are good at imitating others' mannerisms. They might be actors, dancers, surgeons, or athletes.

❋ Logical/Mathematical = Number Smarts

Logical/mathematical intelligence is related to numbers and the relationships among them, the ability to recognize patterns, scientific thinking processes, and making connections between pieces of information. Thinking processes include analyzing, reasoning, classifying, sequencing, comparing and contrasting, calculating, and problem solving.

Strong logical/mathematical learners would enjoy performing experiments and computing metabolic rates. They think conceptually, develop timelines, work on logic problems, categorize patterns, and question natural events. People with logical/mathematical intelligence tend toward careers in science, accounting, computer programming, and engineering.

❋ Musical/Rhythmic = Music Smarts

This intelligence includes heightened sensitivity to the human voice, musical instruments, and environmental sounds. Individuals showing musical/rhythmic intelligence are able to hear patterns and recognize them. They enjoy listening to singing and other musical performances.

People with musical/rhythmic intelligence can learn more if content is related to music. They may be connected with the theater, choirs, orchestras, and bands.

❋ *Naturalist = Nature Smarts*

A decade after introducing the first seven intelligences, Gardner added the naturalist intelligence. People with this intelligence classify and categorize plants, animals, and scenes in nature. They note changes in the environment and create observation notebooks. They enjoy using tools such as microscopes, binoculars, and telescopes.

Certain parts of the brain are dedicated to the recognition and naming of natural things. People with naturalist intelligence may be photographers, botanists, museum or nature guides, or artists who draw nature scenes.

❋ Identifying Multiple Intelligences

Talking with other educators, professional personnel, and parents or guardians can help you identify individuals' learning-style preferences. Your observations of behaviors, performances, interests, and reactions are also helpful. Intelligence strengths can be gleaned through journaling assignments, autobiographies, interviews, discussion group projects, oral reports, and artwork. You can set up special activities and offer choices in learning experiences to give you insight about the ways that particular individuals prefer to learn. The following statements can give you insight into your use of multiple intelligence theory:

____ My students may not be learning to their fullest potential.

____ Even when I'm doing my best teaching, I sometimes wonder why certain learners don't get it.

____ Many of my students know more about a topic than they demonstrate on tests that I give.

____ Some of my learners are highly skilled in areas that aren't included in the curriculum.

____ My teaching doesn't seem to stimulate my learners enough.

____ I need to try new ways to motivate and actively involve my participants in the learning process.

Answering "true" to even one of these statements means the educator needs to study more about multiple intelligences.

❋ *Why Consider Multiple Intelligences?*

People of all ages learn in different ways, at different rates, and for different reasons. All intelligences need to be valued and nurtured. Considering different intelligences provides equal access to learning for all participants and, therefore, helps promote self-confidence. It also supports inclusion of personal and social development and varied teaching strategies as part of the curriculum. See "Using Multiple Intelligences to Improve Nutrition and Health Practices," *Figure* 5-3 on page 67, for an example of how the respective intelligences can be involved in an educational program.

❋ Interdisciplinary Projects

Many educators have heard this comment when they've corrected a student's grammar: "But this isn't English class!" With emphasis on teaming in education today, it's wise to help students transfer learning from one subject to another. Interdisciplinary projects help strengthen several intelligences simultaneously.

Learners need to be helped to see that most content areas are interrelated. Food Science is an integral part of Dietetics, Family and Consumer Sciences, and, of course, Science. Mathematics permeates all subjects. When educators plan lessons together, they can interconnect fields of study and reinforce concepts traditionally taught elsewhere.

Some community education programs, such as Scouts and many school programs, emphasize selecting themes that encompass many content areas. This not only brings educators together, but it also helps learners see the relationships among the subjects they are taking. "Family Life in America's Past" is a theme that could encompass content from Family and Consumer Sciences, History, Math, Geography, English, and/or Art. Some possible learning experiences follow. Can you think of another one that would connect music to the theme?

• Sketch cartoons or draw stick figures to show how family roles have changed throughout U.S. history.

Figure 5-3 — USING MULTIPLE INTELLIGENCES TO IMPROVE NUTRITION AND HEALTH PRACTICES

INTELLIGENCES	LEARNING EXPERIENCES
Verbal/Linguistic	Write scenarios showing people using effective and efficient consumer buying skills in a supermarket.
Interpersonal	Develop a list of resource people and organizations where a person with an eating disorder might go for help. Write and present skits of counselors helping clients and peers helping one another with eating disorders.
Intrapersonal	Make a long-range plan for improving your fitness and nutritional status. Plan fun activities and appealing meals. Develop and use an evaluation instrument for recording progress.
Visual/Spatial	Draw cartoons showing consumers selecting and/or enjoying low-cost, nutrient-dense foods. Sketch foods, showing a standard serving size.
Body/Kinesthetic	Lead the group in exercises that promote total body fitness, including flexibility, strength building, and aerobic activity.
Logical/Mathematical	Use information on nutrition facts labels to plan menus for a day that are approximately 2,000 calories; have between 25% and 30% fat; have at least 67 grams of protein; and meet the percent of recommended daily values for vitamins A and C, calcium, and iron.
Musical/Rhythmic	Write songs and jingles that promote healthy food choices and good nutrition.
Naturalistic	Plan, plant, and maintain a vegetable garden that provides optimal nutrition from foods by using them as they ripen.

- Develop and present skits showing how family life has been affected by topography and climate. Consider areas such as the Great Plains, New England, the Southwest, and the Pacific Northwest.
- Read books to determine how home life was different in colonial times from today. Include child-rearing practices, personal hygiene, clothing, and diet.
- Read stories or watch videos showing how war affected family life during the Revolutionary War, the Civil War, and World Wars I and II.
- Make a chart using actuary tables to show how life expectancy has increased over time.

- Illustrate how portion sizes have changed from times when people worked physically from dawn to dark to today when many people lead sedentary lives.
- Take a walking tour to look at local buildings or examine pictures of structures with architectural features such as gambrel and saltbox roofs, front stoops, and garrison front wall construction. Analyze how such features reflected life at the time when they first became widely used.

The opportunities for interdisciplinary work are limitless. Not all need to be elaborate; they can be as simple as these:

- **FCS, Health, and Math.** Use nutrition facts labels to plan meals and snacks for three days that meet the Recommended Dietary Allowances for dietary fiber, protein, vitamins A and C, calcium, and iron.
- **FCS, Nutrition, and Art.** Use colored pencils or markers to draw attractive and unattractive meals on trays for hospital and nursing home patients. Combine colors, textures, and flavors that are appealing and unappealing. Analyze how the inappropriate combinations could be improved nutritionally and aesthetically.

 # Developing Appropriate Experiences

When you are aware of the personal characteristics, learning styles, and multiple intelligences of your learners, you can make better choices about which learning experiences to use. Few educators have the opportunity to personalize all instruction, but they can include a variety of activities and provide options where appropriate. When a learner is having difficulty grasping a concept, consider how that person learns best and provide appropriate remediation. You can also consciously work to build additional intelligences through the techniques you use and how you present them.

This chapter included different ways of looking at learning. Each can help you analyze your learners so that you can better meet their unique needs. For example, concrete/sequential-oriented learners like to use workbooks and manuals, to watch demonstrations, to use computer-assisted instruction, to be involved in hands-on materials, and to participate in field trips. The abstract/random-oriented learner prefers films, group discussions, short lectures accompanied by questions and answers, and videos. The abstract/sequential learner prefers extensive reading assignments, substantive lectures, audiotapes, and analytical "think-tank sessions." Concrete/random learners like games, simulations, independent study projects, problem-solving activities, and optional reading assignments.

Consider, too, how you learn best and what impact that has on your choice of learning experiences. Educators' efforts seem to be most effective when their own personal learning styles and teaching styles are in sync. At the same time, you must keep in mind that not all your students or clients will have the same dominant learning style you do. You will want to plan your learning experiences to include a variety of teaching methods and media that involve as many senses as possible. Also consider the other influences on the teaching-learning situation when choosing learning experiences. These include the time of day and year, equipment and materials available, and the general philosophy of the community program or school system in which you teach.

References

Gephart, William F., Deborah B. Strother, and William R. Duckett. Practical applications of research. Newsletter of Phi Delta Kappa's Center on Evaluation, Development, and Research, Vol. 3, No. 2, pages 43-46.

Kolb, David A. (1976, 1978) Learning style inventory teacher manual. Boston: McBer and Co.

McCarthy, Bernice F. (1981) The 4 mat system: teaching learning styles with right/left mode techniques. Arlington Heights, IL: Mark Anderson and Associates.

Multiple intelligence theory. http://www.scbe.on.ca/mit/mi.html

Using multiple intelligences to enhance learning.
    http://members.tripod.com/~Rheaultk/index.html

Checkley, Kathy. (1997) The first seven . . . and the eighth, a conversation with Howard Gardner. Educational Leadership, September, pages 8-13.

Building Your Professional Portfolio

Matching Activities to Objectives. Write six objectives at different levels for the same concept. For each objective, plan at least one learning experience that corresponds to that level.

Adapting Learning Experiences. Based on your teaching situation or one you are familiar with, give at least two examples of ways in which the time of day or year, physical facilities, or administrators' or community's attitudes placed constraints on teaching. Explain how you did or would adapt learning experiences to work within the limitations.

Multiple Intelligences. Choose a concept within your area of study. Using the multiple intelligences model, write a learning experience on the concept for each type of intelligence. Which were the most difficult to develop? Why?

Interdisciplinary Project. Develop a one-week plan for an interdisciplinary project that includes your major area of study. Explain how you would convince administrators and other educators about the importance and practicality of this project.

Chapter 6

Teaching Plans

A plan for teaching is like a map or tour guide. It shows your destination and how you plan to get there, yet allows for adaptability and creativity in reaching your goal. If you are driving to a distant place for the first time, you need to plan your trip in considerable detail and carefully map out your route in advance. If you have traveled to a place many times before, you may only have to refresh your memory about the route. In either case, you are free to detour, spend more time at an intermediate point than planned, or take an alternate road for part of the way. Likewise, you, as an educator, need to be flexible about your teaching plans. Learners' suggestions, your analysis of their reactions, or your own new ideas can all prompt modifications to the original plan.

This chapter presents information on teaching plans that you might make for long and short periods of time. If you are in a school setting, you are more likely to call your plans "unit plans" and "lesson plans." If you are teaching in Extension or other nonformal settings such as nutrition workshops, you may refer to your plans as "presentation plans," "session plans," or "workshop plans." In either case, you will start by developing a broad overview type of plan known as a unit plan. A unit plan is usually blocked out, or divided, into segments of time. The next step is to take each time segment from the unit plan and prepare a detailed lesson or teaching plan for that specific segment.

Planning Units for Workshops, Conferences, and Classes

A unit plan is developed for the number of days, weeks, or hours you anticipate spending on one major concept within the curriculum. Unit plans for classes, workshops, or conferences provide the *scope*—what will be taught, and the *sequence*—the schedule telling when various concepts and subconcepts will be covered. A unit plan is broad in scope and lacks the details that are an inherent part of the individual session or lesson plans. These more specific plans evolve from the unit plan. The broad unit plan generally includes the following basics:

• **Description of the educational situation.** This might include general observations about the backgrounds, interests, needs, and ability levels of learners in the group. In addition, a brief overview of the facilities, availability of resources, and administrative and community support might be included. Plans for teaching the unit are derived from the data pertaining to the learners, facility, and community.

- **A justification for choice of concepts.** Justifying your concepts will help you select the most relevant content. It will also prepare you to explain the value of the selected content to administrators and other decision makers.
- **A set of generalizations.** These generalizations show how you expect the learners to link the major concepts. Second- and third-level generalizations are appropriate for broad unit plans. First-level generalizations are too narrow in scope. (See Chapter 3 for more on generalizations.)
- **A conceptual outline.** This is a topical outline of the subject matter in terms of concepts and subconcepts to be covered. The process for developing and blocking out a conceptual outline is found in Chapter 3.
- **Terminal objectives (TO).** These objectives represent higher levels of learning. It may take several days to reach one terminal objective, although occasionally attainment of more than one higher-level objective might be anticipated in a single workshop or class period. Terminal objectives appropriate for use in unit planning are explained in Chapter 4.
- **Major learning experiences (LE).** Only the most important student activities, which allow for the attainment of the terminal objectives, are included in a unit plan. Observations and other information gathered during learning experiences can be used to evaluate learner progress.

Unit plans divided into blocks of time are easy to use because they provide an organized overview of the educator's broad plans for the educational program. The unit plan can block out days for a school setting or hours in a one- to three-day conference or workshop. By planning in advance, media can be requested or developed ahead of time, arrangements can be made for field trips and resource people, and pertinent references can be gathered and studied. Pages 72 and 73, *Figure 6-1*, give an example of a two-week unit plan on food selection appropriate for secondary school. The unit plan on pages 74 and 75, *Figure 6-2*, would be appropriate for a two-day conference for older adults. In this plan, the blocks of time represent various hours.

Note that in both sample unit plans, more than one day or one block of time is devoted to some of the major concepts; others are completed in one day or hour. In the samples, the terminal objectives (**TO**) are at various levels, depending on how high the educator decided to take the learners on each concept. Only major learning experiences (**LE**) have been suggested. These learning experiences enable the learners to meet the objectives, and they correspond in levels of learning. In other words, the learning experience in each case will allow the learners to reach the behaviors specified in the terminal objectives and grasp the concepts given. Labeling each objective in both unit and lesson/session plans with the domain and level of learning facilitates the planning of learning experiences at appropriate levels. Use the codes shown in the chart on page 45 in Chapter 4.

When you plan a unit, the concepts outlined should be attainable through the specified terminal objectives and accompanying learning experiences. A close relationship needs to exist among concepts, terminal objectives, and learning experiences in the unit plan.

Figure 6-1

SAMPLE SECONDARY UNIT PLAN
FOOD SELECTION

	MONDAY	TUESDAY	WEDNESDAY
WEEK 1	**I. FACTORS AFFECTING SIGNIFICANCE OF FOOD**		**II. MEAL PLANNING**
	A. Food habits B. Cultural patterns C. Social values D. Psychological satisfactions E. Family traditions **TO:** Analyze factors that affect the significance food has for individuals and families. (C-An) **LE:** Read and discuss case studies. Share own situations to determine influences on signifcance of food in one's life.	F. Fads and fallacies **LE:** Share food fads and fallacies. Discuss how they relate to the signifcance people attach to food.	A. Food Guide Pyramid and nutrition **TO:** Use the Food Guide Pyramid to ensure meals provide adequate nutrients. (C-Ap) **LE:** Using the Food Guide Pyramid, select foods for a specific individual that would ensure complete nutrition for a day.
WEEK 2	**II. MEAL PLANNING (CONT'D)**	**III. FACTORS AFFECTING FOOD PURCHASES**	
	(continued from Friday) **TO:** Evaluate meals for nutritional content, resource use, and lifestyle characteristics. (C-E) **LE:** Exchange menus written on Friday. Workin small groups to evaluate for nutrition, use of resources, and appropriateness to lifestyles.	A. Income B. Family composition and lifestyles C. Advertising D. Availability **TO:** Determine factors that affect food purchases. (C-An) **LE:** Listen to guest speaker discuss relationships between food purchases and various factors. **LE:** Work in small groups to plan and present one of the following: **(cont'd Wednesday)**	 1. Read handout of a news article suggesting ways to lower the proportion of income spent for food. Present information to class. 2. Develop sociodrama showing how family composition and lifestyles affect food purchases. 3. Prepare visuals on how advertising affects food purchases. 4. Write skit showing ways in which factors above impact food purchases.

Figure 6-1 (cont'd)   SAMPLE SECONDARY UNIT PLAN
FOOD SELECTION

	THURSDAY	FRIDAY
	II. MEAL PLANNING (CONT'D)	

W E E K 1	B. Resources
	  1. Money 4. Equipment
	  2. Time 5. Abilities
	  3. Energy 6. Available foods
	
	TO: Propose changes to enhance resource utilization in given meal situations. (C-S)
	
	LE: View pictures showing meals being served that reflect use of resources. Point out ways resources were used to advantage. Suggest changes.
		C. Lifestyles
		D. Values ⟶
		E. Daily food patterns
		
		TO: Plan meals considering nutritional needs, available resources, values, and food patterns. (C-S)
		
		LE: Work in groups and use case scenarios to plan meals that are nutritionally adequate for special groups and make the best use of available resources.

	IV. PLANNING FOOD PURCHASES	
W E E K 2	A. Food grades B. Food states and forms **TO:** Explain food grades, states, and forms people must choose from in making food purchasing decisions. (C-C) **LE:** Take field trip to a supermarket. Listen to guide explain grades, states, and forms of food. Complete worksheet.	C. Using ads and specials D. Manufacturer and store premiums E. Shopping lists **TO:** Identify factors contributing to consumer skills in planning food purchases. (C-An) **LE:** View skit about grocery shopping; discuss factors characters do and don't consider in planning purchases.

Educational Situation. The 24 junior and senior students in Anytown High School's Consumer Education class have had no previous foods courses. Anytown is a rural community of 35,000 people, with a major city 30 miles away. Most families have middle to low incomes. The majority of students go to work upon high school graduation. The town includes one supermarket and two small food stores. The FCS program has a new facility with a lab for food preparation and Internet access. The principal supports the program.

Justification. Most students will be living on their own within two years. Making wise food choices will enhance their health and financial status. The information presented will assist in sharpening their consumer skills in other aspects of their lives.

Generalizations.
1. If one takes into account factors affecting the significance of food in the lives of those being fed, one's choices will best meet their needs.
2. Successful planning is based on an analysis of nutritional needs, available resources, lifestyles, values, and daily food patterns.
3. Income, family composition, advertising, and availability impact food purchases.
4. Consumer skills in planning for food purchases are enhanced when ads, specials, premiums, and shopping lists are considered.

Figure 6-2　SAMPLE UNIT PLAN FOR TWO-DAY CONFERENCE
AGING WITH ENTHUSIASM

I. PHYSIOLOGICAL CHANGES OF AGING

	9:00–10:00 a.m.	10:15–11:15 a.m.	11:30–12:30 p.m.
D A Y 1	A. What Is Happening to My Body? **TO:** Explain various physcal changes that take place with aging. (C-C) **LE:** View PowerPoint® presentation and model of body as presenter describes age-related changes in body. Discuss.	B. How Will My Life Change? **TO:** Predict ways lifestyle will change with aging. (C-Ap) **LE:** In groups, generate on newsprint a list of ways lifestyle may change with aging. Share.	C. Adaptation and Adjustment **TO:** Propose ways to change environment to maintain a good quality of life as aging progresses. (C-S) **LE:** Working in pairs, discuss case studies of aging individuals and their adaptations for adjusting to limitations. Outline environmental changes needed to maintain quality of life. Share with group.

	III. AGING AND EATING		IV. MAINTAINING CONNECTIONS
D A Y 2	A. Nutrient Considerations **TO:** Explain how nutrient needs change with aging. (c-c) **LE:** Listen and view as leader shares Food Guide Pyramid and Modified Food Pyramid for 70+. View meals using food models that show differences. Discuss.	B. Deficiences and Disorders **TO:** Point out eating habits associated with reduced risk of disorders. (C-An) **LE:** Listen as presenter gives examples of conditions that may result if nutrients are deficient. View pictures showing health outcomes. Complete worksheet on ways to reduce risk of conditions.	A. Social Interactions **TO:** Give examples of ways to avoid social isolation. (C-C) **LE:** Discuss previous information on physical changes and effects they might have on relationships. Break into groups to determine ways to avoid social isolation. Share.

Educational Situation. This two-day conference will draw approximately 100 persons from a five-county area. Attendees will range in age from 55-90 years, be both male and female, and of middle to low income (with many on government assistance). The group is predominantly Hispanic, and Spanish is the first language of most. A grant from the State Department of Health is funding this program. Transportation will be available. The program will be held in the Anytown town hall meeting room. Tables and chairs are provided and a projection screen is available.

Justification. This program is needed to bring together an aging population from a sparsely populated area to share and learn. Many individuals lack accurate

II. AGING AND ACTIVITY

	2:00–3:00 p.m.	3:15–4:15 p.m.	
D A Y 1	A. Preventing Loss of Mobility **TO**: Explain ways to prevent loss of mobility in aging. (C-C) **LE**: View slides and transparencies as leader presents information from scientific studies on age, activity level, and muscle/bone loss. Share ideas on ways to prevent losses.	B. Strong and Fit Exercises **TO**: Repeat basic strength training exercises. (P-GR) **LE**: View documentation on basic strength training exercises. Participate in practice "workout" session.	

IV. MAINTAINING CONNECTIONS (CONT'D)

D A Y 2	B. Family, Community, and Organization Resources **TO**: Propose resources appropriate for individual situations. (C-S) **LE**: View brochures and handouts detailing information on community activities, family services, and organizations available to assist seniors. Decide what you think you would use in your senior years.	*in class activity* *topic sewing const.* *daily subconcept each "has 2 obj"* *-obj has at least 1 activity* *have them do do a lab - how to sew, practice,* *2 week sewing terms, machine parts, use machine make a pot holder*	

information on the age-related changes occurring in their lives. This program will provide that information, allow participants to connect with others, and help them to identify available resources to meet their needs.

Generalizations.

1. An understanding of the aging process assists people in making necessary adjustments in their lives.

2. Activity can help keep one's body healthy as one ages.

3. Proper nutrition contributes to a healthy, aging body.

4. Social interaction and the use of available resources can promote physical, mental, and emotional health during aging.

Individual Teaching or Lesson Plans

The extent to which you plan individual lessons and programs varies greatly, depending upon your teaching experience, knowledge of the subject matter to be covered, and the type of lesson being planned. For the experienced educator, this planning may be primarily mental, with only a few key ideas written on paper. The beginning educator usually has to plan more extensively and in more detail in order to feel confident when teaching. Even an experienced educator's lesson or presentation plans should contain enough information for a substitute with subject-matter background to use them with minimal preparation.

The unit plan provides the broad base from which individual lesson or teaching plans evolve. The "Sample Teaching Plan" for a school setting, *Figure 6-3* on pages 79-81, is based on the second Friday of the sample secondary unit plan. Refer to the sample teaching plan as you read about each component it includes.

❋ *Identifying Information*

At the beginning of the teaching plan, identify the setting, the length of the lesson, and when the teaching will take place. This will help you organize and file your plans. A substitute would also find this background information very helpful. Because the times at which lessons begin and end vary in different settings, it is essential that a substitute have this information. It will also keep you on track.

❋ *Major Concept(s) and Terminal Objective(s)*

The major concept(s) and terminal objective(s) of the lesson plan are taken directly from the unit plan. Placing these at the top of your teaching plan focuses your development of ideas and goals for the lesson. Next you will develop the content notes and learning experiences needed to teach each concept.

There should be a terminal objective for each domain of learning (cognitive, affective, psychomotor) for which you have enabling (more specific) objectives in the plan. The terminal objective indicates the highest level to which you will take the learners in the topic area. Enabling objectives are stepping stones that lead to attainment of the terminal objectives. Objectives are explained in detail in Chapter 4.

❋ *Introduction/Establishing Set*

Whether you use the term "the introduction" or "establishing set," the beginning of a lesson should be appropriate for the learners' ages and ability levels. It must motivate and get the attention of the group. In addition, the introduction should be related to the topic, stimulate thinking about it, and provide for a smooth transition into the body of the lesson. For these reasons, the introduction is usually more effective when it is planned carefully than when it is haphazard. Of course, you can usually change your approach if you get a better idea at the last moment. However, you can't count on devising a stimulating way to begin when you haven't planned in advance.

A carefully planned introduction contributes to your security and allows you to think about the students rather than about what you will say and do. See Chapter 8 for further information on establishing set with students.

❋ *Lesson Body*

The body of the lesson plan consists of enabling objectives, content notes, and learning experiences. It is very important that all three interrelate and are parallel to each other. The three-column format in the sample teaching plan in *Figure 6-3* makes it easy to check whether each objective has parallel content and at least one parallel learning experience. You can read across the plan and check for this interrelatedness. A good system is to number the enabling objectives, content notes, and learning experiences that correlate.

❋ Enabling Objectives

Enabling objectives lead up to the level of learning of the terminal objective but don't exceed it. It sometimes takes several days to achieve a terminal objective, so some of the enabling objectives for those days may be several levels below that of the terminal objective. For any one concept, objectives must be in sequential order.

It is possible to skip a level of learning, but only one level, as you work sequentially up the domains. Also as the content or a subconcept changes, the enabling objectives may revert to lower levels of learning again. Hence, enabling objectives could go in this order: C-K, C-K, C-C, C-An, C-E, (change of concept) C-K, C-C, C-An, C-An, and C-E. You can have more than one objective at the same level for a concept. In the sample teaching plan, the first three objectives build from the C-K to the C-Ap level. Then there are three at the C-C level because the concept has changed and objectives need to return to a lower level. One of these C-C objectives relates to premiums, one to manufacturer and store coupons, and one to shopping lists. Then there is one objective at the C-An level. The C-Ap level was skipped.

Keep in mind that if the concept is finished that day, the last enabling objective in a domain and the terminal objective in that domain will match. If the terminal objective carries forward to the next lesson, the last enabling objective probably will not reach the level of the terminal objective that day.

Because the three domains of learning interrelate, enabling objectives may shift from one domain to another. However, if the objectives in the three domains are separated out, the order of difficulty should be maintained in each. For example, you might be teaching in the cognitive domain on a topic and also trying to integrate some affective learning. You might go from C-K to C-C, then to A-V, then back to C-An, and finally to A-O. While moving from domain to domain, you keep the levels in order within each domain.

❋ Content Notes

The content notes provide the basic subject matter of the lesson or program. The content notes include the points you want to be sure are covered. Notes are written so no content is overlooked and omitted. It is easier to identify key points and examples before class. There are many forms for making content notes, and you will find a format that works best for you. Most teachers find it easier to refer to key points in outline format, rather than complete sentences in paragraph form. Sometimes it is appropriate to formulate key questions and to jot down points you want to be sure are brought out in the responses. (You might highlight questions in color, print them in boldface type, or use another technique for quick reference.) At other times you might want to reference an attached handout or other materials by noting, "See attached leaflet" in the content column. In some cases, you might put key points on transparencies or flip charts, then you elaborate upon them as you teach.

Content notes relate directly to each subconcept that is suggested in each enabling objective and, of course, to the parallel learning experience. Occasionally, one component of content notes pertains to the subconcepts included in two enabling objectives. In the sample teaching plan (*Figure 6-3*), the content notes labeled #2 and #3 cover points related to specials and ads. These subconcepts are referred to in objectives #2 and #3. You can save time and space by clustering content notes in this manner.

Sources for content notes include textbooks, professional journals, popular magazines, newspapers, the Internet, and commercial teaching materials. Your own notes from college courses and workshops may also be valuable sources if the content is still up-to-date and valid.

❋ Learning Experiences

Learning experiences are the activities in which learners take part so that they are able to achieve the specified objectives. Every objective has at least one learning experience indicating what the students will do. Sometimes two activities are planned to provide for attainment of one objective. Learning experiences in the sample lesson plan begin with a verb telling what the students will do. This helps teachers think about activities from the students' point of view. Learning experiences also can be written beginning with verbs telling what the educator will do to involve learners. Either form is acceptable; just be sure to be consistent.

Remember that learning experiences correlate with, or parallel, their objectives in levels of learning. For example, if an objective is at the analysis level, the parallel learning experience should take learners to the analysis level in terms of their thinking.

When listing learning experiences, it is helpful to include the specific media and materials that will be used. Obviously, some learning experiences will require more planning and preparation than others.

Planned learning experiences can be modified. Sometimes you or a student will have an idea that is better than one that you planned. In such a case, you may decide to depart from your lesson plan, at least in part. Educators who are secure in their subject-matter knowledge find it easier to be flexible. Those who are new or less secure about their knowledge or their teaching abilities are more likely to be afraid of departing from previously made plans.

✳ Summary/Closure

The summary or closure ties the lesson or program together by helping students formulate generalizations about the content that has been covered. In the plan on pages 79-81, students are asked to share and discuss the results of the last learning experience to tie the lesson concepts together. See Chapter 8 for additional information on bringing closure to lessons.

✳ Generalizations

Generalizations written for the unit plan are placed on the lesson plans to which they relate. It may take several days to get learners to the point where they can verbalize the generalization. Having a generalization on each plan helps to remind you of the big picture you want your learners to achieve. Each day as you bring closure, you can be working towards this generalization. Generalizations are discussed in detail in Chapter 3.

✳ Teaching Materials and Resources

Listing the materials needed for a lesson helps you organize your thinking and plan ahead. A substitute would find it extremely helpful to have a list of the media, such as posters, videos, and websites, to be used in the lesson.

Resources include student or teacher references such as texts, curriculum guides, and commercial materials. If you include a list of resources and references, the lesson plan can be used again at a later date and the subject matter can be reviewed quickly and easily.

✳ Evaluation

The objectives formulated will influence the methods of evaluation used. By evaluating higher-level objectives, you also may evaluate attainment of enabling objectives in the process. Some learning experiences also evaluate student achievement. It is helpful to indicate activities that serve this purpose. By doing this, it is easy to determine the objectives that remain to be evaluated. When developing a test, refer to the objectives to be covered and write questions that will indicate whether students have met them. Other methods of assessment are discussed in Chapter 7.

✳ Assignments

Including learner assignments in the teaching plan is optional. Assignments might include a project, small-group assignment, survey or interview, experiment, observation, worksheet, or other option to be completed during or outside of class. Assignments to be used as a basis for evaluating student achievement should be directly related to the objectives that have been established.

Figure 6-3

SAMPLE TEACHING PLAN

Audience: Juniors and Seniors at
Anytown High School
Course and Unit: Consumer Education
(Consumer Food Buying)
Class Period and Time:
First, 8:35 a.m.–9:20 a.m.
Day and Date: Friday,
September 13, 2xxx

A. Major concept(s) from unit plan:
- Planning food purchases
- Using ads and specials
- Manufacturer and store premiums
- Shopping lists

B. Terminal objective(s) from unit block plan
Point out factors contributing to consumer skill in planning food purchases. (C-An)

C. Establishing set
Ask students to unscramble the eight words written on a poster, all of which relate to shopping. Each word represents a factor to consider or a step to take before making food purchases. Students who finish quickly can be asked to write a sentence showing how each of the unscrambled words can relate to effective food shopping. (8-10 minutes)

Answers

D	A	S						(ads)
	H	H	L	T	A	E		(health)
S	E	R	O	T	S			(stores)
N	O	S	P	O	U	C		(coupons)
	I	P	A	L	S	S	E	C	(specials)
	T	I	L	S				(list)
G	N	N	I	L	P	A		(planning)
	G	S	R	D	A	E		(grades)

D. Lesson Body

ENABLING OBJECTIVES	CONTENT NOTES	LEARNING EXPERIENCES
1. List sources of ads consumers use to make food purchasing decisions. (C-K)	1. Sources of ads: • Newspapers • Magazines • Radio • TV • Flyers and circulars • Window displays • Internet—World Wide Web	1. Call out sources of ads that influence consumer decisions relating to food purchasing. (2-3 minutes)
2. Give examples of ways to identify specials. (C-C)	2., 3. Ways to identify specials in newspaper ads: • Bold print • Large type • Different colors • Coupons	2. View ads on posters as teacher points out and presents ways specials are emphasized. Call out other ways seen. (1-2 minutes)
3. Point out specials in given ads. (C-Ap)		3. View double-page newspaper ad held up by teacher and name the featured specials. (1-2 minutes)

Figure 6-3 (cont'd)

SAMPLE TEACHING PLAN

D. Lesson Body (cont'd)

ENABLING OBJECTIVES	CONTENT NOTES	LEARNING EXPERIENCES
4. Give examples of premiums that influence shoppers to make food purchases. (C-C)	4. Premiums that influence shoppers: • Coupons • Store discount cards • Games, like bingo • Products sold at discounts, such as dishes, children's books • Food samples in stores • Stamps or tokens accumulated to buy reduced-price products	4. Describe premiums that have influenced people in your family and others' as they planned purchases. (3-4 minutes)
5. Summarize advantages and disadvantages of using manufacturer and store coupons or discount cards. (C-C)	5. **Advantages of coupons:** • Saves money if product would be purchased anyway • Provides considerable saving when coupons are triple-off or double-off and coupons of 50¢ to $1 are used **Disadvantages of coupons:** • May buy products you do not really need • May overspend • Might find store brand still costs less • Takes time to cut out coupons and keep organized	5. Share results of interview done for homework: Ask at least one person, "Do you use manufacturer and store coupons when shopping for groceries? Why, or why not?" Discuss advantages and disadvantages of using coupons. (8-10 minutes) • Increases overall prices to consumers • Shoppers' cards record purchases (privacy)
6. Explain the advantages of preparing a shopping list. (C-C)	6. **Advantages of list:** • Lessens impulse buying • Saves time • Promotes advance meal planning • Serves as a reminder • Helps capitalize on ads, specials, and premiums	6. View a pantomime done by one or two classmates of a consumer shopping for food without a list. Discuss the advantages of using a list when shopping for food. (7-8 minutes)
7. Point out factors contributing to consumer skill in planning food purchases. (C-An)	7. Factors contributing to skill in planning food purchases (skit analysis): **Kim and Pat considered:** • Coupons • Premiums • Prices • Store location	7. View skit, "Kim and Pat Go Shopping." (Skit on next page.) Compile a list of factors the characters do and do not consider in planning food purchases. (12-15 minutes)

Figure 6-3 (cont'd)

SAMPLE TEACHING PLAN

D. Lesson Body (cont'd)

ENABLING OBJECTIVES	CONTENT NOTES	LEARNING EXPERIENCES
	7. (cont'd) • Ads • Specials **Kim and Pat did not consider:** • Planning very far ahead for purchases • Being hungry, leading to impulse buying • Having a shopping list	

E. Summary/Closure
Students will share lists compiled in Learning Experience 7. Teacher will ask what factors Pat and Kim considered. What factors did they forget to consider?

F. Generalization
Consumer skills in planning for food purchases are enhanced when consideration is given to the use of ads and specials, premiums, and shopping lists.

G. Teaching Materials:
- Poster showing ways to identify specials
- Double-page newspaper food ad
- Skit script "Kim and Pat Go Shopping"
- Props for Pantomime and Skit (Shopping basket, various food products, food coupons)

SKIT—"KIM AND PAT GO SHOPPING"

KIM: We'd better go shopping for food for dinner tonight.

PAT: Yes, I'm starving!

KIM: Got something special in mind for dinner?

PAT: No, anything that looks good. Where shall we go shopping?

KIM: Supertown Market gives you a free glass with a ten dollar purchase.

PAT: Aren't prices higher there?

KIM: Maybe. Where do you think we should go?

PAT: Let's try that new place, the Super Savings Store. It's closer than Supertown Market, too.

KIM: Oh, yeah. They've advertised they're giving double-off on coupons this week. I'll take the coupons we have. Are you ready?

PAT: Let's go. Maybe we can buy enough food for tomorrow, too.

H. Evaluation
Objectives 1, 2, 4, 5, and 6 will be evaluated on test; Learning Experiences 1, 3, 4, 5, 6, and 7 and summary/closure also provide evidence of attainment of objectives.

I. Assignment
Due today: Interview at least one person and ask the question: "Do you shop for food in stores which offer coupons? Why, or why not?" Write the answer in two paragraphs on a paper to be turned in.

For next class period: None.

Format Variations for Teaching Plans

Many teachers like to develop their teaching plans on the computer. Those who do sometimes find that other formats for the Lesson Body section work better than the three-column format shown in the sample lesson plan on food selection. Experiment and see what works for you. The format variation, *Figure 6-4* below, has gained widespread usage. (The objectives, content notes, and learning experiences #1, #2, and #3 have been extracted from the "Sample Teaching Plan" on page 79 to illustrate the new format.)

Figure 6-4　　ALTERNATIVE FORMAT FOR TEACHING PLAN

D. Lesson Body

Enabling Objective 1: List sources of ads consumers use to make food purchasing decisions. (C-K)

CONTENT 1:	LEARNING EXPERIENCE 1:
Sources of ads: • Newspapers • Magazines • Radio • TV • Flyers and circulars • Window display posters • Internet—World Wide Web	Call out sources of ads that influence consumer decisions relating to food purchasing. (2-3 minutes)

Enabling Objective 2: Give examples of ways to identify specials. (C-C)

Enabling Objective 3: Point out specials in given ads. (C-Ap)

CONTENT 2 AND 3:	LEARNING EXPERIENCE 2:
Ways to identify specials in newspaper ads: • Bold print • Large type • Different colors • Coupons	View ads on posters as teacher points out and presents ways specials are emphasized. Call out other ways seen. (1-2 minutes) **LEARNING EXPERIENCE 3:** View double-page newspaper ad held up by teacher and name the featured specials. (1-2 minutes)

Building Your Professional Portfolio

Unit Plan. Develop a unit plan for either a workshop or a class on a topic of your choice. Include a description of the situation, a conceptual outline, terminal objectives, major learning experiences, and generalizations. Block out the plan for concepts, terminal objectives, and learning experiences.

Teaching Plan. Develop a teaching plan for a topic of your choice for a workshop or a class. Use either of the formats presented in this chapter.

Interview. Interview an educator to determine the type(s) of teaching plans this individual uses. Describe how the format(s) used by the person interviewed differs from the suggestions in this chapter. Determine the reasons for, and benefits and drawbacks of, the various formats.

Chapter 7

Assessment

Assessment is the contemporary term for what has long been known as evaluation. It is a critical part of the teaching-learning process. In this chapter the two terms will be used interchangeably. Basic definitions for evaluation and assessment include determining the:
- Extent to which objectives have been reached.
- Success of educational endeavors in light of evidence.
- Worth or value of something.

All assessment and evaluation include some subjectivity on the part of the person making the assessment. The goal is to make your evaluation process as objective as possible. The use of testing and nontesting evaluation devices, or instruments, helps to ensure this objectivity.

There are many aspects of the teaching-learning situation that can be assessed: the learners, you as the educator, the environment in which you are working, and the program or curriculum. The main goal of evaluation is to promote improvements in your learners, yourself, your program, and your teaching environment.

Purposes of Assessment

Assessment is carried out for many reasons. The following are key purposes of the evaluation process:

- To assess learner growth and progress.
- To provide feedback to learners.
- To motivate learners.
- To determine where changes are needed in your teaching strategies.
- To determine concepts that need reteaching.

- To provide feedback to parents or guardians.
- To provide documentation for administrators, funding agencies, and state departments of education.
- To assess your abilities as an educator.
- To document the need for change in curriculum or implementation strategies.
- To justify continuation or implementation of a program.
- To report on learner achievement to those at higher levels of education so determinations can be made of the learner's readiness to proceed to the next level.

You can accomplish assessment through both testing and nontesting means. Paper-and-pencil assessments, observational activities, authentic assessment self-report techniques, and learner-developed portfolios all can be utilized to accomplish these purposes.

Linking Assessment to Objectives

In planning your educational program, you formulated the objectives you expected your learners to achieve. As noted in Chapter 4, these objectives may be in the cognitive, affective, and/or psychomotor domains. The learning experiences that you developed guided your learners toward the attainment of these objectives. Now it's time to see if your learners can perform at the levels in each domain that were noted in your objectives. This is the assessment step.

In addition to seeing if your learners have achieved the planned objectives, you may also want to see how well your learners perform in terms of competencies or standards that are external to your program. These can be state or national competencies or standards that provide benchmarks for learner progress. Sometimes these standards or competencies are the basis for questions on state or national licensure exams. If this type of assessment is needed, it's essential that you meshed your objectives with these standards and competencies as you developed your program and teaching plans.

If you have written clear objectives, then the assessment process is simplified. The behaviors you wish to assess are outlined in the wording of your objectives. For example, if your objective in your plan is for your learners "to determine the injury-related muscle problem based on a set of symptoms," then you need to present these learners with a set of symptoms to see if they are able to determine the problem. The evaluation strategies you use must see if learners can perform at the level expected in the objective. In this latter case, the learner was being asked to function cognitively at the analysis level.

Educators who want to evaluate learners' achievement fairly and honestly use a broad base of assessments. Different learners do well on different types of measures. Using a variety of evaluative methods gives all learners an opportunity to do well. Assessment of achievement may be based on homework assignments, work completed during the class or program, projects, reports, laboratory experiences, self-evaluative instruments, and tests. The proportional weight given to each evaluation in determining the composite evaluation should be made clear to students so that they can establish priorities. For example, a chapter quiz might be worth 20 points, while a chapter test is worth 80 points.

Using Tests for Assessment

In addition to determining grades, test results can also be used to analyze learners' strong and weak points and to provide a basis for initiating a conference or counseling session. Teachers can also use test scores to determine which topics they have covered most adequately and which methods of teaching they have used most effectively.

The frequency of testing depends upon the setting and concepts being covered. If only one or two tests are given in a semester course, undue emphasis may be placed upon them. In a workshop, a short, parallel pretest and posttest can measure learning.

In a school setting, it's a good idea to give tests at the beginning of the class period. When learners are told they will be given a test at the end of the period, they are likely to spend class time worrying or cramming rather than paying attention to the material presented. Surprise or pop tests have drawbacks. Students may resent both the teacher and the subject matter. The probability that students will cheat also increases. Although not all students will study for announced tests, students should have the option of deciding this for themselves. Remember that one purpose of giving a test is to encourage students to review and clarify concepts.

Since cheating is a difficult problem to handle, take precautions to minimize its occurrence. See Chapter 18 for specific suggestions for coping with this problem. As a test score increases in importance in determining a final term grade, the likelihood that students will cheat also increases. Basing term grades on a broad base of quizzes, assignments, reports, and projects is more equitable. There's less pressure to cheat when students realize that neither one very high test score nor one very low score will have a great impact on their overall averages.

General Guidelines for Constructing Tests

The following general guidelines relate to writing most teacher-made tests. They may also be used to evaluate and modify any tests that come with a textbook program. After these guidelines, you will find specific information on constructing various types of test questions. Examples of each are included.

1. As you write test questions, keep a tally to be sure the objectives you want to assess are covered in proportion to the instructional emphasis given to each in your teaching. Also check to be sure test questions are assessing learners at a level parallel to the objective. For example, if your objective was to plan meals for an elderly person, your test question must call for writing out an appropriate meal.

2. Use only two or three different types of test questions on a test. For example, you might use multiple choice, short answer, and restricted-response essay questions. On another test you might use matching and extended essay questions. Every time learners have to switch to a new type of question, they have to shift mental gears. It's best to minimize these transitions in a single test. However, you do want more than one type of item on a test. Some learners find certain types of test questions easier or harder to complete. A mixture will more accurately reflect all students' learning.

3. Group similar types of test items together. This organizes the test to minimize the need for learners to keep changing their orientation and thinking process. For example, all true-or-false questions should be grouped in one section of the test, and all multiple-choice questions should be grouped in another section. Within each section, arrange items so they are grouped by subject matter. In other words, keep like concepts together. Include separate directions for each type of question.

4. Test questions should progress in difficulty, beginning with easier questions in the first part of the test. This enables learners to experience an initial success that may motivate them to proceed through the test with a positive attitude. In general, selection questions that ask learners to choose among several possible alternatives are easier than ones that require supplying an answer or writing an essay. Therefore, put selection-type items at the beginning of the test.

5. Word test items and directions clearly and concisely. If the vocabulary used is too difficult, the item may be assessing whether the students understand the meaning of specific words rather than the concepts involved. On the other hand, when the vocabulary is too simple and monotonous, students may be insulted or bored and, consequently, make careless errors. Test-wise students, or ones who are particularly adept in syntax, will have a decided advantage if there are grammatical clues that give away the right answer. This possibility can be eliminated by using "a (an)," "(s)," "was (were)" with nouns and verbs where plurals or verb tenses could indicate the correct responses.

6. Write test items so that an obvious pattern of answers does not emerge, such as "true, true, false, true, true, false," and so forth.

7. Visual and verbal examples used in class and statements from the text shouldn't reappear on a test precisely as they were originally presented. Doing so

assesses memorization skills, rather than the ability to interpret, apply, or analyze subject matter.

8. Avoid using negative statements in a test. If you must do so, call attention to the negative word by underlining or capitalizing it.

9. Avoid placing material in parentheses in test questions. Although your intent may be to clarify by giving an example, in actuality this might cause confusion.

10. Make answer lines appropriate in length for students' handwritten answers.

11. Be sure each test question is independent of all other questions on the test. Answering a question correctly should not depend on having answered a previous question correctly.

12. Check to be sure that the answers to questions are not inadvertently provided in other items on the test.

13. Give a point of reference for attitudes, theories, and philosophies. For example, instead of stating, "Experience is the best teacher," you might write, "John Dewey believed that ideas must be judged by experience."

14. Write and format a test to simplify scoring. For objective questions, place the answer line to the left of each item. That way you can place an answer key next to the answer column for rapid scoring. When tests are longer than two pages, you might have students write all their responses on a separate answer sheet.

15. Place a title at the top of the test. This assists in filing and later retrieval of the tests.

16. Also include space at the top for identifying information such as a name, date, and period.

17. Use continuous numbering throughout the test. In other words, there should be just one question with a #6 assigned to it, rather than an item #6 in each section. This makes it easier to go over the test with the students.

18. Be sure each test question fits completely on one page. Continuing an item onto the succeeding page can be confusing.

19. Indicate clearly the point value of each test item. This helps learners determine the amount of time and effort they should allow for completing their responses.

20. Plan enough time for the test so the majority of students have enough time to finish. A general rule of thumb is to take the test and then at least double the time it took you to take it. This will give you an estimate of how much time students will need.

Constructing Various Types of Test Items

Test questions generally fall into one of the following three categories:

- **Selection-type items.** The learner chooses an answer from given options.
- **Supply-type items.** The learner thinks of and writes the correct short answer.
- **Essay items.** The learner uses higher-level thinking skills to develop and write out a longer answer.

An explanation of each of these three categories of test items follows, along with guidelines for writing and examples.

❋ Selection-Type Items

There are three types of selection-type test items: true-false, multiple-choice, and matching items. In each case, the learner has to choose a correct response from some alternatives that are presented by you, the test writer.

❋ *True-False Items*

Because true-or-false questions are fairly easy to write, they are frequently used in tests. However, these questions must be carefully written to maximize clarity and minimize guessing. Remember that any statements used must be unequivocally right or wrong. Have approximately the same number of true items as false items. When most answers are either true or false, students may focus more on an answer pattern than the content answer. With simple true-false questions, use more to minimize the effects of guessing.

Since the letters *t* and *f* can be easily confused, choose an alternative to save time in grading and to avoid arguments when tests are returned. You could use **+** for true and **0** for false. Another option is to use an answer column and direct students to circle T or F. The words "true" or "false" can be written out, but this increases grading time.

There are ways to make true-false questions more challenging. Students can be asked to correct false statements or to tell why a statement is false. These techniques help minimize guessing and also assess student learning more accurately.

The examples that follow show different types of true-false items. They also show how to write questions for various levels of learning, from knowledge to comprehension to analysis. Many educators erroneously believe that objective test items can be written only at the knowledge level.

True-False Example 1: Simple Two-Response Choice (knowledge level)

Directions: If the statement is true, place a **+** in the blank to the left of the item. If the statement is false, place a **0** in the blank. (1 point each)

__+__ 1. Planning meals in advance helps you shop wisely.

__+__ 2. The selection of the grade of a food product depends upon its intended use.

__0__ 3. Federal regulations require that recipes be given on the labels of canned food products.

True-False Example 2: Correction-Type Response (knowledge level)

Directions: If the statement is true, write **+** in the answer column. If it is false, correct it by writing, in the space provided at the left, the word or words you would substitute for the underlined word to make the statement true. (2 points each)

_____+_____ 1. Most of the design principles used today were developed by the ancient <u>Greeks</u>.

__proportion__ 2. Using fabric with a large design for draperies in a small room is an example of poor <u>balance</u>.

__transition__ 3. Curved lines that create rhythm are referred to as <u>opposition</u>.

True-False Example 3: Series of Statements Based on a Given Situation (comprehension level)

Situation: Marta and Jason have bought an old house that needs redecorating. The rooms in the house are small. Marta and Jason want to make these rooms appear larger through effective decorating.

Directions: Marta and Jason are considering the following list of changes. If the change would make a room appear larger, put a **+** in the blank to the left of the statement. If the change would make the room appear smaller, put a **0** in the blank. (1 point each)

__0__ 1. Use dark colors on the walls.

__0__ 2. Use intense colors on the walls.

__+__ 3. Paint the baseboard, molding, and woodwork the same color as the walls.

__0__ 4. Paint each room a different color.

__+__ 5. Use mirrors for wall decorations.

__+__ 6. Choose furniture that is small in scale.

True-False Example 4: With Reasons for False Answers (comprehension level)

Directions: If the statement is true, place a **+** in the blank to the left. If the item is false, place a **0** in the blank and then, after the statement, give the reason why it is false. Credit will be given only if the reason you supply is correct and to the point. You do not have to give reasons for items marked true. (2 points each)

__+__ 1. On a limited budget, it is more practical to buy furniture that is open stock than that which is custom-made.

__0__ 2. Other things being equal, wood veneer of seven ply will be less durable than solid wood. *Solid wood is more likely to warp.*)

True-False Example 5: Analogy (analysis level)

Directions: If the statement is true, circle the letter **T** in the answer column. If the statement is false, circle the letter **F**. (1 point each)

Ⓣ F 1. Vitamin A is to night blindness as vitamin D is to rickets.

T Ⓕ 2. Iron is to milk as vitamin A is to carrots.

❋ Multiple-Choice Items

Multiple-choice items usually consist of an introductory statement or question, called the "stem," followed by a series of words, phrases, or sentences that are called "alternatives." The stem should consist of a complete idea, not just a single word. All the multiple-choice items in one group should be in the form of either a question or an incomplete statement. Some educators prefer the question form because it is a natural method of inquiry.

Put as much information as possible in the stem so that the stem is longer than the alternatives. Use three to four plausible alternatives below each stem. In a single section of the test each multiple-choice question should have the same number of alternatives for a unified effect. The correct alternatives, as well as the *distractors* (or incorrect responses), need to be similar in content and form. Distractors should seem plausible, or they become giveaways and affect the validity of a test. Remember, too, that when students are in doubt, they frequently select the longest choice, so keep all alternatives about the same length. Be sure every alternative makes a logical complete statement with the stem if you are using the incomplete statement format. Use alternatives such as "all of the above," "none of the above," "two of the above," infrequently. This type of response is often confusing. It increases the probability of guessing. Here are examples of well-written multiple-choice questions:

Multiple-Choice Example 1: Single Best Answer: Analogy

Directions: In the blank to the left of each item, write the letter corresponding to the *one* answer that best completes each statement. (2 points each)

  B 1. What is the best way to dry a 100 percent wool sweater?

    A. On a clothes rack

    B. On a flat surface

    C. In a dryer

    D. On a hanger

Multiple Choice: Example 2: Single Best Answer: Analogy

Directions: In the blank to the left of each item, write the letter of the answer that *best* completes the statement (2 points each)

  B 1. Strength is to nylon as heat resistance is to:

    A. Acetate.

    B. Cotton.

    C. Rayon.

    D. Polyester.

Multiple-Choice Example 3: Most Inclusive Item Without Stem

Directions: Circle the letter that corresponds to the most *inclusive* item in each group. In other words, choose the item that includes all the others listed in that particular group. (1 point each)

  1. A. Educational background

    B. Job experiences

    C. Organizational affiliations

    D. References

    Ⓔ Résumé

❋ Matching Items

Matching test questions are used to show the association of or relationship between two elements, such as words and definitions, events and persons, examples and principles, or causes and effects. A matching section typically consists of two columns. Each column should be homogeneous in form and content. For example, items referring to the function of nutrients should not be mixed in the same column with those indicating the best sources of nutrients. Columns should be labeled according to content.

It is recommended that from five to ten items be used in a matching question. When possible, place the longer items in the left-hand column and the shorter responses in the right-hand column. This helps students identify the correct answer more quickly. Responses in the right-hand column should be arranged in some logical order, such as alphabetically, numerically, or chronologically. This also minimizes time spent in locating a correct answer.

You can reduce the chances of guessing answers by providing a greater number of responses than items or by allowing for response alternatives to be used more than once. However, avoid using one response more than three times, or the validity of the test might be affected. How many times an answer can be used should be specified in the directions in order to minimize confusion for students.

Matching Example 1: Definitions

Directions: For each function in the left column, locate the nutrient in the right column associated with it. Place the letter corresponding to the best choice in the blank to the left of each function. Use each letter only once. (1 point each)

FUNCTIONS	NUTRIENTS
__I__ 1. Keeps gums healthy; aids healing of skin injuries	A. Calcium
__H__ 2. Helps prevent night blindness	B. Iodine
__F__ 3. Builds and maintains body tissues	C. Iron
__G__ 4. Steadies nerves; aids digestion	D. Niacin
__A__ 5. Builds strong bones and teeth	E. Phosphorus
__E__ 6. Regulates the deposit of minerals in bones and teeth; prevents rickets	F. Protein
	G. Thiamine
	H. Vitamin A
	I. Vitamin C
__B__ 7. Prevents goiter	J. Vitamin D
__C__ 8. Helps form hemoglobin in red blood cells	

Matching Example 2: Identifying Illustrations

Directions: Match the illustrations in the left column with the terms in the right column by placing the number of the correct term in the blank in the illustration. Use terms in the right column only once. (1 point each)

ILLUSTRATIONS	TERMS
__2__ A. GARMENT FACING	1. Clipping and grading
__4__ B.	2. Grading
__1__ C. INSIDE CURVE	3. Hemming
__5__ D.	4. Slashing
__7__ E. GARMENT OUTSIDE	5. Staystitching
	6. Trimming
	7. Understitching

❋ Supply-Type Items

In supply-type test items, the learner has to provide a one- or two-word answer to a question without the prompt of a list of choices. There are four kinds of supply-type items: completion, short answer, identification, and association.

❋ *Completion Items*

Completion, or fill-in-the-blank, items are statements in which one or more words are omitted. One-word or single-expression answers (such as "credit rating," "installment loan," and "bait and switch") are preferred. With short answers, grading can be more objective than for answers written in phrases or sentences. The word omitted from the sentence should be a significant one and only one answer should be correct. Write the question so that the answer blank occurs at or near the end of the statement. In that way, the major thought is presented before the blank appears, and the test taker does not need to reread the question. It's important to achieve a balance between providing too little information and too much so that completion items reflect the learners' understanding. All answer blanks should be of uniform length to avoid giving clues. Limit blanks to one per sentence.

You can facilitate scoring by using very short blanks with numbers or question marks within the sentences. Then place a longer answer line to the left of the completion items, forming an answer column.

Completion Example 1: Incomplete Sentences

Directions: Fill in the blank to the left of each sentence with the *best* word or words to complete the statement. (2 points each)

__credit union__ 1. An institution that offers limited cash installment loans only to its members is a(n) __(1)__.

__banks__ 2. The majority of noninstallment cash loans are provided by __(2)__.

__percentage rate__ 3. The amount of interest you pay in a finance charge is determined by the annual __(3)__.

Completion Example 2: Analogy

Directions: Fill in the blank to the left of each sentence with the *best* word or words to complete the statement. (2 points each)

__blue__ 1. Violet is to yellow as orange is to __?__.

__red__ 2. Green and orange are to purple as yellow and blue are to __?__.

__analogous__ 3. Pink and red are to a monochromatic color scheme as yellow, yellow-green, and green are to a(n) __?__ color scheme.

❋ *Short-Answer Items*

The only difference between completion or fill-in-the-blank items and short-answer items is that a short-answer item is written in the form of a question. Again, a short answer is needed. The questions should be clear and concise. There should be just one correct answer. Placing answer blanks to the left of the questions facilitates scoring. An example follows:

Short-Answer Example

Directions: Answer each question by writing the correct word or term in the blank to the left of each number. (2 points each)

__fracture__ 1. What is the technical name for a broken bone?

__osteoporosis__ 2. What is the name of the condition in which bone density decreases and the bones become brittle?

__scoliosis__ 3. What is the name given to a lateral curvature of the spine?

✳ *Identification Items*

The identification test item typically requires the learners to label or locate parts of a diagram or to give specific information about a picture or an object. Pictures, diagrams, and actual objects are more realistic than verbal descriptions and provide interest and variation in testing procedures.

Sketches and diagrams should be drawn clearly and large enough to be seen easily. It is important that lines and numbers indicating various parts of a diagram are easy to understand. Directions must be clear and explicit. Designate a space for recording answers.

Identification Example 1: Labeling

Directions: Examine the food label below. In the spaces below the label, write the names of the parts to which each numbered line points. (1 point each)

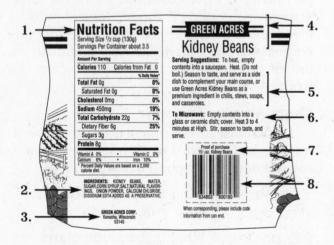

1. <u>Nutrition information</u>

2. <u>Ingredient list</u>

3. <u>Manufacturer</u>

4. <u>Product name</u>

5. <u>Suggested uses</u>

6. <u>Preparation directions</u>

7. <u>Amount of contents</u>

8. <u>Universal product code</u>

Identification Example 2: Passing Around Articles

Identification tests can also be designed so that actual food products, home health care equipment, machine parts or attachments, samples of bandaging techniques, or pictures are passed from one student to another in a planned, sequential order. Gauge when it is time to say "pass" by ascertaining when most of the students have completed their identification. When using this technique, be sure all students understand that they must pass their item at the designated time. Otherwise, some students will accumulate articles while others won't have any to work on. A variety of rotation systems for passing articles can be used. There should be the same number of items (or only a very few more) as there are students taking the test. To begin, each student should be given either one or two articles. Remind learners that the items they receive won't necessarily be received in numerical order. After the entire rotation, the items may be placed on a table so that one person at a time can reexamine them. As an alternative to passing items, you can have students pass by the series of labeled items laid out on a table or counter.

✳ *Association Items*

Association items resemble matching items, except that the learner has to supply the answers for the right column, rather than choose a correct response. Association items are set up just like matching items with headings on each column. The respondents write their answers in the spaces provided in the right column.

✳ Essay Questions

Essay questions can evaluate a learner's ability to use higher mental processes. These processes include interpreting information, applying rules and principles, analyzing causes and effects, and developing and evaluating an original plan. In addition to controlling student guessing, essay questions may more closely approximate the use of information and skills in life situations.

Association Example

Directions: The respiratory system in humans is a common site of infections. In the left column are descriptions of various respiratory infections. After reading the description in the left column, write the name of the type of infection being described in the right column. (3 points each)

DESCRIPTION	NAME OF INFECTION
1. An inflammation of the bronchi	1. (Bronchitis)
2. Inflammatory condition in which small airways in lungs, called bronchioles, become narrowed	2. (Asthma)
3. An inflammation of the lungs caused by bacteria or viruses	3. (Pneumonia)
4. A disease in which alveoli of lungs burst and blend to form fewer, larger sacs with less surface area	4. (Emphysema)
5. An inflammation of the membrane linings of the air-filled cavities in the bones that surround the nose	5. (Sinusitis)

✻ Restricted- and Extended-Response Essays

There are two basic types of essay questions: restricted- and extended-response items. The difference lies in the length of answer the learners are expected to give. Restricted responses are often what are known as "listing questions." Extended-response essays involve writing one or more cohesive paragraphs.

Essay questions are relatively easy to construct, but they do require considerable time for the learners to respond and for the educator to grade. Essay questions are often criticized for having a limited sampling of subject matter, an inconsistency or subjectivity in scoring, and a premium placed on quantity, rather than quality, of response. These weaknesses can be minimized through the use of several techniques.

✻ Guidelines for Writing Essay Questions

1. State essay questions so that they can be graded objectively. This necessitates wording them so that those learners who are prepared know what is expected in the answer. For example, if students are asked to "Discuss the Food Guide Pyramid," they might respond in a variety of ways. A better wording would be "Analyze the dietary intake record below according to the Food Guide Pyramid's suggested daily intake." Students should know how to respond, and you can establish objective criteria to evaluate their answers. As you develop an essay question, identify the major points that a student is expected to cover to make an answer key and determine the question's relative weight or point value.

2. Be specific in terms of how lengthy an answer you want.

3. Require students to answer all items. When students have the option of answering three out of four questions, one student may not know anything about the problem he or she has omitted, while another student may have been prepared to answer all the questions. Obviously, this test would not determine both students' comprehension of the subject matter fairly or to the same degree.

4. Keep in mind that a lengthy response doesn't necessarily represent comprehension of the subject matter or a high level of thinking. A brief answer may result from thinking analytically and critically.

5. Grade the content of an essay question without regard to handwriting, spelling, or grammar. You might grade these separately.

6. Read the first answer on all the papers and check it according to the established criteria for grading. Group the

papers according to the adequacy of the response. Then reread and assign point values to the first question on all the students' papers. Repeat with the second question on all papers, and so forth.

Essay Question Examples

It is easy to develop essay questions incorporating levels of thinking above the knowledge level. For example:

- Explain briefly five ways stress may affect the physical well-being of your body. (Cognitive-Comprehension)
- Describe three differences between guidance and discipline. (Cognitive-Comprehension)
- Analyze the blueprint on display for factors relating to high and low building costs. (Cognitive-Analysis)
- Develop an instrument for rating television programs for children. (Cognitive-Synthesis)
- Evaluate this spending plan for the family situation described below. (Cognitive-Evaluation)

 # Adapting Tests for Special Needs

Learners may have varying special needs that affect test taking. One of the most common is reading one or more levels below grade placement. Such learners are at a real disadvantage when emphasis is placed mainly upon traditional pencil-and-paper methods of evaluation. However, when test questions are read to these students and their responses are based on visual stimuli, many of them are able to convey their knowledge. Ask oral questions concisely and repeat them more than once. Test materials can include photos, drawings, models, or actual items. Learners may be asked for simple oral or written responses, or they may be required to give reasons for their answers. Written responses can best be handled with an answer sheet constructed so that students only have to check off a correct item or write in a number, letter, word, or short phrase.

Special needs students may do better on practical tests and lab work. These can measure skills in areas such as child care, hospitality, vital sign assessment, and patient care. Establish definite criteria for judging acceptable performance so that the results can be scored objectively. Well-developed checklists and rubrics/rating scales can measure student performance on a skill test or on lab work.

✳ Sample Test Items for Limited Ability Readers

Poor readers could answer the following test items more easily. The questions are arranged appropriately in order of difficulty from least to most difficult. Learners with very limited academic ability may only be able to choose from two or three alternatives.

Limited Ability Reader Examples: Food Service

Directions: Circle the one in each group that is the best way to work:

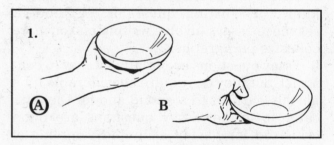

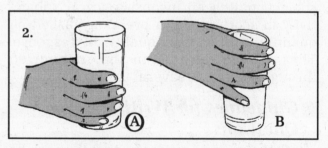

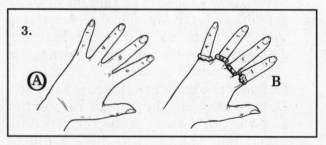

4.

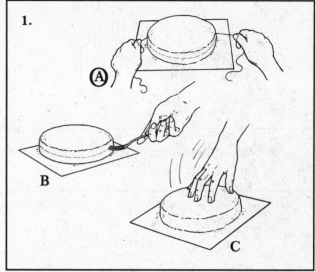

5.

6.

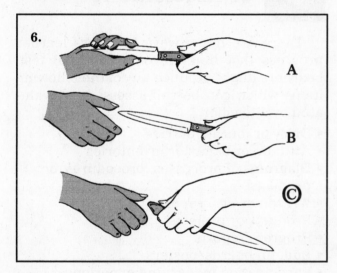

Directions: Circle the last step in cutting a layer cake in half.

1.

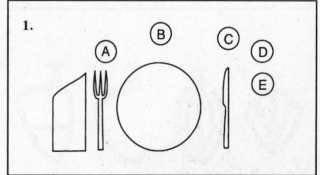

Limited Ability Reader Example: Table Setting

Simulated table settings can be sketched, drawn, or pictured on large pieces of construction paper, poster board, or transparencies, so that the entire class can view them simultaneously. The questions can be asked orally. Student responses are recorded on answer sheets.

The following examples would be appropriate for all levels of learners and provide variety in testing strategy. Their visual and oral components help poor readers.

1.

_C_ 1. Write the letter showing the place for a water glass.

C 2. Write the letter of the item that is in the wrong place.

E 3. Write the letter of the item that is in the wrong place.

Limited Ability Reader Example: Quantity Food Preparation

Directions: Number from 1 to 3 on your paper. Write the letter of the beater that best answers each question.

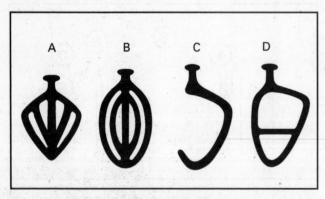

B 1. Which beater would be used for beating egg whites?

C 2. Which beater would be used for mixing bread dough?

A 3. Which beater would be used for mashing potatoes?

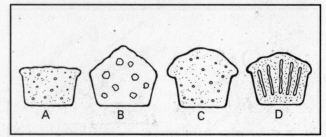

Limited Ability Reader Example: Muffin Analysis

Number your paper from 1 to 3. Write the letter corresponding to the muffin that best answers each question.

C 1. Which muffin was mixed correctly?

D 2. Which muffin was mixed too much?

B 3. Which muffin was baked in an oven that was too hot?

Nontesting Means of Assessment

There are many ways to assess learner progress that don't involve a formal test. Learners might produce any of the following items which can be self-assessed or evaluated by a teacher:

- Diary or journal entries
- Attitude or behavior inventories
- Diagrams of processes, procedures, or products
- Written or oral reports
- Products or projects
- Progress reports
- Bulletin boards/posters
- Participation in learning experiences

Nontesting assessment can be used to assess progress in all three domains of learning: cognitive, affective, and psychomotor. The goal in collecting evidence of progress or mastery on the part of learners is to utilize a wide variety of evidences. This allows learners who are good at some means of providing evidence but not good at others a chance to shine. While some of the items in this list are concrete and easy to assess, others, such as participation, are more difficult. The goal is to eliminate as much subjectivity as possible in the assessment process. The use of checklists, scorecards, and rubrics/rating scales helps assist in achieving this end.

❋ Checklists, Scorecards, and Rubrics/Rating Scales

Checklists, scorecards, and rubrics (sometimes called rating scales) are instruments that can be used by learners to evaluate themselves or their peers and by teachers to evaluate learners' work. Often there is value in having both the educator and learners use the same device to judge the same product or performance and then compare their evaluations. It's also helpful to give learners a copy of the scoring device (or criteria) when an assignment is made, so they know how they will be evaluated.

Many times educators assess learners' performance as they view the students in action. This is called *performance assessment* or performance testing. To provide a reliable, fair assessment of each learner's performance of physical skills and actions, a checklist, scorecard, or rubric/rating scale might be used. Each learner would then be evaluated on the same criteria. This ensures consistency and objectivity over the whole group of learners.

A wide variety of checklists, scorecards, and rubrics/rating scales can be found in textbook programs, periodicals, and commercial publications. It is also relatively easy for teachers to develop their own checklists and scorecards. However, constructing a rubric/rating scale is more difficult and time-consuming. Having the teacher and learners work together to develop evaluation instruments can be valuable learning experiences.

Each of these assessment instruments considers essentially the same qualities, although the emphasis is somewhat different in each. However, it should be noted that a rubric encompasses the greatest depth and necessitates the use of a higher level of thinking to determine ratings.

❋ General Construction Guidelines

Checklists, scorecards, and rubrics/rating scales are discussed individually in the following sections. However, a few general guidelines follow that are appropriate for all three types:

- Decide on the qualities or dimensions of the product or process you wish to assess. Make a list of these.
- List qualities or dimensions in a logical order, if there is one. Think through the sequence in which you are likely to assess attributes of the product or process and put the items in that order in the assessment instruments.
- Determine if you want a total score. If so, plan for this and determine an easy way to total and record subscores and a final score.
- Most learners appreciate written feedback, so provide sufficient space for comments.
- Include a place for identifying information including name, date, and class or organization.
- Use an appropriate title that makes it easy to file your instrument.
- Write clear directions for use of the device.
- Use an easy-to-follow format.

❋ Checklists

Checklists are simple evaluation instruments that consist of a list of qualities to be considered and checked-off or questions to be answered with a "yes" or "no" response. Because checklists are easy to construct and easy to respond to, they often include a fairly large number of subconcepts to be considered. The checklist on the next page, *Figure 7-1*, can be used to evaluate a meal prepared as a laboratory assignment.

In developing checklists, the number of "yes" and "no" responses or checked-off items can be added for a total score. A space for comments requires the learners to use higher-level thinking about the responses they are checking as they evaluate themselves. Use the same grammatical format for writing all items. In this example, all items are in a question form. Another checklist might use all phrases, such as "Planned a well-balanced meal," and "Stayed within budget."

Figure 7-1   ## CHECKLIST FOR EVALUATING A LABORATORY MEAL

Name: _____ Group: _____ Date: _____

Directions: Evaluate your group's laboratory experience by answering each of the following questions and checking the appropriate column. Put comments in the right column. Total the number of checks in each column.

DID WE:	YES	NO	COMMENTS
1. Plan a well-balanced meal?			
2. Stay within our budget?			
3. Use foods that are in season?			
4. Remember to order everything needed?			
5. Have enough to eat?			
6. Plan for all the tasks we needed to do?			
7. Plan for all needed equipment?			
8. Use only dishes and utensils needed?			
9. Wash utensils as we cooked?			
10. Keep the countertop neat and clean as we worked?			
11. Have all the food ready at the same time?			
12. Serve the meal at the appointed time?			
13. Use time wisely in preparing the meal?			
14. Serve an appealing and appetizing meal?			
15. Prepare food that tasted good?			
16. Prepare the right amount of food?			
17. Set the table attractively?			
18. Remember everything that should have been on the table?			
19. Use acceptable table manners?			
20. Include everyone in the table conversation?			
21. Leave our lab section in order?			
22. Complete clean-up in a timely manner?			
23. Hand in our bills and written plans on time?			
24. Work well together as a group?			
25. Share fairly the amount of work to be done?			
Totals			

✳ Scorecards

Scorecards consist of a list of characteristics or factors and a range of point values that might be assigned to each, proportional to their importance. The evaluator assesses each attribute and determines the score to assign. The "Scorecard for Evaluating a Laboratory Meal," *Figure 7-2* shown below, could be used to evaluate meals.

You can see that it lacks the depth of content of some other types of evaluation instruments. Scorecards are narrow in scope. They are, therefore, appropriate for judging such things as an individual food product, one dimension of human interaction, a single work habit, one caregiving task, or a single toy.

The chief limitation of checklists and scorecards is that they have no descriptions of quality. The primary advantage of scorecards and checklists is that their use requires learners to think about the factors listed for consideration.

In the example of a scorecard for evaluating a laboratory meal that follows, nutritional balance is weighted much more heavily than the other items. From lab to lab, the point values could be changed, making other variables weighted more heavily.

| Figure 7-2 | SCORECARD FOR EVALUATING A LABORATORY MEAL | | |

Name: _____ Group: _____ Date: _____

Directions: Score each aspect of your meal by placing a number indicating your evaluation in the appropriate column. This number cannot exceed the highest possible score given. Add comments in the last column. Total your scores.

SELECTION OF FOOD	HIGHEST POSSIBLE SCORE	YOUR SCORE	COMMENTS
Nutritional balance	40		
Variety of textures	15		
Pleasing combination of flavors	15		
Pleasing combination of colors	15		
Foods in season	15		
Total Score	100		

✳ Rubrics/Rating Scales

Rubrics, sometimes called rating scales, are more highly refined measuring instruments than checklists or scorecards because they include descriptions of various levels of quality for each dimension. This provides for rating on a continuum. See the "Rubric/Rating Scale for Evaluating a Meal," *Figure 7-3* on the next page. The descriptions against which work is judged are usually given at three quality levels providing a five-point continuum. Descriptions are assigned 1, 3, and 5 points. In-between ratings are assigned 2 and 4 points. (Occasionally, two descriptions may be used with a three-point continuum.) Care must be taken that each level includes all the aspects described in every other level.

Figure 7-3

RUBRIC/RATING SCALE FOR EVALUATING A LABORATORY MEAL

Name : _____ Date: _____ Period: _____

Directions: Rate your laboratory experience on each of the factors listed by placing 1, 2, 3, 4, or 5, in the blank to the right. For example, if the quality corresponds to the description in the first column, assign 5 points; if described in the second column, give 3 points; if it falls between the two, record 4. Add these points to determine the total score.

CRITERIA:	PERFORMANCE LEVELS					SCORE
	5	**4**	**3**	**2**	**1**	**Points**
A. MENU						
1. Use of Time	Meal simple. Easily prepared in time available.		Meal somewhat complicated. Prepared in time but workers rushed.		Meal elaborate. Not prepared easily in time available.	
2. Cost	Reasonable. No extra or unreasonable expense involved.		Moderate. Some unnecessary expense involved.		Excessive. Foods out of season and expensive.	
3. Contrasts	Good contrast in color, texture, flavor, and temperature.		Some contrast in color, texture, flavor, temperature.		Little or no contrast in color, texture, flavor, temperature.	
4. Suitability	Food preparation suitable for both student abilities and available equipment.		Food preparation suitable for student abilities or available equipment but not for both.		Food preparation too difficult and involved unavailable equipment.	
5. Nutritive Value	All basic food groups included. Meal was very nutritious and well balanced.		Menu included some of the basic food groups. A few items could have been substituted for less nutritious foods.		Menu not very nutritious. Did not include enough foods from the basic food groups.	
B. WORK PLAN						
6. Time Schedule	Time needed to complete all tasks given accurately.		Time needed to complete tasks indicated fairly realistically.		Time needed to complete tasks not indicated, inaccurate, or unrealistic.	
7. Sequence of Tasks	Logical sequence given for all tasks.		Logical sequence given for part of work such as preparation, service, or cleanup.		Sequence not given or illogical.	

Figure 7-3 (cont'd)
RUBRIC/RATING SCALE FOR EVALUATING A LABORATORY MEAL

CRITERIA	PERFORMANCE LEVELS					SCORE
	5	4	3	2	1	Points
8. Division of Tasks	Fair and equitable division of tasks indicated for each member of the group.		Division of tasks indicated but some-what unequal or lacking in detail.		Division of tasks among group mem-bers unfair or not clearly indicated.	
C. MARKET ORDER 9. Lists	All foods needed included in realistic quantities.		Most of foods needed included, quantities question-able for number served.		Did not include all foods needed, quan-tities not stated or unsuitable.	
10. Cost	Costs given, summa-rized, reasonable, within budget.		Cost of foods fairly accurate, cost of meal not summa-rized.		Not given, given for only part of the foods, or inaccurate.	
					Total Score	

Rubrics or rating scales offer the following advantages for teachers and learners:

- They help ensure that grades are assigned fairly and objectively because they employ a consistent scoring system.
- They can inform learners of the teacher's expectations. Learners should be given a copy of the scoring rubric before they begin work on a project. This clearly identifies the standards of excellence for which to strive.
- They help learners understand the strengths and weaknesses of their performance. The completed rubric shows learners specifically what they are doing well and what areas need improvement.
- They can be used as self-assessment tools, if desired, to help learners objectively evaluate their own work.

In this chapter, you have seen an example of a checklist, a scorecard, and a rubric that could be used to rate laboratory meals. They consider essentially the same qualities, although the emphasis is somewhat different in each. Of these, a rubric encompasses the greatest depth of subject matter and necessitates the use of a higher level of thinking to make selections on the continuum. The evaluators are forced to think about their reasons for making certain ratings.

✱ Combination Checklist/Scorecard/Rubric

Many times the characteristics of several types of evaluation tools are combined into one instrument. A rating device with the characteristics of a checklist, scorecard, and rubric/rating scale might be best for you in some situations. Criteria questions, or statements, are listed that the evaluator rates by assigning numerical scores based on a range of point values, or on a continuum. See the example, *Figure 7-4*, on the following page.

Figure 7-4 INSTRUMENT FOR EVALUATING AN ORAL REPORT

Name: _____ Date: _____ Period: _____

Directions: Rate each statement below as it relates to your group's oral report. Place the number of the word or words that best describes it in the space provided to the left of each number. Briefly explain or support your rating in the space after each statement.

SCALE				
Excellent 5	Very Good 4	Adequate 3	Fair 2	Poor 1

SCORE	CRITERIA	COMMENTS
	1. Variety of resources were used to prepare report.	
	2. Material presented was accurate and up-to-date.	
	3. Statements could be verified through facts or statistics given or by sources of information cited.	
	4. Information was presented in a logical sequence.	
	5. Subject matter was covered adequately for the time allowed.	
	6. Provision was made for class members to become involved.	
	7. Everyone could hear presentation.	
	8. Visuals, if any, were neat and could be seen easily by the entire group.	
	9. A demonstration, if used, could be seen by everyone.	
	10. Group members contributed equally in preparing report.	
	11. Group members participated equally in oral presentation.	
	12. Audience seemed interested in presentation.	
Total		

✳ Learner Portfolios

Learner portfolios can also be used as evaluation devices. At the secondary level and above, portfolios are sometimes focused on documenting a student's performance, progress, and skills for the purpose of finding a job or entering an educational or training program. Types of items that might go in this type of learner's portfolio include:

- Resume
- Transcripts
- Achievement test scores
- Certificates of achievement and participation
- Samples of best work (writings, projects, pictures, brochures, etc.)
- Videos of performance in job-related situations or presentations
- Philosophy statements
- Statements of commitment to a career or job focus
- Performance appraisals or job evaluations
- Letters of recommendation
- Skill self-assessments
- Special licenses or endorsements
- Volunteer and community service activities
- Professional organization memberships and involvement
- Sample publications and presentations
- Educational development or career plan
- Evidences of continuing education (workshops, seminars, meetings)
- Interest inventory results
- Recognitions, awards, honors
- Sample applications for jobs, educational institutions
- Pictures related to professional life
- Documentation of leadership efforts
- Sample publications and presentations

Figure 7-5

▰ PORTFOLIO CHECKLIST ▰

Name of Portfolio Preparer: _____

Name of Evaluator : _____ Date: _____

Directions: Check each aspect of the portfolio you are assessing if it exists. Total the number of checks at the bottom. Provide comments in the right column.

CRITERIA	CHECK IF ACCEPTABLE	COMMENTS
1. Amount of material is appropriate.		
2. Items included are relevant.		
3. Documents are well organized and sequenced.		
4. Creativity and originality are evident.		
5. Knowledge and skills of individual are shown.		
6. Progress in knowledge and skill development are reflected		
7. Professional appearance is evident.		
8. Portfolio will be an asset in job search.		
Total		

What you ask individuals to include in a portfolio will be dependent on their age and experiences and the purpose it will serve. When the portfolio is actually used in a job search, the person must select which items are most important to include for that particular situation. No matter what group you are working with, you will want to encourage learners to include evidences of work from your course or program in their portfolios. If the development of the actual portfolio is the focus of your program, then you will be teaching them what to put in a portfolio and how to present it most professionally. You will also be evaluating their portfolios. A sample of a checklist, a scorecard, and a rubric/rating scale that might be used to assess learners' portfolios are included here.

Again, the differences among these three types of assessments can be seen. The checklist simply allows for the indication of presence or absence of criteria, the scorecard allows certain criteria to be weighted more heavily than others, and the rating scale provides descriptions of levels of quality.

※ Authentic Assessment

One of the goals of evaluation is to see how well students can apply and use materials in real-life situations. You can't follow your learners around to see how well they use what they have been taught. However, you can present them with some real-life scenarios or situations in the learning environment to see how they would handle the situation. Based on responses, you can assess their abilities to operate in the real world. These situations might be in the form of case studies or simulations. Two examples are shown on page 106.

Figure 7-6 ——— **PORTFOLIO SCORECARD** ———

Name of Portfolio Preparer: _____

Name of Evaluator : _____ Date: _____

Directions: For each criterion below, assign a point value up to the total possible points to indicate how well each criterion has been met. Total the number of points. Provide comments in the appropriate column.

CRITERIA	POSSIBLE POINTS	POINTS ASSIGNED	COMMENTS
1. Number of items	10		
2. Relevance of items	20		
3. Organization and sequence	20		
4. Creativity and originality	10		
5. Reflection of knowledge and skills	15		
6. Professional appearance	10		
7. Asset to job search	15		
Totals	100		

Figure 7-7

PORTFOLIO RUBRIC/RATING SCALE

Name of Portfolio Preparer: _____

Name of Evaluator : _____ Date: _____

Directions: Read each of the descriptors for the criteria below. Assign a score from 5 to 1 for each variable based on the descriptor most closely reflecting the portfolio you are evaluating. Underline phrases in the descriptors that describe the product you are reviewing. If the portfolio falls between the descriptors, use a 4 or 2 rating. Total the scores. Place comments in the right column.

CRITERIA	PERFORMANCE LEVELS			SCORE	COMMENTS
	5 4	3	2 1		
Content	Includes the desired amount of material. All material is appropriate and well chosen.	Includes enough appropriate material. May also include some of questionable value.	Doesn't include enough appropriate material. Shows poor judgment in selection of items.		
Organization	Organization shows care and thought. Sequence is well chosen to achieve specific goals.	Organization is adequate. For example, chronological order used.	Sequence of materials is disorganized and haphazard.		
Originality	Demonstrates high degree of originality and creativity.	Demonstrates some originality and/or creativity.	Demonstrates little or no originality or creativity.		
Knowledge and Skill Development	Portfolio shows student mastery of knowledge, skill, and/or marked improvement over time.	Portfolio shows adequate level of knowledge and skills. Improvement over time is evident.	Portfolio shows lack of knowledge and skills and/or failure to significantly improve them over time.		
Overall Appearance	Neat and well presented.	Reasonably neat and well presented.	Sloppy; poorly presented.		
Suitability for Job Search	Portfolio would be a strong asset in a job search.	Portfolio would be acceptable in a job search.	Portfolio is not suitable for job search and/or would decrease chances of being hired.		
			Total		

Each of these scenarios has several possible solutions. You could have your learners act out, write, or talk about how they would handle the situations. You will then assess their abilities to apply what you have taught.

Authentic Assessment Example 1

"You are a 4-H camp counselor in charge of a group of eight 10-12 year olds. You sleep, eat, and participate in various activities with this group throughout the day. It is now 2:00 a.m. and you are asleep in your cabin with your campers. There are four cabins of campers in your cluster. One young camper comes over to your bunk and awakens you to tell you he has a bad stomachache and that his arms are very itchy. You turn on your flashlight and see that tiny red bumps cover his arms. The other seven campers are sound asleep. You are the only adult assigned to this cabin. You are about a half mile from where the camp nurse is asleep in her cabin. What would you do?"

Authentic Assessment Example 2

"You are a nurse's aide in a residential facility for elders. It is time in the facility and there is a group of the residents who need assistance with eating. One of the residents, who cannot walk, has been taken out by his family for a drive and early lunch. He required assistance from you and another aide for transfer to his son's car. Just as you are going to help feed people in the dining room, the family member who took his dad out comes up to you and says he must have help getting his father out of the car and back into the facility and bed. His father has eaten but is very tired and needs to use the bathroom. You glance around and notice that everyone is busy assisting residents with eating. What would you do?"

 # Grading Guidelines

You may find yourself in an educational setting that requires you to assign grades to the performance of learners. This is an easier process if you have scores or ratings for the learners on various tasks they have com-

pleted. These scores or ratings can then be combined and translated into a grade. Here are some suggestions to assist you in the grading process:

1. Know your school's guidelines. Your administrator or school board may have some specific guidelines for assigning grades. For instance, in some schools a 90 is an A; in others, an A begins with a numerical average of 92. Find out if your school uses + and – on letter grades.

2. Use as wide a variety of assessments as possible on which to base your grades. For instance, for a nine-week marking period you might have grades for each student on one test, two quizzes, three homework assignments, three participation activities, a poster, an interview assignment, an oral report, two journal entries, and a reaction paper from a panel discussion. With variety like this, learners all have a chance to be successful in some aspects being evaluated.

3. The items to be averaged for a grade need to be converted to numbers for averaging. Many teachers find it easier to assign points to individual items. Then they can just total the points. If you are converting from grades to numbers, be sure the conversions for all students are consistent. For instance, students receiving a B+ must have their B+ converted to the same number, i.e., an 88.

4. Determine how much to weight each of the scores you are going to average for various assignments. Ideally, you would plan all of this out before the marking period begins so students will know how much each item is worth. This can be done through identifying the number of points each assignment will receive in proportion to other assignments. For example, a reaction paper that is worth 200 points gets twice the value of a 100-point mobile project. Be aware of this as you assign points. If you are converting from letters to numbers and then weighting the assignment, you would convert the B+ to an 88 and then multiply it by the proportion of 100% you wanted it to carry weight wise. If it were to count 10% it would be converted to 880 points. These

points would be added in with other scores which have been multiplied by their weights. All scores are totaled and divided by 100. The resulting number, up to 100, represents the person's percentage out of 100.

5. Once you have a set of student averages for which to assign grades, you can look for natural break points in the scores for establishing your divisions between grades. For example, in the following set of numbers, you would break between the 89 and 87 instead of between the 90 and 89 for A and between 83 and 80 for B. Accuracy in scoring is not good enough to be sure that at a different point in time you might not have given students slightly different scores on various items. A breaking point in the set of scores of two or more points should be located. Of course if you have told your learners 80 to 89 is a B, no matter what, you need to stick to that. You also need to decide in advance a lower limit for each grade if no natural breaks appear.

$$
\begin{array}{ll}
95 & \\
94 & \\
91 & \textbf{A} \\
90 & \\
\underline{89} & \\
87 & \\
86 & \textbf{B} \\
85 & \\
\underline{83} & \\
80 & \textbf{C} \\
79 &
\end{array}
$$

6. Grades do matter in the lives of students, so it is important to be careful and accurate in assigning them. Tell learners up front how much various assignments will be weighted. This may be hard to do when you first start teaching, but will become easier with experience.

 # Self- and Peer Evaluation

Assessment is often thought of as something done to others, and, in many cases, this is true. However, there is a great deal of value in self-evaluation—taking an inward look at how you are doing and/or encouraging your learners to do the same. It is hoped that when your learners leave your educational setting they will continue to evaluate their own progress.

This process is one that you must instill in your learners. Giving them opportunities to do structured self-evaluation exercises in your educational setting will promote this on-going process. Some examples include:

- Ask the learners to draw cross-sectional views of various grains without the use of resources. Then have them compare the accuracy of their drawings to those in reference books and make any needed corrections.
- Videotape learners as they interact with young children in a preschool setting. Have them view the video and identify their positive and negative interaction strategies.
- Have the learners keep food diaries for two days and then determine how well they are meeting the suggested intakes from various groups in the Food Guide Pyramid.

Peers can also evaluate each other and provide feedback to each other. In a work setting, peer review is often used. Provide practice for your learners. Examples might include:

- When learners have completed the development of an exercise plan for a person described in a scenario, have them switch plans and critique someone else's proposal, providing feedback on strengths of the plan and areas needing improvement.
- After learners have applied bandages to various types of hypothetical wounds, have a peer assess the correctness of the applications.
- Posters promoting good nutrition for teens can be developed by learners and then they can switch and critique each other's posters, based on the criteria you provided for their development.

It is also important that as an educator you take time to evaluate yourself—a process often called *reflective teaching*. Consistently evaluating your own work and making improvements is what makes you a growing, changing, dynamic teacher. You can accomplish this through reflection on each class or session you present. Critique the strength of your teaching skills and methods. Also assess how well you handle the other responsibilities of your job. Occasionally, use a tape recorder and/or video camera to record a lesson. Reviewing your self-assessments over time will help you see improvements occurring and areas still needing improvement.

 ## Program/Workshop/ Conference Assessment

It's more common to think of evaluating people than programs (courses, workshops, conferences, etc.). Assessing learners' achievement in a program does give a sense of the success of a program. But in addition to assessing learner growth, there are other aspects of a program that need to be evaluated. These include:

- The curriculum or plan of work for the program.
- The processes used to implement the program.
- The resources used to enhance the program.

❋ Types of Program Assessment

Program assessment can be formative or summative in nature. *Formative evaluation* is information obtained about learners, curriculum, processes, and resources during the course of the program. This information is fed back into the program to make positive changes while the program is going on. *Summative evaluation* occurs at the end of a program and provides the basis for change the next time the program is held.

❋ Reasons for Program Evaluation

Programs are usually supported by funding sources. Those people, agencies, or institutions supporting the program want to be assured their money is being spent wisely. Continuation of the program and/or funding may be tied to positive accountability measures. You also evaluate programs so that the curricula, implementation strategies, and/or resource utilization can be assessed and changed to better meet the needs of the clients and educators involved. Change is critical to the maintenance of a relevant program. Without feedback, change is difficult or the need for it may not be seen.

Figure 7-8 ### STRATEGIES FOR EVALUATING PROGRAMS

- Paper-and-pencil pre- and/or post-tests or other assessments of participants' cognitive and affective statuses and changes
- Success of projects completed by students or participants
- Course or program evaluations filled out by participants
- Mini course evaluations, written or oral, gathered throughout the program
- Peer observations and written feedback of actual implementation
- Videotapes of course segments that are reviewed by you, administrators, or peers
- Review of curricula by experts in the field
- Interviews with employers of your learners
- Interviews with clients or parents/guardians of learners
- Learners' "success stories" showing successful application of program information in the "real world"
- Feedback from learners once they are out in the "real world" regarding the relevance of their training

✳ Ways to Evaluate Programs

The most critical piece of program evaluation is having objectives to assess. When the plan for a program is initially developed, write out explicit program goals or objectives. These should clearly spell out the outcomes expected during, and at the end of, the program. The program plan should also identify the ways you will gather evidences to indicate if each goal or objective has been reached. Some of these strategies will be formative in nature, and others will be summative. Those organizations funding or supporting your program will want to receive these data and feedback. The chart "Strategies for Evaluating Programs," *Figure 7-8* on the next page, suggests a variety of strategies you can use to collect feedback about programs and/or classes.

Remember the importance of matching the assessment with the objectives of the program. For example, if a program goal is: "To prepare qualified dietary aides to function successfully in nursing home settings," you will need to assess their qualifications as per standards you set up in your program, their ability to pass any standardized or certificate competency exams, and their performance on the job in nursing home facilities. Probably the best judges will be the dietitians for whom they work. You will need to be in touch with them and may involve them in the evaluation process.

Effective Assessment

Assessment is a significant part of the teaching-learning process. It is directly linked to, and allows you to, assess achievement of objectives. It should be continual and ongoing. You will plan, implement, and use the results of your assessment strategies. Using multiple types of assessment strategies increases your chances of getting a broad base of data that adequately represents the level of attainment of learner and program goals. Testing and nontesting means of evaluation need to complement and supplement each other. Wise use of these results will ensure a relevant, continually changing program.

Building Your Professional Portfolio

Test Writing. Select a topic, prepare a test that includes three different types of test items. Follow the guidelines for preparing each type of test item and for formatting the test. Include clear and concise directions.

Checklists and Rubrics. State an objective in behavioral terms. Then develop a checklist and rating scale (rubric) for judging achievement of the same objective.

Scorecards. Develop a scorecard for assessment of one of the following:
• Taking vital signs
• Hand washing
• Resumes

Program Evaluation. For a specific program, generate a list of evidences you could gather to show program success.

Test Evaluation. Using a test you recently took or gave, critique and revise it as needed.

Chapter 8

Core Teaching Skills

Teaching skills are specific and identifiable techniques and tools that educators use to derive maximum value from the lessons and programs they have planned. The most important, or core, teaching skills are described in this chapter. They include:

- Establishing set
- Questioning techniques
- Using silence
- Reinforcing positive behavior
- Recognizing and obtaining attending behavior
- Using appropriate frames of reference
- Illustrating with examples
- Reinforcing subject matter
- Pacing
- Eliciting learner feedback
- Achieving closure
- Varying stimuli

If you develop expertise in using these teaching skills, others should be easy for you to acquire. Chapter 7 suggested videotaping yourself as an effective way to evaluate your own teaching skills or have someone else give you feedback. Another technique, called microteaching, allows you to work on improving one skill at a time.

Establishing Set or the Introduction

As you read in Chapter 6, effective lessons or presentations begin with a well-planned introduction, often referred to as *establishing set*. This entails developing rapport with participants, setting the stage for the learning that follows, and involving the learners either actively or passively.

- **Developing rapport.** Development of rapport depends upon the situation. For a one-time presentation to a new audience, the educator might greet participants as they enter the room and then begin the session with a bit of personal information that shows a link with the participants. In a school setting, a teacher sees building rapport as an ongoing process. Establishing direct eye contact with students, talking with them as they enter the room, making sincere comments that reflect concern for them, and asking questions that show interest are examples of effective techniques. Whatever the situation, there is a direct correlation between effectiveness in establishing set and the effectiveness of a total lesson or presentation. When you succeed in creating a positive attitude at the beginning of the program, learners are more likely to be involved and interested throughout.

- **Setting the stage for learning.** A key component of establishing set is creating interest in the material to be presented. This doesn't normally require elaborate preparation, though something innovative can be especially motivating. For example, to introduce a lesson on the social development of preschoolers, you might begin with a tape of young children talking to each other.

  Vary the techniques you use. You can link a lesson to material previously learned, to real life, or to another subject area. You might begin with a thought-provoking rhetorical question or an analogy to show the relationship between the topic for the day and some current or historical event. You could refer to a bulletin-board display or exhibit. You might stimulate interest by having materials relating to the main concept of the day in a bag to create an element of surprise. If you are going to use a poster, turn it toward the wall until you are ready to use it.

  For a program on personal characteristics for employability, you might drop an effervescent cold remedy tablet into a clear glass containing water. Relate the bubbling action to friendliness, enthusiasm, and good health required for success on the job. This idea might also introduce a program on patterns of physical activity

and fatigue. In a lesson on posture, you could pretend to be taking participants' picture with a camera. As they sit up straight, you might say, "We would all feel much better if we always looked as we do when we're having our picture taken." When teaching the significance of food, you might begin by serving a small snack and then lead into a discussion of the many reasons people eat what they do. A scrambled word on the board could denote the main topic of the day. You need to plan for establishing set, but you don't need to have a complicated and time-consuming activity.

- **Involving learners.** A variety of factors help involve learners as the lesson or presentation begins. An introductory activity that is both creative and appropriate for the situation and the age of the learners helps focus their attention. Actual involvement in the activity can increase its effectiveness.

  The way you phrase your introductory comments, as well as those during a lesson, can also have a real impact. Reaction is likely to be negative when an educator begins by saying something like, "Today *I'm* going to tell you *all* about . . . " This gives the impression that the session will be very teacher oriented. Learners want to feel included from the beginning, not 20 minutes after the lesson has begun. When educators dominate from the outset by doing all the talking, students are often reluctant to participate. In a leader-dominated situation you hear lots of phrases like "*I* want you to," "tell *me*," and "*my*." In a learner-oriented situation you are more likely to hear "*we*," "*our*," and "*let's*."

  How effective are your introductions? You can check by using the "Evaluation of the Introduction for a Presentation" instrument, *Figure 8-1* on page 112.

Figure 8-1
EVALUATION OF THE INTRODUCTION FOR A PRESENTATION

Use the following scale to rate the presenter's effectiveness and the quality of the presentation.
10 = Outstanding,   8 = Very Good,   6 = Average,   4 = Fair,   2 = Poor

THE PRESENTER	10	8	6	4	2
1. Was well prepared/organized. Comments:					
2. Established rapport with audience quickly and easily. Comments:					
3. Involved audience—actively or passively. Comments:					
4. Stayed within reasonable time limit and appropriate length for topic. Comments:					
5. Used effective voice inflection and volume. Spoke slowly enough to be understood easily. Comments:					
6. Was free of annoying mannerisms. Comments:					
THE PRESENTATION	**10**	**8**	**6**	**4**	**2**
7. "Grabbed" audience's attention right away. Comments:					
8. Was interesting, stimulating, provocative. Comments:					
9. Indicated what presentation would be about. Seemed as if it would lead into the topic of the presentation. Comments:					
10. Seemed realistic and relevant for audience's needs, interests, abilities, and lifestyles. Comments:					

Questioning

Skillful questioning is one of the most important keys to a purposeful and stimulating teaching-learning situation. Some educators are able to formulate effective questions without a great deal of preplanning. This usually results from long practice. However, you probably will find it helpful to formulate questions before class, either by writing them in your lesson plan or by jotting down key words to remind you of the questions you intend to ask. By doing this, you can more effectively guide students toward attaining the planned objectives of the lesson. Preplanning questions also limits asking questions that relate to details rather than to important concepts and generalizations. You can plan higher-level questions that help students to explore ideas and to work toward satisfactory solutions to relevant problems, or you can ask questions that require only knowledge of specific facts. Information is easily forgotten, but developing thinking processes through significant questions that probe for solutions can make an important contribution to the students' lives.

❋ Using Probing Questions

When educators probe, they ask questions that require learners to go beyond superficial, first-answer responses. You do this when you ask these types of questions:

- **Clarification.** Asking learners for more information or what their replies mean.
- **Justification.** Requiring students to defend their responses.
- **Refocusing.** Redirecting the individual's or the group's attention to a related issue.
- **Prompting.** Giving learners hints.
- **Redirecting.** Bringing additional students into the discussion by asking them to respond to another student's reply.

❋ Asking Questions at Appropriate Levels of Thinking

Effective questions place the burden of thinking on the learners. Some questions require lower levels of thinking, such as recalling or recognizing specifics. Others use higher and more challenging levels, such as applying, analyzing, synthesizing, and evaluating ideas. It is generally best to ask questions requiring a variety of different levels of thinking. The proportion asked at each level depends on the objectives of the lesson. If one of the objectives is to recall cognitive information, then you will ask questions that focus on remembering and recognizing facts. However, your objectives and questions should also incorporate the deeper levels of thinking. Higher-level questions can't be answered by memory alone. Questions that require only one-word answers or a simple "yes" or "no" response seldom involve higher levels of thinking, unless they are followed by queries such as "Please *defend* your point of view," "Please *explain* that to us," "How might . . . ?" "What if . . . ?" or "Why . . . ?"

Here are examples of questions above the knowledge level:

- **Comprehension.** "What is an example that illustrates the meaning of the term 'food safety'?"
- **Application.** "How can the principles of child guidance be applied to the situation we just saw in the video?"
- **Analysis.** "What may be the root problem in this situation?"
- **Synthesis.** "If you were given this responsibility, what are the actions you would consider taking?"
- **Evaluation.** "What decision would be the most satisfactory one for you? Why?"

❋ Including Process Questions

Content is *what* you learn, but process refers to *how* you learn it. Process is a method of obtaining, analyzing, and using content. In the Family and Consumer Sciences (FACS) National Standards, the four organizing processes under which most FACS curriculum content falls have been identified as thinking, communication, leadership, and management. Other process skills, such as problem solving, might also be used. Process questions for each of the four process categories have been formulated for each of the 16 FACS areas of study. All of the process questions in the national standards begin with "what," "how," or "why," promoting higher levels of thinking.

- **Thinking.** As a definition, thinking processes embrace complex, multifaceted activities of the mind. The process of *thinking*, in terms of process skills, emphasizes *directed thinking*—or the use of cognitive and metacognitive skills or strategies that increase the likelihood of desired outcomes. Related to the notions of critical and creative thinking, this meaning of the thinking process is purposeful, reasonable, and goal-directed.

- **Communication.** By exchanging thoughts, feelings, opinions, and information, a sender and receiver communicate. The skills involved in communication include speaking, listening, writing, and reading, as well as the interpretive processes of sensitivity, insight, and the ability to adjust communication according to a specific audience.
- **Leadership.** As a process, leadership encompasses all aspects of guiding and persuading individuals and groups (such as families) to develop a purpose and commit to accomplishing that purpose. Leadership requires the use of various strategies to involve people in achieving a shared vision. Shared leadership encourages every group member to help make decisions and take action. Effective leaders are sensitive to the needs, thoughts, and feelings of others while modeling effective communication.
- **Management.** Setting goals, planning, implementing actions to take in order to meet goals, and evaluating outcomes are all part of management. Problem solving and decision making are instrumental to effective management. The complexity of management varies with the context of every situation.

✳ Sequencing Questions

Ask questions in a logical order that provides continuity in the lesson. The sequence also depends on the subject matter and the background of the learners. One approach is to begin with easy questions and move toward more complicated ones. This is effective when the content is complex, or when the participants have difficulty working with abstract ideas. Being able to answer easy questions at first gives feelings of confidence, security, and achievement. This helps build a positive attitude toward the learning situation and may also affect the participants' desire and determination to be successful in answering more difficult questions.

Here is an example of questions ranging from a basic to an advanced level:

- "What are the fibers we have studied?" (Knowledge)

- "What important characteristics does each of them have?" (Knowledge)
- "If you were to purchase a carpet for a heavy-traffic area in your home, what fibers would be good choices?" (Application)
- "Why are these fibers better for this situation than others you might choose?" (Analysis)

Another type of questioning sequence is directed toward a problem-solving or discovery approach to learning. In this case, questioning serves to encourage learners to examine the parts of a whole, to clarify a problem, and to ask their own relevant questions.

In order to work toward problem-solving or discovery learning, an educator might ask:

- "How would you describe the experimental approach we used?" (Comprehension)
- "What might have caused what occurred?" (Analysis)
- "How can you prove your theory?" (Synthesis)

Asking questions such as these encourages learners to engage in thinking above the recall level. It tests their powers of observation and calls on them to give proof of their theories.

✳ Encouraging Participation

Learner participation can be encouraged through effective questioning techniques. You can implement many of the guidelines in this chapter and those listed below immediately. Other techniques may require practice before they become natural and spontaneous for you.

1. **Be sure learners have sufficient background to answer questions successfully.** It can be very discouraging for a person to have to say, "I don't know." A sense of timing is important so that the program or lesson is developed to the point of enabling learners to answer questions intelligently. Help all participants in group discussions develop a sense of achievement. Questions related to simpler concepts can be asked of learners with lower ability, and those pertaining to more complex concepts can be asked

of more intellectually capable individuals. Overall, the questions for a topic should reach the level of the appropriate objective. The objectives should have been written with the ages and ability levels of the learners in mind.

2. **Word questions clearly.** A question like "What do you think about this?" often receives no response or a poor response because learners don't know how to respond to the indefinite wording. More structure is offered when the leader asks, "Why do you agree or disagree with Drew's decision?" Questions beginning with "what about" or "how about" are too broad and vague. "Would you like to" questions allow a "No, I wouldn't!" response.

3. **Ask concise, open-ended questions, not long rambling ones.** When questions are worded clearly and concisely, more students will be able to answer them. A long or awkwardly worded question often doesn't fairly assess students' knowledge because the question itself may not be understood. Formulate questions that require more than a one- or two-word answer to maximize learning.

4. **Vary the wording of questions to create interest.** A few of the phrases you can use to begin questions are: "What might," "Why is there," "Which of," and "If you had." "Please share with *us*" elicits a more favorable reaction than "Please tell *me*," because it is worded more inclusively. You can also simply eliminate such prefaces from your questions.

5. **Direct questions to the entire group, pause, then call on an individual by name.** This technique helps keep everyone alert and encourages each to formulate an answer. When a person's name is designated before the question is asked, others realize they probably won't be called on to respond. However, you can direct a question to a specific person when that learner's attention has been diverted. This allows you to bring the person back into discussion quickly without calling specific attention to his or her lack of concentration.

6. **Call on people randomly, rather than by going up and down rows or around a circle.** When learners know that they won't be asked questions until others have been called upon, they are less likely to pay attention. However, there is no point in calling on learners when their non-verbal cues indicate an inability to answer satisfactorily.

7. **Encourage everyone to participate.** Be aware of who has and has not contributed to a discussion. Try to provide the opportunity for most of the group to participate.

8. **Give people time to answer.** As a beginning educator you may be tempted to answer your own questions rather than give your learners sufficient time to think of their own responses. This may advance the discussion, but it deprives learners of important opportunities for independent thinking. Interrupting students' answers has a similar effect. Try providing a hint if there's no response. Another technique would be to say something like "Let me put it another way," or "I guess I didn't make the question clear," before rephrasing it or changing it to incorporate a lower level of learning. These techniques help build a positive climate for participation.

✳ Using Learner-Initiated Questions

In a nonthreatening, interesting environment, learners usually ask questions that can be used to enhance a lesson or program. Replying to these questions can add depth. However, if a lengthy reply is needed, be sure the topic is worthwhile and will interest a sufficient number of participants. Don't let learners' questions and your own responses extend beyond the point of educationally diminishing returns. In answering a specific question, maintain eye contact and talk to the entire class, not just with the person who asked the question. If necessary for clarity, repeat the question for the group before answering it.

❋ Staying on Track

Particularly in school settings, students often ask questions that lead their teachers into talking about unrelated topics. Some delight in seeing how long they can keep a teacher off the subject. That way, they can't be held responsible for material that was never covered in class. Limited discussion about topics not included in the curriculum can add interest and serve as a motivating force, but each occurrence needs to be carefully evaluated.

Take care to avoid topics that are too personal, highly controversial, or may stimulate very emotional reactions. Issues that might be acceptable topics for classroom discussion in one community or with one audience may be totally unacceptable in another place.

Develop ways to conclude the talk about irrelevant topics. You might say, "This is all very interesting, but let's get back to what we were saying about . . . " Another response could be, "That's an interesting question. Maybe we can discuss it another day."

❋ Responding to Answers

There are many ways to positively reinforce those who respond to questions. You can make comments such as "That's a good answer," "Nice contribution, Charise," "I hadn't thought about it that way," or simply nod your head. Paraphrasing participants' answers adds variety. You can extend answers by restating or adding a thought. Skillful teachers are able to alter students' answers slightly so they are more meaningful and acceptable, while still giving them the feeling that they have made a valuable contribution. Here are some additional tips:

- **Try to avoid telling learners, "No, that's wrong."** This type of remark stifles participation. Students are reluctant to answer questions if they think they might be put down. You can indicate that an answer is incorrect more subtly by saying something such as "The question may not have been clear," or "Part of your answer is right, but . . . " or "That's an interesting thought; however, you may remember . . ." It is also discouraging to be told, "I have

something else in mind," "I'm thinking of another point," or "There's another answer that is right, too." Replies like these make students feel as if they are playing a guessing game and have to read the teacher's mind. This gives the impression that there is only one preconceived and precisely correct answer. Actually, there may be many responses that are right or partially right. Students often think of excellent points that their teachers had never considered.

- **When you follow answers with additional probing questions, participation usually increases.** You might ask for clarification with questions such as "What is an example to illustrate that?" or "What might have caused that to happen?" When you follow up on responses this way, students are encouraged to expand their remarks and to justify their answers. This also clarifies the information for the other participants.

- **When someone is unable to respond to a question, try directing another question to the same person.** You can reword the original question or provide a clue to assist the student in answering. For example, your initial question might have been "Why did the father behave that way?" If there's no response, you might reword the question to "Suppose you were the father. What might have prompted you to act that way?" or "In what ways is this situation similar to the one we discussed yesterday?" By guiding learners toward correct responses, you can help them feel successful. In this way, they also learn that everyone is expected to participate in class discussions.

- **Bring additional students into the discussion by asking them to respond to the same question just answered by another.** This enhances depth of subject matter. A variety of viewpoints can be presented so that all sides of a topic are explored. You might ask, "What can be added to Jared's answer, Eduardo?" or "What is another side of the issue, Chris?"

The types of questions you ask and the way you ask them reflects on your competence as an instructor. Skillful questioning techniques are the basis for all methods of effective teaching. Reading a skit, seeing a demonstration, or going on a field trip may be nothing more than entertainment unless preceded and followed by thought-provoking questions that foster higher levels of thinking. To learn more about the interrelatedness of effective questioning and guiding meaningful discussions, see Chapter 9.

Using Silence

Many educators are uncomfortable with silences or pauses in group discussions. Because of their discomfort, they tend to fill silences by talking unnecessarily or by making space-filling sounds such as "umm." Silence can be a powerful tool in the teaching-learning process because it can provide learners with the opportunity to think. You can use pauses effectively after the following:

- Introductory comments to encourage participants to think about their answers.
- Questions asked of learners to give them time to formulate answers.
- Questions from a learner directed to another learner verbally, or by a look or gesture.
- Student responses that foster additional remarks from other participants.

Reinforcing Positive Behavior

Your positive reaction to desired behavior is an integral part of your role as an educator and facilitator in the learning environment. You give feedback so learners will continue desirable behavior or change their disruptive activities. It's easy to focus on problem behaviors and spend a great deal of time trying to correct those. However, noting and encouraging positive behavior is as important, if not more so. (Chapter 18 discusses motivation and discipline in more

detail.) If you are animated and show interest while you teach, you are more likely to obtain positive participation.

There are also specific response techniques that you can use and behaviors you can develop that encourage meaningful student involvement. You can give reinforcement nonverbally through smiling and nodding or verbally with words of support. Praise is often a single word such as "good," "fine," or "exactly." Sometimes you can simply say, "Go on. This is interesting." or "Tell us more about your idea." When a learner makes a worthwhile comment, you could paraphrase the statement, restate the idea more simply and concisely, or summarize what has been said. This both develops the subject matter further and compliments the student. Learners feel that their contributions are valued and important. Both verbal and nonverbal reinforcement reflect concern for participants' feelings. It is important to give reinforcement in a variety of ways because individuals react differently to various types of support.

By varying reinforcement given for good answers, you encourage student participation. If you overuse expressions such as "OK," they become monotonous and distracting. Besides, replying with "OK" is like saying, "I heard you." It is a neutral response, rather than a positive reinforcement, and does little to encourage students to participate further or contribute again. Although words like "right" and "good" convey positive reactions, if overused they lose their reinforcement value and sound like mechanical responses. Some students become so conscious of teachers' repeated use of words or phrases that they listen for them and actually begin to count the number of times they are said. When this happens, they don't hear *what* is being said but rather only *how* it is being communicated. The chart "99 Ways to Say 'Very Good,'" *Figure 8-2* on page 118, shows that there are many positive alternatives.

Figure 8-2

99 Ways to Say "Very Good"

1. That's right.
2. That's the way.
3. You're doing fine.
4. Now you have it.
5. Exceedingly well done.
6. That's great.
7. GREAT!
8. FANTASTIC!
9. TERRIFIC!
10. Good work.
11. Good for you.
12. That's better.
13. EXCELLENT!
14. Good going.
15. Keep it up.
16. WOW!
17. Much better.
18. Good.
19. Good thinking.
20. Clever.
21. Exactly right.
22. Nice going.
23. Way to go.
24. SUPER!
25. SUPERB!
26. All right!
27. WONDERFUL!
28. That's it.
29. That's good.
30. Congratulations.
31. FINE!
32. Right on.
33. TREMENDOUS!
34. Perfect.
35. Outstanding.
36. How clever.
37. Good effort.
38. I like that.
39. MARVELOUS!
40. You remembered.
41. SENSATIONAL!
42. You did it that time.
43. That's a good idea.
44. Good job, (Bill/Sara).
45. That's really nice.
46. Keep up the good work.
47. That's much better.
48. You make it look easy.
49. I knew you could do it.
50. You're doing beautifully.
51. That's a clever way to do it.
52. You've got it made.
53. You're learning fast.
54. You're on the right track now.
55. You're doing a good job.
56. You did a lot of work today.
57. Now you've figured it out.
58. Now you have the hang of it.
59. You're really going to town.
60. That's coming along nicely.
61. You outdid yourself today.
62. That's the best you have ever done.
63. I've never seen anyone do it better.
64. You are doing that much better today.
65. You're getting better every day.
66. Keep working on it, you're doing well.
67. You're really working hard.
68. Nothing can stop you now.
69. You are very good at this.
70. You've just about got it.
71. That's quite an improvement.
72. That's not half bad.
73. You haven't missed a thing.
74. That's the best ever.
75. You did that very well.
76. You've got that down pat.
77. You're really improving.
78. Well, look at you go!
79. I'm very proud of you.
80. You figured that out quickly.
81. I think you've got it now.
82. You really are learning a lot.
83. You certainly did well today.
84. That's better than ever.
85. That was first-class work.
86. You really make my job fun.
87. You've done it!
88. That's one good way to do that.
89. I'm proud of the way you worked today.
90. I'm happy to see you working like that.
91. Couldn't have done it better myself.
92. One more time and you'll have it.
93. You've just about mastered that.
94. Very impressive!
95. Now that's what I call a fine job.
96. You must have been practicing.
97. Congratulations, you got (#) right.
98. It's a pleasure to teach when you work like that.
99. That kind of work makes me proud of you.

Recognizing and Obtaining Attending Behavior

Look for visual clues that indicate participants' reactions. Facial expressions, the direction of the eyes, the tilt of the head, and body posture can indicate interest, boredom, comprehension, or confusion. Skilled educators recognize such clues and modify their teaching strategies. They may, for example, vary the pace, change the activity, or introduce a different method of teaching to regain the attention of the audience.

Using Appropriate Frames of Reference

Frames of reference provide several different points of view through which participants gain an understanding of content. Any subject is better understood when it is presented from different points of view, rather than just one. For example, fashion merchandising becomes more meaningful to students when it is seen from the perspectives of the garment designer, fabric manufacturer, assembly-line production staff, wholesale distributor, retailer, and fashion coordinator. The key to this teaching skill is the word *appropriate*. You identify many possible frames of reference that can be used in instruction and then make judicious selections from the list, depending on the needs and interest of the participants.

To illustrate how having a frame of reference helps you remember material, try the following exercise. Study the following combinations of three letters in order to list them again in about 30 seconds in any order:

FCS	XRG	ADA
XAT	ZZZ	LCP
IPS	TAS	NED

Which combinations of letters did you remember? Undoubtedly it was those for which you have a frame of reference.

- For FCS, you may have thought of Family and Consumer Sciences if that is your academic area. If it isn't your field of study, you are less likely to have remembered.
- For XAT, you may have realized the word tax was spelled backwards.
- For IPS, you may have seen that it was almost IRS or Internal Revenue Service.
- You probably did not recall XRG without a personal frame of reference.
- ZZZ may have been remembered because it is unusual or because it sometimes indicates sleeping.
- TAS may have made you think of the SAT or Scholastic Aptitude Test.
- ADA is the acronym for the Americans with Disabilities Act.
- For LCP, unless you had some personal frame of reference, it might have been difficult to remember.
- For NED, you may have realized that the letters spell END—the end of the list. Or perhaps you know someone named Ned.

If subject matter is presented using a frame of reference that is meaningful to your learners, it will have added relevance. They will be more likely to recall the information at a later date when it's needed.

Illustrating with Examples

Examples are used to clarify, verify, and substantiate concepts. The more examples used, the greater the retention of subject matter. Multiple examples also maximize the likelihood that one will be relevant to each learner. Here are some ways to use examples effectively:

- Start with simple examples and progress to more complex ones.
- Begin with examples relevant to participants' experiences and knowledge.
- Build on learners' verbal contributions by giving examples to clarify points they have made and to add information.
- Relate examples to the principles being taught or the guidelines being covered.
- Check to see if the objectives of the lesson have been achieved by asking participants to give examples that illustrate the main points.

Reinforcing Subject Matter

The purpose of this skill is to further clarify major concepts, generalizations, principles, and key words that have been taught. You can use repetition effectively to focus, highlight, and direct attention to points that need emphasis. However, students feel belittled and bored if subject matter is repeated verbatim a second time with the same media and teaching methods. Varying instructional strategies enhances the reinforcement of content. For example, your lesson may be focused on the importance of keeping fat intake to less than 30% of total calories. You use the "Nutrition Facts" section of food labels to figure fat content of sample daily meals. In the same lesson, you also emphasize limiting fat intake when discussing weight management techniques. Taking part in different, but related, learning experiences helps reinforce learning. Tailor the activities, media, and examples to each conceptual area and audience.

Pacing

Pacing refers to presenting content at a rate of speed appropriate for the audience, balancing the amount of intellectually difficult material presented at one time, and making a smooth transition from one part of a program to another. Plan transitions to link one activity to another and to move participants from one activity to the next. When pacing is effective, learners have time to absorb the information, but the lesson doesn't drag.

Avoid trying to cover too many difficult concepts at one time. Students need an opportunity to internalize, analyze, and synthesize what they have learned. For example, if you planned to cover career options, internships, résumés, cover letters, and interviewing with a high school group in one day, there would be too little time for the students to grasp the material. Provide opportunities during a lesson for evaluation and student-initiated questions and comments.

Eliciting Learner Feedback

As you present information, you need constant feedback on whether your audience is understanding and learning the content. Questioning, visual cues, and informal appraisals give you immediate feedback. These will help you judge your effectiveness and modify your lessons when necessary. Ask specific questions pertaining to the subject matter, as well as broader questions like "How does what we've been talking about relate to . . . " Questions such as "Do you understand?" are not very effective. Most people are hesitant to admit to the entire group that they don't understand, especially when it appears to them that everyone else does. Using different assessment strategies, such as written project reports, oral presentations, laboratory evaluation instruments, and quizzes, provides feedback from learners with different learning styles.

Gathering feedback does have pitfalls. Consciously avoid relying on a limited number of students as "indicators" or checking your effectiveness based on feedback cues from the same few learners.

Achieving Closure

Closure is more than a quick summary of the material that has been covered. In addition to pulling together major points and helping learners see the relationships among concepts, closure provides them with a sense of achievement.

Closure shouldn't be limited to the end of a lesson. Use it when the major concepts, purposes, principles, or particular portions of a session have been covered to assist individuals in relating new knowledge to past knowledge. You can provide closure at specific points within a lesson to help learners see where they have been, where they are, and/or where they are going. Questions such as these are helpful in bringing closure:

- "How does what we've been talking about relate to . . . ?"

- "What does this mean to you in your life today?"
- "How can you use this information in the future?"

Figure 8-3, below, provides additional tips on achieving closure.

Figure 8-3

A Dozen Characteristics of Effective Closure

1. Pulls major points of the presentation together and reinforces the central idea.
2. Helps audience see relationships among subtopics covered.
3. Clarifies the "bottom line" or what you want the audience to do.
4. Leaves the audience with a feeling of achievement.
5. Helps audience see how content can be used in the present or the future.
6. Involves audience (in actuality or psychologically).
7. Uses questioning techniques effectively (Question, pause, name. Random pattern. No "What about . . . ?" or "Would you . . . ?" type of questions).
8. Uses higher level questions (no yes/no, one-word answer, all knowledge-level, or "Do you want to . . . ?" or "Would you . . . ?" type of questions.)
9. Acknowledges and varies responses to audience's answers, contributions, comments.
10. Remains free of repetitive or annoying mannerisms.
11. Makes ending vivid, memorable.
12. Makes it clear that this is the end of the presentation without having to say "Thank you."

Varying Stimuli

In addition to using specific core teaching techniques skillfully, you will want to vary the teaching environment to enhance learning. You increase interest when you change the seating arrangement and the appearance of the classroom. You can use different accessories, such as posters and student projects. Make a new bulletin board or display. Use a fresh teaching method. You might hold a meeting in another room or have the participants move their desks or chairs into a different pattern.

Although creating interest through variety is usually not identified as a specific teaching skill, it does enhance the teaching-learning process. When you vary habitual patterns, learner attention often increases. This can be as simple as changing the way you move around the room or printing hand-outs on colored paper. Incorporating a variety of teaching methods, materials, and media is also important in creating and maintaining interest.

Improving Your Skills

Skill development is an ongoing process. As you prepare to teach, your instructor, classmates, and supervising teacher can be good sources of feedback. On the job, you may ask a peer, mentor, or administrator to give you helpful suggestions for improving your teaching skills. There are many evaluation instruments available for this purpose and for self-evaluation. The "Rating Scale for Teaching Skills," *Figure 8-4* on pages 122-123, highlights five key teaching skills.

❊ Videotaping

Viewing a videotape of yourself teaching can be enlightening! You may discover habit patterns such as distracting gestures, annoying facial expressions, rocking on your feet, or repetitious verbal interactions. Becoming sensitized to such habits can help you change these behaviors. Try for greater variety in your demeanor and the elimination of any annoying, repetitious mannerisms. Check yourself again periodically. Seeing yourself teaching will highlight your strengths and weaknesses as nothing else will. You could tape all, or just part of, a lesson or presentation. Self-evaluations based on videotaping, as well as peer and supervisors' evaluations, point out areas in which you excel, as well as areas in which you can improve.

Figure 8-4

RATING SCALE FOR TEACHING SKILLS

Person being rated: _____ Evaluator: _____

Directions: Use the key to evaluate the teacher on each of the skills. Record in the score column the number that corresponds to the level of competence. Then compute the total score.

PERFORMANCE LEVEL KEY:
1 = Inadequate   2 = Improvement needed   3 = Average   4 = Good   5 = Outstanding

1	2	3	4	5	SCORE
Establishing Set					
1. Bored students with a dull, unimaginative approach.	Gained immediate interest with a rather ordinary approach.		Gained immediate interest of students with a stimulating approach.		1. _____
2. Did not achieve rapport and created no interaction among students.	Achieved rapport with some students and gained some interaction among students.		Achieved rapport with students and fostered interaction among the students.		2. _____
Framing Reference					
3. Failed to frame a reference—left students questioning relevancy of material.	Had some success in framing a reference that helped students understand material.		Incorporated different points of view to achieve an interesting frame of reference relevant to all.		3. _____
4. Did not relate frame of reference to objectives to make material relevant to students.	Attempted to relate content to objectives, but this was sometimes unclear.		Related frame of reference to objectives and made students realize the relevancy of material to them.		4. _____
Questioning					
5. Did not use functional questions, did not redirect; discussion monopolized by a few students.	Utilized some functional questions, but other questions required more teacher development before other students joined in.		Used content questions to clarify, to justify, and to bring other students into discussion.		5. _____
6. Kept questions on knowledge level; did not encourage higher thinking levels.	Asked some questions on higher levels but tended to stay with lower level questions.		Used content questions to clarify, to justify, and to bring other students into discussion.		6. _____
Reinforcing					
7. Used only limited verbal reinforcement and did not change voice or expression.	Used some variety of verbal reinforcement but used no other means of reinforcement.		Used a variety of methods of reinforcement, including gestures as well as words.		7. _____

Figure 8-4 (cont'd)

RATING SCALE FOR TEACHING SKILLS

	1	2	3	4	5	SCORE
Reinforcing cont'd						
8. Overdid reinforcement to point of sounding fake and insincere.		Seemed to be sincere most of the time when reinforcing.		Was sincere in each reinforcement to each student response.		8.＿＿
Achieving Closure						
9. Did not draw points together or summarize periodically or at the end.		Had some success in drawing points together but had difficulty in choosing when to have final closure.		Achieved closure at appropriate times.		9.＿＿
10. Did not interrelate parts of material or give students a feeling of progress and achievement.		Interrelated some of the material and gave some students a feeling of progress and achievement.		Successfully pulled parts of lesson together and gave students a feeling of progress and achievement.		10.＿＿

 # Microteaching

Microteaching, in its purest sense, means developing expertise in using teaching skills, practicing one at a time. It's a common technique used by those preparing for teaching. For example, you may be videotaped with a small group of learners while establishing set. This teaching skill is critiqued and played back. Then you are videotaped again while establishing set. This procedure is repeated as often as necessary.

Next, a second teaching skill—perhaps using examples—is isolated and worked on until a desirable level of expertise is achieved using this skill. The process continues until a predetermined level of competence has been achieved in using each of the core teaching skills.

In many situations, this pattern may have to be modified. Time, equipment, class size, and other variables affect the procedures used. For example, two or three teaching skills may be worked on during each videotaping session.

 # The Communication Connection

Teaching skills are tools of the trade and they are also tricks of the trade, in the legitimate sense that they help one teacher succeed where another, equally informed and well-intentioned, may fail. Effective communication is the common thread that links these skills. How does effective communication relate to each skill?

Remember that teaching and learning are processes. Teaching skills facilitate the transfer of knowledge from you, the educator, to the learners. But the process also includes using feedback generated as a constant and invaluable guide to help you refine your methods and reach your desired goals.

Building Your Professional Portfolio

Videotape. Videotape yourself teaching. Evaluate your set, questioning, reinforcement, and closure skills. Identify specific strengths and areas needing improvement. Videotape a second time and compare your analyses.

Assessment Tool. Develop an assessment tool that an administrator could use to evaluate an educator's teaching skills.

Extension Lesson. Plan and present a lesson to Expanded Food and Nutrition Education Program (EFNEP) paraprofessionals on one of the teaching skills you have used successfully, such as illustrating with examples, questioning, or using appropriate frames of reference. Include your teaching plan and an evaluation of this experience in your portfolio.

Skills in Action. Write a dialogue among an educator and audience members that illustrates the effective use of at least four core teaching skills. Identify the skills.

Chapter 9
Leading Discussions

Discussions are part of most educational experiences, whether or not that education takes place in a traditional classroom setting. Discussions are often paired with lectures, but they may also be used as the main mode of learning or to reinforce learning. That makes understanding the dynamics of discussions and how to plan, lead, and evaluate them key skills for educators.

What makes effective discussions so important to learning? Besides acquisition of content knowledge, well-run discussions help participants learn to listen to other viewpoints and broaden their perspective. Participants also practice tackling an issue, rather than attacking the person discussing the issue. A stimulating and "safe" climate for discussion helps them develop greater sensitivity in communicating with others. There are few substitutes for the satisfaction of a frank, thoughtful, and relevant exchange of ideas.

 ## Leading Stimulating Discussions

Discussions, like all other methods of teaching, are very dependent on the questioning skills of the leader. Because effective questioning is the base upon which effective discussions are built, review pages 112-117 to reinforce the points made about questioning as a teaching skill.

Stimulating discussions are based on higher-level questions, which can't be answered from memory alone. Such questions call for explaining, using, analyzing, synthesizing, or evaluating rules, guidelines, or principles rather than just stating them. Higher-level questions seldom can be answered with only one word. Beginning questions with *how*, *what*, and *why* fosters thinking at levels above the knowledge level in the cognitive domain.

For success, discussion questions need to be planned in advance. It is easier to stay on track when you know the main questions you will ask and points you need to cover. That doesn't mean all questions and answers can be scripted ahead of time. You will need to adapt your questions based on the flow of the discussion.

It is easy to let a discussion stray from the topic. Some students are masters at changing the subject. Sometimes what comes up is valuable. Other times it simply hinders meeting lesson and program objectives. A caring educator knows when to capitalize on the teachable moment and take care of learners' immediate concerns, even if these topics are not included in the original plan for the day.

✳ Selecting a Discussion Topic

When planning a discussion, select a topic that is relevant to the participants' lives and is easily understood. Particularly in less formal educational settings, you may ask learners what problems they hope to solve and subjects they want to discuss and incorporate these into your plans.

Choose topics that offer several facets to explore and also provide opportunities to consider a variety of viewpoints and perspectives. Discussion topics should be related to a group's real interests, concerns, needs, and experiences.

✳ Initiating a Discussion

You can initiate the main theme of a discussion in a variety of ways. You might provide the needed stimulus through clearly worded and provocative questions that relate to previous experiences of group members, an interesting video, a stimulating story or article, or a presentation of pertinent data. The problem should be clearly stated, and most members should have sufficient information and background to be able to make positive contributions. If group members lack sufficient knowledge or experience relating to the topic, the discussion may be meaningless, or even damaging and prejudicial. A stimulating discussion is based on a firm foundation of learner interest and an environment that invites participation. A comfortable, informal atmosphere in which spontaneous humor might surface at any moment nurtures honest expressions of feeling and opinion.

✳ *Brainstorming*

Brainstorming is one way to initiate discussion. The first step is to gather a quantity of ideas without considering their quality. Participants need to be reassured that their ideas won't be criticized.

For example, you could ask students to list suggestions for the theme of an annual employer appreciation banquet or an open house for parents of young children in the child care program. As ideas are suggested, you or a student writes them down so that everyone can see them. After all ideas are expressed, the participants vote to determine the two or three they like best. Then these are discussed in detail. The advantages and disadvantages of each idea are explored. After this, another vote establishes the *one* idea participants think is best. Such a procedure increases the likelihood that the group, as a whole, will be reasonably satisfied with the decision.

If brainstorming is done in small groups, each group might present the two or three ideas it considers its best. After the best of each small group's ideas are listed, an elimination process may be carried out by a vote of all group members.

Brainstorming is not designed for use in situations that point obviously to one best solution. Neither is the outcome predetermined by the educator or student leader. In other words, the group works together democratically to arrive at *a* solution, not at *the* solution.

✳ The Discussion Leader

As a discussion leader, you model behavior for the learners as you listen, encourage involvement, display interest in each person's opinions, maintain eye contact, and keep the discussion going through a variety of means. Avoid monopolizing the conversation, but sometimes you will have to provide direction and guidance. Be prepared to summarize the main points, make supportive and encouraging comments, or ask pertinent questions. Such sensitivity can prevent the discussion from bogging down or being monopolized by one or two individuals.

In your role as a discussion leader, more than in any other role you assume as an educator, you have to be able to think on your feet. At times you may want to rephrase the ideas of the group in clearer and simpler language. Be careful, though, not to impose your own ideas and values on the group. If you are asked your opinion and want to give it, you might postpone giving it until the latter part of the discussion. It is sometimes difficult to let others do the talking, especially when you disagree with what they say. Above all, as a discussion leader you need to keep emotions under control.

Responsibilities in Leading a Discussion

The leader's main responsibilities are keeping the discussion going and involving everyone, if possible. Watch facial expressions for signs of interest, desire to contribute, and waning attention. Be sensitive to nonverbal cues of disinterest such as swinging feet, stares directed at the window or clock, and doodling. Keep distractions to a minimum to encourage learners to pay attention and to participate.

You might make periodic summaries, and usually you will be responsible for concluding the discussion. Doing this can take the form of asking the participants to identify the main points, to explain how their ideas or opinions may have changed, or to predict how the discussion could affect participants' future behavior.

Setting the Ground Rules

There are many advantages to establishing discussion guidelines with your participants. When they have input into the rules, they have ownership in the process and are more likely to cooperate. Try to keep the guidelines short, simple, and positive. Your group may come up with statements similar to these:

• Be polite.
• Respect other participants' opinions.
• Let one person talk at a time.
• Limit your time speaking.
• Limit the number of times you speak.
• Let others finish without interrupting.
• Follow established methods for showing you want to speak (such as raising your hand).

Seating Arrangements

Experience demonstrates that the people sitting nearest the teacher or discussion leader are the most active participants. People outside this limited area may be hesitant to contribute unless they are skillfully brought into the discussion.

Various seating arrangements can either promote or inhibit communication among group members. It is best to have participants face one another. Then they too can detect both verbal and nonverbal cues. If possible, move chairs into a semicircle prior to the discussion.

In most situations, it is better to sit with the participants, rather than stand. Psychologically, standing tends to place you in an unapproachable and authoritarian position and diminishes group members' participation and leadership.

Discussion Participants

It often takes time for groups to develop the rapport necessary for truly democratic and effective discussions. Show that you expect and encourage variety in the group's responses.

Group members' personalities affect their participation. Some quiet people prefer to let others do the talking yet still may be participating silently. Others may find it difficult to express themselves and feel self-conscious.

Groups often include people who monopolize a discussion by talking too much and too often. They may talk excessively because they are nervous and insecure, or simply because they are confident or enjoy the attention. Monopolizers' comments often pertain to personal concerns and interests. When this happens, others in the group often become inattentive or bored and may direct some of their resentment toward the leader. The ability to manage such behavior is a key to successful discussions. Allow overparticipators a reasonable amount of time to talk and then ask for others' ideas. A comment such as "That's interesting. Now let's hear another point of view," can be made tactfully. You can often satisfy discussion dominators' need for attention while contributing to the progress of the group. Ask such individuals to operate equipment, show visual media and other teaching materials, or write points on the board as they are made.

For those who don't voluntarily contribute their ideas, direct questions to them. This can be handled casually, calling on willing participants as well. If you actively adhere to ground rules and all responses are respected, insecure members may gradually participate more.

Every teacher needs a good sense of humor. However, when joking begins interfering with the purpose of a discussion, a teacher respected by the learners is able to redirect their attention. A comment like "That was good for a laugh. Now let's get serious again because this topic is important to all of us," can put the discussion back on track.

Humor that is clearly intended to embarrass a group member should not be tolerated. That point should be established as part of the ground rules for the class. If an incident does occur, it must be stopped immediately. Often a frown or some other nonverbal sign indicating disapproval is sufficient to get your message to the offender. All group members need to feel that they and their opinions will be respected.

 # Small-Group Discussions

If you are teaching a large group, dividing into smaller groups may enhance discussion. Individuals who are reluctant to speak out when in larger groups often feel more comfortable participating when in smaller groups. The total group's viewpoints and experiences are thereby expanded and enriched. With greater participation, participants discover that they can be part of a democratic process of decision making based on compromise and mutual agreement.

❈ Forming Small Groups

If you meet with the same learners over time, you are responsible for knowing the personality of the group as a whole and individuals' distinct personalities. This background knowledge helps you decide when to use discussion methods appropriate to small groups and how to form such groups.

You may designate group memberships or allow students to form their own groups. The second option has disadvantages. Students, especially teens, are likely to form their small groups on a basis of friendship. Those who are chosen toward the end of the process feel rejected. Since those with various common interests tend to cluster together, diversity of viewpoints is limited. There are effective methods of grouping learners. A few are explained here.

❈ Quick Grouping Methods

One of the simplest ways to form small groups is to ask learners to number off consecutively. The highest number called should be the same as the total number of members desired in a group. Doing this will achieve a random assignment to groups. Organizing groups according to birth months is another possibility. Listing individuals alphabetically by first names and using appropriate cutoff points for group formation will also avoid using the traditional last-name method of grouping. When various methods are used in schools or other programs over a period of time, students benefit from having worked with most of their classmates.

❈ Group-Building Method

To use the group-building approach, tell students to number off by two's ("one, two, one, two," and so forth) until everyone has a number. The students who are "ones" go to one side of the room and those who are "twos" go to the other side. Each "one" is instructed to invite a "two" to join him or her, thus forming pairs. The invited partner should be someone the learner doesn't know or doesn't know well. When all learners have been paired, each pair invites another to join them. If possible, the invitation should go to learners not well-known by those extending it. If groups larger than four are desired, this process can be repeated.

This exercise serves as a means of forming groups with members who have never, or perhaps infrequently, worked together. Members gain a feeling of togetherness as a result of mutual decision making in extending and accepting invitations.

Groups formed in this fashion can work effectively on problems that profit from having participants with differing backgrounds and viewpoints. This method of group building is also useful for getting members of newly formed programs better acquainted.

✳ Puzzle Cutups Method

Pictures related to the discussion topic cut from magazines, advertisements, etc., may also be used to form groups. The pictures may be used without a backing material, or they can be attached to something lightweight, such as a file folder, cardboard, or construction paper. Cut each picture into jigsaw-shaped puzzle pieces. The number of pieces will depend on the desired size of the small groups. One picture is needed for each group.

To organize the class into groups, scramble the puzzle pieces and place them on any flat surface. Then, instruct students to select one piece and locate the classmates who have other pieces that will complete that picture. Through such matching, groups soon form. The teacher can assign specific activities or discussion questions to each group or instruct the groups to turn their pictures over and read the questions on the reverse side.

✳ Facilitating Small-Group Discussions

After groups have been formed, leaders can use a variety of methods to promote discussion and interaction. Inner and outer circles and buzz sessions help to involve students in small groups.

✳ Inner and Outer Circles

The purposes of this exercise are to have learners listen to others, to give them an opportunity to express their thoughts in a concise manner, and to have them summarize or react to what is said by others. This is a timed exercise using incomplete sentences or questions relating to specific subjects.

To set up this exercise, form several groups of ten or twelve. (Multiple groups will operate simultaneously.) Any remaining students act as observers. Directions are given by the leader from the floor.

To begin the exercise, the leader has half of the group take chairs and form a close circle. The remaining students form a circle around the outside in order to watch and listen carefully to the discussion taking place in the inner circle.

Those in the outer circle don't participate in the discussion. Those in the inner circle are instructed to monitor the discussion and to provide as much opportunity as possible for each member to participate.

The inner circle is given the first statement or question and instructed to discuss it for four minutes. At the end of that period, those in the inner and outer circles exchange positions. The learners in the new inner circle are asked to react, in a two-minute period, to what they heard the first group say. Then this same inner circle responds to the original statement or a new one for four minutes. Positions are again reversed and learners now in the inner circle are told to react, in a two-minute period, to any previous statements with which they agreed or disagreed. This process continues until the students respond to all the statements.

After the exercise is over, you might ask participants to express their feelings about the process. For example, did they feel under great pressure to contribute to the discussion? What kind of interaction was there among group members? What were their feelings about silent periods? How did they feel when they heard themselves quoted?

✳ Buzz Sessions

The term *buzz session* is commonly applied by educators to the activity of learners working among themselves in small discussion groups. The purpose of this form of activity is to maximize participation among group members. Three to five people in a group work best. With fewer, there may not be enough interaction. If there are more, some may be reluctant to express their ideas and opinions.

In a buzz session, the teacher or leader stays in the background but offers help as needed. It's the leader's responsibility to go from group to group, giving encouragement and making sure learners stay on task. By keeping up with each group's progress, the leader will sense the right time to give warnings such as "Take only another minute or two to wind up your discussion." It's generally advisable to call time while the learners are still enthusiastic about their topics.

Buzz groups may be used to formulate replies to letters found in advice columns; to offer solutions to situations presented in case studies; to plan menus, time schedules, and market orders; and to develop sociodramas and skits. Almost anything that can be done in a class-size group can be done equally well—or perhaps better—in a buzz group. However, there must be enough depth of subject matter in the chosen topics to warrant the time involved. If the solutions to be suggested or decisions to be reached are not sufficiently thought-provoking, the time spent in buzz sessions may be wasted.

✳ Student Discussion Leaders

In a school setting, students might serve as small-group discussion leaders or facilitators on a rotating basis. This helps them develop both discussion and leadership skills.

At the beginning of a course or class, talk with the group about the role and qualities of a good discussion leader and an effective discussion. Guidelines for both can be established. Some teachers display a poster or prepare a handout identifying the important points for group leaders. This helps discussion leaders evaluate how well they are fulfilling their roles and serves as a reference for all participants. The chart below shows an example.

STUDENT DISCUSSION LEADER'S RESPONSIBILITIES

- Initiate and guide the discussion without monopolizing it.
- Maintain a positive, stimulating, and enjoyable atmosphere.
- Respond to all contributions.
- Listen carefully to what is said and maintain eye contact with the group.
- Analyze the body language of group members. Use these cues to help each member participate.
- Keep the discussion on target by asking questions and summarizing.

Structured Discussion Techniques

More specialized types of discussions can also be effective teaching tools. Panel discussions, symposiums, forums, and debates each bring together different ideas and opinions on various aspects of one subject. *Figures 9-1* through *9-4* illustrate how these formats compare. The thoughts and opinions the audience hears help them analyze a problem or issue. Although the moderator summarizes the material presented in each of these techniques, the listener is expected to draw personal conclusions. Success of all these structured methods depends upon careful up-front planning, preparation, and organization.

✳ Panel Discussion

A panel discussion airs varied views relating to a selected topic but doesn't attempt to reach a decision or consensus. Panel members may be guests or selected students. The moderator introduces the subject and asks one panelist to begin. Each member gives a brief (three- to five-minute) prepared, but informal, talk. After every speaker has presented, panel members are free to react to and ask questions of the others on the panel. Following this informal exchange, the moderator usually opens the program to audience participation. The moderator guides the direction of the discussion, keeps it on the topic, and summarizes the main ideas and the principal sides of the issues.

If a panel discussion was unsuccessful, it is usually because the members didn't study the issue thoroughly or because the topic was too narrow in scope to allow for in-depth discussion. Here are some examples of questions appropriate for panel discussions:

- What are desirable qualities in an employee?
- Are teens today more mature than those of previous generations?
- What are the most effective methods of improving senior citizens' eating habits?
- What community services are available to help families?

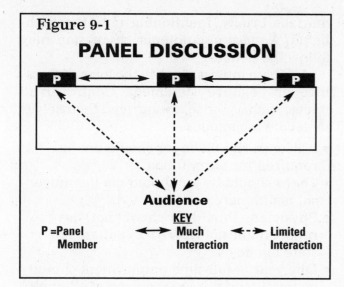

Figure 9-1

PANEL DISCUSSION

P | P | P

Audience

KEY
P = Panel Member | Much Interaction | Limited Interaction

❄ Symposium

In a *symposium* there is one problem under investigation, and each symposium member is qualified to present one aspect of it. Usually each speaker's expertise has been gained through personal experience. Symposium members are given a specific length of time for their presentations. After all have spoken, the speakers exchange ideas or ask questions of one another. There is less interaction among presenters in a symposium than in a panel discussion. Following this exploration of viewpoints by the speakers, the class or audience may also enter into the discussion. The symposium, when used correctly, ensures that the audience gains an overall view of various aspects of the subject.

The teacher, student leader, or chairperson has the responsibility of introducing the participants and their subjects within the general topic, summarizing after all the prepared talks have been given, and leading the ensuing discussion among the speakers. Topics such as these would be suitable for symposiums:

- **Careers in Health Occupations.** Speakers who are employed in paraprofessional and professional areas of health care could speak about needed skills and abilities, desirable personality traits, educational requirements, duties and responsibilities, salaries, and chances for advancement in their respective fields.
- **Meeting the Needs of Special Children.** Parents and siblings of children with mental retardation, physical disabilities,

or special talents might discuss how they meet the special needs of these family members.

- **Single-Parent Families.** Ask representatives (male and female) from a local support group to tell about the problems they have encountered and the solutions they have found most satisfactory in rearing children alone. Teens who live with only one parent may also be willing to give their viewpoints on this topic.

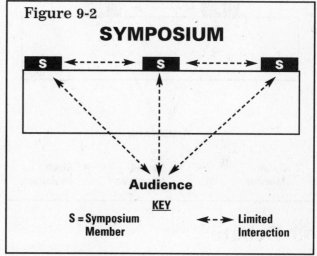

Figure 9-2

SYMPOSIUM

S | S | S

Audience

KEY
S = Symposium Member | Limited Interaction

❄ Forum

In a forum, two, or occasionally three, speakers offer different points of view about a somewhat controversial issue. A forum is more formal than a panel discussion because the forum members don't usually interact much with each other after their prepared speeches. Instead, they answer questions posed by the audience. Listeners have an opportunity to express their own ideas and to ask the forum participants to react to them. A forum moderator must be adept in changing the direction of the dialogue if interest lags, if one or two individuals monopolize it, or if the discourse becomes irrelevant. The moderator summarizes briefly and clearly by reiterating the major contributions.

A forum can be an effective way to introduce a new topic because the speakers are well informed about the topic. The audience is encouraged and expected to ask questions, though they need not have extensive prior knowledge of the subject matter. Some possible topics for a forum are:

- Organic foods are the best foods for good health.
- Financial problems are the leading cause of marital failure today.
- Personal and social skill development is related to good health.
- Men's roles have changed more in the last decade than women's roles.

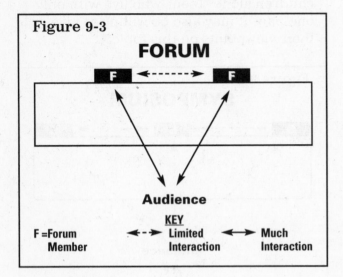

Figure 9-3

FORUM

Audience

KEY

F = Forum Member | ◄--► Limited Interaction | ◄──► Much Interaction

Debate

In a debate, the participants are trying to persuade others. Therefore, the topic must be one about which there are fixed positions or definite "for" and "against" viewpoints to be argued. Teams that take opposing sides debate these issues.

A debate begins when one member of the "pro" team gives reasons for favoring the issue; then a member of the "con" team gives a case for being against it. This procedure continues until each team member has presented evidence and supporting facts. Each should select the strongest possible arguments, make reference to statistics, and quote experts where relevant. This will give authority to the debaters' remarks.

After the prepared speeches, team members have a chance to respond to the statements of their opponents. During this exchange, a new issue cannot be brought up, but new supportive material may be used. Debaters need to investigate the topic thoroughly beforehand so that they can answer questions and defend remarks they and their teammates make. The moderator sum-

marizes briefly, mentioning only the highlights. A class or audience discussion may follow the debate.

A debate topic is given in the form of a positive or negative statement. Controversial issues, such as the following, lend themselves to debate techniques:

- A license should be (or should not be) required for parenthood.
- There should be (or should not be) universal health care.
- Physicians should (or should not) have to report names of HIV/AIDS patients to state agencies.
- One year of full-time employment should be (or should not be) required of all applicants before admission to college.

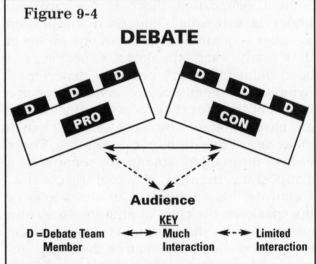

Figure 9-4

DEBATE

PRO   CON

Audience

KEY

D = Debate Team Member | ◄──► Much Interaction | ◄--► Limited Interaction

Evaluating Discussions

Educators can make improvements in leading meaningful class discussions by periodically thinking about and answering the following questions:

1. **Was the discussion carefully planned so progress could be made toward meeting stated objectives?**
   a. Did the physical arrangements of the room promote learner participation?
   b. Was the discussion focused on worthwhile objectives that were clear to the participants and accepted by them as important?

c. Did the participants help determine the objectives and/or discussion topic?

d. Was the approach to the topic stimulating and challenging?

e. Did the discussion move fast enough to be interesting but slow enough to provide for sound, analytical thinking?

2. **Was the discussion appropriate for the learners involved?**

a. Did the discussion present a realistic problem or a situation that was relevant and meaningful to the group?

b. Was the discussion related to concepts or topics that had been covered previously?

c. Did the participants have the background information and experience necessary to make valuable and purposeful contributions?

d. Were the vocabulary and language used appropriate for the group?

e. Was there adequate discussion on essential ideas to arrive at some broad generalizations?

3. **Were participants helped to arrive at their own conclusions and to make their own decisions?**

a. Were participants led to explore all sides of the issue?

b. Were they encouraged to support their conclusions with evidence?

c. Were they guided to consider and apply their beliefs and values?

d. Were they led to consider the possible consequences of their decisions?

4. **Were interpersonal relationships supportive and conducive to learner participation?**

a. Was there evidence of friendliness, acceptance, sincerity, and mutual cooperation?

b. Did participants seem to feel free to express their ideas and to defend their beliefs?

c. Were ideas that participants initiated treated seriously?

d. Was it possible, when individuals digressed from the purposes of the discussion, to refocus their attention without hurting their feelings?

e. Did at least three-fourths of the group participate?

5. **Were the participants given an opportunity to evaluate their growth and gain a sense of progress?**

a. Were learners led to formulate generalizations that related to previously established objectives?

b. Was the discussion summarized clearly and concisely?

As an educator, eliciting feedback from your learners will help you evaluate and improve your teaching competence. You can occasionally ask learners to answer some of these questions to evaluate a class discussion. Let learners know that you appreciate their comments and input by using their ideas when feasible.

Building Your Professional Portfolio

Discussion Plan. Prepare a discussion plan using the following steps:

- Identify a discussion topic.
- Describe the appropriate group for the discussion in terms of age, gender, ability level, number of participants, and setting.
- List four ground rules for the discussion.
- Identify the type of discussion format you would use and justify your choice.
- Describe how you would arrange the room.
- Outline six aspects of the topic to include in the discussion. Write two key questions as discussion starters for each aspect.

Evaluation Instrument. Develop an instrument for assessing a discussion used in an educational setting.

Topic Lists. Generate a list of topics appropriate for each of the following structured discussion techniques: panel discussion, symposium, forum, and debate.

Discussion Dialogue. Write a discussion dialogue involving at least three people. Use the dialogue to illustrate at least six effective discussion techniques. Choose a discussion topic relevant to your employment goal.

Chapter 10

Visual Media

Educators today have a wide variety of visual media available to enhance their teaching and complement the different learning styles of their learners. Of course, one educator may prefer using transparencies rather than a PowerPoint® presentation, just as individual learners like and learn from some approaches better than others. Media can be used to introduce, reinforce, summarize, or highlight material and to stimulate interest. By using a variety of visual media, educators are able to interest and motivate more participants. However, any method or media that is used too frequently loses its appeal, including the latest technology. For instance, the first time a teacher shows a video, students usually react enthusiastically. They would be less enthusiastic about a video the very next day. By the third day, their response to even an excellent video might be, "What? Another video? Is that all we're ever going to do in here—watch videos?"

The key to successful use of visual media is to choose a form that is appropriate for a particular audience and purpose. A three-hour presentation to adults calls for different techniques than a 4-H lesson or a high school class. Similarly, you would probably choose different visual media for a community event than for one in your own classroom. In each case, choosing an effective form of media is as important as the quality of the media itself.

Why Use Visual Media?

Visual and display media can contribute to your educational efforts by serving one or more of the following purposes:

- **Convey content.** In some educational settings, visual media will be used to supplement active teaching. Other times it will stand alone as a teaching tool. In either case, your media presentation should introduce concepts so the intended audience leaves with new and helpful information.
- **Attract attention.** To be effective, the media must reach out and "grab" the viewer.
- **Stimulate action and thinking.** Your goal may be to "sell" a product, idea, or program. Hopefully, after viewing the media, the participants will try to apply the concepts to their lives. At the very least, you should have stimulated thinking about the ideas presented.

- **Reinforce learning.** Visual reinforcement can help viewers grasp concepts that were previously presented orally. Many people are primarily visual learners. Using a variety of senses enhances everyone's learning.
- **Provide positive public relations.** Some forms of visual media are appropriate for helping the public see what your program is all about and the work of people associated with it. This may expand understanding about your program and eliminate misconceptions.
- **Generate interest in a topic.** People attracted to your presentation may have their level of interest piqued by your media.
- **Create affective changes.** Visuals may convince people to regard an issue differently than they had before. For example, a display on hunger in the community might prompt participants to donate to a food pantry.
- **Enhance problem-solving and decision-making skills.** When situations are presented and/or questions are raised as part of visual media, the participants may have to make decisions or work out solutions to problems.
- **Evaluate personal and group progress.** This might take place through media that illustrate the steps to be accomplished in product development or through a progress chart.

Generating Ideas for Visuals

Being aware of your environment is the best way to find ideas for developing your own visual materials. Try the following suggestions:

- Pay attention to billboards and television commercials. Top graphic designers have been hired to sell products for advertisers. Why not sell your program or concept in a similar manner?
- As you read magazines and newspapers and visit websites, watch for graphics and ideas that catch your attention.

- Brainstorm with friends and other educators.
- Look through educational materials. Display ideas are often used and suggestions provided.
- Let your learners be creative and help you. They often bring fresh perspectives.
- Look at product packaging. Consider what attracted you to a product. The concept for a poster or bulletin board may be right in front of you.

Characteristics of Effective Visuals

As you prepare visual media, you need to combine your skills as an educator with those of an artist and entrepreneur. Many of the guidelines for preparing effective display media that follow would also apply to other teaching methods and materials, such as student handouts.

✳ General Guidelines

Regardless of the type of visual media you are preparing, keep these guidelines in mind:

1. **Keep it simple.** The media should convey one idea or message in a forceful and dramatic, yet simple, way. Don't try to present too much information at one time or with one visual.
2. **Match the topic and level to the intended audience.** Choose words that will be understood by the viewers. Select visuals that represent your audience in terms of age, ethnicity, and gender.
3. **Make the finished product neat and professional looking.** You might use a computer to produce attractive lettering. Remember, however, that correct spelling, grammar, and punctuation are critical. Just one misspelled word damages the credibility of a display.
4. **Keep the media uncluttered.** A few large items attract more attention than many small ones, and they are easier to see from a distance. Leave some empty space rather than filling the visual completely with content.

5. **Use a short headline or title.** A brief title has more impact. Starting with an action verb makes viewers think of taking action. A question or open-ended phrase also prompts a response.

6. **Provide a logical sequence, pattern, and/or arrangement.** Remember that people read from left to right and top to bottom. Many other arrangements are hard for the eye to follow.

7. **Make your point or points quickly.** Most people won't spend a lot of time looking at any one visual.

8. **Highlight main points.** For a display, this might mean creating a poster with just a few key points in large type. For a flip chart or transparency, you could use letters in a bright color to draw learners' attention to main points.

9. **Position visuals for the greatest impact and clarity.** With exhibits or bulletin boards, placing the visual at eye level encourages people to stop and look. For other types of media, such as transparencies, flip charts, or PowerPoint® presentations, everyone in the audience should be able to see and read the visual.

10. **Position a visual you must manipulate on the side of your dominant hand.** In that position, you won't have to turn your body to flip pages, move objects, or point to items.

11. **Use real objects and three-dimensional items whenever possible.** Passing a real object around the room or including real examples in a display enhances both interest and learning. When that isn't possible, models are often preferable to drawings and photos.

12. **Let viewers interact with display items.** People often learn more and retain what they learn by touching, feeling, and moving objects. If at all possible, include items that can be handled. Laminating printed material preserves it for reuse.

✳ Elements and Principles of Design

Artists use the elements and principles of design in creating a drawing or painting. Interior designers do the same in planning a room setting. You can use the same design elements and principles to create effective visual materials.

✳ *Elements of Design*

Elements of design are the components that make up a visual design. They are color, texture, shape or form, space, and line. Planning how to best utilize each will result in better visuals.

✳ *Color*

Select colors with care. Color can be used to create a mood, provide associations, and strengthen the theme or message. Yellow, white, and bright colors would be more appropriate than tan or gray for conveying the idea of cleanliness. Green and red or orange and black suggest specific seasons of the year. Certainly, "stop" written in red and "go" written in green are more effective than they would be in the reverse colors!

In creating a visual, try to use no more than three main colors: one for the background, one for lettering, and one for illustration mountings. Of course, color illustrations contain many colors, but their effect is minimal in proportion to the basic colors of the design. When large areas have too many colors, the visual is likely to lack unity.

Choose the combination of colors you will use carefully. Black on yellow is one of the most legible color combinations. However, it may not convey the right message for your subject matter. Research has shown that color combinations rank this way in eye appeal:

1. Black on yellow
2. Green on white
3. Blue on white
4. White on blue
5. Black on white
6. Yellow on black
7. White on red
8. White on orange
9. White on black
10. Red on yellow

Also consider the visual and psychological weight of dark and light colors. Dark colors appear heavier, while light colors have less dominance unless they are very bright.

✳ Texture

Texture, or appearance of texture, can add interest. For a bulletin board, you might choose to use smooth wallpaper with the look of wood grain, brick, stone, or tapestry for the background. You could also use materials that add actual texture, such as burlap, felt, tissue paper, gift wrap, or corrugated cardboard. The look of texture might enhance slides or Power Point® presentation visuals. For a display theme of mapping out careers, you might cover the background with maps. Be sure, however, that the texture doesn't detract from the primary purpose or readability of the visual. It should enhance the theme. Textures are particularly important if viewers will be touching and/or manipulating the media.

✳ Shape or Form

A display should include more than one shape, but too many different shapes can lead to a feeling of clutter and confusion. Research has shown that shapes provide different levels of interest. The oval is seen as the most interesting; the square is regarded as least interesting. Circles and rectangles rank in-between. Following an S shape can give appeal to layouts.

✳ Space

In design planning, people speak of "white" or "free" space. In visual media this is the empty or blank space. To achieve the right amount of free space, start by sketching—by hand or on the computer—a small version of your planned visual. The key is to distribute components well. Don't sacrifice white space just to squeeze in your message. You may actually weaken the visual's effectiveness just by reducing the amount of white space.

✳ Line

Use lines for conveying feeling. They can create motion and move the eye from one place to another. Vertical lines tend to convey poise, dignity, and height. Horizontal lines indicate restfulness, quiet, width, and permanence. Curved lines suggest graceful movement. Slanted lines indicate excitement, action, and sometimes instability.

✳ Principles of Design

The principles of design will help you use the elements to achieve pleasing visual effects. They include proportion, balance, emphasis, rhythm, and unity or harmony. Unity is achieved when all the other principles have been used together effectively.

✳ Proportion

Components in a display should be in proportion to one another and to the whole. That doesn't mean that everything should be the same size, but one component shouldn't dominate the display so much that the other parts go unnoticed. Avoid having a title in huge letters and other information in small print that is hard to read.

The human eye generally finds unequal divisions of space more pleasing than even divisions. Therefore, if you're displaying several objects that are 2 inches wide, don't space them 2 inches apart. Similarly, an odd number of items is more pleasing than an even number.

✳ Balance

You may use symmetrical or asymmetrical balance in your visual. Draw an imaginary line down the middle of your display area. If you arrange items on one half so they mirror the items on the other side, you have created *symmetrical balance*. In *asymmetrical balance*, the objects on either side aren't mirror images of one another, but the "visual weight," or what the items *appear* to weigh, is similar. Visually heavier objects are usually placed closer to the center and lighter ones toward the edges. Asymmetrical balance is considered more interesting and pleasing to the eye.

Imagine that you have eight 4" x 6" pictures to use for a visual display of soy foods. Instead of mounting four pictures on each side, you might choose to enlarge two or three of the best pictures for one side of the display and place the smaller shots on the other half. This would create more interest using asymmetrical balance. In either case, the display shouldn't appear heavier on either the left or the right. However, the bottom should be somewhat visually heavier than the top. For this reason, a slightly wider mat or margin is often used at the bottom.

❋ *Emphasis*

Every visual needs a center of interest where you want your viewer's eye to focus. Emphasis can be used to call special attention to certain features or points in your display. In the display of soy foods, for example, you might want the word SOY to appear much larger than the other words in the title.

❋ *Rhythm*

Repetition and movement can provide continuity of thought and move the eye easily from one part to another as a visual is viewed. Repeating an element such as color, a type of line, or a pattern will lead the viewer around the visual. Motion can also be used to enhance a visual, as in an interactive CD.

❊ Lettering and Graphics

There are now more lettering choices than ever before. You might purchase self-stick letters or reusable punch-out letters, turn to the computer to create crisp looking letters or banners, or even enlist the aid of a calligrapher for a special project. For added interest, you could print the type on paper that has a colorful border relating to your topic. Make the lettering on a visual large enough to easily read at a glance.

If possible, relate the lettering style to the theme. Block letters would be appropriate for a bulletin board on children's toys, while script would be better for a display of different types of invitations. With computer software, you can create many lettering styles, sizes, and colors to provide a professional appearance. Computer-generated visuals in the form of pictures, drawings, graphs, or charts are also available. You could create your own, download copyright-free material from the Internet, or use a software program such as one with clip art. As you design your visual media, remember to check the relationship of the size of your graphics and your lettering so that proportion is maintained.

The examples at the bottom of the left column show how the choice of a lettering style can strengthen and weaken a message.

Similarly, clever use of wording and lettering, geared toward the right audience, can generate interest. These bulletin board titles could be used for high school students:

- **YOU AUTO CONSERVE FUEL.** Use driving and car-maintenance tips for conserving gas. Cartoons might be used to illustrate these points.
- **BOWL THEM OVER.** Use a cutout of a bowling ball. Mount pictures that depict characteristics of a successful job candidate, such as effective communication, being well prepared and organized, good grooming, and appropriate attire. Mount pictures on construction-paper bowling pins that seem to be flying in various directions.
- **$-T-R-E-T-C-H YOUR FOOD $$$.** Store ads, coupons, rebate forms, recipes for inexpensive dishes, and play money might illustrate this bulletin board.

Why not have your learners assist in locating or making graphics for your media displays? This can be a valuable learning experience for them and save time for you. They could look for pictures of foods representing the Food Guide Pyramid groups or prepare graphics that represent the steps in the decision-making process. You could challenge them to illustrate ways to recycle various household containers.

To incorporate magazine and newspaper clippings into a display, you need to mount them for a finished appearance. If you intend to use them more than once, avoid attachment methods such as putting pins through the corners. You can place the pins so that they brace the illustration, rather than make holes in it. You can fasten lightweight illustrations with regular tape rolled in loops, double-sided tape, or a tacky adhesive designed for easy removal.

Copy machines can enlarge pictures. If you need an even larger illustration, transfer the image to a transparency. With an overhead projector, you can vary the size of the transparency image by moving the projector back and forth. Use the transparency as is or trace the enlarged image onto a piece of paper or poster board fastened under the projected image on the wall for use elsewhere.

✳ Titles and Captions

When choosing titles for visuals, think about the purpose of the media you are using. In some cases, the primary purpose of the title is to capture viewers' attention, so you will want something eye-catching, clever, or thought-provoking. For other visuals, you may want to clearly convey the content, so a straight-forward, but interesting, title may be best. *Figure 10-1* suggests titles that could each be used with a variety of topics.

Forms of visual media, such as displays, captions, or labels can also help to attract attention, create interest, motivate learners, and reinforce subject matter. Captions might capitalize on a play on words, current events, a holiday or season, contemporary expressions, popular song titles, or advertising slogans. Captions that imply action are more likely to lead to action. Be sure that labels used to identify items are very clear.

Some other titles and illustrations that serve as reminders of school or community events, important dates, assignments, or to join clubs are: *Don't Forget* with a silhouette of an elephant; *Don't Poke Around* with a picture of a turtle; *Count Down* with a cutout of a rocket; *Hop to It* with a sketch of a rabbit; and *Be Wise* with a drawing of an owl.

Figure 10-1

═ TITLES WITH MULTIPLE USES ═

- **SHEDDING LIGHT ON . . .** Mount a colorful spotlight or lighthouse at the center and surround it with pictures, phrases, or statistics that pertain to a serious topic such as depression, anorexia, date rape, steroids, or emotional abuse.

- **COLOR YOUR (THEIR) WORLD.** With a rainbow as the central theme, you can focus on child development topics, relationship skills, wellness topics, or color selection in interior design.

- **SEEDS WORTH SOWING.** Outline the display board with seed packets. In the center of the board, develop ideas for various concepts. For example, in consumer education, include topics such as staying informed, reading care labels, determining quality and quantity, and keeping records. For career education, use words such as honesty, loyalty, and dependability.

- **STAIRWAY TO . . .** Adapt this title to areas such as career education, better use of resources, or healthful lifestyle habits. Position each term on a different "step" so that it leads into the main title.

- **KNOW TOOLS OF THE TRADE.** Mount actual items or illustrations of the tools necessary for completing a certain task or job. For clothing construction, mount a measuring tape, tracing wheel, seam guide, and rotary cutter. In food preparation, you might include measuring spoons and cups, a spatula, peeler, and other small equipment.

- **FOLLOW STEPPING STONES TO . . . , KEYS TO . . . , FOOTSTEPS TO . . . ,** Use cutouts of stones, keys, or footprints to mount words and pictures appropriate for the specific theme. For example, for Good Health use nutrition, cleanliness, rest, and exercise. For Rewarding Relationships use words such as trust, empathy, respect, patience, and fairness.

- **OPEN THE DOOR TO . . .** Place a simple silhouette of a door in the center of the display. Around it mount large keys cut from construction paper. Label the keys with topics such as friendship, character, communication, health, and careers.

- **CHEER FOR . . . or TEAM UP FOR . . .** Incorporate an illustration of a megaphone.

Bulletin Boards, Display Boards, and Posters

Bulletin boards, portable display boards, and posters can help supplement teaching by emphasizing certain areas of subject matter, teaching by themselves, creating interest in a topic, or making a learning environment more attractive. However, these objectives will only be met if the board or poster attracts attention. Change these visuals frequently. A board that is left up more than two weeks starts to lose its educational value. Ideally, at least part of the board should be changed weekly. Current events, school or community activities, or contemporary expressions may provide timely themes. If your teaching space has several bulletin boards, you may decide to use one for each subject area you teach.

Collect ideas as you come across them. Some educational materials provide ideas for bulletin boards, display boards, and posters. Ads often stimulate creative ideas. *Figure 10-2* below gives some additional ideas for visuals you might create for your classroom. Remember to use the general guidelines for visual media discussed earlier in this chapter.

Figure 10-2

BOARD AND POSTER IDEAS

If you are a classroom teacher, posters and boards can function as effective visual teaching tools. Here are some examples for a variety of subject areas:

- **ARE YOU STRETCHED TOO THIN?** Have elastic bands stretched as far as possible. On each one put a stressor. On the lower half of the board or poster, list ways to reduce stress.

- **AIM FOR GOOD NUTRITION.** Mount an arrow and a bull's-eye target. On the circles of the target, write the food groups or the nutrients: vitamins, minerals, proteins, fats, water, and carbohydrates.

- **LEAD A HEALTHFUL LIFESTYLE . . . BE A FOLLOWER!** Use the computer to generate a separate sheet describing each of the Dietary Guidelines for Americans and then illustrate them.

- **ALWAYS BE CLEAN.** Display various articles or pictures of items that are associated with cleanliness or food safety.

- **FAMILY TIES—THE TIES THAT BIND.** Cover the bulletin board with wrapping paper and attach colorful ribbon to create a wrapped package. Add several bows. Mount pictures of different types of families engaged in activities that help to strengthen family life, such as spending time together, communicating with one another, sharing household tasks, or celebrating a special tradition.

- **WANTED! BABYSITTER.** Mount a mirror under the title. List qualities necessary for successful babysitting. Complete the bulletin board with "Do You Qualify?"

- **PLAY IS THE BUSINESS OF CHILDREN.** Mount pictures of children playing quiet and active games, cutting and pasting, painting, listening to stories, playing with clay, etc.

- **WHAT'S WRONG WITH THIS PICTURE?** Display pictures of well-designed rooms and rooms with obvious design flaws. Learners enjoy identifying the mistakes.

- **TENDER CARE MEANS LONGER WEAR.** Use pictures or real clothing items illustrating these captions: save and read hangtags, repair immediately, store properly, follow cleaning instructions, remove spots and stains quickly.

- **SENSIBLE SAFEGUARDS.** Display articles and pictures of precautions such as locks, railings, and poison labels.

- **LOOK AT THE LABEL.** Display enlarged nutrition, EnergyGuide, or clothing labels. Point out information that is of value to the consumer in making satisfying decisions.

- **BALANCING ACT.** Display a large version of a checkbook register. Provide instructions for balancing a checkbook. For added interest, make a mistake in the checkbook register, such as subtracting a deposit instead of adding it. Ask students to find the error.

While these three visual formats are used often in middle or high school classrooms, portable display boards and posters can be used in other settings. You might use a display board as a visual in an Extension lesson or a poster for a lesson on infant nutrition for new mothers.

You will probably want to reuse some of the boards and posters you create. For bulletin and display boards, sturdy brown envelopes work well for storing pieces. Label clearly and note any components that must be replaced before reuse. Posters are best stored rolled up in a cardboard tube. You might use one tube for each course you teach and label them accordingly.

Exhibits

Exhibits are a versatile way of getting across a message. If you work as an adult educator, you might have an exhibit about your program at an information fair for seniors. Creating school or community exhibits can be an excellent project for a small group, large group, or club such as FCCLA. Making a display together can help learners develop creativity, a sense of responsibility, the ability to work well with others, and leadership skills. Exhibits can provide educational information, create interest in activities, interpret your program to others, and bring favorable publicity.

Exhibits can be set up in a variety of places. There are showcases that can be used for exhibits in some banks, libraries, courthouses, hallways of public buildings, and school lobbies. Displays can be planned for public meetings, fairs, or back-to-school events. Museums and shopping malls often welcome displays as part of health fairs or topics such as National Child Abuse Prevention Month.

In the classroom, an exhibit can showcase students' work. Although the types of student projects will differ over time, everyone should have an opportunity to display work at some time.

Writing Boards

Chalkboards or white boards that require dry-erase markers can be found in almost every educational setting. Whenever possible, material should be written on the board before class. When you turn your back to write on the board during a class or presentation, you risk losing contact with, and the attention of, the group.

The board can be used most effectively during class by writing only key words or ideas on it. Most educators can do this by turning only slightly away from part of the group. Having learners write on the board can also be an effective way of engaging them in various problem-solving situations.

If extensive material has been put on the board before class, try covering it by pulling down a screen hung above the board. By doing this, you can reveal the information gradually by raising the screen at appropriate intervals. Students won't be overwhelmed by seeing all of the material at once, and they won't be distracted by reading ahead.

The board is an excellent place to put reminders that need to be available for several days. These may include vocabulary lists to which you add words as they're used, objectives to be accomplished over a short period of time, dates of events such as the next FCCLA meeting, and assignments with due dates.

Flip Charts

It takes longer to write material on a flip chart than on a chalkboard, but flip charts are fairly durable and can be used indefinitely. Because of the time and expense in making them, use flip charts for a presentation you make frequently or for subject matter that is relatively stable. The principles of furniture arrangement or the family life cycle are practical for a flip chart. Financial statistics would make flip-chart visuals obsolete in a relatively short time. Pictures, cartoons, or sketches can be used to add interest, but make them large enough to be seen throughout the room. If the lettering is small, use of the visual is limited. Use different colors to emphasize important words but not more than three colors. More than that can create a "busy" visual effect so nothing is really emphasized.

✳ Guidelines for Creating Flip Charts

1. **Use a large pad, preferably with a spiral edge.** The pages turn more easily and are less likely to tear than those on pads that are stapled, glued, or taped.
2. **Choose a pad with faint ruled lines or a grid pattern.** This will help you design each page and write neatly. Measure carefully and rough out the lettering lightly in pencil. That way you can make sure the ends of lines won't be crowded and you can avoid dividing words.
3. **Write large enough for everyone to read easily.** Before you start, check what size of lettering is needed from the greatest distance from which it will be viewed.
4. **Avoid putting too much writing on any one page.** A large amount of written material that is cluttered and lacks variety doesn't encourage reading. Never carry a sentence over from one page to another.
5. **Place a protective sheet of paper beneath the page you are writing on.** That way ink won't leak through.

6. **Position the chart high enough to be seen by everyone.** Use an easel or other brace. Place the chart so you can turn the pages without having to move the flip chart.
7. **Index the contents of the chart on the cover of the pad.** Number the bottom of each sheet so you can identify the pages devoted to each topic.
8. **Write your name on the outside cover.** This way, the flip chart won't be misplaced.

 # Fabric Boards

A wider range of illustrative materials can be used with a fabric board than with a flip chart or writing board. A fabric board is portable and the articles on it can be repositioned, providing a higher degree of flexibility than other media. Attachments can be rearranged for comparisons, they can be added sequentially, and they can be taken away. A whole process, or any part of it, can be easily reconstructed. Charts, diagrams, and graphs can be built as learning proceeds.

✳ Making Fabric Boards

A fabric board begins with a piece of lightweight plywood, composition board, or heavy cardboard. Felt, flannel, or other napped fabric such as corduroy is used to cover one side of the board. Stretch the fabric tautly, and securely tack, staple, or tape the edges to the back of the board. A board measuring about 30" x 40" is large enough to be seen by an audience of 150 to 175 people. A somewhat smaller board would be suitable for classroom use.

✳ Preparing Illustrations

For use with a fabric board, magazine pictures or other illustrations need to be stiffened. You can glue them to a lightweight background, such as construction paper or thin poster board. Lamination can also provide body. Avoid using heavy backing materials since they may not stay on the fabric board.

Cover at least half of the back of the mounted illustrations with napped fabric. Glue the fabric to the mounting, keeping the napped side up. When the item is placed against the fabric board, it stays in place because the two napped surfaces have an affinity for each other. To make sure they adhere, the fabric can be stroked gently with an *upward* motion of the hand, and the board can be tilted back slightly.

Fabric board attachments can be reused many times. You can store the items for a lesson in a large, heavy envelope along with accompanying notes or lesson plans. Label each envelope clearly to identify its contents.

✳ Using Fabric Boards

Fabric boards can be used to clarify, illustrate, reinforce, introduce, or summarize information. Their unique asset is the advantage of building concepts sequentially while moving attachments.

Fabric boards can help learners who don't verbalize well or are visual learners to clarify concepts through visual stimuli. For example, pictures of foods of different colors, textures, and temperatures can be used to teach principles of meal planning.

For example, you might use a fabric board to discuss the types of families living on a typical residential street in your town. Computer-generated drawings of houses could be backed with napped fabric. As each family configuration was discussed, the appropriate number of housing units would be placed along the block.

 ## Videotapes and Television

Today's world is one of electronic media, television, and videotapes. Many videos and TV programs are inherently interesting and motivating because they are up to date and touch on contemporary topics of concern. As with any teaching method or media, though, variety is essential.

Videos can be purchased, TV shows taped and shown during classtime, or videos can be made by learners or teachers. One advantage of videotapes is that they can be viewed by an entire group of learners, by a small group, or by individuals. Make sure you are familiar with both the equipment and materials before using them.

✳ Videotapes

Quality videotapes can be purchased on almost any topic you would cover in your program. These range from depression to substance abuse to kitchen safety. Videos can serve as useful springboards for analysis and discussion. Those showing details of skills taught in your program, such as culinary techniques, can be viewed repeatedly until the skills are learned. This frees you from having to repeat demonstrations frequently.

Videotapes, as well as all other teaching media and learning materials, are selected on the basis of whether they enable learners to achieve planned objectives. Always preview videos to ensure that the objectives are met and no inappropriate material is included. As you preview, develop appropriate guidance for participants, including points to look for, questions that will be discussed later, or an explanation of how the content relates to follow-up classroom activities.

Videotapes are relatively inexpensive, but the money spent on them can add up quickly. Teachers at the local or district level often pool their resources to buy tapes and then share them. If there's not a formal teaching materials library in your district, you can set up a similar program with other teachers on an informal basis.

✳ Commercial and Public Television Programs

Television shows can be recorded and shown later for instructional purposes. The entire show can be viewed or relevant portions can be selected for viewing and discussion. Copyright laws don't permit you to keep a tape copied from television for repeated use. Tapes recorded from TV must be erased after their initial use.

Television shows can be excellent for use in areas such as family relations, health issues, parenting, interpersonal relationships, work-family interface issues, self-esteem, eating disorders, and communication. Choose show situations that are relevant to the lifestyles of your audience. Students may not relate to situations that seem too good to be true or unrealistic. Television programs are also appropriate for use in other areas such as decorating or remodeling projects and workplace success. As with any media, guidance for use, clear directions, expected outcomes, and follow-up activities have to be planned, communicated, and implemented.

❊ Creating Videos

A camcorder can be a very useful tool for visual instruction. How many uses can you think of? Here are some ideas:

- You can prepare a lesson in advance for viewing by students when there will be a substitute teacher.
- Sessions can be videotaped for later viewing by students who were absent or need to review.
- Presentations of guest speakers and student reports could be recorded for later replay or to show to other groups.
- Laboratory lessons can be recorded and used later to evaluate skill levels, management principles, and efficiency.
- Children in the child development laboratory can be videotaped and segments of the tapes used to analyze the developmental level of the children and to plan developmentally appropriate activities. Written permission should be obtained from parents before including children in a video.
- Tapes can be made to illustrate interactions such as positive verbal guidance techniques, giving criticism, guidance versus discipline, and constructive and destructive arguments. You could use these to teach communication concepts and to assess learners' sensitivity to communication skills.
- Student skits, sociodramas, oral presentations, and demonstrations can be videotaped and used for self-evaluation or later for discussion. They can be shown to other classes now or in the future.

- Highlights of field trips or FCCLA or 4-H meetings and activities can be viewed later by those who couldn't attend.
- Learner activities can be videotaped and used to market your program with potential clients, agencies, students, parents, advisory councils, school board members, administrators, and/or legislators.

Include appropriate diversity in the people shown. Remember that preteens and teens often prefer to see slightly older students, because it makes them feel more grown-up.

 ## Audiotapes

Audiotapes are most beneficial when accompanied by some type of visual. They can be synchronized for use with slides, transparencies, exhibits, and displays. They can also be coordinated with examples of step-by-step procedures, such as food preparation. Tapes are particularly well suited to conducting interviews and they provide an easy method of reviewing previously covered material. Many learners also enjoy creating radio commercials, brief public service announcements, and other audio formats.

 ## Slides

An educator can use regular photographic slides or computer slides as effective teaching tools. One advantage of slides is that presentations can be customized—choosing and showing the images in the order that best suits the needs of a particular group, commenting about the slides as they are shown, and asking and answering questions. Slides are excellent for some topics, such as showing close-ups of foods uncommon to a region, disease conditions caused by nutrient deficiencies, architectural housing styles, or 4-H record book details. Viewing pictures of outstanding projects developed by an earlier class may stimulate learners to think of meaningful projects of their own and increase their desire to do well.

✳ Preparing Slide Presentations

Place the slides in a carousel or slide holder so the images are upside down and the wrong sides face toward the screen on which they will be projected. It's important to check that the slides are loaded correctly to avoid confusion and wasted time. Slides can be previewed for content with a small hand projector. Use the preview session to plan your commentary to accompany the slides and the questions you will ask during the presentation. As you show the slides to your audience, always stand to the side so that you don't block anyone's view.

 Transparencies

Transparencies have several advantages. They are easy to make, can be shown in a well-lit room, allow the instructor to face the audience while showing them, and can be projected as large or small as desired. Overlays of up to five or six sheets can be used to build a concept sequentially. To facilitate their use, tape overlays together in sequence along one edge or fasten them into a cardboard frame. *Figure 10-3* on page 147 gives examples of transparencies for various topics.

Educational publishers and companies sell both ready-to-use color transparencies and reproducible transparency masters. Commercially prepared color transparency sets often include a variety of teaching suggestions and activities to use with each transparency. Some come mounted in frames, which help keep them flat and easy to handle and provide a place to write notes. However, frames make the transparencies rather large for storage in regular file folders. Transparencies can also be stored in clear page protectors and filed in binders. Because the plastic is clear, the transparency can be put on an overhead projec-

tor without removing it from the plastic protector. No matter which storage system you use, label the materials clearly and keep a list of where they are stored.

✳ Making Transparencies

Transparencies can be made by photocopying an image from paper onto a sheet of transparency film using a copy machine. Special sheets of transparency film are sold specifically for making transparencies. A color photocopier can be used to make color transparencies.

When preparing copy for a transparency, any size of type smaller than 16 point is usually too small to project well, unless shown on a very large screen. Use software that has large-size lettering capability or enlarge the type on a photocopier.

Illustrations can be simple or sophisticated. You can draw simple stick figures to get your point across or use computer images or pictures from other sources. You might use the outline of a relevant object as a border for information presented.

Because transparency film is more expensive than paper, reproduce as much material on one sheet as possible, even if all of it will not be shown at the same time. These small transparency items can be cut apart and the pieces slipped into clear plastic page protectors for projection. This process not only can cut costs, but also avoids creating overcrowded and cluttered visuals.

Color can be added to black-and-white transparencies with markers, pens and tapes produced specifically for this purpose. The pens, both permanent and nonpermanent, can be used to write or draw right on the plastic. Because nonpermanent pens rub off easily, they are used when the writing or color added to a transparency will be removed. Most colors, except occasionally yellow, reproduce and project satisfactorily.

Another form of transparency is less expensive, making it especially well suited for student presentations and other uses. It utilizes clear, stiff plastic that can be purchased by the yard. Recycled plastic project folders measuring 8½" x 11" are also inexpensive and can be split in half to provide two sheets. The ability to write on transparencies is an advantage, particularly when figuring problems such as interest rates. The writing can be erased quickly and easily by rubbing with a tissue or soft cloth; then other problems can be worked on the same sheet. The transparent sheets of plastic are also ideal for tracing images, which can then be projected to the entire class. Students working in small groups can use the inexpensive transparencies to brainstorm ideas, listing them on transparencies for sharing with the larger group.

Figure 10-3

IDEAS FOR TRANSPARENCIES

- **Family Relations.** Concentric circles can be used to show how love grows and changes as an individual matures. The center circle can be self-love; the next, love of parent or caregiver; and so on to love of humankind.
- **Child Development.** Transparencies and overlays could be used to evaluate how clothing features, eating utensils, closet arrangements, bathroom accessories, and furniture can foster or hinder independence and self-reliance in young children.
- **Nutrition.** A "Nutrition Facts" label from a food package might be reproduced. View parts of the label sequentially, as each is explained.
- **Leadership.** Transparencies of pictures of characteristics of a leader can be shown and 4-H members can call out the characteristic depicted in the picture.
- **Design.** Overlays of various colors could be used to illustrate different color schemes when planning an outfit or decorating a room.
- **Housing.** Floor plans of small homes with identical dimensions can be used with different overlays to illustrate room and furniture arrangements, provisions for privacy and storage, and traffic patterns.
- **Safety.** Sketches containing potentially hazardous conditions and ways of eliminating them can be identified and discussed by the viewers.

PowerPoint®: A Technique and a Tool

PowerPoint® is the most commonly used presentation software. It comes as part of a Microsoft® Office package or may be purchased separately. It's very useful for developing professional-looking presentations and for making some other types of visuals discussed in this chapter.

✳ Developing a PowerPoint® Presentation

Presentations prepared using PowerPoint® software can be as simple or sophisticated as you like. The software has many built-in features that make it easy to make even your first presentation look professional. You can continue to learn the additional capabilities of the program.

A PowerPoint® presentation is made up of a series of electronic pages called "slides." These can contain writing, photos, and graphics. Animation, music, and narration can also be added. Your choice of the slides included and their arrangement can easily be changed, as can other features. You might want, for example, to prepare one version that you will present live, and another for viewing by one person or a small group that includes narration.

Preparing a PowerPoint® presentation is more time consuming than many other types of visual media. That makes it most useful for presentations that require a high degree of professionalism, will be given to a large audience, contain many visuals, and/or will be presented multiple times. For example, a PowerPoint® presentation might work well for a presentation to other health professionals at a conference. For a housing course, you could develop a highly visual presentation on period architectural styles that you could use each term.

What other points should be considered before deciding on an electronic presentation? Ask yourself these questions:

- Would such a presentation help accomplish my predetermined learning objectives?
- Would it appeal to my audience? Such a presentation might work well with a group of adults being counseled about diabetic diets, but it wouldn't be appropriate for teaching preschoolers about eating well.
- Could I get the same result using a simpler technique? Is the topic worth the developmental time?
- What would be the learning value of PowerPoint® in this situation?
- What type of follow-up would I use?

Keep in mind that simply using an electronic presentation doesn't necessarily garner learners' interest. Some people use PowerPoint® to essentially write out what they want to say. Then they simply read the words off the slides to their audience. Sometimes they also give the learners printed copies of the PowerPoint® slides, so there's little to motivate the audience to listen. Including graphics, photos, and other techniques in an electronic presentation can add zest to your verbal delivery. Of course, a narrated PowerPoint® presentation could also be appropriate for a few students or clients to use for independent learning.

PowerPoint® software includes a helpful tutorial and automated shortcuts that allow you to develop a basic program quickly. These are the steps to developing a simple program:

1. Choose a design template to pick the look for your presentation.
2. Choose slide layouts appropriate for your purpose and materials.
3. Input type for the slides using predetermined sizes and colors.
4. Add shapes, diagrams, or charts.
5. Add pictures or art.
6. View the slides you have created, make any changes, and sort them into the sequence desired.

More complex features that require more mastery include:

- Importing digital or scanned images
- Customizing color schemes
- Inserting sounds or music
- Narrating your presentation
- Adding video segments
- Adding animation

PowerPoint® presentations are projected onto a screen, similar to overhead transparencies. An LCD projector is attached to a computer to project the images. You can display a PowerPoint® program developed by someone else without having PowerPoint® software on your computer. Most CDs include a PowerPoint® viewer that will automatically start when you choose a presentation. Remember that a PowerPoint® presentation depends on the computer and LCD projector working smoothly with the program. Become familiar with and test out the equipment well before your presentation. Some presenters make a set of slides or transparencies from their electronic presentation as a back-up mode of presentation.

❋ Using PowerPoint® to Create Other Visual Media

This chapter explains the use of various types of visual media. With PowerPoint®, you have the option of using the program as a tool to create other media products. You can incorporate the visual capabilities of this software, such as formats and type styles, to:

- Create 35 mm slides.
- Develop color or black-and-white overhead transparencies.
- Make color or black-and-white paper printouts.
- Design web pages.

Tapping into the Power of Visuals

Perhaps you remember classes you have taken that consisted only of printed text material. Visuals have the advantage of both adding interest and enhancing learning. Most positions for graduates of programs in family and consumer sciences, dietetics, and health lend themselves to frequent use of visual materials. Your chief challenges are to identify the most appropriate visual media for a given situation and to develop high-quality visuals that have a real teaching function. They will help you become a more effective teacher and improve your learners' understanding.

Building Your Professional Portfolio

Analyzing Visual Appeal. Collect at least three examples of visuals that would appeal to a specific target audience, such as teens or older adults. Identify the reasons each would be appealing by analyzing the message, the overall visual presentation, and use of the elements and principles of design.

Preparing a Display. Prepare an effective bulletin board, display board, or exhibit that illustrates the breadth of careers in your field.

Developing Transparencies. Create two original transparencies, one of which uses the overlay process. Explain how each could enhance a specific topic.

Integrating Visuals in Lessons. Prepare a lesson plan that involves the use of at least three different types of visuals. Provide a detailed description of each. Use the lesson plan format in Chapter 6.

Utilizing Presentation Software. Develop an electronic presentation of a topic using software such as PowerPoint®. Give a rationale for using this approach for the topic selected.

Chapter 11

Simulated Experiences

*T*he term simulated experiences applies to a variety of means for taking subject matter off the printed page and bringing it to life, chiefly in the form of small-scale dramas, or slices of real life. The major simulated experiences described in this chapter include:

- Skits. Students take part in problem situations by reading lines from prepared scripts.
- Sociodramas. These situations, known by some as roleplays, usually involve interpersonal relationships. There is no formal, written dramatic framework, such as in a skit. A limited description of the situation is given to the learners, and they take it from there. They act out roles according to convention and their own existing knowledge of, and feelings about, the types of characters they portray.
- Case studies or scenarios. Problem situations are presented to the learners in the form of letters, records, or real-life stories. Responses may be discussed or written.
- Visual situations. A picture or other visual provides the basis for discussion.
- Computer simulations. These software programs present situations for students to work through. In the process, learners must make a series of decisions, each of which leads them down a particular path.

Through simulated experiences, learners have opportunities to experience the difference between doing and merely being told about doing. They discover meaning for themselves, as subject matter is made relevant on a personal level.

 ## Advantages of Simulated Experiences

Skits, sociodramas, case studies or scenarios, and visual situations provide you with tools that have many advantages in a variety of educational settings. In each case, active learner involvement is promoted through acting or group work. Each type of simulation adds interest to the learning environment, motivating learners. These activities provide an enjoyable and common experience on which to base a meaningful discussion and follow-up activities. In addition, you will gain valuable insights into the learners' maturity levels because participants are likely to express emotions they would really feel in similar situations.

The potential benefits of simulated experiences are far-reaching. Through participation, learners may have cognitive and affective opportunities to:

- Frame a reference or see things from another's point of view
- Make decisions
- Share emotions
- Promote self-evaluation
- Develop insight into human relationships
- Increase objectivity
- Improve communication skills
- Use higher-order thinking skills
- Illustrate principles learned
- Find solutions for personal or friends' problems
- Gain confidence

Sources of Ideas for Simulated Experiences

You will need plenty of ideas and your imagination to plan skits, sociodramas, and scenarios or case studies. Some ideas will come from your own experiences, as well as those of friends and learners you have interacted with in the past. Colleagues may share materials they have developed. In addition, reading human-interest stories in magazines and newspapers or letters written to advice columnists may spark ideas. Discussions with counselors, therapists, and social workers can keep you abreast of current concerns and trends.

Skits

Using a skit requires time in advance to either write or locate a script. Keep scripts relatively short, but realistic and meaningful. When you write the script yourself, you are able to ensure that the points you want covered are included. You can also include smaller parts suitable for slow learners, poor readers, or reluctant performers. Since the content of skits is predetermined, you can also preplan appropriate follow-up activities.

✳ Using Skits

A skit will be nothing more than a reading of lines unless you provide opportunities for making it a true learning experience. Give out scripts in advance to those with parts so that they have an opportunity to read their lines several times before presenting. This will result in a smoother and more meaningful presentation. You might also choose a stand-in to become familiar with the skit in case one of the actors is absent on the appointed day.

You may want to change the names in a skit to fit the local situation by using the names of students in the class, your school or organization, and familiar places in the local community. This can heighten interest and make the situation seem more realistic and pertinent, but never do it in a way which might cause embarrassment.

Props can also add realism. When skits are first used with a group, you might supply or suggest the props. Later, learners can be encouraged to identify and bring their own.

If you use a skit someone else has written, read it carefully and make any appropriate modifications. This preparation helps you devise discussion topics and follow-up activities plus identify points to tell the group to look for. Link these to learners' previous learning, interests, needs, abilities, and maturity. By providing this kind of guidance, you help learners see the purpose and relevance of the skit.

Encourage learners to plan the discussions and follow-up activities. Planning stimulates analytical thinking, increases interest and participation, and serves to motivate students to higher levels of achievement.

✳ Learner-Created Skits

Learners often enjoy writing their own skits and may lead the follow-up discussion as well. Using this technique can involve all class members, include topics that are of real concern to learners, and show them that their contributions are worthwhile and important. For example, small groups of learners could write skits on nutrients. Each group could select a specific nutrient and, through a short drama, illustrate the following about it:

1. Historical interest and/or discovery of nutrient
2. Deficiency symptoms
3. Sources of nutrient

You may need to provide reference materials and resources to enable students to look up appropriate information to include in this type of skit. A typical skit emphasizing vitamin C might include a scene from Vasco da Gama's trip from Portugal around Africa to India during which 62 percent of the crew died of scurvy. Later, on the first English expedition to the East Indies, three of four ship captains saw their crews so disabled by scurvy that they were barely able to navigate. The fourth ship, whose daily ration included doses of lemon juice, was untouched by the disease. Soon all British sailors were required to drink lime or lemon juice, and eventually they became known as "limeys."

In the skit about vitamin D, it could be brought out that George Washington, who though he escaped the more serious and crippling effects of rickets, lost his teeth early in adulthood and had to have them replaced with wooden pegs.

To include information about the history, deficiency symptoms, and food sources of vitamin A, the students could act out a scene in which early Greeks, troubled by night blindness, were told by Hippocrates to eat liver dipped in honey. Later, fishermen blinded by the sun glaring on the water ate the livers of codfish and sea gulls to improve their sight. The Greeks and fishermen were not only preventing night blindness, but were contributing to their health by getting enough vitamin A, which had been stored in the livers of animals and birds for future use.

In the skit about riboflavin, which promotes growth, it could be shown that the average American man and woman today are several inches taller than their ancestors. By bringing out interesting facts such as these, you will help learners remember the material better, and they will see its relevance to their lives.

The scripts and possible discussion questions and/or follow-up activities for two skits: *This Communication Will Self-Destruct* and *Diet Confusion* follow.

Figure 11-1

SKITS

SKIT 1: THIS COMMUNICATION WILL SELF-DESTRUCT

The following skit could be used in any program in which interpersonal relationships are emphasized.

Characters: Toby and Dana, a married couple
Setting: Toby and Dana's kitchen

TOBY: What time will you be ready for dinner?
DANA: In just a minute.
TOBY: Dinner is almost ready.
DANA: I'll be there as soon as I can.
TOBY: Dinner is ready. I'm dishing up.
DANA: Hold it. I'm almost through!
TOBY: How can I hold dinner? It will get cold or burn.
DANA: I'm hurrying.
TOBY: Do you know how much time I spent cooking this meal? I was trying to please you.
DANA: You are *so* impatient!
TOBY: Me? You're selfish! All you think of is yourself. You're just like your mother.
DANA: Well, now, I consider that a compliment. It's certainly better than being like *your* mother.
TOBY: Now, what's wrong with *my* mother?
DANA: She's nosy.
TOBY: Now, just one minute. I think you . . .

Discussion Questions:
• Was Toby unreasonable? Why, or why not?
• What did Toby say that led this conversation into a destructive argument?
• What issues came into the argument that were unrelated to the main topic?
• How did both Toby and Dana use poor timing in this situation?
• How could both Toby and Dana have handled the situation more effectively?

SKIT 2: DIET CONFUSION

This skit introduces concepts related to dieting, including the role that celebrities play in body image; media's role; and the impact decision making, and goal setting have.

Characters: Jody, Rosa, and Ella
Setting: Three women in their early twenties are sitting and looking at recent popular magazines. One of the women, Jody, has a magazine featuring celebrities and their diets and weight loss.

Figure 11-1 (cont'd) ━━━━ **SKITS** ━━━━

JODY: I have to lose some weight now! My class reunion is next month and I have to look better! These celebrities look great!

ROSA: Then you just need to start eating less and exercising more.

JODY: That's easy for you to say! This magazine is filled with all these great, but fattening, recipes. I need a quick fix. Eating right and exercising will never have me ready in a month.

ELLA: I just started a low-carbohydrate diet I found in a magazine at the dentist's office, and it's *really* working! I lost 6 pounds in the last week.

ROSA: Watch out, Ella . . . that is too much to lose in one week. Everyone needs some "carbs" for energy and good health.

ELLA: I will worry about that after I lose 12 more pounds. That should only take me two more weeks. . . .

ROSA: Then what will you do?

ELLA: No problem. I may gain it back, but that is OK. At least I'll look good for my vacation at the beach.

JODY: WOW! Here is someone who lost 50 pounds on a high-protein diet. I love meat. I think I might try that one. At least I won't have to eat all those fruits and vegetables. I only like corn, green beans, and apples.

ROSA: But you need a variety of fruits and vegetables for the nutrients your body needs.

ELLA: For some people that's fine. I had an aunt who ate nothing but cabbage soup for weeks and she really lost weight. She hasn't looked so good in years.

ROSA: The idea is to eat a variety of foods in moderation.

ELLA: But this magazine makes it clear that these celebrities lost the weight using this diet, so what is your point? They wouldn't publish this unless they expected us to do the same, right?

JODY: I agree! I'm going to start on this protein diet tonight. Ella, you can have all my "carbs," and I will have all your meat. This weight is coming off!

ROSA: Is either of you thinking about what you'll be doing to your body?

Discussion Questions:
- What factors are influencing each of these women in deciding what foods to eat in order to lose weight?
- What roles are media and celebrity role models playing in their decisions?
- What role are long-term goals playing in their decisions?
- What will be some of the disadvantages of the diets chosen by Jody and Ella?
- What would you suggest that Rosa do to help her friends?

Follow-up Activities:
- Collect information on the pros and cons of various diets. Prepare collages to show their advantages and disadvantages.
- Prepare brochures to be distributed to teens regarding what is involved in "healthy" dieting.
- Collect articles from the popular press on dieting and analyze how and why they are so intriguing to people.
- Ask a dietitian or other knowledgeable medical professional to meet with the group and discuss various diets and their implications for the human body.

Sociodramas

In skits, the participants read the parts and portray the roles of the characters that are delineated for them. In sociodramas, students are free to interpret roles as they actually feel and perceive them. Since the dialogue is spontaneous and unrehearsed, participants usually react as they really would in similar situations.

Most educators don't make a distinction between sociodramas and role-playing. However, there is one difference. In sociodramas, students interpret the parts being played in the way they actually feel them or desire to play them. There is not even a subtle suggestion that a role should be interpreted any certain way. However, in a role-playing experience, students are more likely to feel a commitment to portray a character's role in a way that matches what is expected of a person in that particular situation. For example, when depicting an employment situation in which one student is serving food to another, the learners undoubtedly sense that there is a correct and an incorrect procedure to follow. The players may purposely "plant" errors in their ways of serving and being served, but there is still the knowledge that there are right and wrong ways. Another example might center on a consumer thinking about making an expensive purchase using credit. In this situation there would be an expected pattern of behavior, including certain questions the learner knows should be asked. Similarly, a situation that involves a babysitter asking parents for specific information should demonstrate that the person acting as the babysitter has learned the appropriate content. These would be role-play situations.

The primary advantage that sociodramas have over skits is that they take little or no preparation time. They are extemporaneous portrayals of situations, so only the first few lines and the general plot or theme are planned. What the participants say and do can't be anticipated. This creates a disadvantage—follow-up can't be planned in advance. However, very general questions can be given ahead of time to focus learner attention, such as:

- What seem to be some of the underlying and basic causes of conflict between the characters in this scene?
- Which of the reactions and behaviors shown by the characters are typical of mature and immature individuals?
- What are some ways in which this situation could be improved?

✳ Using Sociodramas

The nature of these techniques requires them to be used with some caution. A sociodrama might work well for open-ended situations that could have a variety of reactions. Role-playing is appropriate for use in situations where concrete information has been learned and can be demonstrated. Students should never be placed in a situation that requires them to divulge personal or family information. In addition, each person's ethical and religious values must be respected.

In some areas, the term "role-playing" is misinterpreted as inappropriately pressuring students to change their personal values. That, of course, is never appropriate.

It is for this reason that a learner should never be forced to play a part in a sociodrama or role-play. However, when teachers know their students well, they can sense which ones would like to take part but simply hesitate to say so publicly. These learners may be encouraged to participate with just the right lighthearted approach.

For example, a teacher might say something like, "Who will be the younger brother? Nobody? Oh, come on, Mark. I know you have a younger brother. I'm sure you could play the part of a ten-year-old boy very well!" If Mark declines this personal invitation, the teacher could reply, "Well, we'll just go on without a younger brother." Or, you as the leader could play the part rather than make a student feel self-conscious and uncomfortable. The first time a sociodrama is used, the class "hams" may be the only volunteers. However, after two or three successful sociodramas, the more reserved students are likely to take part too.

Sociodramas often depict situations involving interpersonal conflict. In order to include episodes that will be most meaningful to the group members, an educator could ask, "What are some common problems teens have getting along with other family members?" This would be a better, and more ethical, question than "What are some problems you have in getting along with your family?" Students' privacy and that of their families are respected.

A typical list from an adolescent group might include:

- Using the telephone
- Sharing a bathroom
- Having to take care of younger brothers and sisters
- Doing chores around the home
- Disagreeing with parents about dating
- Setting curfews

After listing the group's ideas and suggestions, participants could vote for the two or three items that they believe are the most likely to be sources of conflict. Those that receive the most votes would logically be the concerns to be included in the sociodramas.

The group may decide which and how many family members should be portrayed. After the volunteer cast is selected, have them meet someplace where there is a degree of privacy, but where you remain near enough to the rest of the group to provide supervision. Actually, this planning session will take only a few minutes because the participants decide only how the drama will begin and plan just a few of the opening lines. From then on, the dialogue and action should be spontaneous. The students say and do what comes naturally to them.

As the educator, you decide when to end a presentation. The participants may be straining for their lines or the action is about to become tedious. You will want to stop a sociodrama if the participants become very emotional about their roles or they become overly self-conscious. You can simply say something like, "Thank you. Let's stop here and talk about this situation."

Self-consciousness is most likely to happen if the problem situation being acted out is one about which the learners feel embarrassment. However, if this problem persists, you may decide not to use this method of teaching at all with a particular group. Usually though, if you are enthusiastic and excited about using sociodramas, your interest will be reflected in your students' attitudes toward them.

❋ Follow-Up

Without discussion, a sociodrama will remain only a means of entertaining the class. Good follow-up leads the learners to formulate generalizations that can guide them in solving similar problems. The actual participants may be asked to analyze the feelings and emotions they experienced during the enactment of the scene. Then, through skillful questioning, you can lead the learners to a better understanding of others' responses and reactions.

After a discussion of how the situation might have been handled better, another scene could be dramatized incorporating the suggestions for improvement. The same players or another group of participants could take part in the replay. Participants may reverse roles to gain greater empathy for the feelings of other characters.

❋ Variations

Several unique ways of creating situations for sociodramas are possible. You or a student could read or tell the first part of a story. Others could then assume the characters' roles and dramatize a possible ending to the story—without any preplanning.

Another variation is to use pictures of people who are obviously involved in interpersonal problem situations. Learners can act out the scenes as they sense and feel them. Of course, the follow-up discussions described previously will enable these dramatizations to become the bases for meaningful learning experiences.

 ## Case Studies/Scenarios

Case studies, also called scenarios, are stories that usually don't come to a conclusion. They provide a vehicle for involving learners in solving problems similar to those faced in real life. Realistic situations will prompt good discussions. By providing a common basis for discussion, you avoid asking about actual personal and family situations.

❋ Using Case Studies/Scenarios

Case studies can be used in many ways. You can read them aloud or use an audiotape and then use a group discussion to analyze the situation. Another alternative would be to give each person a written copy of the case study followed by questions that require written answers. Their answers, compiled anonymously, could be presented to the entire class for analysis and comparison. Case studies can also be analyzed in small groups. Each group might have the same scenario or the groups might have different situations to analyze. In either case, the small groups' conclusions and recommendations can be shared with the entire class to elicit further discussion.

Case study simulations may be presented as personal letters, letters to the editor, or advice-column letters. Other formats for case studies include narratives, log or diary entries, dialogue excerpts, and simulated counselor or personnel records. The studies will vary in length depending on the type of problem presented, the amount of information to be provided, and the attention span of the learners.

Scenarios may be open-ended or they may include the outcome or decision that was made. The follow-up activities or questions asked about the situations are actually as important as the case studies themselves. Regardless of whether the ending is provided, case studies can be examined for alternative solutions, along with predictions of possible outcomes. When the material is used in this way, learners are given experience in critical thinking and decision making.

The questions used to help learners analyze case study situations are extremely important. To maximize the value of this method, give learners points to look for in the case studies or provide them with follow-up discussion questions before reading about the situations. Learners can use the following four steps in the problem-solving process to analyze case studies:

1. **Identifying the problem.** What exactly is the problem? What additional information is needed?
2. **Identifying alternative solutions to the problem.** What are all the possible solutions?
3. **Examining and weighing the consequences of the possible solutions.** What might happen if this is done? What might happen if another alternative is chosen? How would each solution impact others?
4. **Deciding on a solution.** Of all the alternatives, which provides the best solution? Why? In view of all the consequences, why do you think this is the best thing to do?

The two case studies in *Figure 11-2*, at the right, are followed by appropriate discussion questions. See how these questions help the learners with decision making and foster higher-order thinking.

Visual Situations

In visual situations, pictures, cartoons, drawings, diagrams, posters, transparencies, or slides provide the common basis for discussion. In other words, a discussion is built upon what learners feel about and read into a visual. The pictures often depict interpersonal relationships.

There are many sources of appropriate visuals. A textbook is one and has the advantage of being available to all students at the same time. You might use an existing color transparency or clip a picture from a magazine. The Internet is filled with websites that offer a variety of visuals that might be printed for use in lessons.

❋ Using Visual Situations

It's best if everyone can view the visual at the same time. A picture could be copied onto a transparency to make this possible. If

---

Figure 11-2

CASE STUDIES

CASE STUDY 1:
DOES POPULARITY HAVE A PRICE?

Carlos had only been enrolled at City High for two weeks. He transferred from a small school in a rural area. He was eager to make friends but is finding it difficult. His favorite class was Mr. Duncan's Advanced Biology class. Science was Carlos' best subject. One day, during a quiz, Mr. Duncan stepped out of the room. Eric, a popular student, asked Carlos to give him the answers to the quiz. Carlos really wanted Eric's approval.

Discussion Questions:

- What should Carlos do? Why should he do that?
- Why might Carlos be finding it difficult to make friends in his new school?
- Does cheating make Carlos or Eric a better person? A worse person? Defend your answers.
- Who could get hurt in this situation? Why?
- How could Carlos make a socially responsible decision and still not "lose face"?

Figure 11-2 (cont'd)
CASE STUDIES

CASE STUDY 2: WHO IS AT RISK?

Directions: Read each case study listed below. Be prepared to discuss each situation.

1. Maria is 19 years old. She has not eaten animal-based products since she was very young. As a child, she was allergic to milk. Maria thinks she does a good job of getting all the nutrients that she needs and she doesn't take vitamin supplements. She is very thin but hardly ever exercises. She has been smoking for five years. Although she's often tried to quit, a month is the longest that she has gone without a cigarette.
2. Catherine is a woman in her seventies. Although she was once 5'6" tall, she now is only 5'4" tall. She lives by herself. Her mother and older sister have been in nursing homes since they both fractured a hip about four years ago. Although Catherine hasn't exercised since she was in her teens, she recently started walking around the block to get some exercise. She has started seeing a registered dietitian and now tries to get in two servings of low-fat dairy products each day.
3. Armando is a 21-year-old European male. He is 5'11" and weighs 140 lbs. He is a professional model for Calvin Klein. His job keeps him busy traveling around the world, and he rarely has time for exercise. To keep his weight down, he frequently uses diuretics before an important photo shoot. He also smokes a pack of cigarettes a day.

Discussion Questions:
- What variables put each person at risk for developing osteoporosis?
- What protective factors are evident?
- What action would you suggest each person take at this point to decrease his or her risk for osteoporosis?

- What may have occurred prior to this scene?
- How could this situation be handled? If it were to occur often, how could it then be handled?
- What are feelings and conflicts the parent may be experiencing?

A student might reply to your first question by saying, "The child pleaded with her mother not to leave." You could develop this idea by asking an additional probing question to carry the thought further, such as "What are some ways to help children feel secure so they can cope better when a parent leaves the home?" In visual situations, like skits, sociodramas, and case studies, learning primarily depends upon the educator's ability to ask significant, relevant, and thought-provoking questions that promote meaningful discussions. Some questions can be preplanned, while others must be created on the spot in response to learners' comments and answers.

Computer Simulations

Computer simulations are another interesting visual media that can be powerful learning tools. Learners step into someone else's shoes and experience situations and problems through them. At points in the simulation, students must make choices

a photo is too small for the entire group to see easily and there's no alternative, you can move around the room showing it to each person in the group.

After learners analyze the scene, you, as the educator, start the discussion by asking pertinent questions. For the photo on this page, you might ask the following questions:

based on their character's situation. Their choice leads them down a path to yet other decisions, so each learner's experience is an individual one.

When considering purchase and use of a computer simulation, keep these considerations in mind:

- **The cost of the program.** Weigh the expense against the amount of actual use it will get. How many copies will you need for effective classroom use?
- **The access to computers.** How many learners can use the simulation at one time? Think about how you would fit its use into a lesson if only a limited number can use the program at a time.
- **The relevance of the topic and type of problem solving involved.** How well does the simulation meet your lesson objectives and learners' interests and abilities? What thinking skills would learners practice by using the program? You don't want this just to be busy work or time in front of a computer.
- **The appropriateness of the method.** Would this be the best teaching-learning tool for the content? Is the time required to use the simulation appropriate for the topic?

✳ Using Computer Simulations

If you plan to use a computer simulation, work through the program several times following various combinations of decisions. This will help you to provide the best assistance to your learners as they undertake the simulation.

Your role is to circulate, be sure learners are on task, and answer questions that arise. You will also find yourself promoting the critical thinking of your learners as they ask you questions. When this occurs, question them back and encourage them to make decisions based on what they know.

Preparation for Life

Simulations provide learners opportunities to understand real-life situations from a variety of perspectives. These strategies can bring about both cognitive and affective growth. Changes can be evident if you use the strategies in this chapter to assist learners with analytical thinking and understanding why people think and feel differently about the issues and situations they face in their lives.

Building Your Professional Portfolio

Analyzing Techniques. Prepare a chart that shows the advantages and limitations of using each of the simulated experiences in the educational setting you plan to teach. Identify one specific topic you might teach successfully to your audience using at least four of these experiences and briefly describe how you would use each.

Writing a Skit. Identify a group of learners and a topic for which you could use a skit as a helpful teaching tool. Then write the skit and prepare follow-up questions and activities.

Using Case Studies. Choose one topic that would be appropriate to teach to both high school juniors as part of a class and to adults in an informal educational situation. Write three case studies for each audience that you could use to teach the topic in each setting. Analyze the similarities and differences in how you would use case studies as a teaching technique with the two groups of learners.

Chapter 12

Demonstrations

What do the following have in common: creating a simple window treatment, preparing pasta primavera, performing CPR, and testing for enzymes in foods? All are situations that can be taught effectively through demonstrations, a combination of telling and showing the audience how to do something. Professionals in Family and Consumer Sciences, Dietetics, and Health often rely on demonstrations as a teaching tool. When planned carefully and carried out well, they can be a powerful way to enhance learning.

How can you decide when to use demonstrations? They can be used to illustrate procedures, explain new techniques, and establish standards for individual and group work. Begin by analyzing the objectives you have identified. Objectives in the psychomotor domain are the most common candidates for demonstrations because the viewers are usually expected to repeat the procedure or to adapt it to a similar situation. However, objectives in other domains can also be met through demonstrations. At times, you may decide to demonstrate because it's a less expensive alternative to having everyone try a procedure. Learners may have opportunities to apply the knowledge gained through the demonstration in a laboratory experience, at home, or on the job.

Remember that it's better not to give a demonstration than to present a poor one. If there isn't time to prepare a well-planned demonstration, consider other ways of presenting the material, such as computer-generated slides, transparencies, or a videotape.

 ## Planning a Demonstration

The purposes or objectives of the demonstration should be clear to the presenter and all those who view it. Use these five steps when planning a demonstration:

1. **Outline the material to be covered and determine how to present it.** A concise outline should include an introduction, the major concepts to be covered, and a summary of the main points. Review the outline so you are thoroughly familiar with it. Decide which techniques you will use. How might visuals or handouts enhance the demonstration?

2. **Develop a detailed schedule.** A time schedule will keep you on track so that you complete the demonstration within the time available. Allow time in the schedule for follow-up. If you foresee difficulty completing the demonstration in the available time, look for shortcuts. Sometimes certain steps can be completed ahead of time, others skipped, or a second person can help with the demonstration. Prepreparation of materials can help make a demonstration run smoothly and efficiently. (Learners can often help with prepreparation.) Viewers lose interest when too much time is spent on repetitious and time-consuming tasks. However, don't omit any essential steps. Strive for balance, showing enough of the actual procedure so that viewers understand what is happening without making the demonstration so lengthy that they become bored.

3. **Identify and gather all the items needed for the demonstration.** Make certain any necessary equipment is in working order. Have enough supplies to practice with, as well as for the actual demonstration.

4. **Practice the demonstration.** If at all possible, practice in the place where you will be giving the demonstration. If you can't, duplicate the conditions as nearly as possible. Practice the introduction to help you begin smoothly and with confidence. It should be interesting, while also clarifying the purposes of the demonstration. Position any demonstration equipment on or close to the main demonstration area. You want your audience to see without the need for you to continually move around. A stationary or portable overhead mirror can help your viewers see the procedure more clearly, particularly if the group is large. In some large-group situations, you may need to use a microphone or a video camera with television monitors so that everyone can hear and see the demonstration. Be sure you are thoroughly familiar with all equipment to be used.

5. **Plan follow-up.** As with other techniques, a demonstration needs follow-up to enhance learning. There are a variety of ways this can be accomplished. As you finish your presentation, summarize its main points and emphasize what has been learned. You might use a quick quiz, oral or written. If the demonstration results in a product that could be displayed, plan how to do so, including any necessary labeling. An activity could also serve as follow-up.

The "Demonstration Planning Sheet," *Figure 12-1* on page 161, is a helpful tool. It will help you make certain you adequately preplan all aspects of a demonstration.

 # Demonstration Techniques

The five steps in the previous section outlined how to plan for a demonstration. However, there's much more to developing a quality demonstration. The guidelines and tips that follow have been developed by people experienced in presenting many different kinds of demonstrations. "Check Your Demonstration Techniques," *Figure 12-2* on page 162, gives additional points to consider.

✳ Before You Begin

Even though you have practiced, effectively using the time just before your demonstration begins is a key to success. Check all audio-visual and electronic equipment to be used as soon as you have access to the demonstration area. It's better to know something doesn't work ahead of time. If it can't be repaired or replaced prior to the demonstration, at least you will have time to decide how to compensate.

If you will be giving your presentation in your classroom, you can usually set up the area ahead of time. However, if you are demonstrating in a space that isn't your own, double-check your list of equipment and materials as you pack items to take with you. Include duplicates of any fragile items.

Figure 12-1

DEMONSTRATION PLANNING SHEET

Meeting:	Date:
Location:	Projected Size of Audience:

Key Concepts:

Objective(s):

Introduction—Establishing Set:

Consumable supplies needed:	Equipment needed:

Preplanning and preparation steps to be done:	When?	Completed?

Outline of steps in demonstration:	Points to be made during demonstration:

Closure or follow-up:

Evaluation (Audience reaction; ways to improve next time):

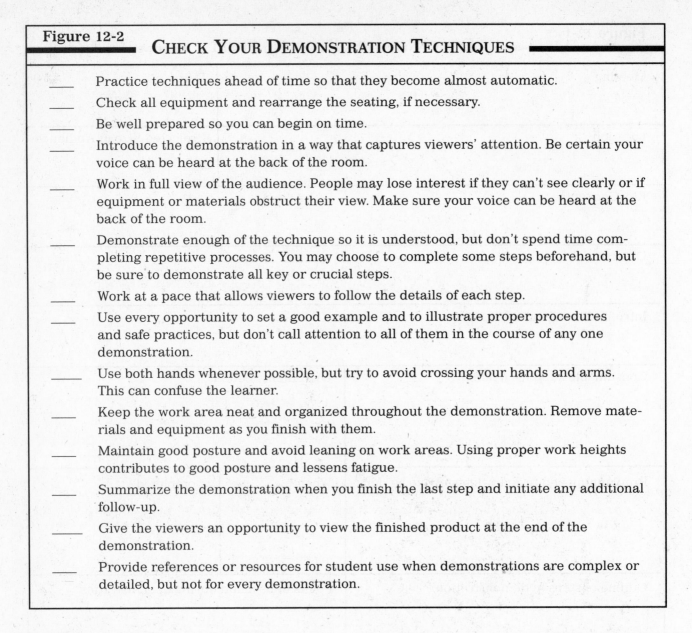

Figure 12-2 CHECK YOUR DEMONSTRATION TECHNIQUES

____ Practice techniques ahead of time so that they become almost automatic.

____ Check all equipment and rearrange the seating, if necessary.

____ Be well prepared so you can begin on time.

____ Introduce the demonstration in a way that captures viewers' attention. Be certain your voice can be heard at the back of the room.

____ Work in full view of the audience. People may lose interest if they can't see clearly or if equipment or materials obstruct their view. Make sure your voice can be heard at the back of the room.

____ Demonstrate enough of the technique so it is understood, but don't spend time completing repetitive processes. You may choose to complete some steps beforehand, but be sure to demonstrate all key or crucial steps.

____ Work at a pace that allows viewers to follow the details of each step.

____ Use every opportunity to set a good example and to illustrate proper procedures and safe practices, but don't call attention to all of them in the course of any one demonstration.

____ Use both hands whenever possible, but try to avoid crossing your hands and arms. This can confuse the learner.

____ Keep the work area neat and organized throughout the demonstration. Remove materials and equipment as you finish with them.

____ Maintain good posture and avoid leaning on work areas. Using proper work heights contributes to good posture and lessens fatigue.

____ Summarize the demonstration when you finish the last step and initiate any additional follow-up.

____ Give the viewers an opportunity to view the finished product at the end of the demonstration.

____ Provide references or resources for student use when demonstrations are complex or detailed, but not for every demonstration.

You may also want to change the seating arrangement before your audience arrives. Choose a plan that will give everyone a clear view. Adjust any overhead mirrors for optimum clarity. Ask someone to sit in the back of the room to help you check how loudly you must talk or adjust your microphone so that those at the back can hear you clearly.

✳ Introducing the Demonstration

Keep the introduction to your demonstration brief, but capture the audience's attention. Link the content of the demonstration to previous learning or personal experience. This often can be done by explaining how the information in the demonstration can benefit audience members personally or professionally. For instance, if you are demonstrating how to make a simple no-sew window valance, mention how participants can save money and still get exactly the look they want by choosing a fabric that matches their décor. If you are showing how to prepare low-cost but nutritious meals, you might tell the audience that the taco salad you are demonstrating could feed six people for as little as $7.00. A fashion merchandising demonstration could show how the lines and colors of clothing can change a person's apparent size. The introduction is also the time to identify any specific questions the learners should be able to answer afterward, based on the demonstration.

If appropriate, you can distribute a hand-out before the actual demonstration begins. This might have an outline of the steps in the demonstration or further explain complicated procedures. It's usually better to wait until the end of the demonstration to distribute handouts with additional information or resources. Otherwise, learners may read the handout materials, rather than watch the demonstration.

❋ Delivering Your Commentary

In a demonstration, what you say and how you say it are as important as what you do. Speak directly to the audience in an interesting and animated way. This helps build enthusiasm and keep the group's attention.

While your commentary should be based on explaining what you are doing, you don't have to announce every move you make. When you do describe your actions, choose impersonal terminology, such as "The second step is . . . " and impersonal pronouns and articles such as "this" and "an." This eliminates the need to use the possessive. It's less awkward to say "Add the rotini to the boiling water," than "Add your rotini to your pot of boiling water."

Although you don't have to talk nonstop during a demonstration, long pauses can make it difficult to hold a group's attention. When it's not necessary to describe the process you are demonstrating at the moment, use the time to add depth to the subject matter, present supplementary material, or ask thought-provoking questions.

Remember to pause if you have to move from one place to another, turn away from the group, or handle noisy equipment. Then complete your sentence or thought before continuing with something else.

❋ Involving the Audience

Demonstrations are usually most successful when there is some level of audience participation. Here are some possibilities:

- Ask questions of the audience as you demonstrate to assess comprehension of what you have explained and demonstrated.

- Encourage viewers to ask questions and talk briefly about personal experiences related to the topic being demonstrated. Ask them to give reasons for using different procedures, for variations, and for alternative methods.
- Let learners take turns being assistants. One or two might help throughout the entire demonstration, or people from the group can be called on to perform one or two steps.
- For food preparation demonstrations, give learners the opportunity to sample the finished product. Capitalize on the motivation built into the fact that people like to eat!
- When possible, have students prepare and give demonstrations individually, in pairs, or in small groups. This technique would work in almost any subject matter area. They might demonstrate such varied procedures as feeding an infant; using, cleaning, and caring for large and small appliances; making accessories and decorative items for the home; and repairing furnishings and equipment.
- Learners can establish criteria for evaluating other students' demonstrations and help provide feedback to presenters.

 ## Techniques for Food-Based Demonstrations

Food-based demonstrations are sometimes used for teaching family and consumer sciences concepts, culinary training, nutrition education, and illustrating health-related topics. They merit some additional guidelines. In addition to demonstrating preparation techniques, the presenter must also model the proper use of tools and equipment, safety precautions, and sanitation procedures—all while producing a satisfactory product. Food preparation demonstrations often deal with perishable ingredients and time constraints. When there is insufficient time to completely prepare a product, a finished or partially finished product may be made in advance. That way, all the key preparatory steps can be viewed and the product can be sampled in a limited amount of time.

Demonstrations of food science topics usually involve experimenting with food products to learn about the scientific principles behind food composition, production, processing, preparation, evaluation, and use. Scientific methods and equipment are used for most experiments and the food involved is usually discarded, rather than sampled at the end of a demonstration.

❋ Getting Ready to Demonstrate

- Dress appropriately for the demonstration. In a culinary situation, this may include wearing a uniform, apron, chef's hat, hair net, and gloves. A registered dietitian demonstrating low-fat recipes might wear a lab coat to create a professional image. In food science, goggles, or other gear appropriate for the particular experiment, would be worn. In every situation, clothes should be simple without any long ties or loose sleeves that could be dangerous near equipment or dip in the food. Keep jewelry to a minimum or remove it. Use gloves as needed.
- Complete as many prepreparation steps as possible before the demonstration.
- Assemble needed items ahead of time. One common method is to group the items on trays for various stages in the demonstration process. Include sufficient equipment, such as several liquid measures, so the items don't need to be washed for reuse during the demonstration.
- Emphasize the importance of sanitation. Before beginning the demonstration, let the viewers see you wash your hands and clean the work surface.
- Emphasize the importance of safety. Explain and show how to use equipment safely. Point out any related hazards.
- When possible, choose low-cost, nutrient-dense foods for demonstrations. This will not only stretch your budget, but also show the group how to cut costs and boost nutrition.
- Have a plan for keeping the work area neat and clean as you work. Place a wastebasket nearby and use trays to move

equipment and supplies no longer needed off the work area as you proceed through the demonstration. If possible, store these used items out of sight, such as beneath the work area.
- For food science experiments, make arrangements for any special needs, such as disposal of chemicals.

❋ Preparing Foods

Demonstrating actual food preparation can be a challenge. You need to make sure that the audience can see and hear what you are doing. At the same time as you are explaining the procedure, you must complete it accurately. Here are some suggestions:
- Place a damp cloth under a cutting board to prevent slipping. Use separate cutting boards for meat and poultry.
- When cutting with knives, keep the food against the cutting surface. Cut away from your body, using the proper size and type of knife.
- When you are using eggs, have extras on hand. Break or separate only one egg at a time into a cup or small dish. Then transfer each egg to the main mixing bowl. You may choose to have the eggs cracked and in a bowl before the demonstration begins.
- While mixing ingredients in a bowl, leave the bowl on the work surface. Place a damp cloth under the bowl to eliminate slipping and minimize noise. Using a clear mixing bowl allows learners to see the contents. When necessary, lift and tilt the bowl to provide a better view.
- Give food on a spoon a firm shake so that the substance falls into the bowl. This is preferable to hitting a spoon or beater on the side of a bowl.
- When pouring a mixture from a bowl, don't allow fingers to touch the food. Use a flexible scraper to remove the mixture quickly and easily.
- When spreading a mixture on bread, leave the bread on a board and use an assembly-line technique.
- Clean up spilled food promptly. Never return it to the food you are preparing.

✳ Being Efficient and Organized

A successful food demonstration depends on organization and economy of time, motion, and materials. Here are some suggestions:

- Put ingredients and equipment needed for the recipe in the order of use.
- If you organize on trays, number them so it's easy to locate them for use in sequential order. As you plan, list the supplies for each tray on a card. For demonstrations you may use again, protect cards and recipes by laminating them or placing a sheet of clear plastic over them. They could be stored together in a page protector inside a binder. As an alternative, you could store the information for each demonstration as a computer file and print it out the next time you use that demonstration.
- Remove each used tray from the work area before replacing it with a clean one.
- After a piece of equipment has been used, place it back on the tray, not on the work surface. This makes clean-up more efficient.
- Place the wastebasket next to the work surface, rather than under it. That way you won't have to stoop down to find it.
- Complete the demonstration with a clean, cleared work surface.
- Plan ahead how to display and/or serve the finished food product. If several items have been prepared, label each clearly. If the group will be tasting a product, include a list of ingredients for anyone who may have food allergies.

✳ Using Food Preparation Equipment and Appliances

In addition to demonstrating how to prepare a food item, you will be demonstrating correct equipment and appliance use. The following list also includes related suggestions that will help your presentation look more professional:

- Before the demonstration, familiarize yourself with any appliances that you haven't used before. You need to know exactly where the controls are and how an appliance operates so you look confident during the demonstration.
- After a small appliance has been used, remove it from the demonstration area.
- When using an electric mixer, remove the used beaters and place them on a tray before moving the bowl.
- Match the appropriate size pan to the burner or unit. Turn off the burner or unit when you are finished cooking. You may show learners how to use the heat retained in electric units for cooking and warming foods.
- When lifting a lid from a hot pan, turn it away from your body and place it upside down on the work surface. Turn pot handles away from the front of the range. Stand to the side when you open the oven door.
- Leave potholders at the range but not near the burners or heating elements. Don't use paper towels or dishtowels as potholders to pull out oven racks or remove food from the oven.
- Place canisters, measuring equipment, product packages, and other items to the side when not in use. If placed in front, they may obstruct the audience's view.

Example of a First Aid Demonstration

One example of a topic that might be demonstrated is the Heimlich Maneuver. Every educator should know basic first aid procedures, including this one, for emergency situations. Most students can learn to perform it through viewing a demonstration and practicing on a special realistic model available from some health agencies. The actual thrusting maneuver should not be practiced on anyone who is not choking, but can be practiced on the model. You can demonstrate correct positioning and simulate the thrusting action without a model. Stress appropriate follow-up measures. The illustrations on the next page identify the steps that would be included in such a demonstration.

THE HEIMLICH MANEUVER

1. **Recognize choking.** If a person who is choking can breathe, cough, or talk, emegency maneuvers aren't needed and may even be dangerous. A person who can't breathe due to choking most likely will not show other signs of injury. Lips and fingernails will turn blue or black. If the victim is unconscious on the floor, death may occur within minutes, so it is essential to act quickly! Have someone call for additional help.

2. **For standing victims, place fist just below the rib cage.** Place one fist above the navel but below rib cage as pictured. Cover this fist with the other hand. Press fist into victim's abdomen. Use both hands to make a quick, upward thrust. Repeat if necessary to dislodge object in the windpipe.

3. **If the victim is on the ground, kneel over the person.** Kneel astride collapsed victim's hips, placing one hand over the other. Place heel of bottom hand slightly above navel but well below rib cage. Press upward into the stomach with quick thrusts. Repeat if needed.

4. **Watch breathing and check pulse.** Be prepared to give mouth-to-mouth resuscitation. Even if the person appears to be okay, he or she needs to be checked by medical personnel.

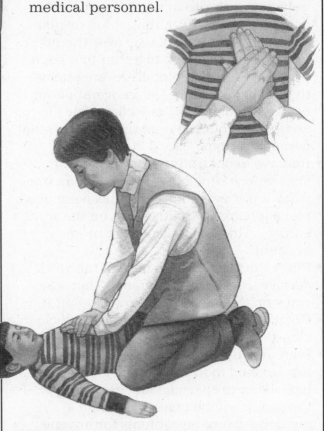

✳ Preparing for This Demonstration

The illustrated example shows the basic steps for a demonstration of the Heimlich Maneuver. Now step back. Review the five steps for a successful demonstration at the beginning of the chapter. Next complete a demonstration planning sheet, similar to *Figure 12-1* on page 161. Although this would be a relatively simple demonstration, working through the process will help you effectively plan other demonstration topics.

Evaluating a Demonstration

The evaluation step can include both evaluation of your presentation by others and self-analysis. While you are polishing your demonstration techniques, other students can help you by completing evaluations of your demonstrations. Your supervisor, or even your audience, may evaluate how well you did once you are on the job.

Figure 12-3 — **INSTRUMENT FOR RATING DEMONSTRATIONS**

Use the key below to rate the demonstration (possible points=50)
KEY: 5=Excellent   4=Very good   3=Good   2=Fair   1=Poor

POINTS BEING CONSIDERED	5	4	3	2	1	COMMENTS
1. Was well prepared.						
2. Organized materials and equipment efficiently.						
3. Demonstrated so all could see and hear.						
4. Kept work surface neat and clean.						
5. Displayed skill in using the technique demonstrated.						
6. Maintained appropriate pace.						
7. Provided an informative and accurate commentary during demonstration.						
8. Involved learners.						
9. Projected favorable image through appropriate attire and demeanor.						
10. Completed demonstration within time limit.						
TOTAL POINTS FOR EACH COLUMN						

TOTAL POINTS _____

For most demonstrations, the same general criteria can be used for evaluation. *Figure 12-3*, "Instrument for Rating Demonstrations," above, is an example of a generic evaluation form. It could be used to evaluate diverse demonstrations, including bathing a baby, teaching weight-bearing exercises, and implementing stain-removal techniques.

Sometimes a more specific evaluation sheet is desired. You could modify a general instrument such as the rating scale. You might also create new evaluation sheets for particular purposes. The "Checklist for Food Demonstrations," *Figure 12-4* on page 168, is an example of a specific evaluation instrument.

After each demonstration, think about what went well and what could be improved. Note those points the next time you present that demonstration. You might complete an analysis like that in *Figure 12-3* as part of your self-evaluation. Occasionally videotaping a demonstration can give you valuable feedback about your performance because you can see exactly what your audience saw.

Figure 12-4

CHECKLIST FOR FOOD DEMONSTRATIONS

Directions: Watch the demonstration carefully. Check Yes or No as it applies to what the demonstrator did or did not do. Write comments in the right column.

THE DEMONSTRATOR:	YES	NO	COMMENTS
1. Welcomes audience.			
2. Introduces herself/himself.			
3. Is dressed appropriately.			
4. Is prepared.			
5. Has professional demeanor.			
6. Is animated and interesting to watch.			
7. Maintains good posture.			
8. Has good eye contact.			
9. Speaks clearly.			
10. Minimizes use of "I."			
11. Demonstrates techniques and/or difficult steps.			
12. Tells why certain procedures are done.			
13. Uses available space efficiently.			
14. Is knowledgeable about use of equipment.			
15. Uses clean and appropriate equipment/materials.			
16. Is neat throughout the demonstration.			
17. Uses glass bowls.			
18. Speaks of ingredients in order of use.			
19. Has prepared ingredients in advance.			
20. Avoids crossing her/his arms.			
21. Has finished product to show.			
22. Is free of annoying mannerisms.			
23. Holds audience's attention.			
24. Maintains appropriate pace.			
25. Doesn't block view with equipment/utensils.			

Building Your Professional Portfolio

Analyzing a Demonstration. Tape a food demonstration on television. Evaluate the demonstration's strengths and weaknesses in a written or oral critique.

Planning and Presenting. Plan a demonstration on a topic in your professional area using the tools in this chapter or others you devise. Then tape yourself giving the demonstration, effectively using suggested presentation guidelines and techniques.

Devising an Evaluation Tool. Create an evaluation instrument for a specific type of demonstration other than food preparation. Include both generic and content-specific criteria. Organize the material logically and present it in a format that's easy to use but which will also provide the presenter with useful feedback. If possible, try out the instrument and make any improvements.

Improving Your Skills. Prepare and give a presentation to others from your class. Have them use an evaluation instrument to rate your performance and also discuss their observations with you. Based on this feedback, identify specific demonstration skills that you can improve. For each, specify how you will work on improvement.

Chapter 13

Experiential Learning: Lab Activities and Cooperative Learning

As an educator, your goal is to prepare learners for real-life experiences. Regardless of your educational setting, you provide opportunities for application of the theories you teach. Experiential learning activities are powerful educational tools because they are specifically designed to connect what is taught to life experiences. Through this process, learners reflect on their experiences in a relevant activity and consciously determine how they might apply their learning in real life.

There are many types of activities that lend themselves to experiential learning. These include simulations, scenarios, games, service learning, problem-based learning, cooperative education, field trips, internships, and mentoring experiences. A number of these are highlighted in other chapters in this book. This chapter focuses on the use of two types of experiential learning techniques: lab experiences and cooperative learning activities.

 ## Implementing Experiential Learning

As noted in Chapter 5, experiential learning is often considered a four-part process. Learners:

- Take part in a relevant experience.
- Reflect on and analyze the experience and its implications.
- Form generalizations about the experience.
- Relate and apply what was learned to life situations.

Experiential learning activities allow students opportunities to observe, simulate, and/or participate in activities that closely reflect situations they may encounter now or in the future. By engaging the learners' minds, bodies, and/or feelings in activities that extend and apply the material pre-sented, experiential learning activities promote the development of cognitive, affective, and psychomotor behaviors. Learners can be taken to the higher levels of each domain of learning as their thinking, feelings, and skills are challenged and expanded through these experiences.

Look again at the list of types of activities that can be used for experiential learning. In doing so, it's clear that use of these types of activities doesn't automatically guarantee that experiential learning occurs. Sometimes these activities fulfill only the first step of the process. Unless a learning experience also includes reflection, generalization formation, and application, experiential learning has not taken place.

Experiential learning activities are likely to be most successful if they reflect the current and future needs of the learners. The settings for the experiences need to be realistic and simulate as closely as possible real, relevant situations. Learners should have an active role in planning and implementing the experience. In experiential learning activities, students are provided opportunities for action and reflection, new experiences, assumption of responsibility, and interactions with the social and physical environments. The teacher assumes a facilitating role in the experience and, in this capacity, monitors progress, assesses learner behavior, and provides feedback.

Experiential learning experiences assist learners with enhancement of decision-making skills and problem-solving abilities, personal growth and development, practical skill development, and self-confidence. Motivation is increased as the linkages between classroom learnings and real-life applications are made. Future expectations on the job and in life are clarified and, therefore, the relevance of classroom learning is experienced. The future is brought into focus and related to the current educational setting.

Types of Lab Activities

Lab activities are opportunities to work with materials, ideas, people, or processes. Lab experiences provide excellent opportunities for learner participation in planning and carrying out learning activities, applying principles, and practicing desired behavior. To be truly educational, laboratory experiences need to be based on concepts that have been covered in the curriculum so that opportunities for application of theory are provided.

Lab experiences provide hands-on opportunities and can be used as part of 4-H training, nutrition education efforts, first aid training, and public health education, to name a few. Laboratory experiences involve a wide array of opportunities for experiencing authentic situations.

Basically, there are three types of laboratories: productive, experimental, and observational. Each has specific characteristics and is most useful for specific types of learning situations.

❋ Productive Labs

In productive labs, the emphasis is on developing psychomotor skills and gaining experience in managing resources while producing a product. The outcome might be an appropriately applied bandage, a children's book, an inexpensive children's toy, a garment, a window covering, stock for soup, a floor plan, a well-made hospital bed, a refinished chair, or the correct execution of CPR. Although the final product is important, the processes used to produce it are equally important. The unique feature of the productive lab is the creation of a product. This can be a product produced following a predetermined plan, a set of directions, or a plan that learners create themselves.

For productive labs, learners should aim for previously established standards of acceptable quality. In some lab activities, a simple scorecard is used and learners are graded. In other instances, such as a culinary class, students continue practicing until they are able to master the skills involved. *Figure 13-1*, "Culinary Arts Party Platter Evaluation," on page 172 sets the standards that culinary students must meet to complete a catering unit. Note that it may take a student several attempts to meet an acceptable level of performance.

❋ Experimental Labs

Experimental labs use a formal process to research problems or questions. The research subject should generally focus on the unknown, rather than on verifying already proven facts that the learners know. The learning experiences suggested here can be developed using scientific and experimental methods.

Experimental methodology usually requires that a control be used for the experiment. Also, for a comparison to be meaningful, a limited number of variables is usually tested at a time. For example, to check the effect chlorine bleach has on nylon fabric as compared with nonchlorine bleach, three samples of the same fabric are tested—one with each type of bleach and, for the control, one with no bleach.

Figure 13-1

CULINARY ARTS PARTY PLATTER EVALUATION

Name: _____ Group: _____ Date: _____

Directions: Have your instructor use this scorecard to evaluate your performance level for each aspect of your party platter. All scores must be level 3 or above for successful competion of this skill. you are evaluating a drawing, do not evaluate for proper cooking.

Type of plate or platter: _____

PERFORMANCE SCORECARD

Performance Standards

Level 4—Performs skill without supervision and adapts to problem situations.

Level 3—Performs skill satisfactorily without assistance or supervision.

Level 2—Performs skill satisfactorily, but requires assistance or supervision.

Level 1—Performs parts of skill satisfactorily, but requires considerable assistance or supervision.

Level 0—Cannot perform this skill.

Attempt (circle one): 1 2 3 4

General Comments:

**PERFORMANCE LEVEL _____
ACHIEVED:**

_____ 1. Follows safety and sanitation practices at all times during this job.
_____ 2. Makes effective use of size and shape, including ovals, circles, squares, and triangles.
_____ 3. Creates an effective focal point.
_____ 4. Uses layout techniques effectively, including symmetrical and asymmetrical balance.
_____ 5. Chooses foods that blend well together in flavor, color, and texture.
_____ 6. Chooses functional garnishes that add flavor, color, and texture.

_____ 7. Presents food arrangements that are neat and artistically garnished.
_____ 8. Uses at least two different cooking methods.
_____ 9. Prepares foods to proper flavor, color, texture, and doneness.

Explain any problems encountered in the quality of product:

Instructor's signature _____ Date: _____

The information gathered in an experimental lab is often compiled in a data table or graph. *Figure 13-2* on page 173 shows a data table for a food science experiment on thickening agents.

The following topics are examples of ones that could be developed into one or more experimental labs. In order to provide a variety of suggestions, each example contains many variables. You may want to use one, or a limited number of, variables in any one experimental lab or plan several related lab experiences.

• **Choosing effective textile laundering techniques for various fabrics.** Experiment with a variety of fabrics made from

Figure 13-2 **DATA TABLE: THICKENING AGENTS EXPERIMENT**

Name of Starch	Line-Spread Average		Appearance of Refrigerated Samples	Appearance of Frozen Samples
	HOT	COLD		
Corn	13	11	thick paste	holds shape; syneresis
Rice	16	17	smooth paste	sponge layers; some water loss
Tapioca	18	15	thick, clear gel	grainy; no syneresis
Potato	10	8	sturdy; holds shape	spongy effect
Flour	23	23	thin paste; soft mound	scalloped; holds shape
Arrowroot	14	12	thick gel	very firm; holds shape

different fibers and with various finishes to ascertain the effects of several laundering techniques. Before beginning, outline the size of each fabric sample on a piece of paper, indicating the lengthwise and crosswise grain. Wash in hot, warm, and cold water for different time periods to note if there is shrinkage and, if so, how much. Note the effects on different fibers and finishes. Evaluate the findings to develop generalizations and implications for choosing and cleaning textiles.

• **Determining product effectiveness on removing stains.** Keeping the fabric, type of soil (preset stains such as blood, grass, coffee), and water temperature the same, experiment using hot- and cold-water detergents, soaps, bleaches, presoaks, enzyme-spray products, and stain removers in stick form to compare results and cost. Use the results to establish guidelines for washing stained products.

• **Analyzing lancet options.** Extract blood for testing blood sugar using various types of lancets and lancet holders. Compare the level of comfort, amount of blood extracted, and ease of use for each and make recommendations for future use.

• **Determining efficiency of bed-making techniques.** Practice making a hospital bed in various ways to determine the most efficient system, while still meeting predetermined standards of performance. Use time trials to determine which person's method is the fastest. What variables must be considered in developing generalizations from these results?

• **Comparing household cleaning products.** Compare a variety of commercial products designated for cleaning ovens, washing windows, polishing furniture, cleaning and waxing floors, and cleaning carpets. Develop a rubric for factors such as effectiveness, time and energy required, and cost. Consider the conditions under which the products were tested and determine what generalizations can be made.

• **Comparing cold storage options.** Store different types of foods in the refrigerator and freezer using various products for wrapping, such as plastic storage bags and freezer bags, foil, waxed paper, and vacuum seals, as well as different types of containers. Leave some products (such as carrots) uncovered in the refrigerator, and others (such as ice cream) uncovered in the freezer. After specified periods of time, compare samples of the products for flavor, texture, and freshness. What conclusions can be drawn from the data?

• **Analyzing hand sanitation products.** Wash your hands with various cleaning agents before handling food. Swab hands after different procedures or use of various products and then swab and label petri dishes. Watch for growth of organisms and identify types and rates of growth. Use generalizations to develop a list of sanitation practices for food preparation.

• **Determining how food preparation techniques affect quality.** Conduct experiments to determine the effects of various preparation techniques on specific food products. For example, compare the color, texture, and flavor of vegetables prepared by steaming, boiling, and microwaving. Prepare piecrusts using a variety of techniques and different fats. Compare the results for taste, appearance, and cost. Vary the temperature and method of cooking with small samples of tender and less-tender cuts of meat. Draw generalizations from each experiment.

- **Testing how cooking method and meat composition affect fat content.** Weigh three different varieties of ground beef to make three exactly equal portions of each, or nine meat patties in all. Cook one sample of each variety to the same degree of doneness by frying. Then cook one of each by broiling and the remaining ones by charcoal broiling. Weigh each portion after cooking to determine the amount of fat lost. Evaluate the samples for flavor and appearance. Record the results on a data table. Develop generalizations from this experiment and identify how this information could be used in the future.

✳ Observational Labs

In observational labs, learners view situations and phenomena to clarify certain concepts. You focus learners' attention by clearly identifying the purpose of observations, the subject of the particular observation, and what viewers should note. Sometimes students may be given an observation form to complete. In other situations, they simply take notes. Experiential learning takes place when observers use the information gathered to develop generalizations and identify how these can be used in future situations.

Learners aren't physically involved in observational laboratory lessons as they are in productive and experimental labs. However, in well-planned observations, students should be just as involved intellectually and learning just as much as in other types of activities.

Here are some examples of observational labs:

- **Lab safety issues.** In a roped-off section of a food science lab or laboratory kitchen, set up equipment and materials to indicate unsafe practices. Have students identify each and describe the possible consequences. They can then use the experience as a basis for developing a set of lab safety guidelines.

- **Milk and cheese products.** Set up a display showing the different forms of commercially available milk and various types of cheeses. Have learners compare flavors, costs, and nutritive values of the different products. They can then suggest ways in which each can be served and used in cooking, as well as form generalizations about cost and nutrition factors.

- **Marketing techniques.** Visit a supermarket to observe the location and placement of specialty and novelty items that are unlikely to be on a shopping list. Have learners note the position of staple foods, dairy products, and nonfood items. Discuss the techniques used that may influence a consumer to buy more than was planned. Discuss factors that influence the choices a person will make. What generalizations can be made? What personal and professional applications might be made from these?

- **Kitchen shape and efficiency.** Have learners watch classmates prepare the same recipe or simple meal in U-shaped, L-shaped, and one-wall kitchens (or whatever layouts are represented in the setting). They can trace the steps of the cooks on floor plans of the kitchens drawn to scale, and then measure the total length of the lines drawn. Determine in which types of kitchens the cooks walked most and least. Draw up a list of ways to minimize walking in less-desirable kitchen layouts. Repeat the observation with a second group of cooks. Form appropriate generalizations useful for real-life situations.

- **Children's programming.** Have learners develop a checklist for judging television programs for children of various ages. Then have each watch several programs and rate them using the checklist. Use the results to make a list of suggestions for improving the programs and send it to the appropriate networks. Also have learners reflect on what they have learned and summarize how this may affect their future work or personal life.

- **Children's clothing.** Develop a display of children's clothes that illustrates features such as:

- Clothes that expand as children grow
- Self-help features that enable children to help dress and undress themselves
- Safety of closures
- Washability and ease of care
- Durability and comfort

Discuss the desirable and less desirable features of each garment. Determine a set of guidelines for selecting children's clothing.

- **Judging maturity in children.** Watch a tape of or share scenes observed in a child care center in which children seemed to illustrate social and emotional maturity or immaturity for their presumed ages. Tell whether adults seemed to handle them well or poorly. Propose ways to determine the maturity level of children of various ages and strategies for handling children of different maturities.
- **Positive guidance of children.** View videotapes of children in a child care facility and rate the performance of student teachers, aides, and others in their guidance of the children. Use an instrument to assess positive human relations and guidance, such as the rating scale, *Figure 13-3* on page 176. Develop guidelines to use when providing positive guidance to children.
- **Safe learning environments.** Visit child care facilities and observe the children, teachers, toys, equipment, furnishings, and kitchen facilities. Note the precautions taken to maintain the children's health and to promote their safety. Evaluate the facilities visited by answering questions such as those in *Figure 13-4*, "Child Care Facility Evaluation List," on page 177. Compare results and draw conclusions.

 # Lab Experiences: Parts and Processes

Whether you are conducting a productive, experimental, or observational laboratory experience, you need to focus on three major parts—the planning, the activity, and the evaluation. Within each of these three segments there are some processes that need to take place for effective laboratory experiences.

Successful lab experiences require careful preplanning and scheduling. Choose situations that are as realistic as possible. By coordinating tasks, precious class time can be used most productively, and all learners will have assignments that are challenging and meaningful.

The actual procedures will vary significantly, depending on the type of lab and subject matter to be learned. In this discussion, a secondary-level productive foods lab experience emphasizing nutrition is used as the primary example. There were three reasons for this choice. First, such labs are among the most complex to plan and carry out successfully. Second, with the increase of hospitality, culinary arts, and food science curricula, food-related labs are among the most common. Third, food preparation labs have traditionally focused mainly on the skills needed to produce quality food products. In an experiential foods lab, the focus is consciously broadened, and generalizations are formed that have real implications for a variety of future experiences. As you study this example, think about how the process could also apply to experimental and observational labs and topics in other subject areas.

※ Planning the Lab

Laboratory experiences require careful planning by both the educator and the learners if they are to run smoothly, and available time is used to the best advantage. The planning section of a lab should include the following:

- The educator sets the objectives for the lab and clarifies them with the learners.
- The timeframe for the lab is established.
- The learners develop plans for tasks to be accomplished and assign responsibilities.
- Each person understands his or her role in the lab.
- The educator and/or learners gather the supplies and equipment needed.

Figure 13-3	GUIDING YOUNG CHILDREN
	PERFORMANCE RATING SCALE

Name: _____ Date: _____ Period: _____

Location of observation: _____

Directions: Read the descriptor next to each Roman numeral that indicates what behaviors you are looking for in each section. Then, for each lettered line, please circle the number above the descriptor that best indicates the performance described. Calculate the total score at the bottom.

I. Demonstrates human relation skills in dealing with self and working with others, such as courteousness, confidence, positive attitude, and effective communication.

1	2	3	4	5
A. Doesn't demonstrate any human relation skills.		Demonstrates some human relation skills.		Demonstrates a variety of human relation skills.

1	2	3	4	5
B. Doesn't communicate effectively with children or others.		Occasionally communicates effectively with children or others.		Communicates effectively through techniques such as using name, praising efforts.

II. Utilizes various techniques in working with children with respect to human development principles, such as working individually with children, allowing each to work at own pace.

1	2	3	4	5
C. Doesn't use any techniques that relate to principles of human development.		Uses some techniques related to the principles of development.		Uses many techniques related to the principles of development.

III. Demonstrates methods of guidance, such as direct and indirect, and positive verbal guidance.

1	2	3	4	5
D. Doesn't give direct guidance when needed.		Occasionally uses methods of direct guidance.		Utilizes variety of direct guidance techniques, such as gentle physical restraint or reassurance.

1	2	3	4	5
E. Doesn't give indirect guidance.		Occasionally uses methods of indirect guidance.		Utilizes variety of indirect guidance, such as setting stage for activities, choosing appropriate toys.

1	2	3	4	5
F. Doesn't use positive verbal guidance.		Occasionally uses positive verbal guidance.		Uses positive verbal guidance, such as "Please sit down. It's time to go outside now."

Total Score: _____

Figure 13-4

CHILD CARE FACILITY EVALUATION LIST

Directions: Answer the following questions with a yes or no and be prepared to justify your answers.

1. Is the child care facility licensed?
2. Is there adequate space indoors to move about freely while skipping, running, and dancing?
3. Is there adequate space indoors to build with blocks, to play house apart from the group, and to paint without being jostled?
4. Is there adequate space outdoors for running, climbing, and tricycle riding?
5. Is the outdoor equipment suitable for the developmental levels of the children?
6. Is there some place outdoors for playing quietly if children choose to do this?
7. Are the toys and equipment sturdy, clean, and safe?
8. Are there blocks, balls, dolls, housekeeping toys, dress-up clothes, wheel toys, and appropriate puzzles?
9. Are there easels, paint, clay or dough, crayons, scissors, and plenty of paper?
10. Are there games and toys that help children learn about shapes and sizes?
11. Are there tables and chairs that are the right size for working comfortably with both feet on the floor?
12. Does the program seem to meet the needs of growing children?
13. Are there quiet times for rest, stories, conversation, and refreshments?
14. Are there free play periods when children can choose what they want to do?
15. Is there time for the children to make things for themselves and to grow in creativity and independence?
16. Are the work periods short so the children do not lose interest?
17. Do the teachers seem to show interest in the children as individuals?
18. Do the teachers seem to be constantly alert to the safety of the children?
19. Are the children supervised constantly?
20. Do the children seem happy?

For productive foods labs, it's preferable to plan, prepare, and serve complete meals whenever possible. This makes the experiences more realistic and meaningful. Give learners some choice in deciding what foods to prepare within a meal pattern. The pattern is established so that certain identified principles of cooking are involved and specific nutrients are included. Having students learn about nutrients in the foods they prepare and eat will be more meaningful than studying nutrition as a separate unit. Instead of studying about calcium, thiamine, and vitamin A in a nutrition unit preceding food preparation, these nutrients can be covered in a meal pattern that includes a milk-rich food, a quick bread, and a green salad. The importance of calcium can be reemphasized, and protein and vitamin C can be studied when preparing foods within a meal pattern of a fruit salad, a meat-extender dish, and a milk-rich dessert.

When using the meal-pattern approach in food and nutrition labs, it may take up to a week to complete the appropriate learning activities, depending on the number of lab units available and the number of students in a class. If six or more students need to be assigned to each unit, consider dividing the students for each unit into two subgroups, Group A and Group B, to avoid congestion and maximize learning. Here is an example of how group activities might be scheduled:

Meal Lab Schedule with Two Groups Per Unit

Monday

Group A: Plan own menu in quantity to serve to both Groups A and B, select recipes, make out market order, develop work schedules.

Group B: Follow same procedure as Group A with own menu.

Tuesday

Group A: Prepare or complete prepreparation tasks for as much food as possible to be served the next day (Wednesday).

Group B: Prepare or complete prepreparation tasks for as much food as possible for serving on Thursday.

Wednesday

Group A: Complete final preparation. Serve meal to entire unit group (A and B). Clean up with help of Group B.

Group B: Work on assignment relating to meal pattern for the week or evaluate management skills and preparation techniques used by Group A. Enjoy meal. Help Group A clean up.

Thursday

Group A: Work on assignment relating to meal pattern or evaluate management skills and preparation techniques used by Group B. Enjoy meal. Help Group B clean up.

Group B: Complete final preparation. Serve meal to entire unit group (A and B). Clean up with help of Group A.

Friday

Group A: Evaluate laboratory experience and complete related assignments.

Group B: Follow same procedure as Group A.

While students in one subgroup are preparing their menu, the others can be engaged in worthwhile activities. These might include reading about and answering questions pertinent to foods and nutrients emphasized in the meal pattern for that week, planning menus for a full day to accompany the one being served, and observing and evaluating the students who are working in the lab at that time. Students in one subgroup might evaluate those in another subgroup by completing checklists or rubrics/rating scales relating to laboratory work habits or by conducting time and motion studies.

✳ During the Lab Activity

Once planning is completed, the learners are ready to start the activity component of the laboratory experience. Some of the processes that occur in this component include:

- Learners carry out the plans.
- Educator supervises the work of participants.
- Educator monitors time schedule.
- Practices of the participants are observed/recorded.
- Participants are guided towards goals.
- Participants are guided in correct use of supplies and equipment.
- Participants are guided to maintain standards and practices.
- Participants are guided in independent thinking to overcome difficulties.

If the lessons preceding lab work have provided learners with essential background material, individuals should be able to work with a reasonable degree of independence and cooperation. However, students don't need to know everything about a subject before participating in a lab experience. In fact, for a foods course, too much time can be spent on meal planning, table setting, and kitchen management concepts before the first lab lesson. By then, students' inherent motivation may be lost. It's often better to choose, or to guide students into choosing, comparatively simple activities at first so they have a sense of achievement. You can provide just enough background in the subject beforehand to enable them to carry out the planned activities successfully. Related concepts can be covered in greater depth as the unit progresses and can be interspersed among subsequent laboratory lessons.

✳ *Providing Guidance During Labs*

During a lab experience, the educator has many roles to fulfill. One of these is observing the managerial processes used and the interpersonal relationships among the learners. At the same time, however, the teacher must continually make certain that all students are safe and learning.

It's inevitable that learners will have questions as a lab progresses. Managing that aspect can sometimes become overwhelming. However, there are techniques that can help you to handle questions effectively.

While students are eager for immediate answers, that isn't always possible or perhaps best. You can set up systems that allow you to get back to students in a timely and orderly way while still maintaining control over your own time.

There are often a few learners who ask for help loudly and repeatedly. Perhaps unintentionally, they want to monopolize the teacher's attention. That's one reason to implement your response procedure before the first lab begins. Point out that using the system will help assure that everyone who needs help will get it. Here are two simple methods you might use:

- Have students write their name on the board or on a flipchart as they need assistance. You help them sequentially.
- Have a set of numbered cards that learners can take as they need help. They can display the numbers or you can call them in order.

Keep in mind that in some types of labs, dangerous situations may be more likely to occur. Make it clear that your students should communicate any emergency situation to you immediately. You don't want your "orderly" system to impede handling a crisis.

The problem of students becoming overly dependent upon the teacher can be a very real one. Sometimes, rather than answering participants' questions directly during a lab lesson, redirect questions back to the students instead. Through skillful questioning you can help them answer their own questions. Also encourage learners to think through a problem and arrive at a possible solution before asking you. They can phrase their question, "Is this what I do next?" rather than "What do I do next?" The latter question suggests that the learner has come to expect the teacher to do most of the thinking and problem solving.

✳ Staying Within Time Limits

Completing labs on time depends on good scheduling. As the teacher, you start by not scheduling too much in a lab period. Students can't accomplish as much as you could in the same time period. In addition, just the logistics of working in a group takes up more time.

A first step is to rough out an approximate time schedule and judge how much time various portions of the lesson will take.

Sometimes you will finalize the schedule. For other lab situations, you may have students develop specific schedules for completing the lesson on time. The work schedule should designate the tasks to be performed by each participant and the time at which each should begin. Remember that asking students to make time schedules using unrealistic time constraints diminishes enthusiasm and inevitably leads to failure. *Figure 13-5* on page 180 shows a sample work schedule for a foods lab. Note that it includes enough detail to show the teacher that every person has specific tasks to perform, that the sequence is logical, and the approximate time allowed for each step is appropriate.

It's often helpful to have a poster indicating a general time schedule for learners' reference. Such a chart can make it obvious to students that they have to use every minute to their best advantage.

For labs that involve use of equipment, it helps to designate the last minutes of the session as check-out time. Many of the problems that are associated with quick and disorderly departure can be avoided. At the designated check-out time, learners should be at their lab station. Then the teacher can quickly check each station and storage area to see that the unit is clean and that the equipment is accounted for and in the proper place. Only after this quick check are the students dismissed to go to their next class.

✳ Evaluating the Lab

The most educationally valuable part of any experiential lab activity should be the evaluation. It is during this time that generalizations are formulated and conclusions are drawn about the work done. Questions are posed, such as "Why did this happen (or not happen)?" Without evaluation, the lab activity tends to become an end in itself, if not just busywork. If learners follow instructions and carry out an experiment or make a product or complete an observation without making generalizations about what they have done, they are unlikely to acquire the understanding originally intended.

Figure 13-5 — WORK SCHEDULE FOR FOODS LAB

CITRUS MOLD, INDIVIDUAL HAMBURGER PIZZAS, MILK

TUESDAY—PREPREPARATION DAY

STUDENT A	STUDENT B
1:00—Pull back hair, put on apron, wash hands.	1:00—Pull back hair, put on apron, wash hands.
1:05—Cook hamburger meat.	1:05—Prepare gelatin using ice cubes.
1:15—Prepare other ingredients for pizza sauce.	1:15—Prepare orange and grapefruit slices.
1:25—Cook sauce, stirring occasionally.	1:25—Add fruit to gelatin mixture.
1:35—Begin to clean up.	1:30—Clean lettuce and store.
1:42—Check out.	1:38—Help with cleanup.
	1:42—Check out.

WEDNESDAY—SERVING DAY

STUDENT A	STUDENT B
1:00—Pull back hair, put on apron, wash hands.	1:00—Pull back hair, put on apron, wash hands.
1:05—Roll hamburger buns flat.	1:05—Warm pizza sauce.
1:10—Pour pizza sauce on buns, bake at 350° for 10 minutes.	1:10—Unmold gelatin salad.
1:15—Help set table.	1:15—Help set table. Place salad on lettuce leaves.
1:20—Serve meal.	1:20—Serve meal.
1:33—Begin to clear table.	1:33—Begin to clear table.
1:35—Rinse dishes and help put them in dishwasher.	1:35—Rinse dishes and help put them in dishwasher.
1:42—Check out.	1:42—Check out.

Use a variety of evaluation devices, changing them frequently. After students have used the same rating device several times, they tend to lose interest in it, which affects the quality of their evaluations. The processes covered in the evaluation component include:

• Discuss and evaluate accomplishments and outcomes.
• Check for attainment of objectives.
• Critique the experience.
• Draw generalizations.
• Draw conclusions.
• Evaluate self and other team members.

✳ *Sample Evaluation Devices for Lab Experiences*

Nontesting means of assessment are commonly used with lab experiences. Match the type of assessment tool to the qualities that need to be evaluated. Chapter 7 includes examples of checklists, scorecards, and rubrics/rating scales.

Other formats can also be used. The example in *Figure 13-6* on page 182 consists of open-ended questions about a foods lab meal. Such instruments can be adapted to many concepts and may be used by individual learners, learners working in groups, or the educator. On evaluation forms used during consecutive laboratory lessons, you can emphasize different concepts, such as nutrition, cost of the menu, and meal service.

It may be easier for a leader or teacher to evaluate specific features while a product, such as a 4-H record book or exhibit, is being constructed rather than to judge many completed projects all at one time. By using periodic evaluations, students can see the strengths and weaknesses of their work as it progresses and make improvements as they continue. There is also value in having learners judge their work as it progresses, compare their evaluations with the educator's, and discuss them.

Simple evaluation devices tend to imply that all the qualities listed are of equal importance. This may not necessarily be true. However, adding comments can minimize this shortcoming. By using a series of checklists, points can be accumulated to help determine a final grade. Be sure to make provision for adjusting the total point value when all the identified techniques are not included in all students' projects. *Figures 13-7* and *13-8* on pages 183 and 184 show instruments that might be used with labs on evaluating children's books and on performing CPR.

 # Managing Lab Experiences

In lab activities, as in all lessons, you are responsible for the successful management and safety of the learners and resources. The following section includes helpful advice on how to handle these responsibilities effectively.

There are many factors that will influence your lab management. Among these factors are:

- The type of lab experience, i.e., productive, experimental, observational
- The number of learners
- The age of the learners
- The learners' previous experiences in the content area
- The ability levels of the learners
- The facility or environment in which the lab is to occur
- The equipment available
- Other available resources, including budget
- Time available for the lab experience

✳ General Tips for Managing Labs

The following points reinforce and supplement tips given in this chapter. If followed, they can help you manage labs so they run smoothly. Think about other suggestions you might add to the list.

✳ *Planning the Lab Activity*

- Establish a specific purpose for the lab, and be sure everyone knows the purpose.
- Give students choices, within limits, regarding products to produce, experiments to do, or situations to be observed.
- Have learners prepare written plans in advance. All learners need to know their jobs and roles.
- Make your expectations clear for behavior, procedures, and products.
- Give clear directions, both written and oral.
- Have all supplies and equipment ready when learners arrive.
- Have lab report sheets prepared.
- Have extra supplies available.
- Check that all equipment works.
- Arrange the room for ease of movement during the lab.
- Work out labeling procedures. Plan where to dispose of or store results of the lab.
- Be sure learners have sufficient background to successfully complete the lab.

✳ *During the Lab Activity*

- Have everyone sit down and listen for last minute instructions before beginning a lab.
- Circulate constantly as the lab is in progress.
- Watch the time and alert learners.
- *Teach* as you circulate and help the learners.
- Stress safety and sanitation.
- Have standard ending or check-out procedures.
- Have a rotation plan for clean up and general tasks that need to be done in the room.

✳ *Evaluating the Lab Activity*

- Provide time for discussion of lab experiences so that participants can draw conclusions, generalizations, and implications.
- Evaluate learners' performances during and at conclusion of the lab.

Figure 13-6

OPEN-ENDED EVALUATION OF A FOODS LAB MEAL

Directions: On a separate piece of paper, answer each of the questions that follow based on the lab experience just completed. Be sure to include your name, class period, and group number.

MENU

1. What factors contributed to a pleasing menu?
2. How could the menu have been improved?

NUTRITION

1. Were all the Food Guide Pyramid Groups represented?
2. Were the Dietary Guidelines followed?

WORK SCHEDULE

1. What timesaving principles were used by members of the group?
2. How could the work schedule have been improved?

MARKET ORDER

1. In what ways was the market order well planned?
2. How could the market order have been improved?

PRINCIPLES OF COOKING

1. What principles of cooking were practiced because of the choice of menu?
2. What new principles were learned by the group during this laboratory session?

CLEANUP

1. In what ways was the cleanup managed efficiently?
2. In what ways could the cleanup have been managed better?

PERSONAL WORKING RELATIONSHIPS

1. In what ways did members of the group work well together?
2. How could the workload have been distributed more fairly?

✳ General Cleaning Duties

Taking responsibility for keeping the lab area clean helps learners realize that the lab is really theirs and not the teacher's. They are also more likely to take pride in it and cooperate in keeping it orderly. Cleanup charts can be used so duties are rotated every few days or once a week.

At the end of a unit or the term, devise a system that will ensure that all students have some responsibility in the final cleanup. For example, when classes have concluded their work in the lab, make a list of all the jobs that must be done in order to "close up shop." Include as many tasks as there are students in all the classes that have been using the lab. Then duplicate the list and cut one copy into strips. Each student draws a slip from a bag or box. On the master sheet, a copy of the list that has not been cut into strips, write students' names next to the jobs for which they are responsible. By doing this, you can check later to see how well each student has performed the assigned task. Those who have done poorly can be asked to do their jobs again, and those who have done well can be complimented and thanked.

✳ Liability and Safety Issues

As the educator, you are responsible for the safety of all the learners. During a laboratory experience, those responsibilities increase. You and your school, organization, or business can be held liable for a learner's injuries if you fail to demonstrate reasonable planning and supervision. This is considered legal negligence. Here are some of the general legal issues to keep in mind:

• **Learners.** You are responsible for teaching your students about safe practices and being certain they know safety procedures. You might teach about lab safety and then give written and/or performance tests. How much learners can be expected to know and remember varies with their age and any relevant disabilities. If your lab situation involves young children, they can't be expected to take much responsibility for their actions.

Figure 13-7

EVALUATION OF A CHILDREN'S BOOK

Name: _____ Group: _____ Date: _____

Directions: Rate the quality of the children's book you are evaluating by using the key below. Place the number of the word or words that best describe each characteristic in the space to the left. Write comments to justify your ratings in the space provided. Calculate the total score.

KEY:				
Excellent 5	Very Good 4	Good 3	Fair 2	Poor 1

SCORE	DESIRABLE CHARACTERISTICS	COMMENTS
	1. Simple plot/Theme	
	2. Vocabulary appropriate for age	
	3. Repetition/Rhyming	
	4. Bright primary colors	
	5. Variety of textures	
	6. Variety of shapes	
	7. Age-appropriate manipulatives	
	8. Durable	
	= Total Points	

Similarly, middle school students are less accountable than older learners. Besides age, you need to get to know your learners well enough to identify those whose behavior may pose a threat. This could range from someone with poor coordination to a student who has a behavioral disorder.

• **Supervision.** While learners are under your care, you are responsible for monitoring their actions and stopping any unsafe behavior. If you must call attention to an unsafe situation, take the time to also give the "why" behind your warning. Supervision also implies constant attentiveness to learners. You should never leave the room while students are in your care unless another responsible adult takes your place.

• **Facilities.** The area in which learners work must be safe. In a school, the administrative and maintenance staffs share that responsibility with you. You must bring problems to their attention and keep learners away from danger.

• **Equipment and materials.** You may often work in lab situations that involve the use of equipment and materials that can pose danger. While a food science, culinary, or textiles lab may include more hazards than a child care observation, consciously identify the possible safety hazards associated with each lesson, advise learners before they begin, and monitor them throughout. You might take additional steps, such as displaying a list of safety rules or posting safety checklists by potentially hazardous equipment.

Figure 13-8

CHECKLIST FOR PERFORMING CPR

Person being tested: _____

Evaluator: _____ Date: _____

Directions: For each step given below for performing CPR, rate a peer regarding whether he/she did each step correctly by placing a check in the appropriate column. Write comments to justify your ratings in the space provided. Total the numbers of *yes* and *no* checks.

COMPLETED THESE STEPS	YES	NO	COMMENTS
1. Checked safety of scene.			
2. Used universal precautions: gloves, mask.			
3. Determined consciousness of victim.			
4. Called 911, if appropriate.			
5. Positioned victim on back.			
6. Opened airway with a head-tilt, chin-lift, or jaw-thrust maneuver.			
7. Looked, listened, felt for breaths for 5-10 seconds.			
8. Ventilated twice when no breathing found.			
9. Checked for pulse for 10 seconds by palpating carotid artery.			
10. If no pulse, started chest compressions at rate of 15 compressions to 2 breaths.			
11. Rechecked pulse at one minute.			
12. Continued until help arrived or too tired to continue.			
Totals:			

- **Following the rules.** Unless you are self-employed, you will be working for a school, organization, institution, or business that will have safety rules of its own. Be sure that you know what these are and follow them consistently. For example, a school may allow only certain types of field trips or require written permission from parents or guardians for participation in out-of-class activities such as FCCLA. It may not allow teachers to drive students home because the teacher assumes legal liability by doing so. An organization may have clients sign release forms for certain activities. Note that permission and release forms don't negate liability on the part of an educator.

- **Emergency plans.** Be certain that you (and learners, if appropriate) know the location of emergency equipment and how to use it. Plan the route you will take if you must evacuate the building and set up a specific location for everyone to meet to make certain everyone is safe. Learn the Heimlich maneuver, take a first aid course, and become certified in CPR.

Keeping everyone safe in an educational setting can be a challenge. However, it's a responsibility you assume when you teach. Treat this topic with the importance it deserves.

The Pros and Cons of Lab Activities

Lab activities often present special problems for novice educators. Sometimes they don't realize how much longer it takes learners to complete a project than someone more experienced, or how much longer it takes a group to perform some tasks than it does a person working alone. If a group is large, there may not be room or sufficient equipment for everyone to work at once. That makes it difficult to provide continuous guidance. If you don't supervise adequately, the learners may not practice the skills they are supposed to be mastering. The freedom and informality of a lab situation can also lead to excessive talking and wasting time if learners aren't highly motivated or if the activity is not well-planned and organized.

Laboratory sessions are expensive, not only in a financial sense, but also in terms of time, material, equipment, facilities and physical energy you may expend. When lab activities become an everyday routine, learning diminishes in spite of the practical experience gained. If you rely too heavily on labs, you also fail to provide the variety and stimulating environment that challenge learners and foster creative activity.

On the other hand, labs can provide excellent opportunities for learning. Students can often have input into the teaching-learning process by direct participation in planning, organizing, and carrying out individual and group projects. Creativity and resourcefulness are encouraged as is resource management. Learners also have opportunities to generalize based on their experiences and to apply their generalizations in new situations.

Lab activities also give learners supervised and guided practice. Learners work with concrete problems rather than with abstractions. In addition, laboratory experiences may help clarify concepts for those who have difficulty with verbalization. For many, the greatest advantage of lab work may be the experience of working and learning to get along well with others in a democratic team-building situation.

 # Cooperative Learning Experiences

Cooperative learning is an educational strategy that is applicable to all subject areas, to all age groups, and to all types of programs. Educators use cooperative teaming because they believe working in teams increases learning, builds self-esteem, and improves interpersonal skills. Research suggests that many students enjoy learning more when they work in groups. In addition, employers often cite the ability to work well with others as a high priority; job success largely depends on the ability to work cooperatively. Cooperative learning has three principal components. As the components are described, you will see that cooperative learning meets the criteria for experiential learning. Students take part in relevant experiences that provide for reflection, application, and analysis. In these processes, problem solving and decision making are promoted on an individual and group basis.

- **Interdependence.** Group tasks are structured so participants must be concerned not only about their own learning, but also about what each member of the group learns. In other words, "We sink or swim together." This interdependence may be encouraged by a variety of techniques, such as the assigning of roles to individuals, requiring cooperative planning of their approach to the assignment, sharing of materials within the group, and preparing a joint answer or response by participants. If the group meets a collective goal, such as all members attaining a score of 80 or more using a selected rubric, then all members of the group receive the same recognition or reward from the leader or peers.
- **Individual accountability.** Each group member is personally responsible for learning the skills and facts related to the group task, and each member must be prepared to demonstrate mastery of the assigned work. The leader may randomly ask one member of the group to explain how to solve the problems, select one

answer sheet from the group to evaluate, or give a quiz to all group members. Learners receive individual scores for use in assigning grades or making awards.

- **Social skills.** Certain behaviors are needed for working successfully with others. Skills such as listening, sharing, encouraging, resolving conflict, and checking for understanding are necessary for group work to succeed. In cooperative learning, these skills are called "social skills." The educator includes instruction in social skills and has groups focus on learning them one at a time.

❋ Cooperative Learning as a Teaching Strategy

Within a lesson, educators usually use cooperative learning after they present new material. Working within their groups, students apply the knowledge that was taught during the lesson. For example, a Family and Consumer Sciences teacher might introduce the concept of self-esteem. After giving students the objectives and purposes of the lesson, the teacher presents basic information about self-esteem. This might include how self-esteem differs from self-concept, how self-esteem develops, and some characteristics of people with high and low self-esteem. Students might be asked to read selected pages from a textbook to learn additional information. Then, using the cooperative learning strategy, the teacher divides the students into small groups to develop a plan, based on a scenario, for improving a teen's self-esteem. The group reflects on what they already know and what they have just learned to develop the plan. After the group completes its work, some form of individual accountability is provided. For example, the instructor might randomly select one member of each group to report on the rationale of the group's plan. After all groups have reported, generalizations can be formulated, and students can use some of the ideas presented to boost their own or others' self-esteem.

Although cooperative learning is similar to group activities that educators have used for many years, it differs in several important ways. In cooperative learning activities, group members take responsibility for the learning of other members, as well as for themselves. They must have the opportunity for face-to-face interaction, explaining what they are learning to each other and helping each other understand and complete assignments. In addition, group members have to utilize social skills that are needed for working well together. The teaching methods for cooperative learning are specifically defined and structured.

❋ The Educator's Role

When cooperative learning strategies are used, learners no longer view their teacher as the main source of information and the solver of all problems. Instead, educators become facilitators or classroom managers as they organize content and learning environments to maximize learning for all involved. Teachers using cooperative learning have five major responsibilities:

- Grouping learners
- Planning lessons
- Emphasizing social skills
- Monitoring groups
- Evaluating learning

❋ *Grouping Learners*

As you plan cooperative learning activities, you must think through the logistics. You will have to make decisions about the size and composition of each group, the arrangement of the room, the distribution of materials, and the assignment of roles.

To determine the size of each group, consider the total group size, the characteristics of the learners, the topic, and the objectives. For example, for an audience seated in an auditorium, groups of two would probably work best. In a traditional classroom with 24 students, groups of four, with desks turned so that the students face each other, may easily be formed. For optimum participation, groups no larger than five are recommended; groups of three or four are usually preferable. Students often stay with the same group for several assignments to foster group commitment.

Some lessons lend themselves to assigning roles for individual group members. A group of three might include a leader, a recorder, and a checker. The leader would be in charge of total participation, the recorder responsible for the paperwork, and the checker responsible for making sure that all group members understand the concepts and skills studied. Some educators prefer these role assignments: facilitator, reporter, and summarizer.

❋ Planning Cooperative Learning Lessons

Regardless of the format you use for your lesson plans, specific and additional elements will need to be included in a cooperative learning plan. These include the following:

- **Criteria for success.** You need to decide how learners will know if they succeeded with assigned tasks. For example, the group work on self-esteem may be considered successful if each group lists specific ways for a teen to build self-esteem.
- **Interdependence.** Every cooperative learning experience needs a structure and a plan that require learners to work together to complete the task. This can be encouraged by having each group member responsible for teaching a procedure to the others, by limiting the materials available so group members have to share, by assigning roles or jobs to each group member, or by requiring a group product or worksheet that shows how all members have participated in completing the task.
- **Individual accountability.** The plan must include a way of assessing whether each learner achieved the objectives of the lesson and developed the required skills. This can be measured in a variety of ways, such as explaining a solution or demonstrating a skill, completing individual worksheets, sign-off signatures on a group project, or filling out a checklist or scorecard.
- **Social skills.** You need to structure expectations for specific social behaviors in each lesson. These expected behaviors are usually ones the group has agreed to work to improve, or you may have identified behaviors that need attention while observing the participants' interaction. For instance, you may have advised the

members of Group A to provide only constructive criticism to one another and to avoid sarcasm.
- **Processing.** The evaluation of progress toward both academic objectives and social skills objectives is important in cooperative learning. The term *processing* is used to indicate cooperative evaluation of group work. During processing, the group may assess how well participants are working together, plan strategies for improving their effectiveness, and set new goals for the next cooperative learning experience. Processing appears in a cooperative lesson plan in the position of closure in a traditional lesson plan.

❋ Emphasizing Social Skills

You and your learners together identify social skills the groups need to develop. Then prioritize them together so the learners concentrate on a few at a time. Social skills identified for development may include:

- Encouraging new ideas
- Giving everyone a chance to talk
- Working quietly
- Participating in the group
- Listening
- Respecting the opinions of others
- Sharing materials
- Fulfilling your role assignment
- Using supportive phrases to encourage others
- Contributing to the project
- Completing work on time
- Criticizing constructively
- Summarizing information
- Questioning ideas and suggestions
- Staying on task

❋ Monitoring Cooperative Groups

While the learners are working in their groups, you will be needed as a resource person, as a validator, and as an evaluator. Move around the room observing and helping groups as needed by:

- Clarifying the assignment
- Answering questions that arise
- Explaining words, processes, or equipment use
- Demonstrating a process or skill
- Encouraging the practice of social skills

- Questioning learners to promote higher-level thinking skills
- Reminding groups to follow the established guidelines

✻ Evaluating Cooperative Learning

Groups can discuss how the respective members were helpful to the group and what they could do next time to make the total group even more successful. For example, Group A may suggest ways to communicate more effectively with each other. Group B may develop a list of words and phrases to use to be more supportive of each other. Group C may decide to work on having certain members participate more.

Evaluation of progress toward academic objectives is an integral part of all teaching and learning. Educators are responsible for assessing every individual's progress toward reaching the objectives. Evaluating social behaviors that produce successful group work is also important in cooperative learning.

Some educators assign two grades to group members. They may evaluate and grade a group report, a decision on which the group has reached consensus, or a tangible creation like a display. In addition, educators give an assessment of each learner's individual work, such as responses to questioning, a worksheet, a demonstration, a homework assignment, or a quiz. In this way, learners are accountable for their group work and for individual mastery of the concept or skill.

Educators who use the two-grade method believe that the ability to work productively in a group is as important to life success as is mastery of technical skills and information. Thus a teacher may use cooperative learning groups when students are evaluating ways to discourage the use of alcohol and other drugs. A group grade could be assigned to each participant based on the group's presentation of a workable plan for action in the high school, middle school, or community. Then each student could be required to write a short essay on the harmful effects of alcohol and other drugs, for which they receive a second grade.

In teaching with cooperative learning groups, as in any teaching, feedback to students is important. Since feedback should occur as soon as possible, you will want to monitor work in progress and not wait for its completion. Both individuals and groups need to know the quality of their work to assure optimum learning.

Building Your Professional Portfolio

Analyzing Experiential Learning. Using an existing activity plan, show how you could modify the activity to use experiential learning effectively. Prepare a written explanation of your changes.

Lab Observation. Observe an educator conducting a lab experience. Identify the type of lab and its topic. Evaluate the strengths and limitations of the management processes used in carrying out the lab. Propose changes you would make if you were conducting the lab.

Lab Orientation. Develop a plan to orient your learners to the laboratory used for a specific subject area. Include the points you would cover and any activities you would use prior to involvement in the first experimental lab activity.

Planning Cooperative Learning. Plan a lesson based on the principles of cooperative learning. Explain how you will involve students in all steps of the process. Justify your plan for grading students on the lesson.

Chapter 14

Games for Learning

Do games have a place in educational settings? Of course they do! The activities that learners enjoy are often what they remember best—and people do enjoy playing games. While young learners spend more time playing games, the popularity of television game shows is proof that they're enjoyed by learners of all ages.

Generally, games are contests among several players operating under a set of rules. Many games foster important skills that come from working as part of a team. There are some games, however, that learners can play alone, such as many computer games. The objective of an educational game, whether played alone or with others, is to win while applying knowledge and understanding of learned material to a situation. Material that has already been presented in a different manner can be reinforced with game playing.

Games can make teaching more fun for you and the learning experience exciting for the people you are teaching. There are dozens of game ideas that can be modified for educational settings. Whether your teaching arena is outdoors at a cystic fibrosis camp or in a middle school classroom, most of your learners will welcome the chance to play an occasional game.

Advantages of Games for Learning

Games offer the advantage of being applicable to learners of various ages and ability levels. If people are grouped on teams, individuals of differing abilities can help each other work toward their shared goal—winning. That helps foster an appreciation of differences. Active involvement, which speeds learning, is a hallmark of games. Games that simulate real-life situations allow the learners to experience some of the daily responsibilities, decisions, consequences, and pressures inherent in life, while dealing with the situations apart from the complex environment in which they may normally exist.

You will need to choose games to match specific learning objectives, keeping the ages and interests of your group in mind. For example, a card game that focuses on fact mastery can make that type of learning more interesting for young teens. Other games can be structured to help learners practice decision making, problem solving, exploration of new ideas, teamwork, creativity, and other higher-level thinking skills. The ability to think quickly and clearly on your feet is fostered through the use of games. Reinforcement of subject matter content is the common thread among educational games.

Learners who might otherwise be unlikely to connect to the material you are teaching may be motivated by a game. Some educators find that once they start to play games with their learners, there are frequent requests for more. Just remember that as with other methods of teaching, if games are overused, they become less effective teaching tools.

 # Guidelines for Using Games

Paying attention to some basic guidelines can help ensure the success of learning games. The following list will keep you on track and make implementing games fun and educational:

1. Rules for playing the game need to be established and understood by players. You can create the rules, adapt them from a common game, or have the learners devise them. Having the learners develop the rules of the game provides a certain level of ownership, which tends to enhance learning. You might display the rules on a poster. Without clear and concise rules, time is often wasted and the educational value lost because of confusion or arguing.
2. Be sure learners clearly understand the objective of the game and what they should review or learn as a result of the activity.
3. Plan a game only if it fits into the curriculum, and learners have the necessary background knowledge to play it successfully.
4. For team games, use fair systems for dividing the group into teams. Avoid those in which learners choose other team members.

5. Have all the materials for the game ready when it's time to begin, including enough materials for all participants.
6. Involve learners in game development, when appropriate. You could have them write the questions for games or develop other components. This helps reinforce the content material and can also save you time.
7. Match the questions or activities for the game to the ability levels of the learners. Don't overwhelm lower-ability students or discourage noncompetitive ones with overly complicated rules or questions. Much of the motivation that comes from playing a learning game results from the feelings of participation and success.
8. Have reference materials available so participants can check the accuracy of any disputed answers.
9. Monitor the group while a game is going on. If your learners are working in small groups, circulate to see how they are doing, and guide the learning process as appropriate. Insist that they treat one another with respect.
10. Have a system for keeping track of scores for teams or individuals. Writing the scores in a highly visible place will help everyone to keep track.
11. Expect some noise. This comes with the territory when you are playing games. Check ahead to make sure your group won't be disrupting an important activity in an adjoining area.
12. Giving small prizes (a pencil, an apple, a sticker, a privilege) for winning can be motivating, but don't let the desire to win overshadow the opportunity to learn. A balance must be achieved, especially when teamwork is being promoted.
13. Discuss the game and its content afterwards. Note any concepts that the learners had trouble with during the game. Use these as a basis for your discussion questions after the game is over. Consider additional follow-up activities to help reinforce these concepts.

Types of Games

The assortment of games found in a toy store or toy department is amazing, as is the array of past and present television games. Discussing the various categories of games with your learners may trigger their ideas for games to play. You probably won't play the actual game, but rather modify it to reflect what you hope your learners have achieved. Most games fall into the following categories:

- **Card games.** Examples include Rummy, Memory, Match 'Em, and Fish
- **Computer games.** A great way to include situational and more complex games
- **Board games.** Base them on traditional games like Bingo or Tic-Tac-Toe or commercial board games
- **Word and pencil-and-paper games.** Endless options exist, such as crossword puzzles, incomplete stories, word searches, spell downs, letter scrambles, and fill-in-the-blank games
- **Sports games.** Can be based on relays, softball, basketball, and kickball
- **TV games.** Look for popular ones that could be adapted
- **Action games.** Such as charades and others that rely on movement

Examples of and directions for a variety of these games follow. They provide ideas for adapting traditional games to the learning arena and developing unique ones. Use your imagination to develop additional ideas.

✷ Card Games

Familiar card games can be used as an effective form of review. Rules can be simple or complex, depending on the specific learning objectives for the lesson. After a card game has been played once or twice, participants may want to change the rules for variety. Games become more interesting as learner involvement increases.

✷ *General Preparation for Card Games*

Create a card game by making a deck of cards with words or pictures, depending on the needs of the particular game. The cards might describe characteristics of children at various age levels, different fibers, clothing styles, careers, employment skills, types of wounds, or various foods. As an example, pictures of foods that are good sources of one or more of the following nutrients can be used: protein, fats, carbohydrates, vitamin A, B-complex vitamins, vitamin C, iron, and calcium. Some empty-calorie foods may be included. You also can include wild cards for added variety.

Make cards by cutting pictures of food from magazines or generating them on the computer, then attaching them to small index cards or inexpensive playing cards from an actual deck. If you need several sets of cards, use a master sheet to draw and label sketches of foods in rectangles the size of playing cards. Duplicate the sheets on card stock and then cut them apart. You can laminate cards or cover them with clear, self-adhesive plastic for longer life. While food and nutrition is used as the content area to illustrate many of the following examples, child development, consumer issues, first-aid strategies, communication, clothing care, furniture styles, and stress management strategies are a few of the many topics for which these games could be adapted.

✷ *Match 'Em*

Match 'Em is an easy game to assemble and to explain to players. One use of the game might be to identify common equivalent measures used in food preparation, as in this example.

Objective: Accumulate the most matched pairs of cards, based on content knowledge.

Preparation: Make a set of 30 playing cards consisting of 15 pairs. For each pair, write a measurement on one card and an equivalent measure on the second. For example, one card may have one-half cup, and another card, eight tablespoons. For participants with limited knowledge of English, you might use sketches to represent measurements. The finished deck must include fifteen sets of equivalents.

Directions: Lay all game cards face down. A player turns two cards face up on each play. If the cards reveal equivalent measurements (not identical), the two cards are placed in a stack in front of that player. If the cards prove to be equivalents, the participant gets another turn. If a player doesn't turn up two equivalents (or recognize them as such), the cards are replaced, face down, and the next player takes a turn. When all of the cards are matched, the matches should be checked against an answer sheet. The winner is the learner with the most matches.

A variation of this game can be played to enhance vocabulary by matching terms that have very similar meanings, such as self-esteem and self-confidence, encouragement and support, creativity and imagination, uncertainty and apprehension. It's also possible to play Match 'Em with food characteristics. For instance, players could match names of herbs and spices with their respective characteristics and uses.

✷ *Four of a Kind*

This game requires students to understand associations among similar items. At the same time, it is based on content knowledge. In the following example, nutrition is the topic.

Objective: Make as many "books" as possible. Each book consists of four related cards.

Preparation: Make sets of four cards that have a common theme, such as foods that represent good sources of the same nutrient or foods from the same food group. Wild cards can represent any food in a group or any nutrient designated by the player holding that card.

Directions:
1. Divide participants into groups of three or four players.
2. The group dealer gives each player seven cards. A discard pile is formed by turning one card face up. Place the remaining cards face down in the center of the table.
3. As players take turns, they may draw two cards from the pile that is face down or pick up the entire discard pile. The discard pile may be picked up only if the top card can be used to form a book. After completing a move, the player must put one card face up on the discard pile.
4. Books are placed on the table as they're made. This may be done only during a player's turn, not during anyone else's turn.
5. The game ends when a player discards and has no playing cards left. Play is also ended when there are no cards on the pile from which to draw and when the discard pile can't be picked up by anyone. The player with the greatest number of books wins the game.

✷ *Going Fishing*

This popular card game can be adapted for many uses. Players must collect cards to complete a set of something. These could be foods from each of the Food Guide Pyramid groups. In interior design, the object might be to collect cards with floor coverings, wall treatments, window coverings, and furniture styles that all are characteristic of a certain style period, such as Early American.

Objective: Select cards that make a complete set.

Preparation: Prepare cards with pictures or words that represent parts of concepts players are to collect. You may choose to include "distractor" cards that don't fit into any of the concept sets.

Directions:
1. Divide participants so each group has two or more players.
2. Scatter cards face down on the table.
3. Each player draws any five cards from those on the table. The remaining cards are left face down.
4. During each player's turn, one card is drawn and one card is discarded face down with the others.
5. Play continues until one player completes a set and is the winner.

✳ Nutrition Points

While this game is devised to reinforce nutrition knowledge, it could be adapted for other uses.

Objective: Identify correctly the Food Guide Pyramid group, the number of servings suggested daily, and the function of a major nutrient in the food appearing on the card.

Preparation: Prepare cards showing a variety of foods. The difficulty level can be adjusted by the types of foods included and the amount of nutrition information requested.

Directions:
1. Cluster players in groups of two or more players.
2. Stack cards face down. Each person turns up a card from the pile.
3. Score in the following manner:
   a. One point for identifying the food group of the item pictured on the card.
   b. Two points for stating the number of servings suggested daily from that food group.
   c. Three points for telling the function of a major nutrient in the food.
   d. Subtract the specified number of points for incorrect answers.
4. Once the players have gone through the entire deck, the person with the highest number of points is the winner.

✳ Trading Game

This game helps students see the relationships among similar items. It can be adapted to any subject.

Objective: Collect cards that are all in the same food group or are nutrient-dense with the same vitamin or mineral.

Preparation: For each food group, prepare 12-20 cards (depending on the number of players) that show foods from the group. As appropriate, include foods with low nutrient density.

Directions:
1. Divide players in groups of three or more learners.

2. Deal the entire deck of cards to the players.
3. Players trade cards in any direction across the table by holding the card or cards face down and calling out the number of cards they want to trade. A player trades with a person who wants to exchange a like number of cards.
4. The first person to collect nine cards in any one of the food pyramid groups receives ten points. At the end of the game, two points are deducted for any card showing foods with low nutrient density. The first player to reach 100 points is the winner.

✳ Truth or Bluff

With Truth or Bluff, learners identify characteristics of content they have studied. It is also a strategy game.

Objective: Get rid of all the cards in your hand.

Preparation: Prepare cards with examples of the content you are reviewing.

Directions:
1. Divide the group so there are three or more players per game.
2. The entire deck of cards is dealt.
3. In turn, each player places one to four cards face down on the table and states what the cards are. For example, a player might say, "These two cards are examples of aerobic exercise." This may or may not be true.
4. The player on the left can either accept the statement or challenge it. If the statement is accepted, play proceeds to the next person. The discarded cards remain on the table. When the play is challenged, the cards must be shown. If the truth was told, the challenging player must take the cards laid down by the preceding player plus all the cards in the discard pile. If the cards were misrepresented, the player who tried to bluff must take these cards and the discard pile.
5. The first player without any cards wins the game.

✳ Computer Games

Various companies and individual developers offer games that you may want to purchase for your program. Many of these games require higher-level thinking skills such as analysis and decision making. It is in these areas that computer games are particularly useful. For example, learners may learn to develop a monthly budget and then use it as situations occur during the month. Other software games may be primarily reviews of facts or vocabulary.

Choosing appropriate programs is more difficult than with a product you can see to evaluate. Often, you will have only advertising information, a written review, or the recommendation of another educator to go on in making a decision. You can also call or visit the website of the company that developed the software for additional information. Sometimes a preview is available.

Chapter 15 gives additional information on choosing software, but the questions below are also helpful in evaluating computer games:

- What is the purpose of the game? Does this fit with your instructional needs?
- Is the game appropriate for the age level of your learners?
- How much time will it take your learners to play the game? Does the time used match the importance of the content and anticipated amount of learning?
- Is the game appropriate for individual use, group use, or both? How does that match equipment availability?
- How can you assess learner progress based on the game?

Computer software is available that makes it easy to develop some types of games on your own. For example, one for word games might allow you to make crossword puzzles or word searches more quickly. In addition, some of your learners may be highly skilled on the computer. You might offer them extra credit for designing a learning game that could be played by the group.

✳ Board Games

Board games are usually played in small groups. A variety of formats are possible and can be adapted to many topics. The three examples shown here lend themselves to most subject areas. Learners can create their own boards and questions for the game.

Zingo

This is an action-oriented game that can be used to review terminology. Zingo can be used in many situations such as naming pieces of clothing construction and kitchen equipment, identifying nutrients and wellness strategies, and citing etiquette practices.

Objective: To cover a row of answers on the Zingo grid in a vertical, diagonal, or horizontal line by answering questions correctly.

Preparation: A card is needed for every player. Each Zingo card should consist of 16 different words or terms written in a grid. (See the condensed version, *Figure 14-1* on page 195.) Not all cards will have the same terms. Learners can be given a list of words or terms, and they can create their own cards by writing in words or terms they select from the list in any order they desire. For cards that contain identical terms, their placement on the grid should be different. Small objects such as pennies or small squares of construction paper can be used as markers to cover responses. You also need a series of question cards corresponding to the words or terms on the learners' Zingo cards.

Directions: This game is a variation of bingo. When a question is read, players cover the correct answer if the answer is on their card. When someone calls out "Zingo," check the accuracy of the winner's answers. If there was an incorrect choice, the questioning continues until someone else wins. Enhance learning by asking students to explain why a choice was incorrect and by giving additional examples to illustrate correct responses.

Figure 14-1 ━━━━━━━ ZINGO ━━━━━━━

Body language	Gestures	Poise	Attention
Conversation	Listening	Respect	Timing
Eye contact	Grooming	Posture	Introductions
Facial expression	Grammar	Smile	Rambling

✳ *Tic-Tac-Toe*

Tic-Tac-Toe is a simple game to set up and play in a group. It can be used with questions on any topic and at varying levels of difficulty. By preparing separate question lists or sets of question cards, the game can be used with several different classes.

Objective: To complete a sequence of three Xs or Os in any direction by answering content questions correctly and working with a team on strategy.

Preparation: The nine-square grid for the game can be drawn on the chalkboard, posterboard, a fabric board, or can be reproduced on paper if multiple groups are planned. If posterboard is used, cardboard Xs and Os with tacky adhesive on the back can serve as markers for the squares. For use on a fabric board, cut the letters from felt. If learners are to play the game independently, write content-related questions on cards. If it will be played as a group, questions can be on a list.

Directions:

1. Divide the learners into teams. You or a learner can serve as the questioner and scorekeeper.
2. To begin the game, the questioner asks one member of the first team a question. Team members aren't allowed to consult each other about answers.
3. When a player answers a question correctly, the team can place their mark on the grid. Team members discuss among themselves where to place the marker.
4. Whether or not the question was answered correctly, the other team takes the next turn. When there's a wrong answer, a player on the other team attempts to answer the same question. Turns for answering questions are rotated among team members.

5. Five points are given to each team for every marker it has on the grid. A bonus of ten points is awarded if a team achieves Tic-Tac-Toe. The team with the most points wins.

✳ *Go Forth*

Go Forth is a board game involving skill and chance. The object of the game is to answer correctly as many questions as possible. It can be played by two or more players, plus one questioner-scorekeeper. Participants can help assemble the game.

Objective: Accumulate the most star cards by the end of the game by answering questions correctly.

Preparation:

1. **Board**—The playing board should be at least 9 inches by 14 inches. Use posterboard or cardboard for a firm backing. The example on page 196 can be used as a guide. Sketches and phrases should be keyed to the subject matter.
2. **Number cards**—Make the cards for the game from colored construction paper or posterboard. Laminate or cover them with clear adhesive paper for greater durability. You will need four number cards, each approximately 1½ inches square. Write the numbers 1 through 4, one on each card.
3. **Star cards**—Stars are drawn on 1-inch-square cards. Approximately 50 cards are needed.
4. **Dot cards**—Dots are also drawn on 1-inch-square cards. Approximately 50 are needed.
5. **Question cards**—Game questions should be printed on one side of cards that measure about 2 inches by 3 inches or on small index cards. On each card, write a content question and the number of spaces that a player should advance for

giving a correct answer. Label one-third of the cards in the deck with 1, one-third with 2, and the remainder with 3. The numbers may or may not relate to the difficulty level of the questions.

6. **Markers**—Choose some objects to serve as markers for players' board positions. You may be able to relate them to the subject area being studied.

Directions: Shuffle the number and the question cards separately and place them on the board in the appropriate spaces. Appoint a questioner-scorekeeper to read the questions that are drawn by the players. Players shouldn't look at the cards.

1. Draw a number card and advance the number of spaces indicated.
2. Select a question card and hand it to the questioner-scorekeeper to be read aloud. If the question is answered correctly, the player draws a star card. If the question is answered incorrectly, a dot card is taken.
3. Continue to draw question cards, taking turns.
4. If players land on a crossover, they have a choice of continuing on the same path or taking a shortcut.

5. When players land on a "count your dots" square, they count the number of dots received for incorrect answers. If they have five or more, they go back to the starting position and begin again. If players have ten or more dots when they arrive at the finish, they must start over.
6. The game ends when the first player crosses the finish line. The player with the most stars is the winner.

✳ Word and/or Paper-and-Pencil Games

Word games give learners a chance to enhance spelling, grammar, and language skills, in addition to content. These can be completed individually or in groups. Some provide verbal practice and others are done silently.

✳ *Hidden Clues Puzzles*

Hidden Clues is a word game that can be used in a variety of ways and in different subject areas. The following example is designed for consumer economics. Learners, as well as the educators, can develop these puzzles or the clues for them.

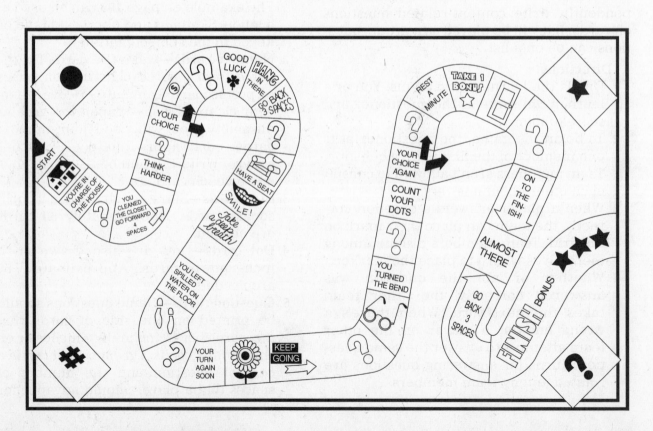

Objective: Unscramble each clue. Next, unscramble the circled letters in the clues to form a related mystery term.

Preparation: First, choose an important concept consisting of approximately five to twelve letters. This becomes the mystery word or term. Next, select words that are a subconcept of or related to that major concept. Each of these supporting words must contain at least one of the letters in the mystery term. Next, scramble the letters in the related words. Circle the letter in each scrambled word that will be used to form the mystery term. Finally, add directions and a space to write the mystery term.

Directions: Unscramble each of the following scrambled-letter clues made to form a word. All words will relate to a common theme. Then unscramble the circled letters to form a term that relates to all the individual clues.

EHKCC	Ⓞ _ _ _ _
TENITRES	_ _ _ _ _ Ⓞ _ _
TPYNAME	_ _ _ _ Ⓞ _ _
TBDE	Ⓞ _ _ _
PPNRLICEI	_ _ Ⓞ _ _ _ _ _ _
OTEN	_ _ Ⓞ _
RYLAAS	_ _ _ _ Ⓞ _
ONAL	_ _ Ⓞ _
TSOC	_ _ _ Ⓞ
IFCNANE	_ Ⓞ _ _ _ _ _
NOYEM	_ _ Ⓞ _ _
RCGEHA	_ _ _ _ Ⓞ _

Now arrange the circled letters to discover the mystery answer. These two words are important to every consumer.

_____ _____

Answers

check	salary
interest	loan
payment	cost
debt	finance
principle	money
note	charge

The mystery answer is: *credit rating*.

After the puzzle has been solved, discuss the relationship of each of the word clues to the mystery answer. For an added challenge, have learners formulate a generalization using some of the scrambled clue words.

✳ Crossword Puzzles

Crossword puzzles can be excellent devices for student self-evaluation and for reviewing key concepts of previously covered subject matter. Visual learners who excel in language arts or particularly enjoy working crossword puzzles may like to make one to share with classmates. This can also be done in small groups. The discussion that relates to making the puzzles serves to reinforce subconcepts of the subject matter.

Objective: To use content knowledge to solve the clues and correctly fill in the puzzle.

Preparation: Choose a concept for the puzzle topic that is broad enough in scope to have many words associated with it. For instance, you could build a puzzle around "prenatal development," but "nutrition for newborns" would be too narrow. Then list as many words or terms as possible that are related to the topic and that learners should know from the lesson. For ideas, use a book index or thumb through the pages of a text or reference book.

Next, for all the terms in the final crossword puzzle, write clues as definitions, questions, or fill-in-the-blank statements—but only one type per puzzle to avoid confusion. Be sure the clues are clearly worded and consistent in format. If the completion format is used, place the blanks at or near the ends of the sentences. See page 91 for more information about writing completion, or fill-in-the-blank, items.

Puzzle-generating software is available that will fit selected terms into a grid, number the cells appropriately, and fill in the unused blank spaces in the puzzle. It's also possible to develop puzzles by hand using graph paper with large squares.

Directions: Learners can work on the puzzles individually or in small groups. Provide an answer key for them to check their completed puzzles.

✳ Sports Games

Learners of all ages may enjoy games based on sports. Adaptations of baseball, football, and soccer are easy to do. Students also enjoy relay games. Sometimes these games can be played outdoors which adds variety to the setting. If that isn't possible, try to rearrange your indoor space to resemble a real playing field.

Many of these games can be played at a range of difficulty levels. Simply write the questions at the level that matches the objective.

✳ *Three Strikes and You're Out*

This is a team game played like baseball. However, players answer questions individually.

Objective: As a team, score the most runs during the game by the team's players correctly answering questions.

Preparation: Set up the room or playing area to represent a baseball diamond. Designate a home plate; 1st, 2nd, and 3rd bases; and a pitcher's mound. Develop at least 40 questions on index cards. You may write questions and answers related to the topic or have the teams write them, as noted below.

Directions:

1. Divide the group into two teams. Let teams select a name and a slogan.
2. If you choose, have each team write at least 20 game questions and the answers, focusing on the material to be reviewed. Once you have checked the questions and answers, have teams transfer each question to one side of an index card with the answer on the opposite side. Label each question as a base hit, double, triple, or home run.
3. Have teams choose which team is up first and have each team designate a line-up sequence for being "at bat."
4. Put all the questions in a container at the pitcher's mound.
5. Team members in the outfield spread themselves around the "field" with one person standing at the pitcher's mound.
6. The team that is "up" sends its first person to home plate.

7. The pitcher (you or a team-designated team member) randomly draws a card, tells if it's for a single, double, triple, or home run, and then reads the question to the first batter.
8. If the batter answers correctly, this player proceeds to the appropriate base. If the batter supplies a wrong answer, it's an out. After three outs, the teams switch. Runs are created as batters are pushed around the bases by other correct answers.
9. Keep track of the number of runs on a "scoreboard" so all can see. Occasionally announce the score. Encourage cheering and support for right answers. The game is over after a predetermined number of innings or time runs out.
10. Review the concepts that seemed difficult for the learners during the course of the game.

✳ TV Games

Since the beginning of television, there have probably been dozens of television game shows that could serve as the basis for an educational game. Watch the popular game shows and modify them to meet your group's needs.

You might divide learners into small groups and have them develop questions for a game modeled after *Who Wants to Be a Millionaire?* For each question they should provide three incorrect answers along with the right answer. Assist the groups as needed in determining the level of difficulty of their questions. The toughest questions, of course, should be reserved for the end of the game when the "monetary" awards (usually points) are highest. During game play, allow the contestant in the hot seat to consult a friend for one answer, poll the audience one time for their response to the question, and have two incorrect answers taken away from the four possible answers provided.

Other favorite television games that can serve as useful models are *Jeopardy*, *Price Is Right*, *Family Feud*, and *Wheel of Fortune*. All were on the air for many years or continue to be televised on a regular basis. Learners will enjoy playing games with which they are most familiar. However, avoid games that belittle losing players.

✳ Action Games

Games that involve a lot of action can be fun for many learners, especially individuals whose strength is the body/kinesthetic intelligence. (See pages 64-67 for more on multiple intelligences.) Action games help to motivate, involve, and keep these learners on task. Charades is an example of an action game. You may take the same concept and create a drawing game.

✳ *Charades*

Charades is a familiar game based on guessing the correct answer from the actions of others. Here, learning is extended by requiring players to give key information about the answer.

Objective: Determine the action being pantomimed and identify the key points that a person in that situation should remember.

Preparation: Think of situations related to the topic that might be acted out. To have a broad selection of topics, playing this game near the end of a unit works best. Examples might be a job candidate dressing for an interview, a careful shopper reading labels at the supermarket, someone taking care of a sick child, a person exhibiting patience, or a cook separating eggs. You may ask each learner to submit an idea or two. Write the situations to be depicted on cards or slips of paper. On a separate paper, list the situations plus the key points that should be identified with each situation. For example, an answer might be the information a shopper should look for on a nutrition label.

Directions:

1. Have individuals or teams pick a situation to act out. This can work either as individuals acting or with two or more teams. Of course, all acting will take place without words. With teams, the participants confer and the team that comes up with the answer first is awarded the point. If the group is small, individuals can act out to the others; individual scores are kept for successful acting strategies.
2. Determine a system for teams or individuals to share answers when they think they have the right answer. Raising a flag or sign can be better than shouting out guesses.
3. If the team correctly identifies the situation, they have three minutes to collectively determine the key points for it.
4. Have a system for tallying scores.

 ## Using Games Effectively

Games, used appropriately, can increase learning. The emphasis should always be on learning while having fun. While preparing games may be time-consuming, the outcome in terms of learner involvement is usually evident. You may develop reusable games over time. Remember that learners can participate in developing the questions, answers, and other components of games. If orchestrated carefully, this participation can be as educational as the actual playing of the game. Creativity and imagination are important as you link games to objectives and learning in the cognitive, affective, and psychomotor domains.

Building Your Professional Portfolio

Learner preferences. Interview learners of different ages to determine the educational games they most enjoy participating in. What types of games don't they like? Based on your findings, develop suggestions for educators teaching various age groups.

Game development. Develop two games other than those detailed in this chapter. Choose from two different game categories: card, computer, board, word and pencil-and-paper games, sports, TV, and action games.

Computer games. Analyze three computer games that might be used in your educational setting. Begin by developing an evaluation device. After you have completed your analysis, write a review of each game that would be helpful for other educators considering purchase.

Using a game. Implement a game with a group of learners. Summarize their reactions and make suggestions for using the game another time based on your observations and their feedback.

Chapter **15**

Learning with Technology

Paul Buzzell, M.S.
Information Systems Specialist,
  Nutrition and Food Sciences
University of Vermont

Stephen J. Pintauro, Ph.D.
Associate Professor,
  Nutrition and Food Sciences
University of Vermont

Many experts acknowledge that the U. S. educational system is in the process of being fundamentally reshaped by technology. Although the Internet has existed since the early 1970s and personal computers have long been in many classrooms, they initially had relatively little impact on educational reform.

What prompted this revolutionary change? The answer can be traced to the development of World Wide Web browser software. It allowed personal computers to evolve from machines used to perform word processing, data analysis, or graphics manipulation to global information and communication networking tools. Even computer novices can easily search and access information from anywhere in the world with Internet access. It is the availability of information on the Internet that will make the greatest difference in education.

In your career as an educator, you will undoubtedly be using computers, the Internet, and other technology in many ways. You may help learners with multimedia projects and lead them on research projects using the Web. Most colleges offer distance education courses and there are virtual high schools—all online. You may well teach an online course to learners whom you may never meet face to face. To do so, you will need not only technological knowledge, but also top-notch communication skills.

 ## The Web

Today, the World Wide Web, more commonly referred to simply as the Web, permeates all aspects of modern society. In very basic terms, the Web is simply a means of retrieving information over the Internet.

At the heart of its tremendous potential as an information retrieval tool is its incorporation of *hypertext links*. That is, by simply clicking on a linked reference in one Web document, you can move directly to a related document located elsewhere on the Internet. Of course, the Web isn't limited to text documents. The Web is capable of delivering a complete multimedia experience to the user. It should be recognized, however, that this remarkable tool is still in its infancy. Educators are just beginning to ascertain the best role for the Web in improving education. However, one fundamental change is clearly emerging. The Web is fueling a shift from a teaching paradigm to a learning paradigm. The role of the educator is becoming less of a dispenser of information to more of a guide in the learning process. With the increased reliance on technology for relaying knowledge, educators are becoming more available to guide learners through the higher levels of learning, such as analysis and evaluation.

Making such a shift, however, requires a substantial commitment and investment in hardware, software, and, most importantly, in teacher education. The Web takes the learning process well beyond the confines of schools. In this regard, the federal government has taken steps to ensure equal and fair access to the benefits of technology for everyone, particularly schools, through the Telecommunications Act of 1996. This legislation has helped bring Internet access to communities, agencies, and schools across the country. The technology continues to evolve with the emphasis on improving the speed and scope of Internet access.

As an educator, you are likely to use the Web often and for a variety of purposes. You may bookmark some websites, such as those of professional organizations, because you trust you will find relevant, accurate updates in your field. Sometimes you may search for teaching ideas. You can tap into the wealth of information available from the U.S. Government at http://www.firstgov.gov. Often you will be searching for specific content for lesson development or an Internet-based activity. Clearly, the Web is one of the most important teaching tools available.

 ## Equipping Your Learning Environment

Before planning technology-based lessons or presentations for your own educational setting, you will need to assess your resources. These include equipment in your classroom or office plus whatever other equipment is available in your school, business, or agency. Your list might include computers; printers; other devices such as scanners and digital cameras; network and/or Internet wiring; and, of course, funding. This chapter is designed to help, regardless of your resources. There are two basic scenarios: you can either work with what you have or purchase some new equipment. Both possibilities will be addressed.

Most schools, businesses, and agencies have computer specialists responsible for purchasing and maintaining technology equipment. Such a specialist can be an extremely valuable resource for you in maintaining and using existing equipment, as well as gaining new resources. Develop a positive relationship with the specialist in your workplace.

✳ Maximizing the Equipment You Have

Attempting to provide computer access to the greatest number of learners, some programs and school districts have purchased low-end computers that are destined to become obsolete within a few years. While many program budgets don't have funds earmarked for adding new equipment to the learning environment, even the tightest of budgets can usually fund minor technological upgrades that will help improve the computers' performance.

✳ *Optimizing Memory*

Getting the most out of the equipment you have should be the first step. Many times maintenance can improve performance and increase your options. If a computer is running very slowly or you are encountering memory errors, replacing the computer may be unnecessary. Computer memory isn't perfect. Occasionally, during storage or retrieval of information, information is lost. This could be compared to you "forgetting" information and, although computer memory is much more reliable than a person's, "forgetting" does occur from time to time. The missing information may not be noticed at times. However, the information lost could also be an integral component of your operating system—rendering the computer useless until repaired. As a hard drive ages or is exposed to harsh conditions, the incidence of information loss can increase. However, routine maintenance can vastly increase the life span of a computer by decreasing information loss.

Most operating systems have maintenance programs to help optimize your system. These include Windows *Scan Disk* and *Disk Defragmenter* and *Disk First Aid* on a Mac. These programs check for errors on your disk and/or organize the information on the disk. These errors could make it difficult or impossible for information to be read from the disk—either due to the disk itself having a faulty section (similar to a scratch on a CD), or information being occasionally stored incorrectly by the computer onto the disk. A defragmenter organizes the information on a disk. For example, many applications or programs have multiple files. If a disk isn't organized, these multiple files could be spread throughout the disk. It makes sense that a computer would perform more efficiently when files used in conjunction with one another are stored near each other on the hard drive disk. A simple analogy would be to compare your hard drive to your desk. Keeping your pencil near a pad of paper rather than on the floor would be much more efficient.

Having a disorganized disk with errors isn't the only cause of computers not performing at their best. If speed is still a limiting factor with your computer after running the maintenance programs, the amount of available *RAM* (random access memory) may be the problem. To check the available RAM on a system, try searching the **Help** menu using the following keywords: "resources," "memory," and/or "RAM." Unnecessary applications may be tying up your computer's RAM. Preventing these programs from running will free up more RAM, adding a little speed. This can be accomplished by either deleting the programs or simply preventing them from automatically starting at boot up.

✳ Avoiding Computer Viruses

Viruses are also a maintenance concern. A computer virus is simply a small piece of computer code or programming that, if allowed to gain access to your computer, may result in anything from erasing some of your files to completely locking up the system. Computers connected to the Internet or a network, and especially those used for e-mail, are most susceptible to infection by viruses. This is due to the fact that a virus often, *but not always*, comes in the form of an e-mail attachment. Scanning your system for viruses is a must—even if the computer isn't connected to the Internet. CDs and floppy disks can also transport viruses. Since viruses come in many forms, an infection may not be apparent immediately. As with all other aspects of computer maintenance, prevention is the primary goal. Many virus-scanning software applications automatically scan all files for viruses, including checking e-mail attachments before they are opened and can infect the computer.

Other physical factors can affect computer performance. Avoid exposing equipment to environmental factors that could shorten its life span. For more details, read the literature that came with the equipment. For example, try not to set a computer up in a window or near a heater where it could be exposed to direct sunlight, precipitation, or temperature fluctuations.

✳ Upgrading Existing Computers vs. Buying New

Upgrading the computers you have may be a cost-effective alternative to purchasing new ones. Another option is the purchase of used computers. As local companies replace their computers, you might obtain their used computers free or at a reasonable cost. Your computer specialist can help determine if such computers would be appropriate for your needs.

Adding more hard drive space or more memory in the form of RAM to an existing computer is a relatively inexpensive way to modestly improve a computer's performance and useable life span. However, processor speed, measured in GHz (Gigahertz), or MHz (Megahertz) in older computers, is often the most limiting factor in computer performance. Processor speed is also the most expensive to upgrade. For this reason, it's advisable to weigh the speed of a computer more heavily than other characteristics when purchasing.

Ports are plugs, located on the exterior of a computer, into which various devices can be connected. The more free ports there are on a computer, the greater are your options for adding compatible devices. Also, inside the computer's CPU (central processing unit), you should find additional "slots" for connecting various types of hardware devices. Avoid buying computers with few or no free slots because that will limit your future ability to upgrade the system.

Laptop computers are a portable alternative to desktop computers. Many people—including educators and students—find this convenience very useful. However, there are some tradeoffs. Limitations of laptops include:

- Low number of free ports and slots.
- Less flexibility when adding hardware.
- Parts typically cost more than desktop parts.
- More complicated power source (laptop batteries are expensive).
- Initial cost is greater than a desktop computer.

Even smaller technologies, such as *PDAs*—Personal Digital Assistants—can be useful. They combine small size with abilities such as scheduling, word processing for entering notes, and even add-ons, such as a temperature probe to record experiment data. While the screen size is quite small, information can be transferred from a PDA to a laptop or desktop computer. Such technology is expected to continue to expand and improve and new devices are likely to become available. It's important to keep up with new equipment that could be used for more effective teaching and learning.

❋ Networking

Computers aren't the only expense to consider when equipping a learning environment. There are matters such as networking computers within your school or agency and selecting and installing printers, projection systems, headsets, and other related equipment.

Networking—linking a group of computers, such as those in a school, together electronically—allows some hardware and software resources to be shared. This can result in considerable cost savings and greater availability. For example, if a computer is running low on hard-drive space, the user can simply store information directly on another networked system. Or, rather than storing every application on every computer, applications can be accessed through the network. Similarly, many software vendors offer special pricing on software that will be shared over a network. This may be considerably less costly than purchasing separate copies of the software for each computer.

❋ Considerations in Purchasing New Technology

Flexibility is key when investing in new technology hardware. It's difficult to predict what the future may bring. Ideally, new equipment should be versatile and easy to upgrade, whether it is computers, printers, projectors, or other devices such as scanners and video cameras. School districts can purchase fewer, better computers if they decide that every learner doesn't need his or her own computer. Another money-saver is to consolidate equipment whenever possible.

Projection systems are one example of how equipment could be consolidated. A projection system projects an image of your computer monitor onto a screen. This is an excellent tool for presentations and discussions and allows a group to view a single computer monitor. Most computers can be set up with a projection system, but be certain of compatibility before committing to a purchase. As an example of consolidation, one or two projection systems for an entire school, or district, may be sufficient. This will allow the purchase of a projector with higher-quality video and audio. The number of projectors to be purchased will, of course, depend on how much they will be used. There is a very wide range of features, prices, and qualities associated with video projection hardware. Some models are permanently mounted on a ceiling, while other lightweight, portable models can be easily transported from classroom to classroom, or even from one school to another. Regardless of which type you prefer, testing it before committing is a good idea.

Sharing a printer is one of the most common cost-saving hardware-consolidation strategies. While printers vary considerably in type, features, and price, the initial expense is just one factor to consider.

Color laser printers can produce high-quality printouts of everything from photos to brochures. However, they are also the most expensive to purchase. When purchasing a printer, it's essential to analyze your current, as well as your future, needs. You might decide that one higher-quality printer could serve many networked computers if reserved for special projects that need its capability, while additional, lower-cost printers could be purchased for routine tasks.

Speed and capacity of printers should also be considered. Naturally, if a printer will be shared with others in a department or program, it should have higher speed and capacity than a situation where every computer has its own printer.

Because printer cartridges are often very expensive, it's wise to price them before purchasing a printer so you can estimate regular replacement costs. It's also advisable to select products from a reputable manufacturer. You will then have some assurance that replacement cartridges can be obtained throughout the life of the printer.

 # The Applications of Technology

The applications of technology in education can be considered from several perspectives. In this section, you will read about using technology to help you present material and organize information. You will also read about some essential software applications, using the Web as communication tool, evaluating Internet resources, examples of possible learning activities including WebQuests, and ethics in the information age.

✳ Applications to Organize and Present Materials

Whatever your teaching situation, you can use technology in many aspects of your job. If you have a nutrition-consulting business, a software program for small businesses could help you schedule appointments, bill clients, and keep records for tax purposes. If you are a state Extension specialist, you might use PowerPoint® software to prepare a training program for local staff members, use a PDA to keep track of your schedule, and use a word-processing program to write articles for a website.

A classroom teacher can both integrate technology into lessons and also use software utilities that facilitate everyday tasks. Such tasks might include preparing lesson plans; managing homework assignments; creating, administering and grading tests; managing grades; and even taking attendance. Software programs to help manage these tasks are readily available. Some are available free (*freeware*) over the Internet, while other, more sophisticated, software applications are available for purchase commercially.

In addition, there are excellent software applications available that integrate all of these teacher tasks into a single course-management application. Some also allow for teacher-learner-parent interaction. Your school district may utilize one of these multipurpose programs district-wide. If you are choosing a program for yourself, you can adapt the capabilities of a program like Microsoft® Office, purchase a commercially available teacher utility program, or download one of the available freeware programs. It depends on your specific needs and budget. Take a moment to consider some of the features and capabilities of these software applications, as well as other options.

The simplest example of lesson-planning software is a word processor. Most word-processing programs are capable of creating documents in an outline format. This greatly facilitates the process of building a teaching or presentation plan. You could also create a lesson-plan template using a basic word-processing program or use one of the software applications specifically designed to assist teachers in the creation and updating of teaching plans. These programs often include features such as built-in formats; the ability to import from other applications, such as graphics, multimedia, and documents; calendar features for scheduling lessons; and the capability to link to any document or Web page and include them as part of the lesson.

Electronic gradebook software can greatly facilitate grading and recordkeeping tasks, while also providing important feedback to learners, parents, and administrators. Many of these software applications allow the teacher to construct exams and assignments and then automatically grade objective questions. The software program may also have the capability to enter the grades into a database, convert the numerical grade to a letter grade (with the ability to construct a curve if desired), notify learners of the graded exam or assignment, and generate a report to learners and/or parents. In addition, some programs can be directly interfaced with administrative grading, attendance, and reporting computer systems.

❋ Integrating and Enhancing Computer Skills

There's no one "right" way to integrate technology into instruction. Variables include the ages and abilities of your learners, the subject matter you are teaching, and your own skills and creativity. Most K-12 students have experience using computers and are comfortable doing so. Some are highly skilled in computer use. The same may not be true for every adult learner. Regardless of age and experience, utilizing technology and the Web have become important means of communication and learning. As the information age continues to become an integral part of daily life, it's important for learners to discover how to utilize the various aspects of technology. Knowing how to access, evaluate, and assimilate large quantities of information and to sort through it efficiently are key skills. Learners also need to learn how to convey their Web-search findings in a professional, efficient manner.

Learning with technology requires the ability to, at minimum, perform basic tasks in three areas: word processing, presentations with graphics, and data handling. Learners also need to be able to integrate all three. If you are working with groups of learners, it's important to find out what skills they have. For example, if all have successfully completed a basic computer class, you could assume those course requirements as their base knowledge. However, a simple questionnaire can give you a clearer idea of what equipment and software students know how to use and their level of expertise. You also can find out what access students have to a computer. Keep this information in mind when making assignments. Whenever a lesson or assignment requires skills that may be unfamiliar, be sure to demonstrate them and provide reference handouts.

As far as word processing is concerned, plan activities and assignments that require learners to branch out. Very few of today's word-processing applications are limited to entering simple text.

- Have learners use more than the basics of a program.
- Set formatting objectives.
- Require that images and other visuals be used in appropriate assigned papers and presentations.
- Encourage creative use of technology in projects and presentations.

To improve information-management skills, learners can benefit from using digital resources for researching and writing papers, rather than just traditional methods. They may need a lesson or refresher on how to search documents electronically for key words.

Familiarizing learners with presentation software packages like PowerPoint® or HyperStudio® will help prepare them for later academic requirements, as well as career applications. If the equipment is available and is appropriate to enhance learning, model its use and help learners master at least the basics.

Graphics, video, and audio are rich media and should be incorporated into your curriculum, if possible. For example:

- Learners can bring in photos to scan. These can be part of an art or design project, a collage, or the basis of a report.
- Photos can be edited using a simple image-editing program.
- Learners can use computer graphic skills to develop brochures, posters, or bulletin board items.
- Learners can make videos of a specific topic such as demonstrating strength training, or food-safety practices, or one identifying architectural styles in your areas.
- Audio narration or sound recordings can enhance visual presentations.
- Learners can utilize technology skills in class presentations.

For some content areas, utilization of database software may be appropriate. Learners can construct and manipulate databases and also develop interpretation skills.

Integrating applications such as these will add variety to your curriculum and will encourage higher-level learning. You will also be helping prepare learners for life in the future by showing them what is possible through the use of information technology.

❈ Evaluating the Quality of Internet Resources

The explosive growth of the Internet gives educators and learners on-demand access to a wealth of global information on every conceivable topic. The difficulty comes in sorting out the credible, high-quality information resources from the enormous number of "junk" websites with limited academic credibility.

Most Web-searching tools allow users to focus their query in order to maximize the usefulness of the results. However, even when the user takes full advantage of these advanced searching options, it's still necessary to be able to evaluate the quality of the search results. Thus, obtaining reliable information from the Web is a two-step process. First, users must construct a focused search strategy. Second, they must carefully evaluate the quality of the search result.

❈ Construct a Focused Search Strategy

The strategies for searching a topic on the Web aren't unlike other traditional library searches. The Web utilizes *search engines* to locate information. A search engine like Yahoo!®, Google™, or MSN™ is simply a computer application that searches the Internet for words and phrases that pertain to what you are looking for. The search engine quickly presents a sorted list of matching results. Most Internet search engines allow the user to incorporate a number of advanced searching options. The use of *Boolean expressions* in your search is the most effective means of finding exactly what you are looking for. Boolean expressions are words such as AND, OR, and NOT. The logic of Boolean expressions is similar among all searching tools. For example, searching with the expression "calcium AND osteoporosis" will yield only documents containing both the words calcium and osteoporosis. However, entering the expression "calcium OR osteoporosis" will result in documents that contain either of the words calcium *or* osteoporosis. Searching using the expression "calcium NOT osteoporosis" will yield documents that contain the word calcium but not the word osteoporosis.

In addition to the use of Boolean expressions, most Web search engines also allow you to restrict your search results in other ways. For example, you can limit a search to only images, or to only words that appear in the title of the document, or to only words that appear in the *URL*. The URL, or *Uniform Resource Locator*, is the Internet address for a Web page, such as www.yahoo.com. Another useful search feature is to restrict your results to documents from a specified *domain*. The domain is simply part of the name of a computer located on the Internet—its domain name. For example, sites with domain names that end with the suffix ".edu" are located at educational institutions, whereas sites ending with the suffix ".com" are commercial websites. Thus, for example, by limiting your search to only domains that contain the suffix .edu, you can eliminate all .com sites from your results. Various Internet searching tools have different rules for how to use Boolean expressions, as well as some of the additional search features. Review the procedures for the searching tool that you are using.

❋ *Quality of the Search Results*

Evaluating the quality of the information obtained from a Web search is a challenge faced by both learners and educators. In some ways it's similar to the challenge of evaluating the quality of traditional print media. Prior to the advent of the Web, learners and educators needed to be able to evaluate the quality of primary research sources and popular print media. Many of the same rules used for this task apply to Web resources. Some of the questions you might ask in evaluating a Web resource include:

- Are the information presented useful for the topic you are researching?
- What is the intent or purpose of the content? Is it intended to present factual knowledge or simply one person's opinion?
- Is the content refereed or juried? That is, has the content been critically reviewed by an independent expert(s) in the topic field?
- Are the author and author affiliation clearly identified? If so, what does the author's reputation and affiliation tell you about the credibility of the content?
- Does the information presented come from more than one source? Is a bibliography included?
- Does the document give the date the content was developed or updated? If the information isn't current, does it matter? For example, some information may be timeless, such as measurement equivalents or the color wheel. However, for many topics presented on the Web, it may be important to consider when it was written. For example, health-related sites should be updated regularly as new medical information and understanding become available.

- Is the content well written or does it have misspelled words and grammatical errors?
- Are there any advertisements on the page? If so, does this suggest that the content may be biased?

In addition to these criteria, you need to consider some issues specific to the Internet. These may include consideration of the URL extension. For example, you may weigh a URL with an .edu or .gov extension differently from a .com site. However, this isn't meant to suggest that .com sites are inherently of lower quality than education or government sites. Many commercial websites provide very high-quality information. Similarly, some education and government sites provide unreliable or outdated information. Ultimately, there's no simple way to be positive that a website's content is entirely accurate. However, by considering the criteria identified here when evaluating an Internet resource, you can judge its value for your purposes accordingly. If you are in doubt about facts presented, check them against those in other sources, or simply eliminate that source.

❋ *Citing Electronic Information*

In addition to searching for and evaluating the quality of information on the Web, learners and teachers are required to respect copyrighted material on the Web unless the material is explicitly marked as "public domain." Standards have emerged for referencing electronic sources. As in print media, there is no single format for these types of citations. However, there are some common requirements. A typical electronic journal article may be cited as follows:

Author. Article Title. Journal Title. Date (Volume: Issue). Web Address. Date Accessed.

This format includes most of the standard features of any "print" citation. The additional components of the citation associated with the electronic nature of the source are the Web address and access date (the date when the person citing the reference actually accessed the information).

Here is an example of a citation using this style:

McKay, M. and B. McGrath. Creating Internet-Based Curriculum Projects. T.H.E. Journal (27:11). Available: http://www.the journal.com/magazine/vault/A2883.cfm. August 30, 2001.

✳ Communication Capabilities

Ultimately, it is the communication power of the Internet that holds the greatest promise and potential for use in education. To facilitate communication between school and home, many schools have taken advantage of tools such as homework phone lines and e-mail to parents. Now the Internet offers much more sophisticated and direct means of communication between school and home, or between school and anywhere on the globe. A school website can provide easy access to information and a way for parents to communicate with teachers or administrators. While e-mail is the most basic form of Internet communication, it has many capabilities beyond a simple messaging system. For example, a video sequence and Web links might be included in an e-mail message to parents. Be sure to make print versions of information available to families without computer access.

Yet another useful and popular application of e-mail is for the creation of mailing distribution lists or Listservs. A *Listserv* is simply a specialized software program originally set up to maintain large mailing lists on the Internet. For example, a Listserv can send e-mail to thousands of recipients in just minutes. By creating a Listserv for a particular topic, you can invite individuals with an interest in that topic to join the "list," or you, as the administrator of the list, can manually add individuals to the list. For example, an instructor can create a mailing list for a women's health program by inputting the names of all of the participants, and communicate to the entire group at once through the list, rather than by individual e-mails. Similarly, learners can communicate with their classmates through the list. Listservs are an efficient and effective means of generating an online discussion.

Web-based discussion boards appear very similar in function to Listservs in that the user can post a question or comment to an entire group at once. However, a significant advantage of a discussion board is that the online discussions are "threaded." That is, the arrangement and order of the posting and comments are organized into topic threads. For example, if someone posts a comment on a particular topic to the discussion board, all subsequent responses to the original posting will be listed beneath the original post. Thus, a user can quickly review all of the discussion related to a particular topic posting.

Both Listservs and discussion boards are examples of asynchronous Internet communication. That is, when you post a message or send an e-mail to the list, you must wait until everyone reads the message and responds if necessary, which may not be for several days. The Internet also has the capability to permit live, synchronous communication between individuals or groups. This type of live electronic communication offers some unique advantages in the educational environment.

The most basic form of live Internet communication is the so-called "chat room." A chat room is simply a software application that permits individuals to assemble as a group in a virtual room, usually centered around a particular interest or topic, and to exchange text-based messages almost instantaneously over the Internet. For example, a teacher of a distance-learning course could establish a chat room on a class website. The chat room, or rooms, could facilitate group discussions or cooperation on a project. Learners, and perhaps educators, would be invited to meet online at designated times to discuss the project. In effect, this allows group communication to continue beyond the normal class time. Much like e-mail communication, chat rooms also have the capability to do more than simply allow the exchange of text messages. Most allow users to exchange files or share other applications. This allows learners to truly participate in a group project, rather than simply a group discussion.

Live videoconferencing over the Internet will certainly supercede chat rooms as the preferred communication tool once broadband Internet access becomes more universally available. Software for facilitating videoconferencing over the Internet is relatively inexpensive and many home computers are configured with small video cameras and the necessary software. Videoconferencing applications allow users to exchange files and work on group projects. Some videoconferencing applications are designed around the requirements of distance education in which the teacher can moderate and control the discussion.

Even without broadband access, educators can take advantage of the capabilities of Internet videoconferencing. For example, if the school has high-speed Internet access and a computer equipped with a video camera and software, the class can connect with anyone in the world similarly equipped. One possible use of this technology would be to bring "virtual guest speakers" into the classroom, live via the Internet. For example, while it may be difficult to schedule an obstetrician or certified nurse midwife to visit the class to discuss pregnancy and childbirth, it could be relatively easy to connect to their clinic for a live interactive discussion with the group over the Internet.

The possibilities of these new Internet communications tools are endless. Learners can remain connected to the class from home while they are ill or if they are traveling. Parents can conference with teachers at a time that is convenient for both. Third parties from anywhere in the world can be brought into the live discussion. Clearly, the ways in which learners, teachers, parents, and administrators communicate will undergo very dramatic changes in the near future.

✳ Technology-Related Classroom Activities

Whether your learning environment has only one or two computers, or you have access to a lab full of computers, there are endless ways to incorporate activities that will enhance both learners' content knowledge and technology literacy. When working with a very limited number of keyboards and monitors, learners can work together in small groups, ideally of no more than three people. Each computer might have one group of students using it while the other groups would be either formulating a plan of action or assembling their findings, or working on another assignment.

Deciding when and how to use technology in activities depends upon various factors. Availability of equipment and your technology knowledge and comfort level have already been mentioned. Your primary responsibility is to meet curriculum requirements, so technology activities must efficiently achieve those goals. You may wish to review the information in Chapter 5 on developing learning experiences and in Chapter 6 on writing teaching plans.

Print and Internet resources, professional meetings, educational technology courses, and discussions with other educators can all be excellent sources of ideas for integrating technology. Internet resources abound. Some websites give general educational information or examples from different subject areas that you could adapt. Others are subject-matter specific. Links from websites that you would rank as top quality often also provide very useful information and suggestions.

When developing activities that require learners to use the Web, you must decide whether you will have them search for websites with relevant information, or if you will predetermine sites for them to use. Both options have benefits. Students need to learn how to conduct focused searches, but these can take considerable time. Guiding students to particular sites gives learners experience in utilizing and synthesizing Internet information, while minimizing search time. Many teachers assign focused-search activities for long-term or out-of-class assignments, but usually predetermine sites for in-class activities.

Figure 15-1 gives some additional suggestions for integrating technology-related activities into your teaching. Give technology-related activities a try and then expand your use of them by applying your creativity and sharpening your own technology skills.

Figure 15-1
Technology-Based Activities

- Group presentations utilizing technology are a great idea because this format allows students to learn skills from their peers. Group learners with varied skill levels together and emphasize the importance of having all members improve their knowledge and skills.
- Many newspapers have online versions. Use relevant articles as the basis for analytical discussions or as the basis for an activity. Some papers' websites, like that of the New York Times, also have lesson plans based on current topics or articles.
- Utilize online tools whenever possible. For example, sites are available that analyze a food diary and make recommendations for changes. Others have tools to calculate mortgage expenses or the amount of carpeting needed for a home. Such sites sometimes also offer simulation activities.
- Connecting with students in other schools or countries can enrich many content areas. Such interaction can come in many forms. Simply sending e-mails back and forth may not seem terribly exciting until learners start relaying multimedia attachments and site addresses. Even more dimensions can be added to these experiences through the use of live chat rooms, discussion forums, and videoconferencing. Joint projects can be conducted.
- Help students learn to publish information on the Web. A text editor program is all that is needed to create Web pages. Web pages are written in html (hypertext markup language). The basics of html are very simple, and they are well worth learning. Even without access to the Web, or a server from which to send Web pages, you can write and test Web pages. Most browsers have an option to open a local file. Try "file," then "open" from your browser's main menu.
- Having learners use search engines to write papers will add another dimension to a curriculum. If they list their key words, search engines, and results, you will be able to assess their information-gathering skills independently of their writing skills.
- If you have access to a writable CD drive, have learners create their own educational CDs. For example, you might have learners create a CD that teaches a specific serging technique or first-aid skill.

✳ *WebQuests*

WebQuests are one specific model for technology-based activities. Since a model was developed in 1995, WebQuests have become a very popular learning tool with students and teachers. A *WebQuest* is an inquiry-oriented activity that is built around a task or end product and based on information that learners gather almost entirely from the Internet. Participants typically share computers, an advantage for programs and classrooms with a limited number of computers.

Based on a model developed by Bernie Dodge with Tom March, both of San Diego State University, a WebQuest has six components:

- Introduction
- Task
- Process
- Resources
- Evaluation
- Conclusion

WebQuests are designed to use learners' time well; to focus on the information itself, rather than looking for it; and to support learners' thinking at the levels of analysis, synthesis, and evaluation. Learners typically work on a problem as a group. Team members each take on a role, often choosing one area in which to become an expert. Then they share what they have learned with fellow team members.

You can develop your own WebQuest or use one developed by another educator. For a WebQuest, Internet sites most appropriate for the activity are predetermined by the educator. This helps learners use their information-gathering time more productively. One existing WebQuest is called "Find a Need and Fill It." The goal of the participants is to improve their own life circumstances or to solve a problem in the community. Another WebQuest involves entrepreneurship. Participants use the Internet to support their team's unique idea for a small business. In a personal budget WebQuest, learners set up a lifestyle and follow a budget.

Topics for WebQuest vary widely. Check education websites and use the focused-search technique to find examples.

✳ Ethics and the Web

Whether learners are working on a WebQuest or doing other research online, the increased use of computers and the Internet has presented educators with many new ethical issues and considerations. These issues aren't limited to only the students' use of the technology. Educators and administrators are often themselves faced with ethical considerations regarding the use of technology. For example, tight supply budgets may tempt teachers to violate copyrights in order to obtain materials for their classes. Some of the ethical issues associated with these new technologies include:

- Copyright issues related to the use of information obtained on the Internet.
- Accessing inappropriate material over the Internet.
- Security of learner information and maintaining privacy.
- Software piracy over the Internet.
- Plagiarism issues.

As an educator, you are responsible for adhering to standard copyright laws and policies, and for instructing your students to do the same. Be sure that in the creation of your Web pages or other course materials, you have not included any information that should be marked as the property of a copyright holder, such as (but not limited to) text from contributors, photographs, or graphics. You should assume that the same restrictions and obligations that govern print documents will also apply in the copyright protection of electronic and digital content.

If you are affiliated with a nonprofit educational institution or organization, you will likely find that copyright holders are cooperative and generous in granting permission to use their materials. Obtaining permission to use copyrighted material is usually a simple process. You can write to the author of the material directly, asking permission to use it. Or, you can take advantage of services that, for a small fee, will attempt to get copyright permission on your behalf. One such service is the Copyright Clearance Center, Inc., accessible on the Web at http://www.copyright.com.

It's unlikely that there will be cyberpolice pursuing all copyright violations on the Internet. There are a vast number of individuals with relatively anonymous access to the Internet. There is also an enormous amount of copyrighted material being placed online every day. As a result, learners should be guided to realize that copyright is much more than a legal issue. The fact that it's unlikely that they will "get caught" isn't the point. Fundamentally, it's a moral and ethical issue.

Computer technology has also raised new concerns regarding privacy and confidentiality. Individuals must recognize that any information placed on a computer, particularly a networked computer, is potentially accessible by others. Thus, educators need to familiarize themselves with the basics of computer security capabilities and limitations. Constant vigilance is essential. Never assume that the security measures you have adopted are foolproof. You need only read newspaper headlines to recognize that the hacking of so-called "secure" websites is commonplace.

Finally, controlling access to inappropriate material, such as online pornography, is always a concern. The nature of the Web is such that learners may very likely encounter such inappropriate material unintentionally. This can happen in the course of conducting a perfectly innocent keyword search. Fortunately there are a number of very effective software-filtering applications available to control student access to "off limit" sites. Most of these filters work by identifying certain words contained within a website. If the word suggests that the site isn't appropriate for student viewing, then the software prevents it from being displayed. Free evaluation downloads of filtering software can be found on the Web. Remember, however, that no filtering software is perfect. Consider incorporating all of the following points to control access:

- Clear rules for student conduct regarding computer use.
- Teacher instruction on the use of the Web and Web search engines.
- Careful supervision of students' computer use.
- Filtering software.

As an educator, you can view these ethical considerations as opportunities for student learning. That is, rather than simply laying out the rules, why not build lesson plans around the issues themselves? For example, have learners assist in the drafting of a class policy regarding the use of copyrighted material and software piracy (or if your institution already has a policy, discuss the reasoning behind it). You could have learners draw up a contract that would be signed by the students themselves, parents, and their teacher regarding the use of classroom technology. Generate class discussions around the issues of pirated software, confidentiality, and hacking; the difference between fair use and copyright violation; and plagiarism. This approach is much more likely to instill high ethical standards in your students and provide them with the tools and skills for dealing with similar ethical issues in their daily lives.

❊ Preparing for the Future

The World Wide Web has dramatically changed the way people communicate, work, play, shop, make travel plans, and, perhaps most importantly, learn. It has infiltrated almost all aspects of daily life and one can only imagine the technological advances that will occur in the years ahead and the impact they will have.

There is no longer a choice as to whether or not to bring technology into our learning environments. The technology itself, and society's adoption of the technology, has made the decision for us. Since today's learners must learn to do well in the information age as it grows and develops at a very high rate, having them experience and use such technologies is a crucial component of any educational program. Educators must continue to explore how to best utilize these technologies in the learning process.

The Language of Technology

Boolean expressions—Whenever you see a Web search tool or database query system that allows you to use AND, OR, and NOT to hone your search, the chances are it uses Boolean techniques. The most common Boolean operators are AND (you're looking for all terms), OR (you're looking for at least one of the terms), and NOT (you're excluding a term). You'll always see the operators referred to in uppercase letters, although you usually don't need to enter them that way to make a Boolean search work properly.

Broadband—A technology that provides an extremely wide and fast bandwidth so that many people can simultaneously use the service.

Browser—A browser is your interface to the World Wide Web. It interprets hypertext links and lets you view sites and navigate from one Internet node to another. Among the most popular browsers are Microsoft® Internet Explorer and Netscape Navigator.

Chat room—A software application that permits individuals to assemble as a group in a virtual room, usually centered around a particular interest or topic, and to exchange text-based messages almost instantaneously over the Internet.

CPU—Central Processing Unit. It is the largest electronic chip(s) in any computer. This is the brain of the computer where almost all information processing is carried out. *Central Processing Unit* can also refer to the "box" which contains this chip.

Digital Subscriber Lines (DSL)—Digital Subscriber Line service is a high-speed data service that works over copper telephone lines and is typically offered by telephone companies.

Domain Name—The official name of a computer connected to the Internet. Domain names are derived from a hierarchical system, with a host name followed by a top-level domain category. Among the top-level domain categories (for the U.S.) are .edu (for educational sites), .com (for commercial enterprises), .org (for nonprofit organizations), .net (for network services providers), .mil (for military), and .gov (for government).

Electronic bulletin board—Software which allows users to leave messages and access information much like an actual bulletin board. These are typically, but not always, Web-based.

Freeware—Software that is made available to the public free of charge from the author.

Graphic User Interface—A way of interacting with a computer based on graphics instead of text. GUIs use icons, pictures, and menus, and use a mouse, as well as a keyboard, to accept input. Examples are the MacOs and Microsoft® Windows.

HTML—Hypertext Markup Language. The language used to create and define most Web pages. It is used to define the locations and characteristics of each element of the page.

Internet—Sometimes called simply "the Net," the Internet is a worldwide system of computer networks—a network of networks in which users at any one computer can, if they have permission, get information from any other computer.

Listserv—A specialized software program set up to maintain large mailing lists.

RAM—Random Access Memory. The memory that can be used by applications to perform necessary tasks while the computer is on. The term "Random_Access" refers to the ability of a processor to immediately access any part of the memory.

Search engines—A database or index that can be queried to help find information on the World Wide Web.

Shareware—A "try before you buy" program. If you decide to keep and use the program beyond the trial period (usually 10-30 days) you are requested to pay a fee to the author.

URL—Uniform Resource Locator. The Web address of a specific website, such as http://www.google.com. Used to identify the type and location of a multimedia resource on the Internet.

WebQuest—An inquiry-oriented activity in which most or all of the information is drawn from the Web. A true WebQuest supports learners' thinking at the levels of analysis, synthesis, and evaluation.

World Wide Web—An amalgam of Internet sites offering text, graphics, sound, and animation resources in an easy-to-use way through the http protocol.

Building Your Professional Portfolio

Enhancing Technology Skills. Choose one piece of technology you don't know how to use, but which could be a helpful teaching or learning tool. Using available resources, make a list of its possible educational uses. Learn basic skills for using the equipment and develop a guidesheet for other new users.

Website Evaluation. Develop an evaluation instrument learners could use for assessing the quality of Internet resources. Also develop a form an educator could use to both evaluate and keep a record of Internet sites.

Internet Activity. Develop an Internet-based learning experience for use in your subject area. Identify the enabling objective and content notes (using the lesson plan format in Chapter 6) that this learning experience flows from. Give your rationale for using the Internet to teach this content.

Computer Ethics. Write a code of ethics for Web users at a specific educational level. Identify the related responsibilities of an educator at that level.

Chapter 16

Engaging Learners in Thinking

Ruth G. Thomas, Ph.D.
Professor, Family Education
University of Minnesota

*I*n the latter part of the twentieth century, interest in teaching that promotes students' thinking capacities intensified. This trend was spurred by several forces. One of these was research and theory development in the 1970s in cognitive science. In addition, translation into English of Vygotsky's (1978) work helped educators become more conscious of how context influences thought—of how the mind develops in ways that reflect one's culture and how one learns to think and perceive as a result of social interaction. These cognitive theories provided a basis for development in the 1980s and 1990s of teaching approaches designed to aid students' learning, remembering, and thinking. Promoting students' thinking capacities interested educational reformers, who worked to move educational practice toward more emphasis on thinking, particularly critical thinking. Technological advances and the globalization of communication and the economy during the 1980s and 1990s that necessitated and made possible new ways of finding, selecting, and evaluating relevant information also revealed new needs for critical thinking. The approaches to engaging students in thinking discussed in this chapter reflect these influences.

The Nature of Thinking

You don't need to look far into the literature on thinking before realizing that there are many different ways of viewing thinking. The kinds of thinking covered here are most useful in those situations and contexts that people encounter in their personal, family, community, and work lives. They involve both thinking and social processes.

☀ Thinking in Action

Thinking in action is reflected in the work of Vygotsky (1978), Schon (1983), and Scribner (1986). This kind of thinking also is referred to as *contextual* and *practical thinking*. One theme reflected in this kind of thinking is that people's expertise in an area of everyday life is as much, if not more, a function of their experience and learning as it is of their intelligence. The importance of context in thinking is a second major theme.

Practical thinking is embedded within the activities of our daily lives. It functions to achieve the goals of these everyday activities. The purposes toward which thinking is directed are influenced by the culture within which people live; the professions, trades, or workplaces within which they work; and the families and communities in which they live. Figuring out how to navigate a boat by the stars is not something toward which the thinking of people in the United States is typically directed. But this was an important problem to solve for people in Micronesia. Figuring out the best buy in the supermarket or how to make a computer do what needs to be done are familiar purposes toward which thinking is directed today in the United States. Thinking in action is instrumental to achieving goals and purposes. The interest of the thinker is in what is to be accomplished rather than in the thinking itself.

Thinking in action encompasses forming, as well as solving, problems. Skilled thinkers do not operate in a linear fashion from problem to solution. Instead, they go back and forth between problem and solution, changing either or both until a fit between problem and solution is determined. This process is illustrated by the following examples.

The breakdown of a car may not simply be a matter of finding the part that failed. Depending on the car's age and potential future service needs, replacement with a different car might be considered. Using public transportation instead of owning a car might be a possibility. Substituting a bike or scooter in place of a car is another possible solution. Thus, the problem is no longer one of how to fix the car, but becomes one of "How can I meet my transportation needs?"

Thinking in action incorporates reflection about the context of the total situation. For example, if you live in a rural area, public transportation is not likely to be an option if your car breaks down. A bike or scooter will not be a good option if you need to travel on dirt or gravel roads. In some countries cars are not readily available to buy, so replacement may not be feasible, at least without a long delay and considerable expense. You need to use initiative and creativity to incorporate your environment in the problem-

solving process. For instance, if you are dealing with the car problem, you might remember that Aunt Susan has a recent model car that she is driving less frequently these days because of failing eyesight. You offer to drive for her in exchange for occasional use of her car. This resolves both Aunt Susan's need for transportation and your need for a working vehicle.

A high school student whose parents have refused permission for traveling with a group on a humanitarian mission to a far-away place takes another look at her own community and finds opportunities she had not noticed in the past. She volunteers to help at a shelter for the homeless and in a Big Sister program for young children in families experiencing hard times.

Such examples reflect the flexibility and creativity that characterize thinking in action. It involves seeing the same thing in more than one light, as having more than one possibility. This creativity and flexibility often come from working together with others—from jointly working on problems and solutions. Because people have different perspectives and perceptions, they are able to see different aspects of a situation. When people share these varied views, the set of possibilities to consider is enriched. Because solutions to real-world problems must often be tailored to a specific situation, flexibility in adjusting solutions and problems is needed. For example, the scooter may be a good substitute for a car for the 25-year-old needing transportation to and from work in Bali, but a golf cart may be a more useful vehicle a 75-year-old in a small retirement community in the U.S. The solution that resolved an issue yesterday may not work again today, or may address a similar issue today if it is modified to some extent.

Thinking in action also conserves mental and physical energy. Approaches generated by such thinking are often ones that require the fewest steps, are the least complex, or reflect shortcuts. People want to make their tasks and jobs easier and are thus motivated to find the most straightforward ways to accomplish them. For example, the task of planning menus evolves into the creation of a set of standard menus that are rotated over time. The task of translating currency from one kind to another when visiting another country becomes the application of a rounded-off conversion factor that is easy to divide or multiply. A high school student who shovels snow for several neighbors with similar size driveways creates a "price per foot" to simplify calculations in billing customers.

Thinking in action is also used to conserve economic resources. The solution to finding a cracked egg in the carton might be redefining it as pet food. A ruined pie is transformed into something usable rather than discarded. An elaborate menu for a family gathering is simplified to conserve time and energy.

The more knowledge you have about a specific situation, the better you are able to formulate solutions and adjust already known solutions to fit new problems. This implies that experiences and learning are important influences on the thinking you are able to do. An example in the world of education would be the comparison between the more experienced teacher and the new educator. Let's assume both are encountering some classroom behavior problems with their seventh graders. Experienced teachers have at their fingertips a whole array of resource materials, successful lesson plans from the past, and a collection of ideas that have worked in other situations for engaging and motivating the learners. On the other hand, new teachers have just the ideas they have learned in university classes and field experiences. In all probability, the more experienced teacher will find it easier to solve the behavior problems. Teachers experienced in an area have developed understanding, expertise, and routines that contribute to their ability to create better solutions more quickly.

✳ Critical Thinking

Paul (1993) has defined *critical thinking* as purposeful thinking in which the thinker systematically and habitually imposes criteria and standards on the issue at hand. It is thinking that argues from alternate and opposing points of view. Critical thinkers identify weaknesses and limitations in their own views. The intellectual standards Paul refers to include qualities such as relevance, accuracy, precision, clarity, depth, and breadth.

Paul has suggested that critical thinking involves evaluating your own and others' thinking in terms of the following:

- Questions being asked.
- Points of view reflected.
- Information being used.
- Interpretations being made.
- Conclusions being drawn.
- Assumptions reflected.
- Results realized. Implications and consequences—where the thinking leads.

According to Paul (1993), critical thinking supports the development of the following characteristics:

- Awareness of the limitations of your own viewpoint.
- Holding yourself to standards as demanding as ones you hold others to.
- Acknowledging weaknesses in your own thoughts and actions.
- Willingness to go without immediate answers and to extend the study of complex issues over time despite ambiguity and opposition.
- Willingness to consider viewpoints you object to or have ignored.
- Willingness to acknowledge weaknesses in viewpoints of your own social group.
- Ability to see issues from another person's point of view.
- Keeping focused on the intellectual task at hand.

Paul has asserted that our context and human nature inhibit critical thinking. He has suggested that we tend to absorb the views of those around us rather than critically evaluating those views. We tend to look at questions, issues, situations, problems, and claims from our own point of view. Our point of view reflects our own interests, rather than helping us evaluate situations fairly and justly. Consequently, instead of "coming naturally," critical thinking must be learned. As an educator assisting your learners in developing this critical-thinking process, you will find that learning to think critically requires considerable effort and commitment.

✳ Practical Reasoning

Practical reasoning combines cognitive, affective, and motivational elements. Critically thinking about multiple points of view, decision making, and moral reasoning are crucial parts of the process. Practical reasoning involves back-and-forth dialogue among people that ultimately leads to action. You engage in the process of practical reasoning because action is perceived as needed, but what the action should be is not clear.

Coombs (1997) defined practical reasoning as any reasoning about the desirability of actions, practices, policies, and programs of action. It may include reasoning about the morality or wisdom of pursuing a course of action and its overall desirability. Examples of questions that engage practical reasoning include: What should be done about the drifting apart that we are feeling in our relationship? Should we continue our public health program in its current form? What should be done about grandmother's living situation in light of her failing health? What should I do with my life? These kinds of questions require inquiry into the situation to understand it and how it came about. Practical reasoning includes considering what values are relevant and important to the reasoner and the merits of possible alternative courses of action. The consequences of possible decisions are reviewed in light of values identified. In practical reasoning, both the long-term and immediate consequences for everyone affected are of concern.

Practical reasoning can be done individually, but is often done with other people. Work teams, families, and community groups often engage in practical reasoning. In addition, situations that stimulate practical reasoning often reemerge over time as circumstances change. For example, revitalizing an interpersonal relationship may be identified as a need more than once in the course of the relationship. However, the reasons for the need and the approach taken to address it may be quite different from one time to the next.

Often practical reasoners discover that what they first identified as the problem is not the problem after all. They come to focus on other aspects of the issue as they examine the situation in more depth. For example, a family set out to do something about their house, which some members viewed as messy (Knippel, 1998). Over the course of their practical reasoning together, they realized that not everyone in the family shared the same degree of concern about the tidiness of their home. A neat house was an expectation some of them had internalized from other people in their past lives. Some family members came to understand that their home reflected their creativity and their enjoyment of expressing their interests. They concluded that what needed changing was not so much the condition of their house, as their perspectives about it. As a result of their practical reasoning efforts, this family reduced conflict over the appearance of their home by accepting it as a condition that reflected their values. They began to feel less guilty as they continued to enjoy their activities. They also found themselves more able to enjoy having friends over without worrying about the neatness of the house.

In summary, practical reasoning encompasses and integrates thinking in action and critical thinking. It is a kind of action-oriented thinking that human beings are regularly called upon to do by the challenges and situations of everyday life. It is a kind of thinking that accommodates and incorporates social participation.

 # Supporting the Learning of Thinking

An educator's orientation toward thinking, learning, and teaching is an important factor in the opportunities provided for participants to engage in thinking. Educators who are interested in what and how learners think give participants opportunities to express ideas. Such educators are likely to engage learners in discussing their own ideas in ways that help participants develop their thinking capacities. Without a genuine interest in what participants think and have to say, it is easy for educators to let conveying of information crowd out learner participation. This "educator-centric" orientation also sends the message to participants that what teachers think and have to say is what is important, and what learners think and have to say does not matter. Educators who are genuinely interested in learners' thoughts and opinions are willing to give learners the time to formulate a thoughtful response or position. These educators are also likely to be cautious about offering judgments regarding participants' ideas and to refrain from frequently sharing their own opinions. Such educators know that it is more encouraging and supportive of learners' thinking if they help their students learn to evaluate their own thinking. When educators introduce their own viewpoints, some learners immediately adopt the teacher's view without thinking it through, considering other alternatives, or coming to know or formulate their own viewpoint. Some educators prevent this by offering their own view as "a perspective held by some people."

❋ Frameworks for Practical Reasoning

Three frameworks for guiding practical reasoning are Sirotnik's (1991) questions, four categories developed by Family and Consumer Sciences professionals, and Freiere's problem-posing approach (Wallerstein, 1987). All of these involve examining the situation to understand it and how it came about, considering what values are relevant and important, and contemplating the merits of possible alternative courses of action in light of their consequences.

❋ Sirotnik's Questions Framework

In discussing critical theory, Sirotnik (1991) has suggested a set of questions intended to guide thinking, dialogue, and action. Sirotnik has indicated that the questions he outlined are based on one translation of Freire's work (Wallerstein, 1987 e.g., Freire, 1973). Sirotnik's questions include the following:

• **"What are we doing now?"** or **"What is happening now?"** This question focuses attention and thought on what has been perceived as something that is not as it should be, but exactly what the problem is

may be vague. Furthermore, the focus of the investigation at the beginning may not necessarily remain the primary focus. In the messy house example, the family discovered that it was their perspectives, not the "messy" house, that needed their attention. The "drifting apart" relationship problem mentioned earlier would be addressed by those involved describing what they see occurring and what the drift is they are feeling. A teen struggling with finding a life direction sees a pattern in the community of children following parents' footsteps into spending life in the community employed in the steel mills located there. A group interested in the pattern of increasing obesity in children in the United States might begin their discussion outlining the changes that have occurred.

• **"How did the situation, condition, issue come to be this way?"** Examining this question enables one to see the role context factors outside the immediate situation might be playing. This question focuses attention on background factors, on the history of the situation, on what has influenced the condition or issue to develop as it has. Without considering this question, the basis for formulating actions that are likely to be effective in addressing a problem is limited. The couple perceiving their relationship as drifting apart might discover that a change in work schedule several months ago for one of them eliminated some special moments. Previously they had time together each day to relax and unwind from the day's activities. They may further realize that an elderly parent's health problem has also now sapped their energies and refocused their attention. The public health program personnel who wondered about continuing their program as it was may find that other agencies have assumed some of the functions theirs had been doing. Or, the program may find that their own agency has gradually taken on many more functions over time and that their mission no longer reflects their activity. The teen notes that few models of life patterns beyond the steel mills are evident, and that a pattern prevails among teens of early childbearing and marriage that leads to responsibility for supporting a family before or soon after completing high school. This question would lead a group looking into the increasing obesity of children to examine factors underlying these trends.

- **"Whose interests are and are not being served by the way things are?"** This question asks practical reasoners to look more deeply into what is happening with respect to the issue or problem of interest and how it came to be. An assumption underlying this question is that most situations and conditions do not "just happen." They come about because persons, groups, organizations, or nations have an interest in things being a certain way. Although some persons or groups may benefit from a particular pattern of circumstances, the well-being of others may be reduced. For example, many people may assume that war is not in anyone's interest. However, some groups profit from wars, such as ammunition and war equipment producers, ship builders, and airplane manufacturers. Insurance companies may benefit from reduction in health services to patients by medical clinics and hospitals, but patient care may deteriorate.

- **"What information and knowledge do we have or need to get that bear upon the issues?"** Information and knowledge are needed to respond to each of Sirotnik's questions. It may be necessary to delve into what is happening now in more depth to gain an adequate understanding of the patterns you think may be occurring and to verify their existence. For example, in one community after a school-age boy was killed crossing a highway to get to a swimming beach, the community undertook a study of the traffic volume, the speed cars actually traveled in relation to the posted speed, and reviewed the records of accidents at this same location over past years. This community also looked into alternative ways of making a safe way for children to cross the busy highway to get to the beach. Community members examined what would be involved in putting in a stoplight, making a walk-bridge over the highway, and digging a walk-tunnel under the highway. They acquired an understanding of possible consequences of each option for preventing accidents and for the traffic flow on the busy highway. The teen seeking to alter for himself the typical life pattern for young people in his community may need to obtain information about other life patterns and careers that will help him envision possible futures. Those examining patterns of child obesity might look at where in the population these patterns are most prevalent and the kinds of information and messages being provided to families by health and educational organizations and by advertising.

- **"Is this the way we want things to be?"** This question helps reasoners consider their values. The community members concluded that they were not going to risk one more accident at the highway crossing by the lake, no matter what happened to the traffic flow. The family that thought they had a messy house wanted peace, less bickering, and continued enjoyment of creative activities. This was more important to them than a higher standard of neatness. A subquestion, "If not, what would be better?" invites envisioning a more desirable situation. When people mentally formulate and describe to others the conditions and situations they desire, the chances of those conditions and situations becoming reality are enhanced.

- **"What are we going to do about it?"** This question focuses attention on developing an action plan for achieving the desired situation. Here is where alternatives are evaluated in light of their consequences and the degree to which those consequences reflect the values that have been identified. Constraints are also part of considering alternatives. For example, in the situation on safely crossing a highway, a stoplight was chosen as both an effective and feasible alternative. It addressed the concerns of parents in the community for their children's safety, and this solution was acceptable to the highway department. In the public health program example, functions that were now duplicated by other agencies were dropped. A new mission statement included functions not now addressed by any other agency. The teen determines to create a new pattern for himself, to seek higher education, and to avoid behavior that threatens that plan. The group concerned with child obesity patterns develops an action plan to help their community address this issue.

Sirotnik's questions help both individuals and groups organize their thinking.

The sequence in which Sirotnik presents the questions reflects a logical flow. A group that is using these questions to support their dialogue and thinking about an area of concern is likely to generate ideas relevant to some of the other questions during their discussion of any one question. Practical reasoning is not linear, but a process that goes back and forth among thoughts. It is helpful if you start the discussion on an issue or concern by posting sheets of newsprint for all to see, each sheet headed with one of the questions. As discussion proceeds, ideas can be recorded under the appropriate question. Because discussion of an issue or concern often requires more than one session, the newsprint sheets on which ideas have been recorded can be saved, and the discussion continued later. On the other hand, educators who are with a group of learners for only one session will find these questions helpful in initiating thinking that is likely to continue after learners leave.

❊ Family and Consumer Sciences Four Categories Framework

Family and Consumer Sciences professionals have identified four categories of questions that organize practical reasoning. These four categories are context, valued ends, means, and consequences. This approach to practical reasoning also emphasizes that practical reasoning is not a linear process, but back-and-forth thinking that shuttles among the four components.

In this approach to practical reasoning, resource materials, such as case studies and newspaper articles, are used to stimulate students' thinking about concerns or issues that involve families and the community. These may be issues such as family violence, young women's deaths related to bulimia, child care availability, or family economics. Fedje (1998) has described her process for teaching practical reasoning as starting with learner review of materials that reflect family concerns. After students have reviewed materials, they are asked to generate questions about the situation(s) they have read or viewed. When they are done generating their questions, they categorize their questions in terms of context, valued ends, means, and consequences.

Context questions ask about political, social, economic, historical, and cultural aspects of the situation. Valued-ends questions concern what would be desirable, what is important, and differences in what would be viewed as desirable among persons concerned with and affected by the issue. Means questions focus on generating strategies for creating a more desirable situation. Means are not limited to physical acts but may include changing one's perspective or accepting another group's position. Means may also include organizing groups and taking political action. Consequence questions ask about the long- and short-term effects of actions being considered and what will happen to various groups that would be affected. Consequences are also examined in relation to the valued ends that have been identified.

Once learners have categorized their questions, they are asked to generate further questions about the case study or other material that has been used to stimulate their thinking. Students are asked to generate questions in each of the four categories. After this opportunity to practice generating the four kinds of questions, learners are provided with a new case relating to another concern facing family members. They again generate questions in the four categories. This is repeated with new cases until learners can readily generate the four kinds of questions.

At this point, learners are ready to focus more intently on significant continuing concerns that all or most families face in one form or another and that reemerge over time as circumstances, conditions, and people change. For example, the question of what should be done about the drifting apart in a relationship is one that couples may find themselves raising more than once in the course of their relationship as new stresses, responsibilities, health conditions, and emotional ebbs and flows affect the time and attention they are able to give to each other. The question of whether to continue a public health program in its current form is one that social and educational programs face periodically as their audiences, agencies, institutions, and contexts change. The question of what should be done about grandmother's living situation in light of her failing health may be answered one way at one point in time, but is likely to reemerge if health deteriorates further. The question of what to do with my life is one faced by young people whose life is before them, but again by middle-aged persons who may feel caught in unfulfilling routines and responsibilities, and by those nearing retirement. These kinds of questions are experienced by people across generations, time, and cultures.

Once students have a grasp of what continuing concerns are, Fedje engages them in identifying significant continuing concerns reflected in society and finding illustrative case studies in newspapers, magazines, movies, and television shows. This helps students connect specific, concrete instances of concerns in people's lives to bigger, societal-level continuing concerns. Having learners generate questions in the four categories about case studies helps them see more clearly how the questions help define concerns and come to conclusions about what to do. Then Fedje introduces a change in some circumstance in the situation. This might be the loss of a job, injury of a key person in an accident, or birth of a child with a special condition. Learners consider whether the new development stimulates additional questions in the categories. This helps students see how change in only a single aspect of a situation can have profound impact on the situation, as well as the questions.

Learners are then asked to apply practical reasoning to their own lives by writing a paper in which they identify a continuing concern that relates to their family life. In the paper, learners are asked to write a short description of the situation, to generate questions in the four categories, and to discuss how they might use the questions in dealing with the situation. Fedje holds individual conferences with students, reviews drafts of their papers along the way, and engages the group in reviewing and critiquing each other's drafts as ways to support learners' efforts in developing their papers.

The four-categories approach to practical reasoning reflects the reality that people's thinking about complex problems emerging from real-life situations is not linear, but more multidimensional. This characteristic can give such thinking a confused appearance to both observers of it and the person experiencing it. The four-categories approach organizes this thinking and strengthens it by calling the thinker's attention to blind spots and gaps that might be missed.

✳ *Freire's Problem-Posing Framework*

Freire's framework (Wallerstein, 1987) explicitly acknowledges the emotional and motivational connections to thinking. His work concerns awakening the ability of oppressed people to transform their lives in directions that are more consistent with their interests and well-being. Freire's problem-posing framework developed around his concern for social change. It is useful as a framework for structuring classroom learning that engages learners' thinking around such issues.

Wallerstein (1987) has described three phases outlined by Freire that characterize the problem-posing framework: listening, dialogue, and action. In the first phase of listening, the teacher listens to learners both inside and out of the educational setting to understand their concerns and the context that surrounds those concerns. For example, the educator or youth worker spends time with youth in extracurricular or community activities. The adult educator listens to adults as they discuss their concerns and their daily lives in restaurants, over backyard fences, and in community gatherings. Learners are also asked to bring objects, documents, and other artifacts from their lives and communities to the class. These may include things that are associated with various emotions for them, including pride, concern, fondness, and repulsion. For example, the educator may ask learners to bring artifacts that have been in their families over more than one generation. The learners explain the significance of the items to their families. Through such listening, educators come to understand the issues or themes that predominate in the lives and thinking of the people they serve. The educator comes to understand learners' situations from the perspective of the learner.

The educator also involves the learners in listening activities with their peers and people in their communities, neighborhoods, and workplaces. This promotes understanding of what others' lives are like and what issues and themes predominate in the conversations. Learners are asked to observe in ways that give them fresh outlooks on what they might otherwise miss. The blinders of the familiar are removed, for example, by asking learners to imagine they are "space people." They visit homes, places of work, neighborhoods, and schools assuming they are seeing these situations for the first time. Learners are asked to record what they see and what they notice as patterns. In this role, they may answer questions such as: "Are different kinds of interactions used for one group of people and other kinds of interactions used for another group?" "Are privileges extended to one group or person and not to others?" "Do groups differ in the kinds of futures they see for themselves?"

Learners are also asked to interview people in a variety of familiar settings. Sample interview questions might include:

- "What do you hope for in the future?"
- "What bothers you in your life today?"
- "How do you live your life here?"
- "What is it like to come from ___?___ to live in the United States?"
- "What are your hopes and dreams?"
- "What have you found difficult in life?"

Learners are then asked to share their observations and interviews with their peers. The activities for this may take many forms, including note-sharing, photographs taken, stories written that reflect their observations, or skits that portray their observations and experiences.

The educator listens for the most intense and central issues or concerns that emerge from the listening phase. These become the foci for the dialogue phase. Because issues that are of deep concern to people are connected to strong emotions, sometimes direct discussion of them may be too painful. The intensity of emotions connected to the issues may make it difficult to see all aspects of the problem or situation. For example, in the situation mentioned earlier in this chapter of a child being killed by a fast-moving car on a highway as he crossed to a swimming beach, the emotional pain surrounding this situation may make it very difficult for a community and the parents and friends of this child to discuss it as simply a "continuing concern." Considering the possibility that their own life could be different from what has always been the case in their community may create hope in teens that may initially make the realities they face more painful. Other issues may be too threatening, embarrassing, or overwhelming. For example, workers concerned about wages and working conditions may fear reprisals from bosses if they voice their concerns. Parents concerned about their children's exposure to television and World Wide Web material they feel is inappropriate may feel powerless to influence the programming of these media. Consumers who have been "taken" by a merchant may fear being viewed by others as gullible.

To assist in these situations, a code puts the information that has been gathered about people's concerns into a symbolic form. A code contains the issues but is not the real situation. It is used to focus, stimulate, and begin the discussion. This provides a more neutral representation of the issues that can be focused on. The specific form of the code can vary. It may be an object, a documentary film, a story, a photograph, a skit or play, a written dialogue, a song, an artistic work, or a collage. The code's role is to re-present learners' reality back to them in a way that allows them to project their emotional and social responses onto it in a focused fashion. Its purpose is to promote critical thinking and action. Codes present open-ended situations and issues. Consequently, participants have the role of suggesting their own options for action. For example, a video produced by the

Cooperative Extension Service called "Family Matters" depicts the lives of two families and contains issues relating to family economics, unemployment, couple relationships, and concerns about children's education and child care. These issues and concerns connect to many families' real lives, but discussing them in terms of the families in the video is easier, initially, than talking about a learner's own father's unemployment, parents' fight over money, or unattended children.

Problem-posing questions are used to assist participants in interpreting the presented code. This decoding activity helps participants recognize, validate, and relate the code to their own concerns and those of others. It also moves discussion toward consideration of action. It explores the problem, its causes, and the visions and ideals people have. These aspects of the discussion reflect the continuing concern, its context, and people's valued ends in the four categories framework. The questions are also similar to those of Sirtonik. In the questioning, learners are asked to:

- Describe what they see.
- Define the problem(s): What is happening (in the code)? How does each person (in the code) feel?
- Share similar experiences (their own or those of others they know): How is this problem similar or different from what you or others you know have experienced?
- Consider why there is a problem: Who benefits and who loses from this situation? What do you think would be better? Why?
- Strategize what they can do about the problem: What can the people (in the code) do about the problem? What can you do in your own life? What do you think other people should do? What have you done in the past?

The action phase involves deciding on and carrying out courses of action. Participants may need to learn how to complete certain actions. For example, if one course of action involves getting a bill introduced into the legislature, participants may need to learn what the process is for doing this and develop their skills in communicating with legislators and organizing groups to support the bill. This learning can be accomplished through bringing resource people into the classroom, arranging for field trips to the capitol so students can see the bill formation and enactment process in action, and arranging opportunities for students to meet in small groups and develop roleplays that give them practice in needed skills. In the skill practice groups, an observer watches the interaction, and the other group members spontaneously enact a relevant scene such as approaching a legislator about sponsoring a bill. The observer cuts the action at a critical point and gives feedback to the actors, who then replay the scene based on the suggestions of the observer and their discussion of the observations. If time allows, roles are rotated, and another scene is enacted by the new actors and critiqued by the new observer.

✳ Putting the Three Frameworks Together

Teachers differ in their abilities to relate to the different frameworks for practical reasoning. One of the frameworks might be a better fit for a particular purpose. For example, the Sirotnik (1991) framework is readily understood by learners. It is usable in a shorter period of time than the four categories and problem-posing frameworks. A shortcoming of the Sirotnik framework, however, is that it pays less explicit attention to consideration of consequences of possible actions than does the four categories framework. However, the examples discussed in connection with the "What are we going to do about it" question illustrate consideration of consequences. Teachers may have a harder time relating to the four categories framework because it is not a set of procedures. Fedje's (1998) presentation of the four categories framework, however, addresses this issue to some extent. That is why her treatment of the four categories framework has been emphasized here. With sufficient guidance and support, students do grasp and can use the four categories framework.

Friere's problem-posing framework (Wallerstein, 1987) provides the most extended support for identifying and formulating continuing concerns from the learner's, rather than the educator's, perspective. This is a valuable characteristic if teaching and learning are to be relevant to the participants' lives and engage their interest and motivation. The problem-posing framework also gives more explicit attention to carrying out action that has been selected or formulated. It offers the opportunity to carry the practical reasoning process through the full cycle. This includes taking action and evaluating the impact of this action by examining what has happened to the original concern once the action has been taken. Since extensive attention is given to identifying and formulating the concern in the first phase and to implementing action, the problem-posing framework requires the most time. It would be an appropriate framework to use to engage students in practical reasoning focused on an issue of concern over an entire term or year.

Figure 16-1, on page 226, presents a visual depiction of the overlapping components of the three frameworks for practical reasoning: Sirotnik's Questions Framework, the Family and Consumer Sciences Four Categories Framework, and Freire's Problem-Posing Framework. The four categories of the Family and Consumer Sciences framework (context, valued ends, means, and consequences), the three phases of Friere's framework and Sirotnik's eight questions (in italics) are depicted. As the chart reflects, the problem-posing framework, with its big segments of listening, dialogue, and action, lumps many things together that the other two frameworks pull out for focused attention. These other frameworks enrich, elaborate, and support the problem-posing framework, particularly the dialogue phase.

✳ Critical-Thinking Frameworks

This section presents two frameworks that are useful in engaging participants in critical thinking. As pointed out earlier, critical thinking is engaged in as a part of prac-

tical reasoning. In other words, if you work through the practical-reasoning frameworks presented previously, you will have engaged your learners in critical thinking. It is helpful for some purposes, however, to have thinking frameworks available that focus more specifically on discussion of specific claims, issues, questions, concepts, or proposals. Whereas the practical-reasoning frameworks are useful in dealing with as yet unformulated problems and issues, Paul's (1993) frameworks provide ways to approach thinking about already formulated positions. Use of Paul's frameworks can lead to reformulation and modification of your learners' positions and understanding of other positions. Although the ideas his frameworks contain are not unique, the way that Paul has organized them is helpful for educators.

✳ *Critical Analysis Framework*

Paul (1993) has formulated a framework that professionals and students have found helpful in organizing and guiding their thinking. An adaptation of this framework is presented in *Figure 16-2*, on page 227. The four dimensions of the "Critical Analysis Framework" are substructure, origins/roots, competing views, and implications/consequences. The claim, belief, proposal, or concept of interest is examined in terms of each dimension.

The similarities of some aspects of this framework and its questions to the Family and Consumer Sciences four practical-reasoning categories framework and questions are apparent. The origins/roots dimension is like the context category in the four categories practical-reasoning framework. The implications/consequences dimension is like the consequences category, and the competing views dimension could bring up issues related to conflicting interests, as in the valued-ends category of the four categories practical-reasoning framework. The major difference, however, is that rather than focusing on an issue or continuing concern and moving toward action, Paul's framework moves thinking towards deeper understanding of a claim or idea. Consequently, the Critical Analysis Framework is useful for examining

Figure 16-1 — OVERLAPPING COMMONALITIES OF THE FRAMEWORKS FOR PRACTICAL REASONING

CONTEXT

Problem-posing dialogue phase

Has this situation always been like this? Has it changed over time? What has led to its current state?

How did the situation, condition, issue come to be this way? (Sirotnik)

What information and knowledge do we have and do we need to help us understand the history and forces that have produced this situation? (Sirotnik)

VALUED ENDS

Problem-posing dialogue phase

What would be a more desirable situation, set of conditions?

What would be viewed as desirable by this group? By that group?

How would we describe this situation if it were the way we think it should be?

What would parents, adolescents, the community at large think of our description?

Who would benefit from the situation we have described as more desirable?

Whose interests are and are not being served by the way things are? Who benefits from the current situation? (Sirotnik)

What information and knowledge do we have and need to get from whom/where in order to understand and appreciate the various perspectives and interests involved? (Sirotnik)

Is this the way we want things to be? (Sirotnik)

If not, what would be better? What information and knowledge do we have and need to get that would help us generate ideas about and description of a more desirable state of affairs? (Sirotnik)

CONCERN

Problem-posing listening phase

What are we doing now? (Sirotnik)

What is happening now? (Sirotnik)

What information and knowledge do we have (or need to get) that bear upon identifying, describing, and understanding the current state of affairs with respect to ____? (Sirotnik)

MEANS

Problem-posing dialogue phase

What could be done about the situation, issue?

What could be done that would have the desired effect on the situation?

What resources are available to us or that we could gain access to?

What have others done when faced with a similar situation and seeking a similar goal?

What information and knowledge do we have (or need to get) about possible actions that could be taken? (Sirotnik) That might be effective? That would be consistent with the value positions of those involved in and affected by the situation?

What are we going to do about it? (Sirotnik)

CONSEQUENCES

Problem-posing dialogue phase

What will happen in the short run if we take this action?

What will happen in the long run if we take this action? Where might this action ultimately lead?

What will happen to whom if we take this action?

What would happen to each of these groups if this action were taken?

How is the situation we are concerned about likely to be affected if we take this action?

Might this action have unintended consequences?

ACTION

Problem-posing action phase

Figure 16-2

CRITICAL ANALYSIS FRAMEWORK

	Competing Views What would people who have a different view say about this?	
Origins/Roots Where did this idea and its underlying assumptions and central concepts come from? Who is proposing, promoting it, and why? Who is making this claim and why? From what historical, cultural origins does it emanate?	**The Claim, Belief, Proposal, Concept Being Examined**	**Implications/Consequences** Where does this idea lead if we take it to its ultimate conclusion? What will happen if this idea is pursued, adopted, believed by many people, acted upon?
	Substructure What assumptions underlie this idea? What reasons are given for believing it? What evidence is provided? What concepts are reflected in it?	

From Paul, R. *Critical Thinking: What Every Person Needs to Survive in a Rapidly Chaning World*. Revised 3rd edition © 1993. Foundations for Critical Thinking (www.criticalthinking.org) (cct@criticalthinking.org) Used with permission.

proposed solutions, claims, conclusions, or concepts. An example of each of these follows:

- **Proposed Solution.** We should build a footbridge over the highway to prevent deaths due to accidents.
- **Claim.** Making contraceptives available to teenagers will increase their sexual activity.
- **Conclusion.** Preschoolers benefit in important ways from early education.
- **Concept.** Logical consequences as a mode of child guidance.

The "Critical Analysis Framework" is useful for considering ideas and proposals raised in a meeting and in a classroom. It organizes thinking, generates relevant questions, and reveals perspectives underlying what is being examined. Because it can be quite specific in its focus, it can be used to guide the discussion of an idea within a single class session. Consequently, it is a framework that is useful when learners are together only once or for a very limited time. It is also useful when competing alternatives, ideas, or solutions are being advo-

cated. It provides a way to subject each of these to the same kind of scrutiny and examination, exposes hidden agendas, and supports a deeper understanding of each. Thus, it can help a group of people make more informed and critically considered choices.

Use of the framework in a classroom can proceed in many different ways. It is important to clarify with the learners at the onset what is being examined (what is in the center of *Figure 16-2*). Once this is clear, you will guide the discussion around the diagram. Starting with the substructure may seem logical because this dimension produces further clarification of what is being examined. In starting there, however, it is almost inevitable that ideas related to the other dimensions will emerge. In the beginning, it is helpful to set up four sheets of newsprint, four headings on a blackboard, or four pages on an electronic display so that ideas can be recorded where they fit as they emerge. You can still proceed from substructure to origins to competing views to implications and consequences as a general direction while being flexible in accepting ideas generated that are relative to another dimension.

✳ *Critical Dialogue Frameworks*

The critical analysis framework, discussed in the previous section, is useful for people doing their own critical analyses by themselves and for a group that is examining an idea. The Critical Dialogue Frameworks are intended as guides for interaction among people that allow participants to express and examine multiple ideas, rather than just looking for a single answer. Paul (1993) has suggested initially providing participants with highly supportive experiences and progressively increasing the challenge and complexity as they gain experience with critical dialogue. The dialogue frames nurture skills that are useful in the conversations most of us have daily with other people. These include:

- Listening fully to another's perspective.
- Drawing out another's perspective.
- Reconstructing and expressing another's perspective.

Critical dialogue is not the same as debate. The goal is not winning, making the other position or person look bad, or manipulating the other person to adopt a certain position. Instead, the goal is understanding. The strong, as well as the weak, aspects of alternative views are acknowledged. To encourage these orientations, participants might be asked to argue one side of an issue first and then argue the opposite view. The issues explored need to be ones that participants care about; otherwise the process is simply a shallow exercise and real critical thinking is not engaged.

Because identification of issues is important, ask your learners to list issues of concern to them that pertain to the course or subject. Issues may also emerge from class discussions and be agreed upon by the group as ones of interest. As the term "issue" suggests, there must be more than one view or position regarding it. Once issues are identified, then introduce the critical dialogue frame. The following sections discuss three types of critical dialogue.

Socratic Dialogue

Socratic dialogue is a good framework to use with inexperienced critical-dialogue participants. This type of dialogue offers support for the participants in formulating and expressing their views or positions with respect to the identified issue or question. The purpose is not to put learners down or expose their weaknesses. Rather, it draws out the learners' positions and helps them clarify and articulate their views.

To implement the Socratic dialogue, the student needs a partner who will ask questions designed to draw out the learner's position. This partner can be the teacher or another student who has received some coaching in being a good listener and Socratic questioner. A good way for the partner to start out after the student has stated a beginning position on some issue is to ask for elaboration, clarification, or meaning. For example, the partner could ask, "Please say a little more about. . . . " or "I'm a little unclear about. . . . Could you please explain what you mean by that?"

As the speaker responds, the partner listens for concepts and asks for their meaning. The partner might then probe as to how that meaning differs from other similar interpretations. For example, "When you use X in this context, how does it differ from Y?" The partner also listens for assumptions and asks for their basis. For example, "It seems that you are assuming X. If that is correct, what makes that assumption seem true? Justifiable?" The partner also asks for reasons why the speaker holds those views or assumptions. When they are provided, the partner considers their validity and implications. For example, a question might be, "If we agree to use that as an argument, what will happen to X?" The partner tries to figure out the core beliefs or conclusions within the position being articulated. The partner also asks the speaker about implications of the beliefs being expressed. The partner looks for consistencies among all these dimensions and asks about contradictions that seem evident.

The partner doesn't try to interject his or her own view or a contradictory position or tell the speaker the argument is strong or weak. The partner's goal is to understand the speaker's position and what it's based on and where it leads by posing questions that help the speaker consider and express the position. The partner must be a very good listener and good at resisting the temptation to evaluate or contradict the speaker's position or to suggest a "better" competing position. The partner who is genuinely interested in what the speaker has to say will find the role easier and be more successful in drawing out the student's position.

Reconstructing Another Point of View

This critical dialogue framework raises a unique challenge for the learner. The positions that the learners must formulate and express are not their own but someone else's. Ideally, it is a position with which the learners disagree. Learners must argue these positions as if they are their own and point out the strengths, as well as acknowledge the weaknesses. The goal is to understand and appreciate the other view. This requires the students to take on another's position, think it through, and see the world from that perspective. By doing this, students use the opposing view as a lens from which to view the questions, events, and situations being examined. People often just oppose views that are different from their own without really understanding them. Paul has stated that the most difficult views to reconstruct are those that are opposed to your own. This is true because opposing views compete directly with the value system underlying your own views. They threaten your value system, and you are likely to see them as dangerous. Those you identify with are much easier to reconstruct. There are also views that are difficult to construct because you are unfamiliar with them, and you may have trouble getting interested in reconstructing them because they may appear irrelevant to your own view.

Students may do the reconstruction on their own and present the view as an argument to a group. Group members then ask Socratic dialogue questions, or the student and a partner may have a Socratic dialogue similar to that outlined in the previous section. The position the student expresses at the initiation of the dialogue, however, is the reconstructed position. This position is then elaborated on with the assistance of the partner's questions. As in Socratic dialogue, partners do not interject their positions. Instead, the partner's role is to draw out the thinking of the student, which in this case is the student's reconstruction of another's position.

Dialectical Dialogue

This dialogue framework is arguably the most challenging for the learner because it is more complex, incorporating the other two critical dialogue frameworks. This dialogue involves critical discussion of two contrasting points of view. Like the others, it involves two persons, but both are questioners, and both are formulating not just one, but two, positions. Issues that reflect at least two contradictory points of view are especially well suited to this dialogue framework. These are positions where one cannot be true if the other is true. For example, positions that only traditional marriages be allowed and that nontraditional marriages should be allowed are contradictory. Similarly, an argument for government subsidy of day child care and one against such subsidy are contradictory.

In this type of dialogue both persons offer a point of view that contrasts with the other's point of view. The idea is to take an issue and reconstruct one side or the other and have a discussion that is fruitful without making the other side look bad. Students think of reasons that can be offered in support of the position they are arguing. Both persons question each other regarding the other's point of view. After a while, if there is time, the partners switch sides, each arguing the position that opposes the one they were just expressing. The goals of this framework are to help learners enrich their points of view, become more aware of the limitations of their views, and acknowledge the strengths of other views.

Although an educator can be an effective partner in the other two types of critical dialogues, Paul has recommended that students be partners in the dialectical dialogue. Pitting an educator's view against a learner's is not conducive to the learner's deep understanding and ability to think through the merits of a position.

❋ Thinking in Action Framework

The "Thinking in Action Framework" helps the learners understand that context interacts with thought, action, and purposes and can modify all three. Learners come to appreciate the use they make of the context and the resulting adjustment of action plans that they do on a continual basis. Once learners are aware of these patterns, they are able to see ways to incorporate the context into their thinking, action formulation, and evaluation.

The context is a source of both problems and solutions. It introduces unexpected occurrences, situations, and conditions. For example, a woman who thought her flight to Florida would land by 7:00 p.m. finds herself still in Chicago at midnight waiting for a mechanical problem to be solved. The context also contains resources that can be incorporated in formulating action to address the issues. For example, the context provides technology that allows the woman to call her brother in Florida and let him know the situation.

The context is also a source of learning because we find new possibilities as we fix the numerous snags that we experience throughout the day. The man who allowed plenty of time to get to an interview finds that the road he planned to take has been torn up and blocked. He finds another route he had not been aware of that is more direct than the one he knew.

As human beings, our goals, purposes, and interests make some aspects of context salient and others go unnoticed. For example, farmers and resort owners take special note of weather, a contextual feature which people who work in offices may not be concerned about except on weekends. If you have just learned that you have a child with diabetes, you are suddenly aware that there are many children with diabetes whom you hadn't noticed before.

The context is always changing—far more than we realize. This fluidity of context is illustrated by a woman who needed a lawnmower for the following season. In February she bought a used lawnmower that didn't work from her boyfriend's brother and got it fixed. She spent as much on repairs as a new one would cost, but she wanted to cement her relationship with the boyfriend and his family. In May, the lawnmower would not start, despite its overhaul. She had broken up with the boyfriend over the winter. A neighbor showed her how to start it, and she was able to use it to meet her need for cutting the grass. The woman's primary purpose was no longer a factor. However, her second purpose, lawnmowing, now became primary. The context provided a solution—a sympathetic neighbor who was knowledgeable about motors and willing to help.

To help students understand how context interacts with thoughts, actions, goals, and purposes on a personal level, you could ask your students to share a recent experience they had in which things did not go as they planned. Learners are asked to write experiences down, being sure to include the following:

- **Background.** What led up to this activity, event, or situation? What had gone on before?
- **Purpose.** Why was this activity taking place? Why had this been planned? What was the intent or idea behind it?
- **Activity.** What was happening? What was the activity you or other people were engaged in?
- **Reasons for Activity Choice.** Why this particular activity rather than some other?
- **The Problem or Unexpected Occurrence.** What snag or glitch occurred?
- **Alternatives Considered and Their Evaluation.** What alternatives were considered? How was each alternative evaluated?
- **Resolution.** How was the situation resolved?

When learners have prepared their stories, they are shared in small groups. The groups are asked to find the following features of thinking in action reflected in each of the stories:

- Connection to purposive, goal-directed activities of daily life
- Back and forth action between problem definition and solution and between people
- Incorporation of context
- Flexibility and creativity
- Conservation of energy and other resources
- Dependence on available knowledge in the situation

Finally, the groups are asked to reflect on all of the stories they have heard and to identify any further features that they believe characterize thought in action. They are then encouraged to use their understanding in addressing the issues that arise for them in their day-to-day life in the days ahead.

Thinking: A Critical Aspect of Education

The discussion of thinking in this chapter has focused on engaging learners in thinking relevant to their everyday lives. The approaches discussed here are not for teaching about thinking, but rather, they are intended for involving students in thinking. Through such engagement, learners are able to develop their capacities for thinking. These capacities are social, emotional, and cognitive. The thinking frameworks are adaptable for use with a wide range of learners of varying ages, educational backgrounds, and experiences.

References

Birren, J.E. and Fisher, L.M. (1990). The elements of wisdom: Overview and integration. In R. Sternberg (Ed.), Wisdom: Its nature, origins, and development. New York: Cambridge University Press.

Coombs, J. (1997). Practical reasoning: What is it? How do we enhance it? In J. Laster & R. Thomas, Family and consumer sciences teacher education: Yearbook 17, Thinking for ethical action in families and communities (pp. 49-64). Peoria, IL: American Association of Family and Consumer Sciences and Glencoe/McGraw-Hill.

Fedje, C. (1998). Helping learners develop their practical reasoning capacities. In R. Thomas and J. Laster (Eds.), Family and consumer sciences teacher education: Yearbook 18, Inquiry into thinking (pp. 29-46). Peoria, IL: American Association of Family and Consumer Sciences and Glencoe/McGraw-Hill.

Freire, P. (1973). Pedagogy of the oppressed. New York. Seabury Press.

Knippel, D. (1998). Practical reasoning in the family context. In R. Thomas and J. Laster (Eds.), Family and consumer sciences teacher education: Yearbook 18, Inquiry into thinking (pp. 16-28). Peoria, IL: American Association of Family and Consumer Sciences and Glencoe/McGraw-Hill.

Paul, R. (1993). Critical thinking: What every person needs to survive in a rapidly changing world (Revised 3rd ed.). Santa Rosa, CA: Foundations for Critical Thinking.

Schon, D.A. (1983). The reflective practitioner. New York: Basic Books.

Scribner, S. (1986). Thinking in action: Some characteristics of practical thought. In R.G. Sternberg and R. Wagner (Eds.), Practical intelligence: Nature and origins of competence in the everyday world (pp. 13-30). New York: Cambridge University Press.

Sirotnik, K. (1991). Critical inquiry: A paradigm for praxis. In E. Short (Ed.), Forms of curriculum inquiry (pp. 243-258). Albany, NY: State University of New York Press.

Vygotsky, L.S. (1978). Mind in society: The development of higher psychological processes. Cambridge, MA: Harvard University.

Wallerstein, N. (1987). Problem posing education: Friere's method of transformation. In I. Shor (Ed.), Friere for the classroom (pp. 34-44). Portsmouth, NH: Boynton/Cook Division of Heinemann.

Building Your Professional Portfolio

Classroom Strategies. Interview teachers and find out strategies they use to promote critical thinking. Write a summary of your interviews.

Integrating Critical Thinking. Choose two topics related to your field of study. For each, write an analysis-level objective and a corresponding analysis-level learning experience that would promote critical thinking:

- Energy conservation
- Housing selection
- Food-intake patterns
- Lifestyle changes
- Weight maintenance

Critical Thinking Questions. Develop questions that foster critical thinking for each of these topics:

- Care of elder family members
- Personal health assessment
- Investment options
- Balancing work and family

Critical-Analysis Dialogue. Write a dialogue involving either an educator and learners or two learners where critical-analysis dialogue is illustrated.

Chapter 17

Integrating Basic Skills into Your Curriculum

Sandra W. Miller, Ph.D.
Professor Emeritus, Family and Consumer
    Sciences Education
University of Kentucky

Charlotte Tulloch, Ed.D.
Teacher Educator, Special Populations
University of Kentucky

*T*he headlines confirm it. Student performance on academic achievement tests continues to fall below expectations in many districts and states.

There have been reports about the inability of high school graduates to write an intelligible letter, complete application forms acceptably, and make change correctly for customers. These limitations have contributed to the increased emphasis on acquisition of basic skills in elementary and secondary education.

Various definitions of the term "basic skills" have been suggested. Family and consumer sciences and health educators believe the knowledge and skills in their disciplines are "basic" to the quality of life for individuals and families. For the most part, the education reform movement defines basic skills as mathematics, science, writing, reading, and social studies. Sometimes critical thinking, covered in the previous chapter, is also considered a basic skill. And for learners in the 21st century, Internet literacy may also be considered a basic skill. In each of these areas, "basic" refers to skills at least appropriate for grade level, not to low-level skills.

 ## Basic Skills

There are natural overlaps between basic skills and all other subject-matter areas. When people are confronted with a compelling problem or puzzling situation, they don't ponder which part is math, which is family and consumer sciences, health, and so on. Instead they draw on knowledge and skills from all subject areas that might prove helpful.

Students often learn more and are more motivated when basic skills are reinforced through applied fields because they are able to see the relevancy of those skills to their lives. It's apparent that reading is relevant as consumers read product labels and directions. As job seekers draft letters to prospective employers, the importance of good writing skills is clearer. Learners see the value of math as they estimate costs and comparison shop, or when they take and record vital signs. Science comes alive as students learn principles underlying food preservation, the body's use of food, or treatment of infections. Students see the purpose of social studies as they study the relationship between price and demand for consumer goods, such as household products, or factors that promote and reinforce gender stereotyping.

While the overriding goal of family and consumer sciences or health isn't to teach basic skills per se, these skills are essential if your students are to acquire competencies in these disciplines. Thus, when your learners are unable to perform these basic skills, you have the responsibility to teach the skills within the context of your field.

Sometimes teachers of different subjects work together to teach basic skills. One approach is for two or more teachers from different disciplines to teach their learners together, sharing facilities. For example, family and consumer sciences, math, and social studies instructors might collaborate to teach world protein distribution and consumption. Their goal would be for the students to learn more about percentages in mathematics, protein content in meats and other foods, and protein distribution and consumption among the world's population. The teachers would mix their students, move into each other's classrooms and labs, and share resources. Another collaboration example, a multidisciplinary one, is to focus on a single theme across a variety of disciplines. Regional agricultural products are a possible focus in which agriculture, family and consumer sciences, health, mathematics, and social studies teachers could independently have lessons with their respective students as their contribution to the project. The topics might range from nutrition to math skills as they relate to how the commodities are sold. Social studies students might address the future of family farms.

Personnel exchanges may also be used in integration. For example, a math teacher may visit a family and consumer sciences or health classroom to reinforce relevant mathematics. Or, a family and consumer sciences instructor may give a PowerPoint® presentation to a social studies class about early homes and how culture influences housing. The same teacher might demonstrate food preparation skills to foreign language students learning about international cuisine. In return, a French teacher might teach a foods class the pronunciation and origin of food terms such as *hors d'oeuvre*, *en brochette*, *canapé*, and *crepes*.

❈ Mathematics

In many content areas it's important that learners use mathematics to solve problems and understand content. Understanding paycheck statements; figuring sales taxes and discounts; calculating unit prices; the cost of credit; the number of rolls of wallpaper to purchase for a room; and interpreting children's growth charts are but a few of the tasks where basic math skills are needed. *Figure 17-1* on page 235 provides ideas for linking various content areas with math.

Some general tips for helping students hone their math skills include the following:

- Never assume that all students are proficient in math applications, such as calculating averages, percents, or fractions. Do several practice problems with them.
- Be sure handouts that include mathematics are error-free and that you can accurately and confidently demonstrate the relevant skills.
- Use actual items whenever possible. The hands-on approach will make the activity seem less abstract and help capture learners' interest.
- Vary classroom activities more often when math is involved. Many students have an aversion to mathematics. The attention span for learners doing a difficult task is limited.

❈ Science

In science classes students gather information through laboratory, field, and research work and draw conclusions based on their observations and data. There are many opportunities to show how the scientific process relates to various aspects of everyday life.

Experiments can be powerful learning opportunities. For example, the relationship between physical well-being and an adequate diet can be shown through animal feeding experiments that might be conducted cooperatively with a general science, biology, or agriculture class. Principles

Figure 17-1

MATHEMATICS LINKS

There are many creative ways to link math to your subject matter:

- Provide students with restaurant menus. Have them simulate dining out with some learners as servers and others playing customers. Have students practice computing meal costs, tips, change, and dividing the bill among the members of their dining party. They may also be able to compare the practicality of buying a complete meal rather than à la carte selections. Finally, you may want to have participants determine the cost of preparing the same meal at home.
- Have learners compute their Body Mass Index (BMI) and their target heart range. Discuss the use of each as a tool in a wellness program.
- Give students recipes and have them halve or double the recipe, prepare it, and evaluate the resulting product.
- Give learners an imaginary $1,000 to invest for five years. Have them calculate the return on their money at various interest rates.
- Provide the dimensions of several rooms in a home. Have students determine the number of square yards of floor covering that is needed. Based on the price per square yard, have them calculate the cost of various floor coverings. An alternative is to have students actually measure the classroom and compute costs for replacing its flooring.
- Have learners plan an entrepreneurial project. For example, they might make and sell denim purses or stuffed toys at craft fairs. Or, they might develop a food product, such as jars of salsa or packages of dried mixes for soup, dip, or hot chocolate. Have students compute the cost of necessary materials, the product's selling price, and the profit that would be achieved. How many would they have to sell to make a profit of $100, $500, etc.?
- Let learners choose a vehicle to "buy" from newspaper or online ads that include descriptions. Have them calculate the monthly cost of owning the vehicle, including the loan payment, insurance, fuel, and license.
- Have a mock shopping trip in the classroom. Attach price tags to garments hanging from a rack. Ask students to figure the cost of purchasing two garments, including sales tax. Have them determine the cost of a garment after discounts of 20, 30, and 40 percent. Even students who perform well in math class may find such real-life applications difficult and can benefit from the practice.
- Have students use census data to create graphs depicting rates of birth, marriage, divorce, death, etc.

behind frozen food preparation can be illustrated with an experiment involving correctly and incorrectly wrapping foods to be frozen, storing them in the freezer for a period of time, and then evaluating them for flavor, texture, and appearance. Learners are both physically and intellectually involved in the activity.

Demonstrations are another effective way to teach scientific principles. They could be used in a foods or food science course to illustrate the nutritive composition of some foods, such as oil in peanut butter, starch in potatoes, and sugar and fat in selected fast foods. Experiments can show chemical reactions in food preparation when various substances are combined: the production of carbon dioxide when baking powder and water or baking soda and an acid are mixed, or the reaction of easily oxidized fruit when it's treated and not treated with an acid. Making yogurt can be used to illustrate the effects of acids and enzymes on milk products.

As students learn about child development or health, they encounter various science-related topics, ranging from prenatal development to genetics to immunizations to brain development. Learners might research why breast-feeding has been deemed more beneficial than formula, or how doctors rate newborns using the Apgar scale.

Science has an important role in the study of housing and construction as students learn about electrical systems, plumbing, heating, cooling, and ventilation. For instance, a brief refresher course on the properties of electricity may be necessary as ground fault circuit interrupters and circuit breakers are studied.

A nutrition educator might teach the chemistry involved in diabetes. In another setting, the topic might be an explanation of the role of metabolism in weight loss.

Many scientific concepts cross subject-area lines. For example, physics principles can be applied through the study of convection and conduction, microwave and pressure cookery, and light diffusion. The effects of advancing and receding colors can be incorporated into lessons on interior design and apparel selection.

✳ Social Studies

There are many ways to link content to social studies through geography, history, government, economics, and sociology. Increasing global interdependence in today's society affects consumerism, nutrition, foods, textiles, apparel, housing, and health. Cultural diversity is incorporated into the study of human development and families.

Learners may be able to trace customs in their own families to their cultural heritage and share these customs with the group. They can read about ethnic foods and analyze food customs unique to various regions of the U.S. and the world.

The global perspective in child development and human relations can be explored by asking individuals who were raised in another country to share views on child-rearing and traditions associated with children. Learners can use the Internet and other resources to study the social development of children in various countries, seeking information on cultural values, education, life expectancy, health care, family interactions, and traditions such as games and recreation.

History comes alive and is much more meaningful when connected to the content areas that are being studied. Interior design and clothing students can learn about the evolution of styles through the years. Learners might compare lifestyles in Colonial times with those today. For example, analyzing children's furniture and clothing from Colonial days indicates that children were considered little adults rather than active, creative youngsters who were still developing. Students might compare the times when doctors made house calls and a variety of home remedies were tried versus the use of prompt-care centers and prescriptions that prevail today.

Issues of hunger and homelessness can be addressed through serving meals at a soup kitchen or collecting canned goods for a food pantry. Students can participate in programs, such as Habitat for Humanity and other service learning projects.

Movies, TV programs, and commercials might be studied to see if and how they promote and reinforce gender stereotyping. Students can compare any differences between the way males and females are depicted in physical appearance, personality, and activities in which they're involved. If a problem is part of the story line, students can determine what it is, who has the problem, who resolves it, and how.

Oral histories of older adults can be recorded to compare lifestyles or household activities of the past with contemporary ones. Interviews give students contact with older adults, a practice that can facilitate understanding of later years of life, diminish stereotyping of seniors, and allow the seniors to assist in the education of youth.

✳ Writing

Good writing skills are vital because people rely on written communication on the job, with e-mail, and often in family life. Many educators share a belief that young people must learn to write and write to learn. The best way to improve writing skills is to provide opportunities to write. Incorporating writing into daily lesson plans can be accomplished in a variety of ways, besides traditional subject-matter reports and papers. Learners can take part in activities like the following:

• Keep real or imaginary journals and diaries. Students should have the freedom to write as if they're thinking aloud.

- Summarize a reading assignment they have completed. This will help learners quickly assess whether or not they comprehended the material.
- For several minutes at the beginning of a class period, write about what they learned in yesterday's session. Or, at the end of class, write about what's just been learned.
- Define vocabulary words and use them creatively in sentences.
- Write vivid descriptions of clothing designs, meal plans, room settings, a home's exterior, or children observed at play.
- Evaluate classroom and laboratory projects.
- Write invitations and thank-you notes to resource persons.
- Write an essay, have a peer or teacher critique it, and then rewrite the piece.
- Compose book reviews of children's books or other books relevant to the subject area. Movie reviews are another possibility if the subject matter pertains to a topic that is being studied.
- Write letters to legislators, to the editor of a magazine or newspaper, or to retailers and manufacturers.
- Write a news release about an activity the class or group is doing or write about events from a reporter's point of view.

Many learners today feel more comfortable writing at a computer keyboard than writing by hand on paper. Some may be able to record their thoughts more quickly this way and enjoy the ease of editing and making changes. You may choose to have them print a hard copy of their draft so you can give feedback along the way.

For some assignments, such as journals, the goal is to clarify thinking and develop the art of writing. Occasionally, you may assign topics such as "A Purchase I Made That Wasted My Money" or "How to Deal with a Three-Year-Old's Temper Tantrum" or "In Ten Years I Hope to Be . . . " You may choose to collect these assignments to read and/or grade or not, but you should award credit for completing the activity.

Learners may also be required to research and write about concrete topics, such as child abuse and its prevention, addictions such as smoking and alcohol, and diseases like mononucleosis. In addition to content, these more formal reports should be evaluated on the clarity and technical aspects of the work. Are words spelled correctly? Are words capitalized as necessary? Are appropriate words and correct grammar and punctuation used? Is the writing style appropriate to the situation? For assignments created with word processing, is the formatting correct? Students need to be made aware of the points on which their work will be assessed. You may choose to use a rubric for this purpose.

In addition to writing journal entries and reports, learners can practice real-life writing activities. These might include filling out job applications or scholarship forms, writing résumés, completing insurance forms, and writing step-by-step directions.

✳ Reading

Reading is often regarded as the most important basic skill because all content areas depend upon it. Reading competency is essential in the working world since almost all occupations require reading and writing. Many workers spend a minimum of two hours daily reading print, charts, graphs, and computer screens.

In a perfect world, all students who entered your classroom would be proficient readers; yet obviously that won't be the case. It's possible to structure lessons to help the students who struggle with reading. While reading teachers emphasize specific skills, your focus will be on those skills your learners need to understand the information being presented. You will use reading to teach more content. *Figure 17-2* on page 238 suggests techniques to improve reading skills.

For learners with a negative attitude toward reading, reinforce an awareness of the different materials they will need to read throughout life. Of special significance to teens are the state's drivers license manual, e-mail, catalogs, magazines, and menus. Other materials include ads, recipes, equipment manuals and directions, contracts, and medicine labels. You might lead a discussion about the possible consequences if a pre-

Figure 17-2

TECHNIQUES TO IMPROVE READING

Here are some approaches to improving reading skills:

- Help learners become acquainted with reading materials being used. For example, when using a new textbook it's helpful for students to understand the overall layout, chapter organization, and the clues that indicate what's important, such as bold print, underlining, and highlighting.
- Introduce reading assignments, whether they are one page or a chapter. Explain what learners are supposed to glean from the assignment and why they are reading it. You might assess what they already know about the topic and discuss how they can build upon their prior knowledge. Familiarize them with new vocabulary and define key words. Point out any advance organizers. Suggest that learners focus on the title and the first sentence of each paragraph, since these give direction to the content that follows.
- Motivate learners to read. For example, before giving a reading assignment on marriage, ask an open-ended question such as "What makes a good marriage partner?" Showing objects featured in a reading or cartoons, posters, and pictures related to the reading can also generate interest. For

example, you might pass around various types of bandages described in a chapter on first aid.

- Encourage learners to jot down questions or ideas that come to them as they read. They might use self-stick notes.
- Assign readings of an appropriate length and difficulty. Several short readings can be easier to tackle than one long assignment in which learners may get lost or lose interest. The more difficult the reading, the shorter it should be. For example, students might be able to quickly read a chapter on good grooming, whereas technical information about fibers and fabric construction would be better divided into more than one reading assignment.
- Pose questions that require learners to go beyond picking out isolated pieces of information. For example, for an assigned reading on the types of advertising, ask learners to list the types and then give their own examples, not the ones provided in the text.
- Use word games to allow learners to practice basic reading skills in a way that does not seem like work. Crossword puzzles, word searches, and word scrambles are games that can help reinforce the meaning and spelling of new vocabulary words.

scription bottle, recipe, map, or babysitter's instructions were misinterpreted.

It's helpful to informally assess students' reading skills at the beginning of a course. A variety of methods can be used. For example, you could devise a reading guide based on a text chapter or reading selection. This could include main points or main heads. Depending upon your purpose, you might add comprehension questions beneath each or have students write in the main points. Reviewing the completed guides can help you identify individual and group strengths and weaknesses. Check the Internet or talk to someone from the language arts department for additional simple diagnostic tools, such as the Cloze procedure.

✳ Reading Levels

Written materials that are too far above or too far below learners' reading levels can be a turn-off to them. Generally, short words and sentences are indicative of lower reading levels, whereas words with several syllables and long, more complicated sentence structures are found in materials with a higher reading level. There are several formulas available to help determine the reading level of material you are considering assigning to your learners. Information about the Fry readability formula, one that has been used for many years, is available online. Remember that the larger the number of samples used in testing the readability level of a resource, the more accurate the score will be.

Reading level, as determined by a readability formula, should be just one of the factors considered when evaluating the reading appropriateness of a text or similar material. Other factors to evaluate include:

- Is the writing style interesting and clear?
- Is the overall look inviting?
- Is the print easy to read?
- Do the headings within the material help readers understand the organization and key points?
- Are key terms that may be unfamiliar set off and explained at first use?
- Is a glossary included, preferably with pronunciation guides for terms difficult to pronounce?

Comprehension is more difficult for concepts that are abstract rather than concrete. The less factual and more abstract concepts are, the more difficult the material is to read and comprehend. For example, "discipline" and "maturity" and "economics" are rather abstract concepts. Simple definitions can't fully clarify them. It's only after reading, study, and experience that some concepts become clearer.

✳ *Reading in Class*

Avoid asking struggling readers to read aloud to the entire class or large group. There are more effective practices for student reading than the dreaded "round robin." However, oral reading in class can be effective if used appropriately. For example:

- Assign students to small groups or pair with a reading buddy. Have them silently pre-read a section and then read it aloud to their group or buddy. Guide them so that each reads about an equal amount. Explain to them how they should discuss the reading or look for particular points or issues.
- Allow students to read a section silently before reading aloud. They might even be alerted the day before so they have time to practice.
- The teacher or a learner who reads well might read aloud a short section as needed. Reading an appropriate, interesting book to the class, a chapter or section a day, may help to present desired concepts in a new way, facilitate discussion, and provide struggling readers an oppor-

tunity to share in a good book. Just be sure to stop reading before students stop listening.

- Be sensitive to the content. Don't ask learners to read something aloud that might embarrass them.

Using a Variety of Reading Materials

A variety of types of reading materials besides texts are suitable for classroom use. Newspapers, magazines, paperbacks, pamphlets, catalogs, Cooperative Extension bulletins, and Internet websites may be excellent resource materials. Relevant equipment manuals and other everyday reading can also be very useful.

By using different types of written resource materials, you will increase interest in the topics you are teaching. Most learners relate well to these familiar materials. Once their interest is piqued, you are more likely to be able to reinforce basic skills.

Using familiar reading materials also helps to keep materials current and relevant. Newspaper flyers provide current supermarket prices. Magazine and newspaper articles reflect concerns and issues of the day. Many such materials are inexpensive or free, allowing for frequent replacement and updating.

Some examples involving a variety of reading materials follow. Many of these can be adapted for use in studying a variety of content areas and simultaneously reinforcing basic skills. Your ability to use these materials effectively is as important as the quality of the publications themselves. Guide learners in using periodicals, pamphlets, newspapers, and other written materials to ensure optimum learning. Encouraging students to read them isn't enough.

✳ Newspapers

Newspapers are an excellent resource to supplement textbooks. Health students can read about the latest medical advancements. FCS students can follow news and legislation that affect children, teens and families; find healthful new recipes; and read about what local people are doing to improve life in their community. Character education can be taught with feature articles that appear in the newspaper.

Newspapers can be used with learners of any age. Struggling readers are proud to be seen reading a newspaper, rather than some remedial materials that might carry a stigma. Critical thinking can be promoted as students look for differences in opinion or outlook while comparing multiple editorials and articles covering the same issues or situations.

Since not all your learners will have daily access to a newspaper—or perhaps even be familiar with the newspaper—it's likely that you will have to provide articles or newspapers. Many publishers have programs that make copies of their paper available to schools and programs at a reduced cost. More than 700 newspapers in the U.S. participate in a program called Newspaper in Education (NIE). Administered by the Newspaper of American Foundation, the NIE programs provide a wide variety of curriculum materials to teachers. Many of the teaching materials are linked to learning standards in the respective states. Contact your local newspaper publishing company to find out if they participate in the NIE program or visit the foundation online.

Figure 17-3, "Teaching with Newspapers," below and on page 241 illustrates a few of the ways that different components of a newspaper can be used in teaching family and consumer sciences and health. Many of these learning experiences could be coordinated with assignments and projects in other subjects.

❋ Paperbacks, Periodicals, and Bulletins

Paperbacks may have special appeal to learners especially if they are bestsellers or currently popular. Attractive paperbacks may be less threatening than textbooks to some readers.

Many paperback books dealing with consumerism, interpersonal relationships, health issues, and lay psychological theory could enhance learning on related topics. If possible, have a selection on hand to lend to learners. You can save money by buying them at a used bookstore that exchanges paperbacks. The array of paperbacks available also enables learners at various maturity levels and from different cultural and socioeconomic backgrounds to satisfy their diverse needs and interests.

Because magazines focus on many issues that are important to students, they can be an effective tool in the classroom. The timeliness of material in current issues makes them especially appealing. If there are students who regularly receive magazines at home, you might ask them to bring in articles related to topics discussed in class. Articles can be shared and discussed. Magazine pictures can be used for making notebooks, mobiles, collages, posters, bulletin boards, and other visuals.

Bulletins from agencies such as Cooperative Extension, health, or other service agencies provide current, pertinent information. Agencies may not be able to provide classroom quantities, but often they will supply one or a few copies for teachers to put in a resource file for students. Learners will then have relevant,

---

Figure 17-3

TEACHING WITH NEWSPAPERS

Hundreds of newspaper publishers provide guides and workbooks that instructors can use to teach their students by reading various components of the newspaper. These include news stories, columns and features, editorials, advertisements, and even the comics and the weather. Many involve using math, language arts, science, social studies, and critical-thinking skills. These are just a few possible activities.

- Read newspaper articles about local, state, and national efforts to solve problems relating to drugs, school violence, health care issues, eating disorders, unemployment, child abuse, pollution, disease control, and

Figure 17-3 (cont'd)

TEACHING WITH NEWSPAPERS

other pressing issues. Discuss the responsibilities of citizens to question or support pertinent legislation and programs.

- Collect articles about home accidents. Suggest ways by which these mishaps might have been avoided. Discuss whether response to each accident was appropriate or inappropriate.

- Practice reading and writing skills by choosing an article that pertains to subject matter being covered in class. After reading the article carefully, have students write a brief synopsis to share with classmates.

- Hold a "press conference" in which students pretend to have just discovered another nutrient, developed a new synthetic fiber, found a cure for a disease, or invented a revolutionary household appliance. Or, feature a real nutrient, new fiber, new cure, or appliance. Write news stories describing how this new product will change consumer practices and affect personal and family living and health.

- Identify trends in interior design by reading features about furnishings and home improvement. Compile a design resource file by clipping articles, photos, and ads.

- Analyze advertisements to differentiate between those having a primarily emotional appeal and those providing factual data. Determine what the emotional ads are suggesting to the consumer. Decide which ads both appeal to emotions and provide meaningful consumer information.

- Discuss the psychological effects of various phrases such as "for . . . three days only," "only two to a customer," "must be sold immediately," "last chance to buy," "stock up while they last," and "limited quantity available." Find examples of other phrases used in ads that are designed to persuade consumers to act quickly. Distinguish between "for sale" and "on sale."

- Analyze ads to determine their target market. Then design ads that try to persuade different types of people to buy the same hypothetical product. Create advertisements that appeal to money, beauty,

style, health, and status consciousness. Also create ads that attract particular groups such as young children, teens, middle-aged women, men, parents, and retirees.

- Read the food ads and plan menus for a week, using as many specials as practical. Discuss why supermarkets sometimes sell items below cost, advertise specials, and promote features such as double coupons or extended store hours. Discuss the value of advertising for both the consumer and the seller.

- Analyze classified ads in a newspaper over a period of time to determine the types of employment for which there are the greatest and least demands locally. Analyze possible reasons. Select a job from the classified ads and write a letter applying for that position. Develop an appropriate résumé to include with the letter.

- Use the classified sections of several newspapers and have a scavenger hunt to locate all the jobs advertised relating to specific areas, such as home health care, dental hygiene, child development, clothing and textiles, food and nutrition, resource management, or any other areas being studied. If listed, analyze the rate of pay offered and education required.

- Read letters in personal advice columns, but not the replies. Have students write replies and then compare them to the columnist's reply. Discuss the possible effects of the proposed courses of action.

- Analyze cartoons or comic strips to determine values held by the artist as reflected through various characters. Find examples of a cartoon character being or not being honest, persistent, respectful of others, tolerant, etc.

- Pretend to buy a few stocks and follow the market every day. Compute gains and losses at the end of a specified period of time. Analyze reasons why some stocks may have increased in value while others declined. Follow the same procedure with mutual funds.

"real-world" materials available on topics ranging from health care to food management to money management to the care of aging relatives.

✳ Internet

The Internet has opened up a vast, worldwide library of written materials. Most educators and learners have some access to the Internet at school, an office, or at home. Beyond these sources, public libraries and other agencies also provide Internet access. Thus, learners can study or explore a topic online at the same locations where they might research a topic in books.

Searching for materials online can be appealing, even to individuals who aren't inclined to read. Thus, the novelty may attract some learners. Internet material also has an advantage in that information can be "published" almost instantly, instead of having a long delay while a book is being edited, printed, and distributed. The ease of publication is, however, also a disadvantage because anyone may publish almost anything on the Internet. As a result, the World Wide Web has both valuable, accurate information as well as questionable websites and unreliable information.

Because of the wide range in quality of information on the Internet, it is essential for educators to help learners examine Web materials critically. Refer back to pages 207-208 for a list of criteria for judging the credibility of websites. As learners surf the net, remind them of the conduct that you and school officials expect of them. They should never reveal personal information and should notify you right away if they encounter inappropriate material.

Many learning activities can combine the use of material from the World Wide Web with conventional printed materials. A few suggested uses follow:

- Require students to include the Internet in research projects. Make arrangements for them to conduct Web searches in the classroom, computer lab, or library.
- Research topics that are currently being considered for state or national legislative action, such as child care, school violence, and health-care costs. Have learners formulate opinions and then compose and send e-mails sharing their concerns and ideas with appropriate legislators.
- Develop brochures on relevant topics. Have learners use data found on the Web and copyright-free graphics.
- Have learners explore how personal bills can be paid online. Compare the process with paying a bill in person or by sending it through the mail.
- Research a topic currently in the news by searching in newspapers across the country. Media websites provide access to many newspapers by state. Some newspapers put much of their content online while others may not. Follow an ongoing issue for several days or weeks and report on its development. Look for discrepancies or differences in interpretation of issues among various online newspapers.
- Examine cost-of-living information for several cities. Explore what the costs and benefits would be for living in a particular city or region. Compare one city or region with another.

 # Publicizing Basic Skills Integration

Familiarize yourself with any district, state, or national standards your school uses for language arts, science, math, and social studies. This will help you identify ones you already incorporate in your program and others that are relevant.

Let administrators, other professionals, learners, and the public know about your efforts towards teaching basic skills, especially in real-world contexts. This will enhance respect and recognition for you, your learners, and your program. Make a matrix identifying how your program and basic skills competency standards interface. Post the matrix in your classroom. Present it at open houses, to your school board and advisory council, and at parents' and faculty meetings. *Figure 17-4* on page 243 provides a sample matrix.

Figure 17-4

SAMPLE BASIC SKILLS MATRIX

Mathematics Basic Skill Competencies	Management Concepts		
	Saving energy in the home	Managing a checking account	Using financial services
Read a Celsius or Fahrenheit thermometer to the nearest unit marked.	X		
Identify data relevant to the problem being solved from the statement of the problem.	X	X	
Identify appropriate units to measure mass.			
Estimate the answer to a computation problem.	X	X	X

Develop a portfolio of your best basic skills activities. Show the portfolio to your administrators, advisory council members, parents, other instructors, and counselors. Invite administrators to your program when you are doing an outstanding project incorporating basic skills. When you have visitors to your classroom, tell them both your subject matter and basic skills competencies for the lesson. You might say, "Today's objective is to assess the leading chronic disease conditions among middle-aged Americans. Our basic skills competency is graphing. Students will construct graphs that illustrate the numbers of males and females aged 40-60 affected with various chronic diseases."

❊ Cross Credits

Many school districts and states have increased graduation requirements, thus making scheduling of career and technical courses difficult. As a result of this and other factors, some districts and states have approved cross credits. Sometimes these are referred to as equivalent credit, dual credit, or optional credit. They are awarded for career and technical courses that emphasize a particular basic skill. For example, in some states and districts a student can earn a science credit by taking food and nutritional science, a social studies credit through a money management or consumer education course, or communication credit through a personal development course. This practice makes scheduling more flexible and allows students to experience practical application of academic skills. Point out to the appropriate decision-makers how you are successfully integrating basic skills into your curriculum every day.

References

Miller, S.W. & Tulloch, C.R. (Eds.). (1989). <u>Teaching basic skills through home economics</u>. Washington, DC: Home Economics Education Association.

Miller, S.W. & Tulloch, C.R. (1996). Basic skills in family and consumer sciences education. In S. Redick (Ed.), <u>Review and synthesis of family and consumer sciences teacher education research 1985-1995</u> (pp. 259-267). Peoria, IL: Glencoe/McGraw-Hill.

Richardson, J.S., & Morgan, R.F. (2000). <u>Reading to learn in the content areas</u>. Belmont, CA: Wadsworth.

Vacca, R.T. & Vacca, J.L. (1999). <u>Content area reading: literacy and learning across the curriculum</u>. New York: Longman.

http://www.naa.org/foundation/nie.html Newspaper in Education. (Accessed December 15, 2001)

Building Your Professional Portfolio

- **Integrating Competencies.** Select an academic area and a topic from your course or workshop. Develop a matrix illustrating integration of competencies in the selected academic area with concepts covered in your class or workshop.

- **Readability Levels.** Test the readability of a textbook using the Fry scale. Calculate the overall readability level after three samples, ten samples, and twenty samples. Explain any differences in the overall scores. Then analyze the text for other factors influencing readability. Summarize your conclusions about the appropriateness of the text for a particular grade level.

- **Integrating Basic Skills.** Develop an outdoor experience that would include all the learners in a given situation. Determine ways in which science, math, social studies, language arts, nutrition, and health concepts would be incorporated.

- **Being a Guest Expert.** Create a presentation for a history class explaining how components of family and consumer sciences, such as food preparation, family dynamics, housing, sanitation, consumer economics, and clothing, were different in Colonial times or another era.

Chapter 18

Motivation, Discipline, and Student Responsibility

When beginning educators are asked what their biggest concerns are, motivation and discipline usually top the list. Actually, motivation and discipline in teaching situations go hand in hand. Learners who are motivated and interested in their work aren't likely to present behavior problems. They are usually willing to take responsibility for their learning. By providing purposeful, stimulating, and interesting activities, you can help build a positive classroom climate—an environment conducive to learning for all students. The discipline or guidance methods you choose also affect learning. Your ultimate goal is to instill responsibility and self-discipline in your learners to prepare them for independent learning throughout life.

 ## Motivation of Learners

Motivation is a state created within an individual that propels that person to action. The term "motivation" is derived from a Greek word meaning "to move." As the leader of a class or group, it's your challenge to move your participants to action, both individually and as a group. The degree to which individuals are motivated falls along a continuum from panic to sleep. Your job is to keep moving your learners towards the ideal level of motivation halfway in between.

Motivation energizes an individual and keeps attention focused. People who are motivated are more receptive to learning. Motivated learners want to receive the knowledge you are trying to share. They tend to learn more quickly and present fewer discipline problems.

✳ Extrinsic vs. Intrinsic Motivation

Motivators—the things that "push" learners to learn—tend to fall into two categories: extrinsic and intrinsic. Part of your job will be deciding which to use when. Extrinsic rewards are those that aren't directly related to the achievement itself. Although they result from the achievement, these rewards provide something extra. Perhaps students can choose not to take the final exam if they maintain a B average or better throughout the semester. In Family, Career and Community Leaders of America, club members may be promised a party if they complete their projects by a certain date. Parents dangle an extrinsic reward when they offer money for a good report card. In all of these cases, the learners are being motivated by external forces.

Intrinsic motivation comes from within the individual. It means wanting to do well for the sake of learning. It brings a sense of satisfaction and self-fulfillment. Perhaps the learner's goal is related to achieving a certain GPA or class rank, to pleasing a parent, or to making the Honor Roll.

Some parents and educators disagree with motivating learners extrinsically. They reason that such rewards have to cease at some point because, in life, people aren't necessarily compensated for all their accomplishments. Others argue that extrinsic motivation sometimes evolves into intrinsic motivation. This might happen if, through working for an extrinsic reward, the learner also gains a sense of personal achievement. For this transition to occur, the reward needs to be as closely related to the accomplishment as possible.

❋ Factors Impacting Motivation

If you think about what motivates you to do your best, chances are those same factors are at work for your learners. When asked to complete the following statement, "I am motivated to work hardest when . . . ," these responses are offered frequently:

- The teacher or leader is enthusiastic and organized.
- The material seems relevant to my life.
- I like what I'm doing.
- I understand what I am doing.
- I feel like there will be benefits from what I'm doing.
- There are obstacles or challenges to overcome.
- There's some friendly competition.
- I am having fun.
- My efforts are reinforced.
- The material is interesting.
- There's a deadline that I'm working toward.
- I feel involved.
- The people I'm working with are cooperative.
- My curiosity is aroused.
- I feel like people care that I succeed.

Within these statements are many of the keys to motivating learners. Your job as an educator is to create an environment where your learners feel their own self-worth and can relate to thoughts such as these. For many learners, the most important motivator is the final one on the list. Showing that you, the educator, care is a powerful motivator for learners.

❋ A Model for Motivation

Figure 18-1 below depicts a model or flow chart for thinking about how to motivate learners. There are three aspects of the model:

- **Elements of Motivation.** These provide the foundation.
- **Task Components.** These suggest ways of motivating.
- **Reward Systems.** These give ways to help learners feel positively about themselves.

Figure 18-1	A MODEL FOR INCREASING MOTIVATION
Elements of Motivation ↓	Capitalize or build on the learners': • Needs • Interests • Goals
Task Components ↓	through learning experiences that include: • Activity　• Curiosity • Materials　• The unexpected • Variety　• Good teaching skills • Challenge • Friendly competition
Reward Systems	that will allow each learner to: • Be correct • Have fun • Receive attention, praise, privileges, rewards, and tangibles

❋ Elements of Motivation

In order to motivate your learners, it's helpful to start with where the learners "are." This means turning your attention to their needs, interests, and goals. Once you find the "hooks," you can capitalize or build on these elements. Find ways to link the content you are covering to the learners. Don't assume that they will make the connections on their own.

In capitalizing on learners' needs, it's helpful to first consider the basic human needs proposed by Maslow. Do what you can to see that your learners' needs are met in the following areas:

- **Physiological.** Learners can't concentrate if they're hungry, thirsty, tired, or lack shelter.
- **Safety.** Learners must feel safe physically and psychologically before they are free to learn.
- **Love and Belonging.** Learners need to feel that people care about them and that they are part of a group before they are ready to tune in to your teaching.
- **Esteem.** You are in a position to help learners build their feelings of self-worth, in turn enhancing their ability to learn. Like all people, your learners have a need for self-respect and understanding.
- **Self-Actualization.** Learners want to become all they can become when all their other needs are met. To help your learners reach this state, do all that you can to see that their other basic needs are taken care of.

As you plan lessons, try to link your concepts and activities to your learners' needs. Many topics within Health and Family and Consumer Sciences—relationship skills, conflict resolution, nutrition, and home safety—are closely connected with basic needs. When your learners see how the material will help them meet one or more of their needs, they are likely to be more motivated to learn. Make a point of indicating specific situations when the subject matter is apt to be especially valuable. You might begin a lesson with "You will be able to use this information when . . . " or "You will need to know this if . . . " or "In the workplace, these skills will . . . "

Building a firm basis for motivation also means capitalizing on your learners' interests and goals. Dealing with students' attitudes toward learning and their interpretations of subject matter may require you to sensitively find out about their lifestyles, viewpoints, and concerns. Do they work? Do they participate in sports or other activities? Do they drive? Are any of them parents? Are there any vegetarians? Do some learners have special medical conditions? What are their concerns for the future?

By observing your learners, you will learn so much. To get to know them better, you can use activities that encourage learners to share things about themselves. Listen carefully to what they say in the group and in conversation with you. Another strategy is to have learners fill out inventories of their interests and goals.

Here are some examples of ways to capitalize on interests and goals:

- Many teens are preoccupied with their appearance. Linking healthy skin and shiny hair with the foods they eat will help motivate teens to learn about nutrition.
- When meeting with a group of adults interested in becoming volunteer leaders in your county 4-H program, find out more about their individual interests. That way you can incorporate examples tailored to their interests as you explain the program.
- Getting a driver's license is a goal of most teens. This goal can be the jumping-off point for motivating them to learn about car insurance and related consumer issues. Learning about collision coverage would have relatively little meaning for someone who never expects to drive.
- Elders with osteoporosis may avoid going places because they fear falling. Your exercise program can stress strategies for safe mobility to help alleviate their fear and meet their need for safety.

❋ Task Components

After assessing and attempting to build on your learners' needs, interests, and goals, you move on to planning and implementing learning experiences that provide additional motivation. Characteristics that enhance motivation include:

- Planning varied learning experiences that actively involve students in the learning process.
- Using visuals and tangible materials to enhance opportunities for visual and tactile learning.
- Including activities that pose physical or intellectual challenges, plus a bit of friendly competition.
- Arousing curiosity through intriguing questions and unexpected ideas.
- Implementing the teaching skills described in Chapter 8 successfully.

Here are some examples of the effective use of task components:

- In a self-defense course, the participants view demonstrations of a variety of strategies. Then they practice those strategies with individuals who simulate a variety of dangerous situations.
- In a high school class, students view slides of physical outcomes of diseases, such as skin cancer, lung cancer, or STDs. These graphic presentations are usually motivating because they have a significant emotional impact.
- Weight loss and weight management programs have weekly weigh-ins to instill competition among participants.
- A guest speaker who relates a personal problem or tragedy, such as drunk driving or an addiction, can leave a lasting impression with listeners.
- Good questioning skills can raise the points you wish to make as you teach a lesson on the benefits of not smoking.

❋ *Reward Systems*

It is human nature to want to be correct and receive attention and rewards. These rewards can be tangible objects, praise, or privileges. In order to motivate, many educators feel that they need to provide rewards. One of the most motivating rewards is being able to walk away from a class knowing that you not only learned something, but had a good time, too.

Here are some examples of the use of motivational rewards:

- In a program on lowering cholesterol, provide participants with a bag of healthful snacks when their cholesterol falls by a certain number of points.

- Praise learners for progress with a variety of positive reinforcers. Refer back to "99 Ways to Say Very Good" on page 118.
- Allow learners who have done particularly well on an exercise, quiz, or worksheet to have some unexpected free time. All age groups see this as a reward.

❋ Motivating by Building Self-Esteem

You teach through your verbal behavior and actions. Anything you say or do may affect a learner's self-concept, feelings, and attitudes, either for better or worse. Undoubtedly, you can recall an instance when an adult's words had an enormous impact on your own self-concept.

There are many ways to build the self-worth of learners, which in turn motivates them to act appropriately. Learn names as soon as possible and speak to participants by name. "Hi Michael" shows more interest than a generic "hello." Educators have to establish an atmosphere of mutual respect and trust that makes each individual feel worthy. Leaders can't demand respect; esteem and honor must be earned. Take time to listen to what your learners have to say, and use their ideas and suggestions whenever possible.

Educators who are attuned to others' feelings show this with remarks made in a positive manner. If someone seems to disagree with a statement that another learner has just made, you might say: "Amanda doesn't seem to see it that way. How do you feel about it, Amanda?" Try to remember attitudes that were previously expressed and show this by making a comment such as "Yesterday Shawna expressed the opinion that . . . " By remembering an individual's contribution and referring to it later, you are validating that person. In essence you are saying, "You and your ideas and thoughts are valuable." When you take a learner's present or past comment and build or "piggyback" on it, you help to build self-esteem and motivation.

✳ Educators' Behaviors That Affect Learner Motivation

It's important to realize that learners, like educators, behave in terms of what *seems* to be true. Teaching and learning are accomplished not necessarily according to what the facts are, but according to how they're perceived. This has real implications for your behavior—intentional and unintentional.

For example, you communicate a sense of acceptance or rejection with your body language—your posture, gestures, and demeanor. Educators who have a habit of standing with their arms folded may inadvertently convey the message "Don't approach me." Similarly, the teacher who always sits behind a desk rather than moving around the room may be communicating "I really don't care about you," or "I am the authority in this room." Slouching and slumping posture may be interpreted as indifference and boredom, whether that's true or not. Conversely, maintaining good eye contact, smiling, and giving participants your full attention say to them, "I think you are important."

Similarly, some teaching methods and attitudes spur motivation while others dampen it. For example, your enthusiasm about the subject matter can carry over to your learners. If they see you really care about helping them change their eating habits or finding ways to deal with conflict peacefully, they are more likely to respond enthusiastically.

When you present information, do so in interesting and meaningful ways. Listening to daily lectures delivered in a monotone doesn't motivate learning. It may actually diminish it. Using a mix of teaching strategies is much more likely to spark and maintain learners' interests. Ask for and use learners' input. Encourage them to think creatively and solve problems.

Behavior of educators that is inconsistent, distant, cold, and rejecting is less likely to enhance self-concept, motivation, and learning than behavior that is warm and accepting and consistent. Self-confidence and self-respect are strong motivating forces. The educator who realizes this will take every possible opportunity to help learners feel wanted and worthwhile. It is important to acknowledge that *all* people have the same need for recognition, attention, and achievement.

✳ Giving Effective Feedback

The feedback students and participants receive on their efforts and work has a major impact on both motivation and learning. Often, it's the person struggling who most needs encouragement. A constant barrage of negative comments rarely results in positive change.

Writing appropriate remarks on students' papers is time-consuming, but personal comments often have very positive effects on learner achievement. In fact, a personal comment can have more motivational value than the grade assigned. In a research study, a large number of students' papers, with grades ranging from A to F, were divided equally into three groups. The first group's papers were returned with only a letter grade. Those from the second group included a stereotyped phrase, such as "Keep up the good work," "Needs improvement," or "You can do better." The third group's papers had a comment showing personal and professional concern for the learner. Not surprisingly, on the next assignment, the individuals who had received only a grade on the first assignment made the least progress while the students who had received personal comments showed the most improvement. In fact, the learners in the latter group who had done failing work on the initial assignment made the greatest improvement of everyone.

When evaluating learners' work or participants' effort, try to both begin and end with positive comments and to intersperse negative remarks between the favorable ones. Negative criticism is more likely to be accepted and acted upon if it's preceded by positive comments. Finishing with a positive comment leaves the person with a better feeling than ending on an unfavorable note. It's almost always possible to find something good to say about the effort shown, the performance, or the product. Negative criticisms can be made in the form of suggestions. For example, you might write, "Next time you might want to try . . . " Another tactic is to ask questions that prompt the learner to think about ways the assignment might have been handled differently. You could ask, "Did you consider . . . ?" or "What do you think might have happened if . . . ?"

Overall, strive to give more positive or neutral feedback than negative. It's often just a matter of how a comment is phrased. For example if a lab experiment doesn't turn out as expected, "What do you think caused this?" is more effective than "What did you do wrong *this* time?"

Discipline to Enhance Learning

While motivation is a major concern at all levels of learning, discipline is primarily a K-12 issue. Older learners have a choice about whether or not to be in an educational setting. Their added maturity and the less-restrictive environment of post-high education also help keep problems to a minimum.

Discipline in the educational environment implies that educators have the right to teach and learners have the right to learn. Those rights need to be protected. The ultimate goal of a discipline policy is to instill in the learners the ability to self-discipline, self-monitor, and be responsible. Discipline should not be confused with punishment. Today, discipline is often referred to as *instructional guidance*.

When discipline is thought of as control, the result may be uniform behavior and a quiet room, but there will also be limited creativity and less flexibility. When discipline is regarded as punishment, negative and aggressive responses are likely to surface. Some students may react with behavior that seems to say, "Let's see how much we can get away with and how much we can annoy the teacher." When discipline is regarded as more of a learner's responsibility, attainable goals are more likely to be set and reached.

There are no hard-and-fast rules for effective classroom discipline. The reason is that there are differences from one area of the country to another, from one school to another, and from one class to another.

Effective solutions depend on the types of learners, teachers' personalities and abilities, school administrators and their policies, the curriculum, and the unique interaction of all of these factors.

The type of student misbehavior to be dealt with varies greatly. Daydreaming during class, defying authority, and acting violently are far apart on the continuum and call for quite different responses.

Problem students usually represent only a small proportion of the participants in a program or class. However, for inexperienced teachers, one or two disruptive learners can seem like a room full of problems. Think positively. The majority of students are conscientious and hardworking.

It is unfortunate, but necessary, for educators to accept that there are some factors that influence discipline over which they have limited control. These may include not only school policies, but also administrative support, the overall school climate, the backgrounds of the students, parental support, class size, and classroom configurations.

✳ Developing a Philosophy of Discipline

As an educator, you need to formulate a philosophy of discipline that is comfortable for you. To be effective, it should be compatible with your teaching style and personality. Think about factors such as how much formality, control, quiet, and organization you need. What type of learning environment were you most comfortable with as a student?

Teachers who aren't secure about their own self-worth, their knowledge of the subject matter, and their ability to teach effectively may unwittingly express these insecurities in their behavior in the classroom. This, in turn, opens the door to additional discipline problems. Educators must have enough self-confidence to set reasonable limits on students' behavior and to follow through with predetermined actions if they respond inappropriately.

An instructor's insecurity may be expressed by a controlling manner with aggressive and harsh disciplinary actions or by passivity. The saying, "You usually get what you expect," is often a self-fulfilling prophecy when it comes to classroom discipline. Learners who are expected to be cooperative usually are, and those who are expected to misbehave often do. The teacher's attitude is of utmost importance. Educators who manage their learning environment effectively certainly are more likely to enjoy their work.

As you formulate your own philosophy of discipline, you have a wide range of models for instructional guidance to consider. Some approaches are considered teacher-centered approaches while others are learner-centered. Since extremes in discipline aren't particularly effective, aim for a spot in between where you act deliberately and purposefully but with self-confidence.

To assist you in finding your style, several philosophies will be discussed. As you read about these concepts, you can pick and choose the pieces that will work best for you. You may also decide to research other philosophies to create one that will work for you. As you gain experience, you will continue to refine your philosophy and methods.

❈ Preventive Discipline

Preventive discipline focuses on minimizing problems. Many, many behavior problems can be prevented through some sensible, yet simple, strategies. Regardless of the overall discipline philosophy you adopt, you can use many of these ideas. Three key areas include getting off to a good start, being well organized, and having positive interactions with learners. *Figure 18-2* on page 252 gives additional ways to prevent discipline problems.

❈ The Right Start

Never underestimate the importance of "setting the right tone" in your teaching situation from the very beginning. During the first few days, learners form opinions about you, the group, and the situation. Some may test you to determine the limits you place on various forms of behavior. In other words, learners decide how cooperative they intend to be.

Plan to be in the room when learners arrive. It's a good practice to stand in the doorway at the beginning and the end of every session and talk to the participants, preferably by name, making them feel welcome.

The first five minutes of any meeting are very important in establishing control for the remainder of the session. This is especially true of the first days of classes. Get everyone's attention as quickly as possible. Doing so helps establish the practice of getting down to business promptly.

Give students something definite and interesting to do the first day so they learn at least one new piece of information before they leave. Don't be concerned about how much material you cover the first week of class, as long as there is a positive learning atmosphere. As you begin to develop rapport with students, try to involve them in helping select material to be covered to ensure that it meets their needs.

❈ Being Well Organized

There is no substitute for being organized when teaching. Disorganization, unscheduled class time, poorly planned activities, rough transitions between activities, and a lack of continuity of subject matter inevitably lead to confusion, lack of participant interest, and behavior problems.

Inexperienced educators tend to have the most discipline problems, often because they are overwhelmed with routine "custodial" duties. In addition, they find it necessary to spend much more time on planning than more experienced professionals.

Educators who create a positive classroom climate are perceived to be good managers and well organized. Organization includes:

- Being well prepared for class, getting the class settled to begin on time, having materials ready to use, and preparing professional-looking handouts and visuals.
- Acting deliberately by knowing what needs to be covered, keeping the group moving forward, using an appropriate tone of voice, and being in charge while maintaining a warm and friendly demeanor.

- Knowing the subject matter well enough to provide up-to-date information, being able to explain and clarify it, making it interesting and stimulating, and being able to answer questions.
- Involving learners in planning and implementing activities that involve higher levels of thinking.
- Handling misbehavior fairly and consistently without damaging participants' self-concepts.
- Being self-disciplined by following school or agency rules, being truthful, and not threatening unless the "threat" or action can be carried out.
- Having a neat, organized learning environment. An orderly room invites orderly behavior.

✳ *Interacting Positively with Learners*

New educators may feel they don't have time to work on building relationships with the learners. Actually, educators who have achieved a healthy professional relationship with their learners are more likely to be able to foster positive relationships among group members. This, in turn, helps create a more productive environment for teaching and learning.

Whether educators have been teaching for two months or twenty years, they need to act like adults in charge of a democratic environment and not like pals to their learners. Many students who have little discipline at home feel secure when they have parameters, know where they stand, and recognize that they will be treated fairly and with con-

---

Figure 18-2

ADDITIONAL PREVENTION STRATEGIES

The following tips may also fit into your style of instructional guidance.

- Establish clear rules where rules are needed. Make sure the learners know what the rules are.
- Make sure that your rules and practices support, rather than conflict with, school or agency policies. For example, if students are to be out of the halls during class periods, don't send one on an errand during class.
- Let learners assume independent responsibility. Find jobs for them to do. Keeping busy minimizes discipline problems.
- Avoid unnecessary disruptions and delays.
- Plan independent activities, as well as organized lessons. Learners enjoy variety.
- Keep lessons moving at a good pace. Change the pace when you sense the lesson has gone on too long.
- Monitor attention during lessons. When you see attention drifting, change the pace and/or activities.
- Maintain accountability. Require that learners regularly present evidence that they have reached objectives.
- Stimulate attention periodically.

- Give clear, deliberate directions.
- Bring effective closure to lessons. Set expectations for the next time you meet, in addition to reviewing what was covered.
- Smile. Use humor. Plan for at least one laugh a day.
- Work out a system for distributing materials that doesn't consume a lot of time.
- Give passes for students to leave the room sparingly, but be flexible because emergencies do arise.
- Make a list of learners who seem inattentive. Work to involve them. Move a disruptive learner's seat close to your desk. By having some degree of control over each learner, you have a better chance of guiding the entire group.
- Sit in the back of the room when you show a video or have a guest speaker. That way, if you need to single out learners who need to change their behavior you won't disturb the entire group.
- With K-12 students, get to know parents or guardians and don't hesitate to contact them when their help is needed. It's easier to get cooperation from parents in discipline situations when a positive relationship has already been established.

sistency. Learners are most likely to conform when they are clear about what is expected of them.

Martin and Quilling have suggested that you can set the stage for effective discipline by developing positive interactions that include:

- Listening to the concerns of others.
- Communicating until understanding is achieved.
- Exhibiting a positive regard for people.
- Establishing a give-and-take relationship.
- Being organized and consistent.
- Using others' time efficiently.
- Stressing the positive and encouraging effort.
- Respecting the rights and property of others.
- Recognizing and reinforcing desired behaviors.
- Being friendly and pleasant.
- Being a positive role model.
- Evaluating objectively.
- Admitting mistakes.

As you go about the daily business of working with young people, both in and out of the classroom, be friendly, warm, and pleasant without becoming a part of their social group. Students want teachers they respect, not buddies. Wearing professionally appropriate attire will help you establish and maintain a professional relationship with students.

❋ Assertive Discipline

Canter and Canter are credited with starting the assertive discipline movement that is used by many schools and educators today. This philosophy is applicable to both formal and nonformal educational settings. Assertive teachers communicate their needs and wants clearly and firmly to their learners and are prepared to reinforce their words with appropriate actions. Rules and consequences are the same for all learners. The underlying tenets of assertive discipline are that both the educator and the learner have the following rights:

As an *educator*, you have the right to:

- Establish a classroom structure and routine that provides an optimal learning

environment, in light of your own strengths and weaknesses.
- Determine and request appropriate behaviors from the learners that meet your needs and encourage the positive social and educational development of the learner.
- Ask for help from parents or an administrator when you need assistance with a learner.

The *learner* has the right to:

- Have an educator who will help the learner limit inappropriate and self-disruptive behavior.
- Have a leader who will provide the learner with positive support for appropriate behavior.
- Choose how to behave and know the consequences that will follow if misbehavior occurs.

❋ *Action Discipline Plans*

The implementation of assertive discipline relies on the utilization of what is known as an *action discipline plan*. Discipline problems can be minimized when educators establish a well-managed environment for effective discipline and develop and implement a plan. An action discipline plan consists of written expectations of learner behavior, identified rewards for learners who behave appropriately, and established consequences for those who don't. *Figure 18-3* on page 254 shows a sample action discipline plan.

Educators will be less subject to job dissatisfaction and burnout if they enter teaching with realistic expectations of acceptable learner behavior and preplanned consequences for misbehavior, and then make these clear to students up front. This *doesn't* mean, however, that an instructor should begin a new session by reading and distributing rules for behavior.

It's much more effective to work with the learners to establish criteria for behavior when a new course begins. Three to five *positive* guidelines for behavior are an appropriate number. State guidelines in general terms so they are applicable to various situations. With your guidance the students might develop a list similar to this:

Figure 18-3
Sample Action Discipline Plan

Expected Learner Behaviors
1. Come prepared for day's activities.
2. Listen to and follow directions.
3. Clean up work area after use.
4. Use good manners in dealing with others.
5. Respect the property of others.

Rewards for Appropriate Behavior
1. Complimentary note sent home
2. Additional computer time
3. Homework pass
4. Ten minutes of class time for socializing

Consequences for Misbehavior
1. Write name on board.
2. Change seat in classroom.
3. Give detention at lunch time.
4. Give after-school detention.
5. Call parent or guardian.
6. Have conference with principal and teacher.

• Respect the rights of others.
• Use lab equipment appropriately.
• Be cooperative.
• Be courteous to others.
• Be prepared.

Display the behavior or guidelines in a prominent place. Lists of rewards and consequences can be established in the same way.

✳ *Implementing the Action Discipline Plan*

Once the plan has been developed and posted, refer the learners to the plan frequently as you implement it. Be sure to point out when learners are following the expected behaviors, as well as their shortcomings. It's motivating to hear yourself praised for taking the assignments to a classmate who is ill or for having everything you need for class. Educators sometimes forget to focus on the positives.

Be consistent in both the application of rewards and consequences as you implement the action discipline plan. For implementing consequences, apply them in the order in which they're listed.

The longer you wait to assert control with a group of learners, the more difficult it will be to establish. Learners quickly sense whether or not you will enforce control. Nevertheless, it's important to keep a sense of perspective and avoid challenging minor offenses. Don't let situations become magnified out of proportion. It's possible that you are the only one annoyed by a situation. For example, you might overlook some whispering. After all, it's possible that the learners are talking about the subject matter. *Be certain* a student made an offensive comment or misbehaved before you take action that might cause a confrontation in class or put you on the defensive with the learners. Sometimes you will need to go along with a joke. It's vital to maintain your sense of humor; you will need it often.

Control is often associated with rules and policies. However, it's important to establish only the rules and policies you intend to enforce. When many rules are in effect and you try to enforce all of them, you spend a great deal of your time and energy doing so. On the other hand, rules that aren't enforced serve to encourage learners to challenge other rules.

✳ *Responsible Classroom Management*

One learner-centered approach to instructional guidance is called *responsible classroom management*. It is based on the teachings of noted psychologists Jean Piaget, Abraham Maslow, Mortimer Adler, Erik Erikson, Lawrence Kohlberg, and Richard Havighurst. This approach assumes that all students can experience success in school. It seeks to instill in students an internal motivation to be responsible for their learning and the self-discipline to control their behavior.

Teachers are responsible for developing an environment that gives learners a sense of acceptance and belonging. They also deal with students as individuals, each at a unique stage of development, and tailor their interactions with each accordingly. Responsibility and performance are acknowledged, but tangible rewards are not used.

Standards replace rules and meeting those standards is considered an expectation. When students misbehave, they must suffer the logical consequences of their actions. This is meant to help them correct their behavior and develop the decision-making and problem-solving skills needed in adult life. Behavior Improvement Agreements and parental involvement are other tools used to help students meet established standards.

✳ Handling Special Circumstances

Whatever approaches you choose for instructional guidance with your learners, you may still encounter special discipline problems. Three of these are cheating, confrontations, and violence.

✳ Cheating

Learners' reasons for cheating are varied, and it isn't always easy to decide how to handle this problem. It's impossible to prevent cheating from occurring altogether, but there are measures that can be taken to minimize it. When it's difficult to provide sufficient space between learners or when you suspect a problem with cheating, you might develop two different test formats by arranging the same questions in different order. While learners are taking a test, walk around the room. Don't utilize the time to concentrate on work at your desk.

When cheating is suspected, proceed with caution. Accusing someone of dishonest behavior in the absence of concrete evidence puts you in an untenable position and may have a detrimental effect on the learner's future actions. The situation can often be handled subtly. For example, you might take the two identical papers of learners who sit next to each other and write across them, as if on one sheet: "It's unusual that your two papers are exactly alike." No further action may be required. It's likely that the pair will be grateful that an issue wasn't made of the situation and doubtful that they will repeat the behavior in your class. Fortunately, when learners respect a teacher and perceive that they are treated fairly, they may be less likely to cheat than when opposite conditions exist.

If several learners are involved in cheating, never penalize the entire group for their actions by giving another test the next day or making an extra assignment. The infraction isn't the responsibility of the rest of the class. In addition, evaluation and academic work shouldn't be associated with punishment.

✳ Confrontations

When public accusations and confrontations occur, both parties may suffer damage to their reputations, regardless of who is right or wrong. Relationships may be strained long afterward. Retaliation may even occur. If a confrontation does take place, avoid harboring resentment and suspicion. That isn't conducive to a positive teaching-learning relationship.

When there's a disagreement between you and a learner, avoid arguing with the individual in front of the group. Try to talk quietly with the person at the end of the period, during a free period, or before or after school. Remind the learner of the behavior you expect. Be positive; focus on the desirable consequences of cooperating rather than on what will happen if there's more unacceptable behavior.

✳ School Violence

Unfortunately, violence in society spills over into schools. A conflict outside of school may play out on school property or in the classroom. Other times, trouble may erupt from school-related issues. Whatever the cause, both predetermined policies and constant vigilance can help schools and teachers prevent episodes from occurring. Some schools have on-campus police, scanning devices to prevent weapons, and similar measures. Many have adopted formal plans and policies to minimize violence. However, teachers need to be alert to changes in behavior, students' gossip about conflict, and other clues to potential trouble. When appropriate, include topics such as stress reduction, conflict resolution, and anger management in your curriculum. Your safety and that of your students must be your primary concern. If any situation seems to pose a threat, notify your administration. If the threat is immediate, ask a nearby teacher for backup.

✳ Correcting Misbehavior

When it's necessary to correct students for misbehavior, each situation has to be evaluated on its own merits. However, it is important to be consistent in the way problem behavior is handled. Try to listen to a learner's explanation carefully, patiently, and with empathy. There is little value in severe discipline, in punishing a class for the misbehavior of one learner, or in making the offending student write "I will not . . . " a hundred times. Lowering a learner's grade for inappropriate behavior is also a poor practice. The problem is not the person's achievement but the person's behavior. By lowering a grade, you are associating punishment with learning.

If you are certain that a learner is responsible for an act of inappropriate behavior, avoid forced confessions and apologies that might only serve to encourage the person to lie. In many instances, you already know the facts. Tell the individual you are aware of what was done, and that you do not want to see it repeated.

Among the most difficult interactions are those in which learners deliberately challenge your authority. If you are to meet your professional responsibility, you must try to help your learners exhibit acceptable behavior and become involved in the learning process, even if they are uninterested and uncooperative. However, you must also deal with the immediate situation. That's when clear classroom rules and consequences come into play. They allow you to react deliberately and with authority, rather than with emotion or threats. Staying calm, speaking slowly, and remaining focused on the main problem can all help defuse the situation.

 ## Student Assumption of Responsibility

Learners are more motivated and self-disciplined if they assume responsibility for their actions, including their learning. Individuals' acceptance of responsibility in the learning process is essential if they are

to meet state and national standards and to reach their potential.

In the past, a primary role of the family was to teach youth to be responsible citizens. With present-day lifestyles, schools have had to assume a greater role in teaching young people to be responsible for some of their own education.

The best way to teach responsibility is to expect responsible behavior of learners. When a helpful instructor always has a pencil, paper, or spare textbook ready for students who forgot theirs, students will conclude that irresponsibility is acceptable. Because employees who aren't punctual may lose their jobs, teachers who tolerate frequent tardiness aren't helping learners accept responsibility. Basic skills, in one sense, aren't only language arts, math, and science, but also being punctual, courteous, and cooperative.

In assessing accountability in schools, standardized student achievement test scores are often used to determine the effectiveness of the educational system, as well as the competence of individual teachers. This approach presents a fallacy because learners should assume some responsibility for their learning, too. Continued transference of responsibility from students to teachers or situations causes students to conclude that they don't have to be responsible for their own learning.

Students who have responsibilities at home are more likely to assume responsibility for their learning as well. It has been shown that there is a relationship between assumption of responsibilities at home and in school. Not surprisingly, assuming responsibility at school also seems to be associated with number of siblings, self-motivation, and high grades.

✳ Teacher vs. Student Responsibilities

Should an educator be accountable for the individual who doesn't want to learn and who doesn't attend school regularly? As noted previously, it is the teacher's responsibility to *try* to reach this type of individual, but each learner brings background factors to the class over which the teacher has no control. Home conditions, family attitudes toward education, aspiration level, academic ability, and self-concept are associated with motivation toward doing well. Teachers cannot, and should not, be held responsible for everything that happens in the educational setting. Everyone in a particular class or program has some responsibility toward what happens in that group.

It's the instructor's responsibility to provide experiences to help the learner achieve objectives, but the individual has the responsibility of meeting those objectives. Learners can be helped to assume responsibility in the learning process by establishing goals that lead to improved performance. They may be allowed to select learning activities that interest them, but these activities shouldn't interfere with other students' learning. No learner has the right to bother others. Some students may need help in learning to respect the rights of others. They need to be responsible for self-discipline and self-control, both in academic activities and personal conduct. They also need to accept the consequences for their decisions about their behavior.

❋ Promoting Learner Responsibility

You have a crucial role in helping learners assume responsibility. Working toward goals, developing leadership skills, cooperative learning, and focusing on character development are all ways to promote learner responsibility.

❋ Goals and Expectations

Both teachers and learners have goals and expectations in the educational setting. Provide opportunities for learners to share their goals and expectations with you. You need to do the same with them. Take time to discuss the alignment of the two. Work on building consensus. Also allot time for learners to formulate personal and class goals and to share and affirm those as part of the educational process. Assist them in being accountable for attaining those goals by providing specific evidences of achievement on a regular basis. Accountability is critical in the world today. Practice can start in a safe environment like the classroom. Peer- and self-evaluation are ways to assist learners to be comfortable with this process.

❋ Leadership Development

Some of your programs—especially 4-H and FCCLA—will clearly focus on leadership development. You may have learners who are involved in peer mediation or violence-prevention programs. In other cases, you can build leadership development into your lesson plans. Providing learners with some of the following opportunities will promote leadership skills:

- Arrange for guest speakers.
- Greet and introduce guests.
- Check attendance.
- Collect and distribute materials and papers.
- Plan a time schedule for a group event.
- Enter data into computer programs.
- Lead small- or large-group discussions.
- Be scorekeeper/timekeeper for games or other activities.
- Write follow-up and thank-you letters.
- Design, collect items for, and prepare bulletin boards and other visuals.
- Compile information for a newsletter.
- Conduct group meetings.
- Check parliamentary procedure used.
- Research a topic of interest and present findings to peers.
- Design graphics needed.
- Collect fees and report income and expenditures.
- Keep track of fund-raiser orders.

It's surprising and unfortunate that many adults haven't had the opportunity to carry out many of these tasks. Leadership takes practice. You need to be willing to relinquish some of your control to give learners a chance to take responsibility. A task may not be done exactly as you would do it, but it will provide them with self-confidence and motivation.

❋ Cooperative Learning

Working together is imperative to success in the real world. Provide opportunities for learners to work cooperatively on group or team endeavors. In that process, ensure that they are given a chance to practice some of the following behaviors that promote successful cooperative learning:

- Assigning roles or responsibilities to team or group members
- Delegating tasks
- Setting goals as a group and as individuals
- Allocating time to accomplish tasks
- Reporting results
- Collaborating with others
- Communicating regularly with each other
- Evaluating group progress
- Sharing tasks
- Dealing with differing values, attitudes, and personalities
- Distributing resources according to task assignments
- Researching aspects of a problem
- Assuming one's share of the group workload
- Preparing a personal timeline for completing tasks for the group

Each of these tasks promotes responsibility among learners. In addition, learners who assume and accomplish these tasks are more likely to be motivated. Refer to pages 185-188 for more on cooperative learning.

❋ Character Education

Character education continues to be a high-profile topic. Some instructors have learners read the newspaper to find positive and negative examples of character. Others have them consider examples found in books and popular movies.

A popular source of materials is the CHARACTER COUNTS! Coalition. It is a nonpartisan alliance of educational and human service organizations dedicated to fortifying the character and ethical behavior of America's youth. Six pillar values constitute the agenda of the Coalition: trustworthiness, respect, fairness, citizenship, caring, and responsibility. The responsibility pillar encourages youth to:

- Do what you are supposed to do.
- Persevere: keep on trying.
- Always do your best.
- Use self-control.
- Be self-disciplined.
- Think before you act—consider consequences.
- Be accountable for your choices.

Whether you are working with students in a school, 4-H program, or a teen pregnancy program, or with adults, character education can often be easily and logically integrated into your teaching.

❋ Measuring Student Assumption of Responsibility

It can be valuable to have learners evaluate themselves regarding their assumption of responsibility in the classroom. It helps them become aware of behaviors expected of a responsible person.

Figure 18-4 on pages 259-260 shows a slightly updated version of the scale that Douglas developed and administered to 198 students and 10 of their teachers. Students rated their level of assumption of responsibility; then the teachers rated the students. Douglas found a high level of agreement between learners' and teachers' scores. Interestingly, she found that students who had jobs rated themselves lower than other students did. Perhaps these students were learning the importance of assuming responsibility in employment situations. You could learn more about your learner by administering your own survey. The results could also serve as the basis for incorporating personal responsibility into your teaching.

Figure 18-4

Scale for Student Assumption of Responsibility in the Classroom

Person being rated: _____ Evaluator: _____

Directions: Responsibility involves doing something you know you are supposed to do without having to be told to do so. Keep that definition in mind as you read and answer each of the statements below. Each indicates a responsibility a learner might show in the classroom. Decide how often you believe the individual you are rating shows the responsibility stated and place a check in the appropriate column.

CLERICAL RESPONSIBILITIES	ALWAYS	OFTEN	SOMETIMES	SELDOM	NEVER
1. Brings necessary materials, such as paper, pen, pencils, and assignments.					
2. Keeps books in good condition.					
3. Keeps graded papers organized.					
4. Corrects mistakes when papers are returned.					
5. Follows rules for computer use.					
6. Uses own possessions rather than borrowing.					
7. Writes neatly and legibly.					
8. Helps keep the room neat and clean.					
9. Brings a pass when tardy.					
10. Promptly returns papers that must be signed.					
11. Promptly returns borrowed items, such as reference books.					
12. Promptly takes care of fees.					
PERSONAL RESPONSIBILITIES					
1. Uses available class time on assignments.					
2. Completes assignments on time.					
3. Promptly makes up work missed during absences.					
4. Brings other work to do after completing class work.					
5. Studies for tests.					
6. Asks questions when explanations aren't understood.					
7. Uses sources allowed to complete work.					
8. Contributes positively to discussions.					
9. Is well groomed.					
10. Voluntarily seeks extra help when needed.					

Figure 18-4 (cont'd)
Scale for Student Assumption of Responsibility in the Classroom

PERSONAL RESPONSIBILITIES (CONT'D)	ALWAYS	OFTEN	SOMETIMES	SELDOM	NEVER
11. Is seated when the tardy bell rings.					
12. Is quiet when the tardy bell rings.					
13. Follows directions.					
14. Works to best of ability.					
15. Concentrates on the class work during the class period.					
16. Avoids disturbing others.					
17. Attends to personal business outside of class.					
18. Obeys school rules.					
19. Obeys class rules.					
20. Asks questions relating to topic.					
21. Accepts consequences of own behavior.					
22. Follows class routine willingly.					
23. Attends school regularly.					
24. Behaves when visitors are present.					
25. Speaks at an appropriate level.					
RELATIONSHIP RESPONSIBILITIES					
1. Respects the instructor.					
2. Respects instructor's belongings.					
3. Waits for a turn for help.					
4. Is courteous.					
5. Listens to others when they talk.					
6. Respects other students' belongings.					
7. Encourages other students to be quiet.					
8. Allows the instructor to settle problems.					
9. Helps other learners understand information.					
10. Cooperates with the teacher.					
11. Cooperates with other learners.					

References

Douglas, C. (1980) <u>Assessment and analysis of student assumption of responsibility in the classroom</u>. (A dissertation in home economics.) Lubbock. TX: Texas Tech University.

Jensen, R. and Kiley, T. (2000). <u>Teaching, leading, and learning</u>. Boston, MA: Houghton Mifflin.

Kellough, R. and Kellough, N. (1999). <u>Secondary school teaching: a guide to methods and resources</u>. Upper Saddle River, NJ: Merrill/Prentice-Hall.

Martin, B. and Quilling, J. (1981). <u>Positive approaches to classroom discipline</u>. Washington DC: Home Economics Education Association.

http://www.charactercounts.org   CHARACTER COUNTS! Coalition. (Accessed January 14, 2002)

http://www.fcclainc.org   Family, Career and Community Leaders of America. (Accessed January 12, 2002)

Building Your Professional Portfolio

- **Building Motivation.** Using the model of motivation, describe how you could use the elements of motivation, task components, and reward systems to enhance motivation in the educational setting you expect to teach.

- **Organized Management.** Develop a set of forms you could use in the classroom to organize tasks and routines. Explain how such devices can help enhance learning and minimize problems.

- **Assertive Discipline.** Develop an Action Discipline Plan for your learning situation. Include expected behaviors, rewards, and consequences.

- **Handling Misbehavior.** Identify common behavior problems you might encounter in the classroom. For each, describe the method you would generally use to correct the problem.

- **Student Responsibility.** Develop a rating device for assessing a class' overall level of student responsibility. Use the device as you observe a group of learners for at least two class periods. Summarize your observations and identify ways student responsibility could be improved.

Chapter 19

Diversity, Equity, and Special Learning Needs

Mary Helen Mays, Ph.D., MPH, MBA, RD/LD
Interim Director, Program and Grants Administration
Community Voices, El Paso, Texas

What a difference a century makes! In 1900, as well as in most of the decades that followed, Americans had clear expectations regarding the roles people were to play. Women were typically homemakers and mothers. Their roles in society revolved around supporting their families and the paid work of men.

Not only have opportunities improved for both genders, but also for people of color and for individuals with disabilities. Segregation is no longer tolerated, racial slurs aren't considered funny, and children are seldom kept home or sent away to special schools or institutions because of a disability. In most instances, they are educated alongside other children in inclusive classrooms.

As an educator, you need to model sensitivity, tolerance, and openness to the uniqueness of each learner. Respecting and accommodating diversity are critical to teacher success.

 ## Historical Perspective

As a nation of immigrants, Americans viewed their nation as the "melting pot" of the world. People of different cultures were expected to conform to the widely held ideas of American life. The standard cast white males as leaders, discouraged use of the traditions of one's homeland, and often punished those who chose to use a language other than English.

During the last 100 years, many people dedicated their lives to changing stereotypical ideas such as these. Not only did women achieve the right to vote, they have flown shuttles into space. Some men now stay home and act as the primary caregiver for their families while their spouse is employed. The melting pot has become more like a rich, colorful, and delicately woven tapestry. Like thousands of threads, each individual represents a unique resource of strengths, skills, and potential. When human beings work together, more can be accomplished.

In the past century, there has been considerable progress in reducing prejudices and biases toward diverse groups, but there is more to be done. As the 21st century unfolds, educators need to be diligent in working with learners and families to see the potential in all people, regardless of gender, culture, age, or race. America will continue to grow and be strong as the commonalities among all people are recognized, their differences are acknowledged, and their strengths are built upon.

Cultural Diversity

How would you define "cultural diversity"? Is it individuals who speak a language different from yours? If you are Christian, is it all the people who are not? If you are young, where do middle-aged people and elders fit into "cultural diversity"?

In fact, there are several interpretations of "culture." A common definition is that culture is any set of coherent norms and traditions that help the members of that group engage and function in the world. Culture shapes values, education, language, religion, work, relationships, and parenting. Your culture shapes the meaning you give to information and knowledge and how you share them.

Often "culture" is used to refer to a person's national or ethnic heritage, but it can mean more than that. Many people, whether they recognize it or not, live a multicultural life. For example, someone might be influenced by both American and deaf cultures. People who refer to themselves as Mexican-Americans are making a bicultural statement about being American while simultaneously acknowledging their cultural heritage.

Paley (2000) has pointed out that many black children regularly use one speech pattern while playing with each other and another when playing with white children and talking to their teachers. They seem to move between speech patterns with ease.

Because society is multicultural, educators need to know about various cultures, including topics such as language, values, history, architecture, celebrations, parenting, home furnishings, clothing, health, hygiene practices, and foods and their preparation. Family and consumer sciences professionals are concerned with the quality of life for all individuals and families. This provides a unique opportunity to search out and disseminate information about different cultures through discussions and other learning activities in a variety of courses and programs.

✳ Learners with Limited English Proficiency (LEP)

Immigrants continue to come to the United States in search of a better life. Over six million children ages 5 to 17 live in homes where a language other than English is spoken. This number represents about 17 percent of the total number of students in the United States. Many of these young people have had limited opportunities to become proficient in English. However, they may well be fluent in one or more languages such as Spanish, Russian, or a Thai dialect.

The Office of Bilingual Education and Minority Languages Affairs (OBEMLA) defines learners who come from homes where a language other than English is frequently used as "language minority students." However, there's not a consistent definition across the nation for limited English proficiency. Many states use this term for learners from a non-English language background and/or those who have difficulty understanding, speaking, writing, or reading English.

Historically, English as a Second Language (ESL) has referred to programs designed for students whose first language was not English. Another term, ESOL, English for Speakers of Other Languages, is also used. Today, the term Limited English Proficiency (LEP) identifies learners who aren't proficient in English but are able to fully participate in an English-only learning environment. "Bilingual Education" is typically used to refer to programs designed to meet the needs of "language minority students" by using the learners' native languages while they acquire necessary English-speaking skills.

✳ Strategies for Facilitating Learning in Multicultural Environments

Due to the increasing mobility of people, educators in every corner of the U.S. find themselves working in multicultural environments. The following strategies may be helpful in promoting positive relationships with people from other cultural groups:

- **Foster clear communication skills.** Stumbling blocks to good communication are the beliefs, assumptions, attitudes, and values that people bring to a discussion. These factors are used, often unconsciously, to filter or interpret messages. You can use popular books and television programs as a basis for discussion of communication differences among diverse groups.
- **Nurture respect for the viewpoints of others.** Inspire your learners to appreciate and respect perspectives other than their own. When your learners first experience different cultures, they may be uncomfortable. Encourage them to discuss their thoughts and feelings respectfully. Educators who facilitate students' understanding and expression of their own beliefs and values may find learners who have an increased understanding and acceptance of others with beliefs and customs unlike their own.
- **Cultivate links between the classroom and home.** Work to include parents in your efforts to address multiculturalism. Encourage parents to participate in the planning of programs or activities. Develop newsletters or other ways to communicate with parents about the progress and purpose of multicultural programs. Invite parents to participate in field trips or other cultural events. Conduct family workshops about cultural diversity. These activities help reduce the sense of cultural isolation that some learners and parents may feel.
- **Recognize different learning styles.** Learning styles, discussed in depth in Chapter 5, influence many aspects of classroom management and instructional design. Successful learning is most often supported when educators use a variety of teaching strategies to accommodate students' diverse learning styles. The multicultural classroom is no different. By understanding learning-style differences you can help students be successful.
- **Work for equitable participation in the classroom.** Research has long indicated that teachers interact more frequently with male students than female students and white males more often than males of color. Through understanding the class-

room dynamics of interpersonal communication, teachers are sensitized to structuring the learning environment to encourage equitable participation among students. You might maintain a personal tracking system to check how many times each learner is called on, then find ways to increase the participation of students who tend to keep quiet. Try increasing the amount of waiting time after asking questions. Research indicates that allowing some silence after asking questions encourages learners who may be reluctant to participate. Consider seating students in a way that breaks up clusters of similar students, such as females or Asian students. Also plan some activities that require learners to move around and mix with each other. When people get to know others as individuals, the unknown becomes less threatening.
- **Focus on the importance of teamwork, particularly in diverse groups.** Today's learners will enjoy greater future success if they are skilled in working with people from varied cultures. When there are team members who represent a broad perspective of values, ages, physical abilities, traditions, and beliefs, then creativity in problem solving is likely to increase.
- **Call each student by name, pronouncing it correctly.** When names are difficult to pronounce, it's helpful to write them phonetically on the board. You might tape-record all students pronouncing their names and telling a little about themselves. That way, attention isn't drawn to one or two learners.
- **Avoid unintentional "put-downs."** You may have heard remarks such as "You people are such good entertainers" or "Do you know Amir Merzhad in Chicago?" or "I know what it's like to be discriminated against, too." Often meant to "break the ice" or merely as friendly remarks, statements of this sort may not be interpreted that way by the people hearing them. Some comments may be considered racist. Others may be regarded as patronizing—too solicitous or artificial. Remarks of this type inhibit communication rather than enhance it. There are also some terms that are offensive when said in a particular tone or in certain contexts. If

you are unsure about how to refer to a person by cultural background, simply ask that person what term he or she prefers. Because cultural groups are diverse, there are probably no terms that are pleasing or appropriate for all.

- **Stay calm if you are accused of prejudice or bias.** Avoid being defensive and immediately denying the accusation. Since you probably aren't sure exactly what the person is referring to, try to get more information. For example, you might ask, "What have I done that seems prejudiced?" or say, "I am not aware I have been. When you see me do or say something that appears to be biased, please point it out to me." This approach can encourage dialogue. If the learner is able to point out specifics, you might gain valuable insight into how others perceive your actions. On the other hand, the learner may have no concrete evidence of bias on your part but may simply make the remark to see your reaction. Sometimes learners are unable to identify a specific act, but they may articulate how they feel. In that case, attempt to operate from the *reality* of that person's *perception*, if possible.

 # Equity

You may teach a learner who is coping with a serious illness, one who wears a salwar kameez to class, or one who looks like a fashion model. Another student may be obese, have a family member in prison, or be considerably smaller than his or her classmates. In another program, your learners may include a teen mom, a state senator's daughter, a student who lives with gay parents, or one who has a learning disability. No matter what your learners' backgrounds and issues, equity in your classroom or program means equal opportunity and treatment for all students. The climate should be comfortable and welcoming for everyone.

Educators need to recognize inequity in educational opportunities and carry out specific interventions that constitute equi-table educational treatment. Although schools aren't totally to blame for problems created by stereotyping, they are one of the major socializing agencies in the nation and need to assume some responsibility.

❊ Changing Stereotypes

Individuals should be treated as persons and not primarily as members of different groups. Their shared humanity and common attributes should be stressed, not their differences.

Sex equity is one area where stereotypes may exist. Neither gender should be stereotyped or arbitrarily assigned to a leading or secondary role. Some couples choose a lifestyle where the male is the primary wage earner while the female's role is full-time homemaker and mother. Other couples make a conscious decision not to have children. A growing number of men and women choose to remain single, some opting for single parenthood. Others make a commitment to a partner of the same sex.

The key is that lifestyles or roles should not be portrayed as "right," "wrong," "better," or "worse." Just as schools are implementing policies against bullying, many have policies concerning sex equity. Individuals shouldn't be disrespected for their preferences and choices in lifestyles. It's more productive for educators to help learners examine and verbalize their views of the advantages and disadvantages of traditional and less traditional roles for both males and females.

❊ Developing Sensitivity Through Class Activities

A variety of learning activities can help learners consider the effect that various types of stereotyping have had on their lives. The following suggestions may help you generate other ideas:

- Brainstorm to give examples of verbal expressions that perpetuate stereotypical behaviors in children. Examples include:
  "Big boys don't cry."
  "That's a girl toy."
  "That book is for girls."
  "Do you want to grow up to be a sissy?"
  "She's a tomboy."

- Have students access data from the website of the U.S. Census Bureau. It contains statistics such as the number of working mothers; the number of types of families and households; business ownership by race, and the overall diversity of society. This information can be used as the catalyst to discuss the implications of changes in stereotypical roles and the larger effects on society.
- Brainstorm familiar stereotypes—the meddling mother-in-law, spoiled youngest child, provocative secretary, sleazy lawyer, forgetful senior citizen, etc. Discuss why such stereotyping is unfair and should be refuted. Ask students how they could discourage the stereotyping of peers, especially those whose appearance differs from the norm.
- Use sociodramas to focus on role conflicts. For example, someone might portray a male customer in a hardware store telling a female employee that he wants to see a man about mixing some paint. Two students might take the roles of working parents trying to decide who will stay home from work that day to care for a sick child. Sociodramas can also provide valuable practice for handling awkward situations, such as how to respond when someone tells a joke with an ethnic slur. Encourage the learners to think of and act out other role-conflict situations.

✳ Portraying Equitable Treatment

While great strides have been made in this regard over the past 20 years, it's important to make a conscious effort not to reinforce the old stereotypes. Pay attention to the people and characters depicted in classroom posters, to the guest speakers you invite to address your learners, and to expressions you use and comments you make as you teach. All should match the diversity of society.

- **Occupations.** Many people are comfortable with traditional occupations. If this is a learner's plan for the future, respect that choice. However, keep in mind that learners should see both men and women and people of any cultural background in all roles and occupations. For example, women may choose to be homemakers, but they may also aspire to be engineers, police officers, electricians, pilots, and politicians. Men may choose to become dietitians, radiology technicians, family therapists, or nurses. People of both genders and all races and ages should be shown at various levels within a profession. All work should be treated as honorable and worthy of respect. Emphasize that both individuals and society benefit when each person can choose the best possible way to use his or her skills and abilities.
- **Family types and aging.** It's important to recognize that your learners come from a variety of family backgrounds and choose appropriately diverse learning materials. There are nuclear families, households with unmarried partners, and blended families. Some children have gay parents and may be secretive about their families. About four million households in America are classified as multigenerational—consisting of three or more generations. Children being raised by their grandparents is no longer considered unusual. In addition, older adults should not be portrayed as always being infirm. Showing diversity both helps individual learners relate better to material and reminds all students that diversity exists.
- **Generic language.** Help learners to recognize that generic terms, such as "doctor" and "preschool teacher," should be assumed to include both women and men, as well as people of any age or color. It's seldom relevant to use modified titles, such as *male* nurse, *female* bank president, or *black* musician. Similarly, don't stereotype tasks as "woman's work" or "a man-size job." Avoid descriptions that exhibit a surprised attitude toward men and women who perform competently in nontraditional jobs.
- **Names.** People should generally be referred to by their names, not by their roles. For some older women and women from various cultural backgrounds, including African Americans, it can be considered disrespectful to use a first name unless you know that person well. In the classroom, be sure to include

names from a variety of cultural backgrounds when developing activities such as scenarios. Also alternate the order in which names and roles are mentioned rather than always putting males first.

 ## Learners with Special Needs

One aspect of diversity includes individuals with physiological challenges. Unless you have had some professional experience with individuals with physical and learning disabilities, you may, at first, be concerned about how to teach such students effectively. It helps to remember that each person, whether having a disability or not, is an individual with her or his unique needs and talents. Whatever the disability, you will soon find abilities waiting to be discovered and nurtured.

While the educational environment will need to be modified to facilitate learning, teachers should work with an impaired student with the expectation of self-sufficiency and capability. You should expect students with impairments, indeed all students, to participate fully and independently in class. Expect them to succeed.

If you teach high school or adult learners, the students themselves can give you ideas about what works for them. It may be more difficult for younger learners to verbalize these concepts for you, but by asking, you empower them and teach them to advocate for themselves. In any case, teachers should try to establish comfortable, open communication with learners with special needs. Individuals with physical challenges want to be as self-sufficient as possible. Most often, they will let you know when they need assistance. You can always say, "Let me know when and how I may help you."

Your attitudes toward students with disabilities set the model for other learners in your class. The inability to see or hear clearly doesn't affect a person's intelligence or other physical abilities. Make certain your classroom is one in which every learner is respected.

Sometimes teachers feel guilty if they find they dislike an individual with a disability, just as someone might feel about disliking an elderly person. The important point is that you like or dislike the individual for any of the reasons that would lead you to like or dislike any other person, not because of their disability or age. And, of course, you would never let such feelings affect your dealings with a student.

❋ Inclusion

If you were preparing for a teaching career 30 years ago, you might be anticipating leading a classroom with all or no special education students. Today, it is much more likely that special needs students will be mainstreamed into your regular classroom, primarily due to legislation that was implemented in 1975. The Education for All Handicapped Children Act (Public Law 94-142) guaranteed that *all* children were entitled to a public education. In 1990, the act was renamed the Individuals with Disabilities Education Act or IDEA (Public Law 101-476). It mandated inclusive schooling in the *least restrictive environment*, meaning that children with disabilities should be educated with children who aren't disabled. This law was again amended in 1997 and is referred to as IDEA '97 (Public Law 105-17). It ensures that all students able to learn are involved in the general curriculum.

A common misperception exists that, in order to be part of an inclusive setting, students with disabilities have to be able to follow the curriculum in the same way as their classmates. This is not the case. The law requires that students with disabilities be provided with "supplemental supports, aids, and services." These might range from a peer tutor to large-print books or a classroom aide.

Parents of learners without disabilities often voice concerns that students with disabilities may disrupt the class or take a disproportionate amount of the teacher's time. Both concerns are legitimate. Intervention would be needed for any student who is so disruptive as to interfere with the functioning of the class. Concern about the teacher's time is justified. Regular classroom teachers should receive assistance when students with disabilities are mainstreamed into their classrooms. The ideal inclusive classroom is one in which the students with disabilities benefit, the students without disabilities benefit, and the teacher receives ongoing support. Teachers typically find that the strategies used for mainstreamed students are appropriate and effective for all learners.

✳ Individualized Education Plans (IEPs)

IDEA '97 also focuses on the *Individualized Education Plan (IEP)*. Every child in a public school who receives special education and related services must have an IEP that is truly individualized for her or him. This plan serves to guide teachers, administrators, parents, and often the students themselves, in how best to structure the learning environment for this person. The IEP is a legal contract among all parties who sign it.

The IEP process is coordinated by the school system. It is an opportunity for teachers, parents, school administrators, specialized personnel, and the learner to collaborate on meeting the learner's unique needs. Evaluation begins when a child is suspected to have a disability. Qualified professionals and parents review the outcomes of evaluations. Together, they decide if the student is a "child with a disability" as defined by IDEA '97. Parents can request a hearing to challenge the eligibility decision. If the student is determined to be eligible, the IEP team must develop an IEP for the student within 30 days.

The student's parents and the student, if appropriate, should be actively involved throughout the development of an IEP. Before services can be provided, parents must give consent for the child to begin receiving services. Services should commence as soon as possible after the IEP is completed and agreed to by all parties.

If parents disagree with the IEP and placement of the student, they can discuss these issues with the IEP team and attempt to come to an agreement. If this isn't possible, mediation can help.

IDEA '97 requires that certain information be included in each child's IEP, as outlined in *Figure 19-1* on page 269. It is the school's responsibility to ensure that the IEP is carried out as written. Parents are provided a copy of the IEP and the student's teachers and service providers have access to it. It is essential that all involved are clear about their own specific responsibilities for carrying out the IEP.

Each IEP contains annual goals based on the learner's unique needs. During the academic year, the school is responsible for assessing the student's progress toward these goals and documenting this progress in the IEP. Progress reports must be provided to parents, and they need to be told if the learner's progress is sufficient for him or her to reach the goals by the end of the school year.

IEPs must be reviewed at least once a year. Additional reviews may occur at the request of either parents or school officials. If appropriate, the IEP may be modified.

Learners must be evaluated every three years to find out if they continue to meet IDEA's criteria for a "child with a disability" and to determine what their educational needs are. Certainly, students may be evaluated more often if conditions warrant or if school personnel or parents request a new evaluation.

✳ Learners with Hearing Impairments

If you are scheduled to have a learner with a hearing impairment in your class, your first step should be to read the student's existing IEP. You might talk to other instructors who have taught this person for advice on techniques that work well. You can collaborate with instructional specialists, occupational therapists, speech therapists, and other individuals in your professional environment for ideas on how to enhance learning for students with hearing deficits. One of your best sources of information will be the student. He or she can advise you about ways you can maximize his or her learning.

It is helpful to understand the source of the learner's hearing loss. In general, there are three types. *Conductive loss* affects the sound-conducting paths of the outer and

Figure 19-1

INDIVIDUALIZED EDUCATION PLANS

An Individualized Education Plan (IEP) is required by law to contain ten basic pieces of information about the learner and the educational program that will be designed to meet the individual's unique needs. Briefly, these are:

1. **Current performance.** This is usually based on observations and a variety of tests that help determine how the student is currently doing in school and how the child's disability affects her or his involvement and progress in the general curriculum.

2. **Annual goals.** These are goals that can be reasonably expected to be accomplished within a year. They may be broken down into short-term objectives. Goals may be academic, social, physical, or related to another educational need. All goals should be measurable.

3. **Special education and related services.** All of the special education and related services that the learner will receive must be identified. The IEP must include any modifications to the program or support needed to assist the student.

4. **Participation with nondisabled children.** If the student is to be limited in his or her participation in the regular class and other activities, this must be defined in the IEP.

5. **Participation in state and district tests.** The IEP must state what modifications in the administration of achievement tests, if any, will be required. If the test isn't appropriate for the learner, the IEP must state why and must identify how the student will be evaluated.

6. **Dates and places.** The IEP must state when services will begin, where they will be delivered, how often they will be provided, and how long the services will last.

7. **Transitional service needs.** For students 14 or older, the IEP must address courses needed for the student to reach his or her post-school goals.

8. **Transitional services for leaving school.** For those 16 years of age or older, the IEP must define what transitional services are needed to help the student leave school.

9. **Age-of-majority rights.** In some states, beginning at least one year before the child reaches the age of majority, the IEP must include a statement that the student has been told of any rights that will transfer to him or her at the age of majority.

10. **Measuring progress.** How the student's progress will be measured and how this will be reported to parents are required.

middle ear. The degree of loss may be decreased by use of a hearing aid or surgery. People with conductive hearing loss often hear better in noisy environments than people with normal hearing. This is because they become accustomed to others speaking to them in loud voices. *Sensorineural loss* affects the inner ear and auditory nerve. Hearing loss may range from mild to profound. Learners with this type of hearing loss may speak loudly, experience more high-frequency loss, have difficulty distinguishing consonant sounds, and may not hear well in noisy surroundings. The third type, *mixed loss*, results from both a conductive and sensorineural loss.

There is a close relationship between hearing loss and the development of speech. As a result, learners with hearing deficits may also have speech impairments. The level of speech difficulty depends on when the individual lost her or his hearing—before or after oral language skills developed.

When working with learners with hearing deficits, keep these points in mind:

- Visual information is especially helpful for learners with hearing impairments. Incorporate more of this mode of learning into your class. Other learners will also benefit. Allow the student time to access visual information independently.

- Circular seating arrangements allow the student to see everyone in the group. If seating must be in rows, seat the learner (and interpreter, if there is one) in front. Be sure to include the hearing-impaired learner in discussions.

- Have the learner's attention before you begin to speak. A visual cue, such as a wave, is often helpful.
- Look directly at the learner when speaking, even when an interpreter is present. Don't speak loudly, but speak clearly. If the learner doesn't understand, rephrase your ideas or thoughts. If all else fails, communicate in writing.
- When speaking, avoid actions that might make lip-reading difficult. For example, having your back to a window can make it difficult to see your face clearly.
- While some learners with hearing deficits may be able to read lips, be aware that many speech sounds have identical mouth movements. For example, *p*, *b*, and *m* look exactly alike on the lips when spoken. Also, many sounds such as vowels are produced without using clearly distinguishing lip movements.
- If a hearing-impaired student signs, learn at least basic signs for better communication.
- Repeat questions and comments of other learners, especially those seated behind the learner. Acknowledge the speaker so a student with a hearing impairment can focus on that individual.
- When in doubt, ask hearing-impaired learners privately how you can best assist them.

✳ Learners with Visual Impairments

Visual impairments can range from a need for large print materials to total blindness. As with other physical challenges, you should plan to work in partnership with specialists within the school system, the student's parents, and the student to determine ways to best facilitate learning.

Put yourself in your student's place as you mentally replay several lessons from your course. Which teaching techniques and student activities would present difficulties for this visually-impaired student? How can you modify your teaching to make the learning more accessible for the student? Here are some general suggestions:

- Understand and respect the skills of visually-impaired students.
- Provide the same or equivalent information and experiences to visually-impaired students as to sighted learners. Treat them equally.
- Speak directly to them and interact with them on a daily basis.
- Learn about the alternative means that visually-impaired students may use, such as a cane, Braille, tactile stimuli, or audiotapes and CDs.
- Be attentive to the types of interaction you have with students. When writing information on the board, say what you are writing. Spell words aloud, if needed. When talking about objects, be descriptive with attributes such as shape, weight, and texture.

✳ Learners with Attention Deficit Disorder

Attention deficit disorder (ADD) continues to be a controversial learning disability diagnosis. Some people argue that the condition is overdiagnosed, while others claim that it is underdiagnosed. Many express concern over the use of stimulants as a treatment for the disorder. Historically, children with ADD have been labeled as "learning disabled," "brain damaged," "hyperkinetic," and "hyperactive." None of these terms adequately defines or describes this condition.

ADD is a neurobiological disorder characterized by serious and persistent difficulties in three areas: attention span, impulse control, and hyperactivity. These often result in poor performance in school, even if a child is highly intelligent. It is a chronic condition that may begin in infancy and continue through adulthood. It's estimated that between three and five percent of America's school-age population is affected by ADD. That translates to about one in 20 students, prompting some health professionals to refer to ADD as the most common childhood disorder. It has been suggested that ADD is linked to food allergies, sugar in the diet, and poor parenting. These theories have been debunked, but researchers do believe there is a genetic link to ADD.

There are two types of ADD. The first is *attention deficit hyperactivity disorder*

(ADHD). Hyperactivity distinguishes it from the other type, *undifferentiated attention deficit disorder (UADD)*, With the latter, the primary and most significant characteristic is inattentiveness, resulting in distractability and disorganization. The hyperactive behavior of students with ADHD makes them more obvious in a classroom than those with UDHD, who tend to be quiet and passive.

In both cases, the degree to which characteristics are displayed is recognizably different from other students of the same age. Students may often have difficulty following instructions, blurt out answers, and move from one uncompleted task to the next. Such characteristics usually occur at home, at school, and during peer interaction, rather than in just one setting.

Teachers who work with students with ADD find that effective management of the learning environment facilitates their learning. If a student with ADD has been diagnosed, he or she will probably have an IEP. You may teach learners, however, who are undiagnosed. This includes adult learners. Here are suggestions for helping students with ADD learn more effectively:

- **Seat a learner with ADD near your desk.** Do this without making an issue of the seating arrangement. This will allow close interaction between you and the student while also limiting the student's view of others, reducing the amount of environmental stimuli the learner receives. A U-shaped seating arrangement is another possibility because it allows you to easily make eye contact with the learner.
- **Provide good peer role models for students with ADD.** Peers they look up to are especially effective in this role. Peer tutoring and cooperative/collaborative learning are beneficial ways of including these positive role models in students' lives.
- **Reduce the amount of distracting stimuli.** Possible distractions include an abundance of posters; noise from heating and air conditioning; and being near doors or windows and high-traffic areas in the room. It is helpful to keep the classroom door closed.

- **Limit the number of changes that you expect students with ADD to handle.** Changes in schedules, disruptions of work patterns, and new physical environments should be limited or managed. Post a schedule of the day's topics or events. It will help daydreaming students to figure out what's going on when they come back to reality.
- **Set up quiet areas for study.** In the classroom, encourage all students to use the quiet area so students with ADD don't feel isolated. Encourage parents to establish a quiet, stimuli-reduced study space at home. Study times should be set and maintained as a routine part of the student's day. Encourage parents to periodically check the student's completed work and make certain it goes back in the student's backpack. It's common for students with ADD to complete their homework, but not turn it in.
- **Make sure directions are clear and concise.** When giving instructions to your students with ADD, maintain eye contact with them. Break down directions into smaller, simpler units. Multiple commands often frustrate and confuse learners with ADD. Check that students understand directions before beginning a task. Repeat them calmly, as needed. Provide written instructions as often as possible.
- **Maintain a supportive learning environment.** If you act in a positive manner, learners will be encouraged and feel good about their abilities. All students, especially those with ADD, should feel comfortable asking for help or clarification with directions, projects, or assignments. Encourage students to think through problems and seek their own answers. Plan to gradually reduce the amount of help you give the class, yet anticipate that students with ADD will need relatively more assistance.
- **Help students develop organizational aids.** In teaching, for example, show how linking a new concept to a familiar one or using graphic organizers help learning. Show how color-coding can improve organization. Require that the student write all assignments in a notebook. You

may need to help some students with ADD with this process. Both teachers and parents can sign off on the student's completed work, using the notebook as a means of communication.

- **Modify assignments to meet the needs of students with ADD.** For example, learners with ADD are capable of critical thinking, but you may need to assist them through the process. Directions written in a step-by-step format with check-off boxes may help learners stay on-task. More time may be needed to complete some assignments.
- **Modify testing procedures, as needed.** Periodically review your evaluation criteria and methods to be sure that students' knowledge is being tested, not their attention span. Allow additional time to complete tests. Especially for district and state tests, you may be able to make reasonable accommodations, such as providing a quiet room for taking the test, reading the test to the student, allowing extra time, breaking a test into shorter sessions, and reducing the number of students in the room. What isn't acceptable is shortening a test, changing a short answer test to multiple choice, or anything else that would alter the content of the test.

Self-esteem is a problem for many individuals with ADD. However, suggestions for increasing self-esteem in these students are, in fact, effective with all learners. Look to each learner's unique talents, abilities, and strengths. Encourage positive self-talk; praise immediately and often for appropriate behaviors and good performance. Physical activity helps build self-esteem. Biking, swimming, bowling, and karate are often recommended for learners with ADD. These activities are noncompetitive to mildly competitive and engage the individual in focused, physical activity.

All students need adequate supervision and appropriate guidance or discipline. As discussed in Chapter 18, the consequences of misbehavior should be predetermined and stressed to students. Enforce classroom rules and expectations consistently and fairly. Obviously, you should never allow ridicule, criticism, or teasing that is linked to the student's ADD. Never publicly remind students who have medication for their ADD to take their medicine or ask if they have taken it.

✳ Success Stories

Prior to the passage in 1975 of the legislation mandating appropriate educational opportunities, an estimated one million special needs students were kept out of school and many others weren't getting appropriate services. Now, three times the previous number of students with disabilities continue on to college. Compared to then, the number of 20-year-olds with disabilities who are working has doubled. Such figures are impressive, but, unfortunately, students with disabilities are still twice as likely to drop out of school. Dedicated teachers can help see that number decline and can boost the talents and skills those with disabilities can add to our society.

References

Franklin, J. (2000). Living with attention-deficit disorder. *Curriculum Update*, Fall.

Kluth, P., Villa, R.A., and Thousand, J.S. (2001/2002). Our school doesn't offer inclusion and other legal blunders. *Educational Leadership*, December/January.

Lamme, L.L., and Lamme, L.A. (2001/2002). Welcoming children from gay families into our schools. *Educational Leadership*, December/January.

Paley, V.G. (2000). *White teacher*. Cambridge, MA: Harvard University Press.

Rasmussen, K. (2000). Meeting the special needs of all children, inclusion or intrusion? *Curriculum Update*, Winter.

http://www.census.org U.S. Bureau of the Census. (Accessed January 28, 2002)

http://www.ed.gov/offices/OSERS/IDEA Individuals with Disabilities Education Act 1997 Ammendments. (Accessed January 24, 2002)

Building Your Professional Portfolio

The Cultural Diversity Debate. Some segments of American society are against embracing the ethnic cultures of immigrants. Research the reasoning used by people with this viewpoint. Explain how you would handle parents' varying viewpoints on multiculturalism if you were a middle school or high school teacher.

Culture and Communication. Choose at least six ethnic cultures prevalent in an area where you might teach. Research customs and behavioral expectations that affect verbal and nonverbal communication in those cultures. Determine how this information might directly affect the ways you interact with learners and parents from these cultures.

Equity in Learning Resources. Develop an evaluation instrument to rate equity issues in teaching/learning materials you might use, either a textbook or nontext materials.

Adapting Teaching for Special Needs. Choose one lesson, presentation, or dietetic counseling session you have previously developed or used. Analyze and identify ways you would modify your teaching for a learner with a specific impairment.

Chapter 20

Working with Adolescents at Risk

Susan D. McLaughlin, M.P.A., CPP-R
Primary Prevention Services Coordinator
State of Connecticut Department
of Mental Health and Addiction Services

*T*he term "at risk" conjures up a variety of images such as depression, abusive and defiant behaviors, violence, substance abuse, truancy, and promiscuity. Efforts in the 1980s and early 1990s to define and label "at-risk" behavior were intended to get young people the help they needed to prevent the progression or development of more serious behaviors. While this led to an emphasis on problem behaviors and dramatically increased resources to work with these identified youth, it also served to ignore those who exhibited no obvious problems or risk factors. As the science of prevention has evolved in recent years, however, understanding of adolescence has expanded. As an educator, you can create a learning environment that helps build strong, resilient teens.

Understanding Adolescents

Some teen learners live in homeless shelters; others change schools due to frequent moves. Many suffer from abuse or low aspirations. Learners may present and reflect the ills of society, dysfunctional family dynamics, and personal troubles in school hallways and classrooms, as well as in the community. Appropriate support structures are a necessary and essential part of the educational system. At the same time, addressing students' holistic needs allows the educator to focus on teaching and emphasizing positive learner achievement. Educators can implement generic methodologies that will help strengthen the health and well-being of each learner and the class, or group, as a whole.

This chapter focuses on how to create conditions that foster health and resiliency. By looking at "the whole child," it's possible to enhance students' success in the classroom, as well as in other aspects of their daily lives. By infusing prevention strategies into your routine, young people can experience greater levels of health, wellness, achievement, and satisfaction in their schools, families, and communities.

❋ Characteristics of Adolescence

Teens are fraught with contradictions. Many are extremely self-absorbed while obsessed with appearance and relationships. Surrounded by dozens of opportunities, they complain of "nothing to do." They work to express their individuality, yet they learn to fit in. Moods swing; tastes change. They test boundaries and take risks. Previously accepted authority and dogma may be questioned and challenged.

The "job" of the adolescent is to become a healthy, well-adjusted adult who has a strong sense of purpose, feels good about herself or himself, and makes a positive contribution to the world. To accomplish this goal, youngsters experience profound and all-encompassing changes from their pre-teen years through their early twenties—changes that permeate their mental, physical, and emotional beings. These normative and transformational experiences include:

- **Physiological, hormonal, and developmental changes.** These form the evolving palette upon and within which young people negotiate and establish their emerging identities.
- **Transitions.** These require moving into the realms, expectations, and responsibilities of secondary school and/or higher education, the world of work, and more independent lifestyles.
- **Loss.** This includes letting go of childhood roles, beliefs, body image, interests, and activities.

These three pervasive influences of adolescent development create the common denominator of the adolescent experience, which, in itself, is fairly overwhelming. For learners to assimilate and integrate what's happening to them in their lives with what you are expecting of them academically, it's essential to address the whole child.

❋ The Whole Child

In addition to the natural challenges of growing into adulthood, "The Holistic Model," shown in *Figure 20-1*, illustrates the "self" surrounded by each of four equal aspects or realms: the physical, mental, emotional, and

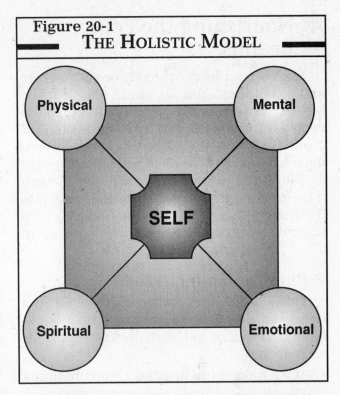

Figure 20-1
THE HOLISTIC MODEL

spiritual parts of the person. The changes presented in the previous section impact each aspect of the self:

- **Physical.** This encompasses the body, physical health, and fitness of the individual. Nutrition and patterns of exercise, posture, and breathing have primary impact here.
- **Mental.** The cognitive sphere includes knowledge, decision making, and problem solving. The application of healthful life skills is in this realm.
- **Emotional.** The emotional realm is the seat of feelings and the ability to know and understand these feelings and to communicate them in appropriate and timely ways.
- **Spiritual.** The spiritual realm is the nucleus of self-esteem, self-respect, and responsibility; the personal understanding of the self in relation to higher forces; and a perspective of meaning and significance in the world.

Each of the four realms needs to be acknowledged and nourished. The intended result of this attention, along with the recognition and understanding of the generic adolescent experience, is the emergence of the whole child: a healthy, confident, competent, and compassionate individual committed to self, family, and community.

✳ Nourishing the Four Realms

Each of your learners has four pathways to understanding. You do, too. The Holistic Model transcends the language of personality types, as well as the learning styles discussed in Chapter 5. Utilizing brief interventions in each of the realms will enhance your learners' educational experiences and maximize the integration of your teaching into their lives. These interventions will also help minimize distractions caused by adolescent life experiences.

✳ *Physical Realm Activities*

Many educators have discovered the improved disposition and functioning facilitated by frequent, yet brief, directed activities such as these:

- **Take a moment to breathe.** Deep breathing oxygenates the brain and boosts concentration. Direct the group of learners to take three slow, deep breaths at the beginning of class or before a test. For best results, tell them to breathe in through the nose, hold it for a moment, and exhale through the mouth. Take a deep breath together after a difficult task, when someone is upset, or whenever you need to refocus the group.
- **Stretch and move.** Adolescents' bodies are programmed to be active, yet during most of the school day they are sedentary. A few gentle arm, shoulder, and neck stretches; torso rotations; and leg flexes release tension and simultaneously energize the body.
- **Use music to soothe and motivate.** You might play quiet background music during a specific seat activity. (However, watch for any signs that it is distracting to learners with ADD.) You might link an energizing activity to a song, such as having the learners march in place, then touch their right elbow to their left knee and left elbow to their right knee ten times. Such activities, called "neuro-linguistic programming," connect the left and right hemispheres of the brain and help maximize brain functioning. Other possibilities are to sing together or have a group hum. Learners may balk at these suggestions initially, but most will enjoy participating.

✳ *Mental Realm Activities*

Education takes place primarily in the mental realm. Practice cognitive skills by demonstrating how to transfer critical thinking in institutional settings to situations in the learners' daily lives. These are ideas you might try:

- **Post a model for decision making or problem solving.** A simple model is the stoplight: a poster of the red, yellow, and green circles of light. Red is the reminder to stop and think, to consider the situation, and clearly define it. Yellow is for caution, thinking about possible options and consequences. Green prompts that you are good to go, but you also need to remember to evaluate the results of your choice.
- **Encourage learners to review and evaluate their participation and progress.** For example, have learners use journals or personal response sheets once a week. As detailed in Chapter 17, they can respond to structured prompts such as "What I am most proud of this week" or "This is what I would do differently the next time."

✳ *Emotional Realm Activities*

Feelings are literally what people feel. Emotions are what they experience internally as a result of these feelings. Typically, emotions are ignored in the academic setting, yet they are an integral part of the learner and have an impact upon learning. Family and consumer sciences instructors have a distinct advantage in this realm because a portion of the subject matter is linked to emotions. Emotions will be discussed, for instance, when learners study relationships, child development, and parenting, as well as the emotional needs that are satisfied through housing. The following suggestions can be used with any class. They work best when they are discussed, shared, negotiated, and consistently monitored:

- **Help learners develop positive communication skills.** Encourage them to speak for themselves, to use "I statements" when confronting a challenging interaction, to refrain from comments that judge another person, and to maintain compassion in words and deeds.

- **With student input, develop a list of "Working Agreements."** Similar to the action discipline plan discussed in Chapter 18, these class agreements might include "respect for people and property," "one person speaks at a time" (also known as "share the air"), and "the Ouch rule." This rule says that any person offended by a remark can say "ouch," and the originator has the opportunity to withdraw or discuss the remark. The "Working Agreements" can be posted, referred to and adhered to, and reworked as necessary.

✳ *Spiritual Realm Activities*

The spiritual realm goes beyond a specific religion or dogma. It involves an individual's connection to a greater meaning, a sense of purpose within the world.

- **Encourage pride and satisfaction, and acknowledge achievement.** False modesty serves no one. You might say, "You have done a great job on this project. I am proud of you. You should be proud, too."
- **Create opportunities for students to contribute to the group.** Rotate simple daily tasks, like distributing or putting away materials. Have students make contributions to, or be responsible for, bulletin boards and displays.
- **Foster peer support.** Cultivate time for students to share their expertise and help one another.
- **Encourage personal quiet time.** Suggest daily journaling or time spent in a favorite spot outdoors.

 # Intervention Opportunities: Now or Later

The subject matter in Family and Consumer Sciences, Health, and Nutrition holds great promise for helping your learners lead productive, happy lives and make positive changes. However, as stated earlier in this text, often there is little you can do about environmental factors that impact individuals, such as familial, societal, or genetic factors.

The good news is that your teaching methods, supplemented by the inclusion of intervention activities, will influence the level of a learner's self-esteem. It's this core belief in self that drives self-confidence and success in the classroom and, by extension, in the world. Adolescent behavior is a strong indicator of self-esteem. By paying attention, you can determine if adolescents are in need of special care from you and/or would benefit from a referral to another helping professional.

It may be normal adolescent behavior to feel depressed sometimes, to flirt with a risky behavior, or have an occasional problem at school. *Figure 20-2*, the "Intervention Opportunity Model" below, gives a graphic depiction of what happens when trouble-indicators evolve into more serious behaviors and proceed unchecked. Trouble indicators include depression, high-risk behaviors, and problems in school.

✳ The Model Explained

The number of people ages 14 to 24 taking their own lives has tripled during the past 30 years. Equally alarming is the statistic that since 1980 the suicide rate for younger children, ages 10 to 14, has increased 128 percent.

Experts say that more than 90 percent of youth who complete suicide have given ample warnings and distinct clues regarding their despair. At the core of this despair

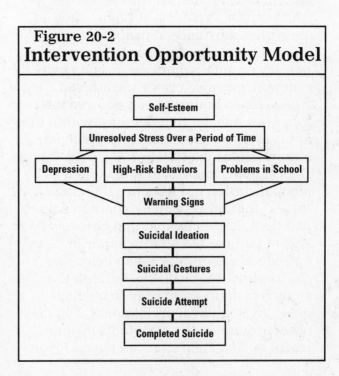

Figure 20-2
Intervention Opportunity Model

are loss and separation, feeling disconnected and alone, helplessness, and hopelessness. Risk surveys administered to high school and college students consistently report that more than 30 percent have considered suicide at some point in their lives, and 10 percent have actually made an attempt. Some studies report higher percentages.

There is a strong and irrefutable link between the impact of our fast-paced, consumer-driven, contradictory culture and the natural hazards of adolescent development. The media exploit sexuality, present a distorted body image, and actively promote alcohol and legalized gambling. The pervasive message is that money, good looks, and possessions are the keys to happiness and success.

No wonder that the adolescent, who is by nature wrestling with major issues of loss and contradictions, is extremely vulnerable. Strong coping skills and a steady support system help keep the adolescent afloat and afford a smoother transition into adulthood. Individuals whose foundations are less solid are more easily overwhelmed. The following list consists of a progression of behaviors you may witness in adolescents who don't have solid coping skills and support systems:

- **Unresolved stress over a period of time.** Just navigating the difficult road of adolescent developmental transitions can cause stress. Problems at home, such as life with a substance-abusing or terminally ill family member, or living in poverty or in an otherwise unsafe environment, can also create unresolved stress. As an educator, you observe the "spillover effects" that manifest within the areas of depression, high-risk behaviors, and problems in school.
- **Depression.** Depression is classified as a mood disorder, but it's more than the "blues" that most people experience now and then. It is estimated that between 7 and 14 percent of children experience an episode of major depression before age 15. Treatment is available, but first the victims of depression have to be diagnosed by a medical professional. You may observe some of the symptoms in your learners. See *Figure 20-3* on page 279 for a list of symptoms and behaviors of depression.
- **High-risk behaviors.** These are behaviors that are dangerous to self and/or others. Drinking, speeding and reckless driving, experimenting with illegal or harmful substances, smoking, shoplifting, and fighting are examples of high-risk behaviors that are overlooked or tolerated by some adults as being "typical" or "a right of passage." Gang activity, starvation, or bingeing and purging are further examples of pushing the limits beyond an acceptable level of personal safety.
- **Problems in school.** These include sporadic or poor attendance, dramatic fluctuation in grades, academic failure, cheating, and behavioral problems. Defiance and rule-breaking are also problems observed in school, and these situations can be exacerbated by students' inability to manage conflict.
- **Warning signs of suicide.** Look for the pattern of several related signs, as indicated in *Figure 20-4*, "Warning Signs of Suicide," on page 279. The duration of a given pattern for two weeks or more should warrant concern, unless the behaviors are normal for a particular individual. Check for the presence and intensity of a particular crisis or event—moving, a breakup with a girlfriend or boyfriend, a failing report card, or school suspension. Such an event could represent a precipitating factor or be "the straw that breaks the camel's back."
- **Suicidal ideation.** At this stage, suicide begins to be considered as a conscious option. The degree of seriousness can wax and wane over time. Often, it's a fascination, an indulgence. Individual life events, coping skills, and support systems have a strong impact on outcome at this stage.
- **Suicidal gestures.** These are superficial attempts and can include youth who self-mutilate, slash the body in an attempt to feel pain, or who ingest a handful of pills, and call for help.
- **Suicide attempts.** By and large, adolescents who make serious attempts on their lives don't want to die. What they want is to stop living in such pain, and through their tunnel vision they see death as their only option. The fact that adolescents tend

Figure 20-3
Warning Signs of Depression

Millions of children, teens, and adults in the United States suffer from major depression, making life and learning very difficult. Here are possible symptoms and behaviors that your learners may exhibit. Depending on an individual's age and gender, behaviors may vary. An official diagnosis of a major depressive disorder usually results from an individual having five or more of these symptoms:

- Persistent feelings of sadness or emptiness
- Loss of interest or pleasure in activities that were previously enjoyed
- Pessimism and hopelessness
- Feelings of worthlessness and helplessness
- Daily fatigue and loss of energy
- Bad temper, irritability, easily annoyed
- Fearful, tense, anxious
- Little interaction with other learners
- Change in sleep habits—insomnia, early morning awakening, oversleeping
- Appetite loss or overeating
- Restlessness
- Dropping grades
- Repeated emotional outbursts
- Difficulty concentrating, remembering, and making decisions
- Physical symptoms with no apparent medical cause—headaches, digestive disorders, chronic pain, aching arms or legs in children

to make their attempts at home between 2:00 p.m. and 6:00 p.m. illustrates their ambivalence towards this act and the hope that they will be rescued. The availability of handguns, however, is largely responsible for the dramatic increase in completed adolescent suicides. Households with guns are almost ten times more likely to have a teen suicide than homes without guns. In such instances, the probability of being found in time is slim.

Fortunately, the vast majority of your learners will never descend through this model. However, if you observe learners displaying the trouble indicators and warning signs, you need to intervene. Take action promptly with the appropriate personnel, such as school administrators, the social worker or psychologist, guidance counselor, or nurse.

❊ What Educators Can Do

Your mission is the education of your learners, which can be compromised by their inability to be fully "present" and attentive. As you work to fulfill this mission, take time to acknowledge the adolescent experience and nurture growth within the structure of the program. Many of the situations causing ongoing, unresolved stress need to be brought to the attention of other appropriate professionals. An exception is the bul-

Figure 20-4
WARNING SIGNS OF SUICIDE

EARLY WARNING SIGNS	LATE WARNING SIGNS
• Difficulties in school • Talking about suicide, death • Depression • Neglect of appearance • Increased substance use • Dropping out of activities • Changes in sleeping habits • Isolating oneself from others • Feeling that life is meaningless • Loss of interest in activities • Hopelessness • Restlessness and agitation • Helplessness	• Feelings of failure • Sudden improvement in mood • Overreaction to criticism • Preoccupation with one's failures • Overly self-critical • Collecting means to kill oneself • Anger and rage • Making final arrangements • Pessimism about life, the future • Ending significant relationships • Giving away possessions • Inability to concentrate • Having a suicide plan • Preoccupation with death • Taking unnecessary risks

Connecticut Committee for Youth Suicide Prevention.

lying and harassment many students are subjected to at school. Never turn your back on this demeaning activity in the classroom or hallways. Not only does it damage self-esteem, but bullying and harassment have repeatedly been proven to be factors in tragic episodes of school violence.

In your efforts to create an optimal learning environment, you encourage and promote your learners' personal coping skills and problem-solving abilities. The following strategies have been found to be effective:

- In assessing your level of concern about a learner's possible depression, refer to the Holistic Model. Apply what you observe to the physical, mental, emotional, and spiritual realms. Clusters of clues across the realms could indicate the need for consultation with or referral to an appropriate professional.
- Be vigilant about high-risk behaviors. Monitor behaviors relevant to your setting and set firm guidelines with consistent consequences. Challenge your learners to think through their choices and to thoroughly weigh consequences and risks prior to their actions.
- You are the first line of defense when problems arise in your program or classroom. Maintain as strong a connection with the learners' parents as possible. When you refer students to the guidance office, social workers, or other sources of help, follow up. The fate of too many young people has floundered in a pile of paperwork or at the hands of overburdened or inattentive staff.
- When warning signs begin to appear, use the Holistic Model as you would when concerned with signs of depression. Remember that depression is a common warning sign. Evaluate what you know about the person in the physical, mental, emotional, and spiritual realms. In each area, what gives you cause for concern? Consult with other staff, possibly coaches and other educators, who see the indiviual in different situations. Make sure each of you appraises the strengths you observe in each realm as well. This is important information that will be the foundation upon which recovery can be built.

- Professional help is essential when suicidal gestures or attempts have taken place. The individual should be monitored closely for at least a year, because the greatest risk of a repeated attempt is during the next three to six months. With proper treatment and support, most people can rebuild their lives and proceed without further suicidal trauma.

Too often educators struggle with a learner in serious trouble or find themselves looking back after a tragedy and second-guessing how it could have been averted. Use "The Intervention Opportunity Model" on page 277 as a reminder that there is almost always an opportunity to intervene, to address the behavior of concern, and to make an appropriate referral.

 # Creating Conditions That Foster Health and Resiliency

Over the past two decades, professional youth workers and other caring adults have searched for the answers to this question: Given similar difficult backgrounds of trauma, abuse, and neglect, why do some youth fail and spiral through the depths of substance abuse, emotional breakdown, crime, and suicide while others soar to personal and professional success? The turning point in the at-risk movement was when professionals began to discover and examine the factors that create this contrast in outcomes.

The findings were that those who emerged intact from overwhelmingly difficult circumstances shared basic protective factors and positive conditions in the home and school environment. These include a sense of personal safety and identity; connection to caring adults, often one adult; and a sense of personal power and control.

Conditions that foster health and resiliency promote health and well-being in each of the physical, mental, emotional, and spiritual realms. In turn, this enhances student learning. Consequently, creating these conditions also decreases the need for special interventions aimed at dealing with and preventing negative behavior. Individual self-esteem and achievement increase and elevate each other. Learning escalates when the group becomes more cooperative and cohesive.

❋ The Circle of Courage

A comprehensive model illustrating the need and strategy for creating conditions that foster health and resiliency is grounded in a traditional Native American philosophy of child rearing. It is explained in contemporary terms as "The Circle of Courage."

Native American philosophies of child management represent what is perhaps the most effective system of positive discipline ever developed. These approaches emerged from cultures where the central purpose of life was the education and empowerment of children. Researchers are studying this holistic approach and how it can be understood, scientifically validated, and replicated.

Fostering self-esteem is a primary goal in socializing children, as well as in specialized work with children and adolescents at risk. Without a sense of self-worth, a young person from any cultural or family background is vulnerable to a host of social, psychological, and learning problems. (Brendtro, Brokenleg and Van Bockern, 1990.)

This "The Circle of Courage" concept is depicted in *Figure 20-5* below. Its premise is that each person and each child has a place,

role, meaning, and purpose in the world. The circle begins with this concept, which is central in the element of belonging, and proceeds sunwise, or clockwise, through mastery, independence, and generosity and then back to belonging, where the circle continues. One element builds upon the other, strengthening and nourishing the whole child. "The Circle of Courage Principles," *Figure 20-6* on page 282, explain this concept.

❋ *Building Belonging*

A sense of belonging can be fostered in many ways. Besides those suggested here, refer back to page 248 in Chapter 18, which discusses enhancing self-esteem. Incorporate the element of belonging by remembering:

- Names are important. Learn each individual's name and use it frequently. At the beginning of a new course or program, you might have learners put name tags on their desks. This also helps them learn each other's names.
- Learners need to feel safe in order to concentrate. Do what you can to ensure the safety and comfort of the room; each person's workspace should be respected and secure within reason. If possible, regulate the temperature for comfort.
- Learners need to know the parameters of your rules, policies, and expectations. Be clear and consistent.
- The "Working Agreements" or agreed-upon rules, discussed earlier, help give learners a sense of ownership and responsibility for what happens in the group. They reinforce that inappropriate behavior isn't tolerated.
- Learners usually know about support systems, but they often need reminders, reinforcement, and encouragement to make use of them. Make sure participants know when you are available to provide extra help and for personal meetings. Discuss the network of help and support available for students and how to access it.
- Encourage individuals to think about their own personal support network.
- Class meetings that are weekly, monthly, or otherwise as needed give students a

Figure 20-5
THE CIRCLE OF COURAGE

GENEROSITY

INDEPENDENCE

BELONGING

MASTERY

Used with permission from Circle of Courage, Inc. P.O. Box 57 Lenox, SD 57049 Adapted from art by: George Blue Bird.

forum to share feelings and discuss appropriate classroom-related business. Hold meetings routinely, not just when there is a problem. Such meetings will help protect class time by preventing nonacademic issues from encroaching on lessons.

- Provide opportunities for working cooperatively, both in pairs and in small groups.
- Encourage a sense of cohesiveness. Mark participants' birthdays on a calendar so they may be recognized. If there are occasions where food is served, such as an end-of-term party, have students bring in their favorite foods or a food that represents their cultural background.
- Encourage contributions to classroom and department displays.

✳ *Building Mastery*

As the principles of mastery indicate, students must feel they are worthwhile, capable people. Help them practice the principle of mastery:

- Use journals or personal response sheets for participants to record and monitor individual progress and experiences.
- Provide opportunities for learners to evaluate and grade their own assignments and projects as a supplement to, but not a replacement for, the grades you assign.
- Encourage appropriate self-praise and sharing of successes.
- Provide opportunities for participants to share their personal interests. While studying fitness and wellness, learners

Figure 20-6	"THE CIRCLE OF COURAGE" PRINCIPLES
Principles of Belonging ↓	• Network of meaningful relationships and adult role models for security and support • Trusting relationships, limits, rules, and a positive and caring environment • Ability to identify and express emotions and attitudes • Discovery of interests, capabilities, and backgrounds of self and others • Skill in making friends • Peer approval and support
Principles of Mastery ↓	• Competence • Success and accomplishment in things regarded as valuable and important • Exploration of ideals, heroes, role models, standards, and values • Awareness of individual strengths • Recording and evaluating progress • Receiving positive feedback • Self-praise for accomplishment
Principles of Independence ↓	• Mission, purpose, and motivation • Self-empowerment through setting realistic and achievable goals • Responsibility for consequences of own decisions • Sense of own ability • Achievement, hope, and success
Principles of Generosity	• The "Give Back" or "Give Away" (the giving of self, time or tangible "things" without expectation of return) • Opportunities to give to and share with others • Personal contribution • A feeling that combines security, uniqueness, purpose, success, and accomplishment

might want to lead brief demonstrations, such as karate, yoga, or dance. Another might share a scrapbooking hobby during a unit on organization.

- Let students demonstrate areas of competence by peer tutoring. Assign skills and topics for them to master in order to teach their classmates, possibly with a WebQuest.
- Allow the completion or repeat of failed or missed assignments. Completion of these provides feedback valuable for student self-assessment.

✳ Building Independence

Moving smoothly from dependence to independence is difficult for most teens. You can help them practice the principle of independence:

- At the beginning of the term or program, have learners consider and commit to short- and long-term goals. They can record the goals in their journals and submit a copy to you so they feel accountable to someone. The goals can include levels of academic achievement and how learners will apply acquired knowledge in their lives, as well as more personal goals for behavior and peer relationships. Participate in this process to ensure the goals are realistic and achievable.
- Be as comprehensive and as specific as possible when providing feedback on learners' work. As emphasized in Chapter 18, note strengths and positives, as well as areas for improvement. Learners can use and build upon this feedback as they move toward greater competence.
- Consistently enforce consequences and the importance of taking responsibility for one's actions.
- Encourage learners to discuss and debate what is personally important to them, to clarify their priorities, and to reevaluate when necessary.

✳ Building Generosity

Generosity brings learners a sense of self-fulfillment. You can encourage generosity in a variety of ways:

- Support volunteerism and also create curriculum-appropriate opportunities for learners to share a skill mastered in the classroom with a school group or at a community facility.
- The class can "adopt" a younger class or community group, such as Scouts, and tutor, read, or help in other ways on an ongoing basis.
- Every learner can be responsible for completing a minimum number of hours with an elder or differently-abled person, a community organization, or a health or child care facility.
- The group can decide upon a legacy, something they will leave behind for those who follow, such as painting a mural, writing a class poem, or implementing a beautification project for the classroom, school, or community.

Generosity, by nature, makes a person feel good on many levels. In the context of "The Circle of Courage," the satisfaction of personal contribution leads to an increased sense of self-worth and belonging. This strengthened "belonging" leads to further competence within *mastery* and *independence*, moving the young person forward to deeper levels of success and accomplishment. Ultimately, the greater the positive connection with each of these principles identified in the model, the greater the health and resiliency of the person.

✳ Using the Circle for Change

Incorporating these or similar strategies into your program will provide participants with skills and opportunities essential for success in school and in their daily and future lives. By adopting "The Circle of Courage" as a guide, you tip the scale in the learners' favor by strengthening protective factors and promoting health and resiliency.

You will encounter individuals who need shoring up in one or more of these elements, or who have broken down altogether. "The Circle of Courage" teaches that without *belonging, mastery, independence,* and *generosity,* there can be no courage, but only discouragement. It has been said that discouragement is courage denied, and when "The Circle of Courage" is broken, the lives of youth aren't in harmony and balance.

As you consider the behaviors and trouble indicators of your own learners, you can try to determine how they are "out of balance" by referring to "The Circle of Courage" model. Consider some of the following troubling behaviors:

- Some youth who feel rejected are struggling to find belonging through distorted behaviors such as gang loyalty, sexual promiscuity, cults, or overly dependent behaviors. Others have abandoned the pursuit to belong and are reluctant to form human attachments, are lonely, isolated, or distrustful. Their unmet needs can be addressed in *belonging*.

- Frustrated in their attempts to achieve, some teens seek to prove competence or mastery in distorted ways, such as cheating, overachieving, illegal acts, or becoming a youthful version of a workaholic. Others retreat from difficult challenges by giving up, avoiding risks, or living with feelings of inadequacy. These youth need involvement in an environment with abundant opportunities for *mastery*.

- Some teens fight against feeling powerless by asserting themselves in rebellious and aggressive ways. Those who believe they are too weak to manage their lives are submissive, irresponsible, undisciplined, or easily led by others. They need opportunities to develop the skills and confidence to assert positive leadership and self-discipline through *independence*.

- Without opportunities to give and share with others, it's difficult for young people to develop as caring persons. Some may become experts in playing the martyr, slip into codependent relationships, become used and/or abused, or plunge into lifestyles of hedonism and narcissism. Young people must experience the joys that accrue from helping others and witnessing selfless activities to realize the true spirit of *generosity*.

As you observe and reflect upon young people's behavior and achievement, you can use the Holistic Model to assess strengths and competencies. This will allow a more balanced picture of the individual and help determine appropriate action. Actions taken can then be reflections of the elements in "The Circle of Courage."

 # A Model for Action: Putting It All Together

Putting it all together in a workable and effective package requires acceptance of a basic prevention strategy: "No progress has ever been made against an epidemic by treating only the casualties." Each adolescent is, by nature, experiencing losses; transitions; and physiological, hormonal, and developmental changes. The consequences of these circumstances are present in the learning environment. Paying attention to them will help students to stabilize and to integrate these changes with what you expect of them.

Incorporating brief interventions in each of the physical, mental, emotional, and spiritual realms of the Holistic Model will enhance your participants' experiences and maximize their ability to apply what they learn to their daily lives. By encouraging examination of each dimension, the Holistic Model also offers a simple and effective technique for assessing student health and well-being. It is imperative to evaluate strengths and supports because they form the foundation upon which progress is made.

Adolescent behavior is a strong indicator of self-esteem. By paying attention, you can determine if youth are in need of special care and/or would benefit from a referral to another helping professional. While the vast majority of your participants won't descend through the Intervention Opportunity Model, it's a valuable tool for helping you recognize trouble indicators and warning signs. There is almost always an opportunity to intervene.

In a young person's life, the determinants of success include a sense of personal safety and identity, connection to a caring adult, and a sense of personal power and control. These "protective factors" come together in "The Circle of Courage." This model illustrates the progressive beliefs that engage the child through belonging, competence, responsibility, purpose, achievement, hope, success, and personal contribution. Educational philosophies, policies, and activities that reflect the tenets of "The Circle of Courage" and integrate the physical, mental, emotional, and spiritual realms serve to create conditions that promote health and resiliency.

✳ What the School Can Do

Classroom health is typically a reflection of the school climate. The degree to which learners feel safe, valued, and supported is, to a large extent, determined by the tone set by the school administration. This environment, in turn, is affected by central administration. It is within this framework that you create the setting for learning.

In an optimum learning environment, many support systems are in place to maintain student health and well-being. Programs and opportunities that augment the work of guidance counselors, social workers, and school psychologists include the following:

- **Prevention and educational efforts.** These are usually initiated by the administration, including regular assessments of needs and gaps in services for students. Ongoing staff training can include peer-resistance skills or drug-refusal skills, for example. The entire staff can learn how to practice and incorporate these healthy life skills throughout the curriculum to ensure that they're enforced and utilized. There can be routine dissemination of information to staff and students related to mental and emotional health issues on how to manage stress or deal with conflict. Library displays and parent newsletters highlighting these or other issues help to reinforce school efforts in these areas. Prevention and education efforts can be greatly enhanced by maintaining positive, ongoing relationships with the local human service organizations, community clubs, recreational sports leagues, parent groups, and the faith community. Partnering in special projects and sharing information with these groups will help to promote a sense of connection and community.

- **Community service.** Volunteerism can be a powerful catalyst for creating positive conditions, if promoted and supported by the school. Some schools now require a minimum number of volunteer hours as a graduation requirement. Schools can partner with local youth services agencies in coordinating volunteer job banks, such as raking leaves or running errands. Beautification projects, such as maintaining a garden at a park or senior center or removing litter from an adopted stretch of road, are examples of opportunities to participate in meaningful ways in the life of the community. See Chapter 23 for more about service learning.

- **Peer programs.** These peer-helper or peer-advocate programs train a cross section of students in listening, helping, and referral skills. Trained students then help other students as a resource to their peers. In more structured programs, peer helpers are assigned to freshman homerooms or paired with transfer students, students returning from treatment centers, or those experiencing life transitions such as divorce or major illness. Some programs also offer peer tutoring, conflict mediation between students, or present educational programs about substance abuse to younger learners.

- **School resource teams.** Comprised of teachers, administrators, and other support staff, teams undergo training, meet regularly, and adapt their services to the unique needs of the school population. They provide early identification of students in distress or proactive response in a crisis. Peer advocate groups; advisor/advisee programs; issue-focused guidance groups, such as for children experiencing family trauma; and consistent referral and follow-up procedures support intervention efforts of the team.

✳ What You Can Do

You are well aware that you serve as an important role model for your learners. Take the time to make a self-assessment using the Holistic Model. Are there areas in your life that could use extra attention?

Look at your personal needs. It's difficult to be there for your students if you aren't fully present in your own life. Teaching is a remarkable and rewarding experience. It can also frustrate, drain, and otherwise discourage you. You need to maintain your strength and resolve, and you must be healthy to do that. Airplane passengers are instructed, "If you are traveling with a small child, put the oxygen mask on yourself first." You must take care of yourself before you can tend to someone else effectively. Some considerations for personal health and well-being include:

- Be in good physical shape. Eat a balanced diet and keep sweets and alcohol to a minimum. Get enough sleep and exercise.
- Develop and maintain your own personal stress management plan. Practice deep breathing and positive affirmations.
- Practice problem-solving techniques. Set realistic goals for yourself and stay with them. Record thoughts and experiences in a daily journal, including processing a bit at the end of each teaching day. This is a powerful "downloading" technique and will do much to improve your stress level.
- Take an inventory of your personal relationships and nurture the ones that encourage and support you. If necessary, improve your skills in assertiveness and active listening. Use "I messages."
- Practice speaking your truth, being honest with yourself and others. Connect with mental health professionals for support as needed.
- Compile a list of "My 20 Favorite Things to Do" and do at least one of them every day. It may be as simple as e-mailing a friend or brewing a cup of flavored coffee.
- Maintain a daily spiritual practice, be it prayer, meditation, or a few minutes of quiet solitude. Take time to consciously "quiet the chattering mind." Begin and end each day with thoughtful intent.
- Develop a relationship with nature and spend time outside on a regular basis, whether it's gardening, taking a walk, or simply sitting on your porch.
- Treat yourself with the same care and respect you would extend to a treasured friend.

For some, this list is a reminder of what you are already doing. For others, it's a collection of things that would "be great if I had the time." For most of you, the reality lies somewhere between the two. There's a saying about starting a new endeavor: A shift of a few degrees at the beginning of any voyage will mean a vastly different position far out to sea. It isn't necessary to do everything at once. Choose something and stick with it.

 # Making a Difference

The purpose of this chapter is to present a guide, a model, for you to build upon. Think about "The Circle of Courage" and use it as a guide to consider what happens to foster belonging, mastery, independence, and generosity at the building level. What else can be done to ensure that students feel safe, secure, and welcome in the building and to know they are valued and supported? How else can they be given opportunities to explore relationships and "give back" to the school or program in meaningful ways? Whatever you can use, or adapt, will help support you in creating healthy and resilient learners who can be secure and successful in all facets of their lives. Your efforts are an integral part of this mission. Enjoy the journey.

References

Brendtro, L., Brokenleg, M., and Van Bockern, S. (1990). <u>Reclaiming youth at risk. Our hope for the future</u>. Bloomington, IN: National Educational Service.

http://www.jasonfoundation.com Jason Foundation. (Accessed February 1, 2002)

http://www.nimh.nib.gov National Institute of Mental Health. (Accessed February 6, 2002)

http://www.mhsource.com/narsad/ National Alliance for Research on Schizophrenia and Depression. (Accessed February 25, 2002)

http://www.oregoncounseling.org Oregon Counseling. (Accessed February 6, 2002)

Building Your Professional Portfolio

• **Teen Stress Survey.** Develop a survey to identify which stressors teens find most difficult to handle. Administer the survey to at least one class or group of teens. Summarize the results and identify concrete ways you could improve the teens' coping skills for the top-rated stressors.

• **Identifying Resources.** Identify and contact school and community resources teens could turn to for help with serious problems such as substance abuse, pregnancy, and gangs. Find out the specific types of help each offers, detailed contact information, and other relevant facts. Organize your findings into a format teens could easily use.

• **Using "The Circle of Courage" Model.** The chapter identifies ways you can help teens practice each of the four elements of "The Circle of Courage." Using those as the basis, develop a more complete list. Include both attitudes and actions you can adopt and activities for students.

• **Learning More.** Choose one serious problem common among teens to research. Find out the causes of the problem, its prevalence, and ways to minimize its occurrence and lessen its effects. Identify ways you can incorporate this information in your teaching situation.

Chapter 21

Managing Educational Resources

Management skills are essential to effective teaching. In your role as an educator, you will use, improve, and teach management techniques. This is an on-going process.

Resource management is a key component of overall management. It's likely that your job will include identifying, choosing, organizing, controlling, using, and evaluating available resources in order to successfully meet your program goals. Resources range from human such as time, energy, and skills—to your learning environment and learning materials. In addition, you may have financial responsibility for your program's budget. How well you carry out these responsibilities affects the overall success of your program and the quality of your learners' education.

You will also have opportunities to help your learners gain management skills. Consider the positive impact that developing such skills now will have on enriching their lives in the future.

 ## Filling the Manager's Role

Were you thinking of a career in management when you chose this field of study? Perhaps not, but the chances of taking on that role are very high in this profession. If you are uncertain about your management skills, they can be developed through training and experience. In your position, there will be limits within which you can make management decisions. You need to learn to operate within these confines and to determine to whom you can turn for help in solving difficult management problems. It's important to take action through appropriate channels. Don't be afraid to ask for help in making decisions. You may make mistakes, but the important thing is to learn from them and to avoid repeating them. As Ellen H. Richards, the founder of the American Home Economics Association and the first female graduate of the Massachusetts Institute of Technology, once said:

What if a few mistakes are made?
How else shall the truth be learned?
Try all things and hold fast that which is good.

❋ Characteristics of Effective Managers

To effectively carry out a management role, you must possess or develop certain abilities and qualities. As you look at the following list, mentally check off the traits you now possess and note those you need to develop in order to enhance your role as a manager.

Consider your ability to:

- Make timely decisions.
- Be confident in your decision making.
- Sense problems in a group or in yourself.
- Visualize desired results.
- Seek information from available resources to figure out how to solve problems.
- Make complete, well-conceived plans.
- Organize people.
- Use and adjust plans to accomplish results.
- Realize limitations of resources and devise ways of using alternative resources.
- Give clear, concise directions in a pleasant manner.
- Work under pressure.
- Lead people in getting activities accomplished.
- Analyze completed work and judge results in an objective manner.
- Be willing to change.
- Work harmoniously with others.
- Be energetic.
- Have keen observational skills.
- Recognize individual differences and strengths in others.
- Remain objective.
- Be optimistic.
- Communicate well.

If you possess many of these characteristics, you are on your way to being an effective manager. Others will come with experience.

❋ Resources to Be Managed

In your work as an educator, you will need to manage many types of resources. Some are human resources; others are nonhuman. It's your responsibility to manage time, energy, money, space, equipment, teaching supplies and materials, other people, and paperwork. In some cases, you will not only manage the resources, but also will be responsible for selecting the resources. While each of these resources needs to be managed individually, you will be most successful when you see the big picture and manage each resource within the total context of your educational setting. For example, teaching materials are managed best when you also consider the budget you have, the available storage space, and the length of time you will be meeting with the learners who will use the materials.

Management of one facet of your life affects others. This is clearly evidenced in your ability to manage and dovetail your personal and professional lives.

 # Managing Time and Energy

Time has been referred to as the great equalizer. Everyone has exactly the same amount of time to work with each and every day. Energy, on the other hand, is a more personal thing. How much you are able to accomplish in a block of time is largely determined by the amount of energy you wish to or can expend during that time period. With fast-paced lifestyles, people are always looking for ways to boost energy and to best use or save time. The following suggestions are some that educators have used and found to be helpful. Choose those that will work for you.

- **Make and use lists.** Few people can remember everything. Keep a list and also make notes in your calendar or planner. Keep them handy at all times. Don't rely on your memory alone, especially on a hectic day. As you accomplish tasks, cross them off. That is the satisfying part of list making!
- **Use calendars.** A large calendar with the month or year at-a-glance is helpful at home and at your workplace. You may want carry a week-at-a glance or month-at-a-glance calendar with you. Computer calendars are another good option. Some automatically match the day's appointments with items from the "To Do" list due that day. Experiment to find what works best for you and use it.

- **Prioritize.** It's easy to become overwhelmed by the length of your to-do list. The tasks and duties that demand attention can be classified into three categories:

  A Must be done now
  B Ought to be done at this time
  C Need not be done right now

  Look at your list and assign each task one of the three priority levels. Then start to work through the list, beginning with the things that are classified as **A**.
- **Have an action folder.** In the special folder or spot in your work area, put those items requiring attention before the end of that hour, morning, or day. Using a bright folder is helpful.
- **Plan the work and work the plan.** Life involves making one set of plans after another. Part of planning is, of course, having goals that you want to reach. When developing a plan, whether daily or weekly, take into account your working time, meetings, and appointments. Fill the time slots with the things you need to do. Be realistic. Don't try to cram too much into a short time frame.
- **Make up your mind quickly.** Don't allow yourself to spend a disproportionate amount of time on less important decisions. Collect the information you need to make a well-informed decision, make the decision, and then move on. Use what you learn from the decisions you have made to make better ones in the future.
- **Practice "block thinking."** Concentrate all of your thoughts on one problem or project, attempting to block out other concerns or issues until you have accomplished this task.
- **Dovetail.** Whenever possible, try to accomplish two tasks at once. For instance, if you need to buy food for a demonstration in class, also pick up the items you need for your family while you are at the store. Avoid two trips. While cutting out pictures to use in a lesson on toy safety, look for other pictures you will need for upcoming lessons.
- **Eliminate double work and backtracking.** For example, if you are about to contact participants for a panel presentation, ask yourself the following questions:

Do I have sufficient facts at this time to make the contacts?
Should I check out procedures first?
Should I contact anyone else first?
Are there additional things I need to discuss with any of the participants?
- **Make time for paperwork.** Set a regular time to go through papers. That way you won't overlook important items. Try to choose a time when your concentration is good and you feel energetic and enthusiastic.
- **Create a good filing system.** Papers and folders can pile up quickly. Soon you have difficulty finding what you need and waste valuable time. Efficient filing systems are discussed in more detail later in this chapter.
- **Go through mail once.** Sort as you go through the mail and other correspondence, including e-mail. Sorting near the wastebasket and recycling container will remind you to toss things you don't need to keep. Take prompt action on other items. File what needs to be filed as soon as possible.
- **Simplify communication.** Sometimes a personal contact is the most appropriate form of communication. However, there are many times when using the telephone, memos, or e-mail will suffice. Whatever the method, state your message clearly and specify any needed follow-up.
- **Delegate.** You can relieve a great deal of stress by teaching others how to take care of some time-consuming management tasks. For example, learners can improve their own management skills through opportunities to create bulletin boards, contact and introduce guest speakers, find pictures of various concepts for use in projects, send for information and resources, enter data on the computer, and organize storage space. A volunteer or aide might copy and collate handouts, set up for a lab session, or help with record-keeping. Sometimes family members can also be a great resource. For example, children might carefully remove labels from cans for a lesson on food labeling.
- **Take time for you.** Exercise, sleep, eat well, and look your best. Refer back to

page 276 in Chapter 20. Have a daily plan for getting exercise and eating in a healthful manner. These actions really do increase your energy level. You will be much more efficient if you make time for these activities in your life. A person who feels well and looks good will perform well. You will be a role model for your learners.

- **Avoid feelings of guilt.** This can be easier said than done. Don't feel guilty about not having enough time to do everything. Do your best, but accept the fact that there are just so many hours in each day and there are some things you will not get to. Feeling guilty does nothing except add stress, leading to poor use of time and loss of energy.

 # Managing the Physical Learning Environment

Most educators work in a school setting. The suggestions given here relate directly to such an environment. However, most of them also work in, or can be adapted to, other settings.

The opening of the department or facility at the beginning of the program is a good time to analyze the use of space and resources and to plan any improvements. The physical facilities of the area should be flexible enough to provide:

- Experiences which allow learners to see, hear, interact, experiment, demonstrate, discuss, study, and work alone or in groups.
- Adequate seating, laboratory space, computer space, and storage space for the current enrollment.
- Unobstructed traffic flow throughout the department and rooms.
- Maximum use of all storage spaces for equipment, teaching supplies, and instructional materials.
- A variety of activities covering all aspects of the curriculum.
- A work/conference center for you.
- Proper heating, lighting, ventilation, and sound controls for maximum learning, health, and safety.

Your learning environment may be small or large. It may be outdated or very modern. Manage what you have to the best of your ability and take initiative to acquire additional supplies and equipment that are needed.

❋ The Teaching Space

You may have a standard classroom, meet in a church basement, or teach in the woods at a camp. Whatever the setting, consider the number of learners who will be in the space and determine how crowded or comfortable it will be. Look at the flexibility you have to move furniture and equipment around. Sketch possible new arrangements. Your goal should be to achieve the optimal environment for learning in light of your learners, the content, the activities you have planned, and the resources and visuals you want to use.

❋ *Arrangement*

To optimize learning, arrange the tables, chairs, or desks so as many people as possible can see one another. To project or display visuals, look for a spot where most people can see them without major disruptions and changing of seats. Try out visuals in advance by looking at them from various parts of the room. Position projection equipment so that it doesn't block the view of any learners.

Think carefully about traffic flow and traffic patterns within your room. Learners should be able to access their seats without stumbling over other people or furniture. Computers, pencil sharpeners, bookshelves, and other supply areas should be easily accessible without causing one learner to disrupt the group.

❋ Supplies and Resources for Teaching

To involve learners and provide variety, teaching requires a lot of supplies. Supplies and resources you may typically be using include handouts, transparencies, models, newspapers, magazines, brochures, videos, textbooks, learning games, computer programs, posters, bulletin board and display materials, real objects, and food items. The list goes on and on. Common supplies, such as markers, newsprint, tape, tacks, staples, scissors, tape, and glue, also need to be kept on hand.

❋ Selecting Resource Materials

You will want to make the best selection of resources to meet the needs of your learners and the educational environment. Here are some general guidelines to keep in mind as you select various teaching resources:

- Select resources that best help fulfill the objectives you have set forth for your learners. The teaching materials should provide the opportunity for the learners to reach the behaviors specified in the objectives.
- Determine that the content presented is reliable and authoritative.
- Be sure that resources are current and up to date. Learners will be distracted by materials that show out-of-date items, such as old automobiles, bulky computers, telephone booths, and hairstyles and clothing that were trendy a decade ago. Illustrations and pictures need to be as timeless as possible so the resource does not become dated quickly. Cartoons and line drawings add interest and lessen this potential problem.
- Be sure that the media and supplies you choose are appropriate for your learners' level of conceptual development.
- Choose teaching materials and supplies that will be the best means of developing the concepts you want to convey.
- Assess reading materials for reading level. Be sure it matches that of your learners. Refer back to pages 237-239 in Chapter 17 for information on readability tests. If you are working with low-ability learners, look for materials that have an appropriate balance of visuals and reading. Visual cues can help enhance reading skills. Check the size of the type, keeping in mind that poor readers and older adults often find small type difficult to read.
- Select reading materials that have eye appeal. Look for the effective use of color, white or free space, pictures integrated with written text, and clever titles.

- Assess the visuals and illustrations. Will they appeal to the targeted group and be related and placed near the appropriate content? Do the captions and explanations enhance learning?
- Be sure that diversity is represented in both the written and visual parts of the materials you select. As discussed in Chapter 19, including a variety of people representing the spectrum of the real world is important as you teach diverse audiences. Ideally, the diversity of the group you are teaching should be reflected in the materials you select.
- Assess that the presentation of more than one point of view is given on controversial issues and that both the advantages and disadvantages of the alternatives are explored.
- Choose materials without stereotypes and biases. You want to be sure that equity is preserved.
- Determine whether the cost fits in your budget. Sometimes more costly materials are worth the expense if you can use them repeatedly over time.
- Weigh whether the amount of advertising in free materials is distracting or the content is slanted.
- Assess the size of a document. Small brochures are often dropped on the way out of the room. Oversized materials can get torn because they don't fit in a notebook or the file folder.
- Determine if replacements are available if parts get lost. Games and models will become useless if parts can't be replaced.

❋ Selecting Textbooks

The choice of textbooks requires careful consideration. While the previous guidelines for selecting reference materials apply, textbooks offer a few unique features requiring evaluation. The use of an evaluation device, such as *Figure 21-1* on page 293, may be helpful, whether you are asked to be on a textbook selection committee or are selecting a text for your program. Such an instrument can help you narrow your textbook selections down to one or two top choices. The criteria included are those most relevant to textbook evaluation. Many others have been discussed in other chapters.

Figure 21-1   TEXTBOOK EVALUATION FORM

Name of Text: _____   Author(s): _____

Publisher: _____   Copyright: _____

Directions: For the textbook you are reviewing, circle the appropriate number by each statement (5 = Strongly Agree, 4 = Agree, 3 = Neutral, 2 = Disagree, 1 = Strongly Disagree). Compute a total score for each textbook reviewed, and use the total score for comparison purposes. Pay particular attention to the subtotal for each category.

	SA	A	N	D	SD
Appropriateness and Scope					
Author's point of view is acceptable to the community.	5	4	3	2	1
Author's point of view is in agreement with program philosophy.	5	4	3	2	1
Content covers appropriate objectives/competencies.	5	4	3	2	1
Content is at the appropriate reading level.	5	4	3	2	1
Subtotal _____					
Accuracy					
Author is qualified to write the book.	5	4	3	2	1
Content is up to date and timely.	5	4	3	2	1
Content will not quickly become outdated.	5	4	3	2	1
Content is accurate.	5	4	3	2	1
Content is sufficient to cover fundamental areas.	5	4	3	2	1
Subtotal _____					
Format					
Format is attractive, with an appropriate mix of text copy and illustrations.	5	4	3	2	1
Organization of content will facilitate learning.	5	4	3	2	1
Writing style is interesting and upbeat.	5	4	3	2	1
Explanations are clear and accurate.	5	4	3	2	1
Suitable vocabulary is used and defined.	5	4	3	2	1
Learning objectives are identified.	5	4	3	2	1
Illustrations are well-designed and reinforce content.	5	4	3	2	1
Photographs are up to date, interesting, and appropriate.	5	4	3	2	1
Print is clear and easy to read.	5	4	3	2	1
Summaries and/or reviews are included.	5	4	3	2	1
Individual and/or group activities are suggested.	5	4	3	2	1
Provisions are made for individual differences in interests and abilities.	5	4	3	2	1
Table of contents, glossary, and index are sufficiently detailed.	5	4	3	2	1
Cover and binding are attractive and durable.	5	4	3	2	1
Subtotal _____					
Bias					
Book is free of racial bias.	5	4	3	2	1
Book is free of ethnic bias.	5	4	3	2	1
Book is free of religious bias.	5	4	3	2	1
Book is free of gender-role stereotyping.	5	4	3	2	1
Book is free of age discrimination.	5	4	3	2	1
Book is free of job denigration.	5	4	3	2	1
Subtotal _____					
TOTAL SCORE _____					

When previewing textbooks, you can learn valuable information by examining the authorship, copyright date, and publisher's data about the book. If the book is a revised edition, you can determine the extent of revision by noting changes in the table of contents, illustrations, format, and selected pages from the previous edition. The publisher's promotional materials usually indicate the general age group for which a textbook is designed.

A book's most obvious feature is, of course, its cover. The cover can do much to attract a learner's interest, to establish a positive attitude toward wanting to read the book, and to stimulate curiosity about what's inside. A colorful cover that won't easily appear dated is an asset to any textbook. Inside, a two-column format is easier to read than a single wide column. Type should be large and clear enough to be read easily. The paper shouldn't reflect light unduly, but it should have sufficient gloss to keep it clean. Consider the durability of a book, as well as its thickness and shape. A very thick textbook may have a negative psychological effect on learners. Books that are unusual in size and shape may be difficult to carry and store on shelves.

Supplemental materials that suggest learning experiences and provide resource materials are valuable to teachers and learners. These activities may relate to general concepts or particular topics in the texts. They provide ideas for the teacher and encourage learners to delve further into areas in which they have special needs or interests. Projects to be carried out at school, at home, and in the community may be suggested. Case studies, teaching aids, and thought-provoking questions for discussion may be proposed. The suggested learning experiences should appeal to learners at various achievement levels and should help the instructor individualize instruction. While the availability of supplemental materials shouldn't induce you to select an inappropriate text, having quality teaching and learning aids to choose from can save time and help you teach more effectively.

✳ Large Equipment

Some learning environments contain large or expensive pieces of equipment, such as refrigerators, freezers, quantity food service equipment, computers, digital cameras, industrial sewing equipment, sergers, hospital beds, washers and dryers, and playground equipment. Obviously, these are major investments that need to be chosen with care so that they last a long time. You may also need to make decisions about furnishings, such as window and floor coverings and tables or desks.

✳ *Selection*

After assessing your facility you may realize you can make a few substantial changes each year to improve it, but that there are some things that cannot be changed. For example, it's unlikely that you will be able to buy all new equipment in one year, but you may be able to purchase some things and repair others. In either case, consider these points to make the wisest decisions:

1. Weigh the initial cost of the item against its frequency of use.
2. Consider the amount of space, maintenance, and care required.
3. Consider the time and energy the equipment will save.
4. Weigh the alternative of the time and the cost of using resources existing elsewhere in the community. You might use a laundromat instead of buying a new washer, rent equipment used only occasionally, or repair something, rather than replace it.

Not only is it wise to do some comparison shopping, it may be a necessity. It's common for employers to require three or more bids for major items before issuing a purchase order. Be sure to consider the durability of the product. Read periodicals such as *Consumer Reports* to find the current recommendations. Compare warranties and guarantees on the products. Find out how repairs are handled. Read all contracts carefully before signing anything.

As you select large pieces of equipment, consider the types of equipment your learners may be expected to use in the workplace. If possible, replicate those in your learning environment so learners develop readily transferrable skills.

Planning ahead for replacement is essential. Determine the age and condition of any large pieces of equipment and estimate when each item is likely to need replacing. While it's unlikely that you will be able to replace several large items in any one year, you should build the costs of gradual equipment replacement into your yearly budgets.

❋ Maintenance

Maintenance of the department or learning environment should be a continuous process, with periodic evaluations of the extent to which your management goals are being attained. Ideally, these goals would be reached:

- The department is ready for use when needed.
- There is a place for everything, and everyone who uses the facility knows where things belong.
- Equipment is checked, in good condition, and ready to use.
- Human and nonhuman resources are being used to best advantage.
- Participants are learning from the duties they are performing and are developing managerial skills.
- Habits of cleanliness, orderliness, and safety are being maintained.

At the beginning and end of each program time frame, take time to clean, organize, and inventory the materials and equipment in the teaching setting. In the long run, this makes the facility more comfortable and sanitary. It will save money, time, and energy during the program to have equipment in good working condition and materials readily available. This would be a daunting project to do alone, but with the help of learners, you can plan cooperatively a list of tasks to accomplish. Divide the tasks among the group, designating when and how they will be done.

❋ *Organizational Tips*

During the course of a day, many different learners use the facilities in which you teach, and, perhaps, several teachers. It's vital that each group leave the setting in good condition so subsequent groups can proceed with their work as planned. Post a list of procedures for using department facilities where it can easily be seen. Make a large poster of guidelines for department use. Include a catchy title to encourage cooperation.

Labeling cupboards, drawers, and shelves makes it easy to keep equipment in its proper place. If you have a foods lab, you might paint numbers or dots of different colors on cooking items, utensils, and dishes to designate the unit kitchen where they belong. By using plain dinnerware of varying colors for different kitchens, the dishes can be combined for special occasions. Afterward, they can easily be returned to their respective units.

Here are some suggestions that facilitate keeping the learning environment orderly, attractive, and efficient:

- Develop a checkout and return system for books, materials, and equipment borrowed by both learners and teachers.
- Designate a lost-and-found area and have learners look there for misplaced items.
- Provide space near the door for learners to leave clothing and books that won't be needed.
- Have duplicate cleaning supplies and equipment so that housekeeping tasks can be shared and performed quickly.
- Conceal supplies and materials needed for future activities by using a decorative screen or one that can double as a bulletin board.
- Designate certain shelves or places for various instructional materials so that learners, assistants, or aides know where to return them.
- Plan lessons so that more than one group can use the equipment, materials, and supplies while they are out. This is particularly helpful with food and nutrition classes.
- Repair or replace worn items as quickly as possible, especially if they may pose a safety hazard.

Most school programs require an annual inventory of equipment, utensils, and supplies on hand near the end of the academic year. Learners can help take inventory, and this activity can be related to on-the-job experiences, as well as clarification of principles of storage and efficient management. The completed inventory forms are usually kept on file in an administrative office. Keep at least one copy in your files.

✳ *Cleanliness*

One of the best uses of available human resources in keeping the learning environment clean is including learners in the process. Assistance from learners can serve a dual purpose—maintaining cleanliness and orderliness while also learning from the duties performed. Some students may resent having to spend time cleaning. They may protest that these are menial jobs, or that it's the custodians' job, or that they don't come to school to perform clean-up duties. Meet their objections with the facts. Care of the workplace is included as a management standard for any skilled job, ranging from the carpentry shop to the hospital operating room. There are many ways to assign jobs, from regularly assigned duties to playing cleaning games. You can work with learners to make a checklist of cleaning duties or develop one yourself. To assign tasks, you might list two or more small jobs or one big job on an index card. Leave a couple of cards blank. Have the learners draw a job card from the stack, identifying the duties they are to complete. Those drawing blanks are supervisors. Another method is to make two copies of your master list. Cut one into strips for learners to draw. Use the second to record each person's assignment. Creating a cleaning contest is another way to spark interest.

Students need to know what's expected of them before attempting a chore. Some learners are truly puzzled when told to "clean up." Nothing is more convincing to students than a demonstration of what good cleaning is. Standards of cleanliness vary widely. If your learning environment has kitchen units or food science lab units, have one unit arranged and cleaned to a minimum of what you expect your learners to maintain. Have them look at it carefully as an example of what you consider clean. Let them see if you have missed anything and make suggestions. Let them protest standards they think are unattainable. Then hold them to the accepted standard of cleanliness that has been agreed upon. You might incorporate the lesson with one on safety and kitchen sanitation practices.

Have learners take turns supervising with you. Treat the inspection as an educational exercise. Students will learn to be effective managers and will enforce standards on their peers.

✳ *Storage*

Your facility may have lots of storage space or very little. In either case, you will want to make the best use of what you have. Many organizing aids, such as inexpensive plastic storage containers, can be used to supplement and/or organize storage space. Label containers with their contents so stored materials are easy to find. You may want to keep a record of what is stored where. Protect items, as needed, from dust and moisture. Put valuable items behind lock and key. A good storage system results in a neat and organized learning environment. It adds to the professionalism you portray.

Some teachers have to move from room to room for various classes. In this situation, many use a cart for moving essential items and the day's materials from place to place. If you move from building to building, consider a hand truck for transferring heavy loads.

 # Managing Finances

The value of money used to operate a program lies in what it can do for the educator and learners in achieving the program goals. The amount of money can be less important than the way it's managed.

As the educator, you have the right to know what funds are allocated to your program. In turn, you are obligated to spend the money in specific and appropriate ways for the best advantage of the program operations.

✳ Budgets

Depending on your employer, you may be required to allocate your funds by outlining a budget for the year. Budgets can be an indispensable management tool. Yours might look like the sample budget shown in *Figure 21-2* below.

Studying records from the previous year or two should help you to predict this distribution of funds. However you manage it, your obligation is to do the best you can for the program with the funds allotted. A characteristic of a good budget is that it allows for flexibility. In the sample budget, the educator may find a way to reduce spending for the health class in order to purchase more materials for use in another unit during the year. Repairs may cost more than $200. It's wise to retain some funds for unexpected expenses until near the end of the fiscal year. Keep notes of what is needed as the school year progresses, because you must be prepared to justify all expenditures that are planned.

Note that the sample budget includes the cost of replacing a refrigerator. Sometimes such large, expensive equipment is paid for from special capital funds controlled by the administration, rather than from a department or program budget.

Involving learners in creating budgets helps gives them a feeling of ownership in the program. It also can be a valuable learning experience in money management.

When prices are charged for products made and services rendered by learners in classes, it is usually required that any profits go back into the program. With guidance, students can help decide how these funds will be reinvested.

Remember to prepare the budget based on the actual needs of the department. The best budget is one in which the income and the expenditures balance at the end of the year. Neither a deficit nor a large surplus is desired. Either condition can imply poor management.

✳ *Purchasing*

It's important to learn and follow the correct procedures for purchasing. Most program administrators will have you submit a requisition form or purchase order for approval. This includes an itemized list of what you are ordering, the price of each item, and the supplier's name and address. Upon approval, a requisition or purchase order number is issued to authorize the purchase. You may then pick up the purchase or have it shipped. When you receive the merchandise, you will probably turn in a receipt and fill out a receiving form so that the vendor will be paid.

Maintain records of what you spend. Use the computer or develop a simple ledger-sheet format to record all expenses. Keeping track of requisition or purchase order numbers will help you trace any problems. Proper record-keeping protects you

Figure 21-2	SAMPLE DEPARTMENT BUDGET	
CATEGORY	**AMOUNT**
Health program for Scouts and 4-H	$200.00
Pregnant and Parenting Teens Health Class	200.00
Nutrition for Teens class	350.00
Management for Living (cleaning products, resource books)	100.00
Child Development for Babysitters (educational toys, videos)	300.00
Consumer Education (resource booklets, games, field trip)	250.00
Repairs	200.00
Replacement of refrigerator	900.00
Miscellaneous	100.00
TOTAL	$2,600.00

from misunderstandings regarding the way you handle the program money. *Figure 21-3* on page 299 shows a sample ledger sheet.

No matter what form you devise to keep these records, they must:

- Be carefully and accurately prepared.
- Be easy to interpret.
- Present facts clearly and honestly.
- Follow, as far as possible, standard procedures.

❋ Saving Money

In most programs, money is far from plentiful, and you will need to control expenses. When cuts are made in funding sources, you may face a frozen, or even decreasing, operating budget for your programs. The problem is compounded when you are trying to increase student enrollment and maintain a quality program. Finding ways to accomplish goals economically becomes a priority. The following suggestions may be helpful, especially for food and nutrition courses which are more expensive to run than most.

- Investigate whether equipment repairs can be made free of charge by others in the school, such as a technical education class or custodian.
- Visit local businesses, such as department stores, florists, craft and fabric stores, and other specialty shops, to request materials that could be used as teaching aids. These might include fabric remnants and fabric swatches, wallpaper books, rug and upholstery samples, silk flowers or ribbons—even food and bandaging materials.
- Use manufacturers' coupons, often available online, to save money on supplies, household products, and food for the department.
- If possible, photocopy handouts and student worksheets on both sides of paper.
- Use free videos and brochures in lieu of a food demonstration when the cost of ingredients is prohibitive.
- Encourage learners to consider less expensive substitutes for ingredients in recipes, such as store brands instead of nationally advertised brands, crunchy cereals in place of nuts, and canned cheese soup for cheddar cheese sauce.

- Identify stores that give discounts to school or community programs.
- Read ads for store specials and plan some lessons around the sale items.
- If possible, obtain quantity foods, such as dried milk, through a school cafeteria or government program.
- Buy lower-priced seasonal foods in quantity and freeze for later use, if storage space allows.
- Grow herbs that can be used in cooking and as garnishes. Their decorative value is an added benefit.

 # Handling Paperwork

Every program has records and reports to be completed and the responsibility for this time-consuming task will be yours. Make this part of department business as efficient as possible. Accuracy, neatness, and promptness are real necessities in preparing reports. Carelessly prepared reports may reflect carelessness in other responsibilities.

❋ Types of Records, Reports, and Materials

Commonly required records, including several that have already been described, include:

- Inventory of equipment and supplies at the beginning and end of the year. Your administrator may provide inventory forms.
- List of expenditures for supplies and new equipment. Ledger sheets serve this purpose. Documentation of reimbursements should be saved.
- List of needed repairs. School districts usually make large repairs or improvements during the summer.
- List of anticipated purchases of equipment and instructional materials. This aids administrators in making budget allowances for the coming year.
- Copies of all program-related reports, including travel, annual program, attendance, grades, and number of participants.
- Copies of block, unit, and teaching plans.

Figure 21-3 — SAMPLE FUNDS LEDGER SHEET

DATE	REQUISITION NUMBER	VENDOR	PURCHASES	CLASS PROGRAM	AMOUNT	BALANCE
8-25	Beginning Balance					$2600.00
8-30	1236Y	Bell	2 Videos	Child Development	$190.00	2410.00
9-2	4481Y	Glencoe/McGraw-Hill	Resource Book	Management	55.80	2354.20
9-4	4536Y	N&G Discount	4 Storage Bins	Management	25.00	2329.20
9-4	4552Y	Scott Bus Company	Field Trip Bus	Consumer Ed.	105.00	2224.20
9-30	5231Y	Conlan's Foods	Groceries for September	Nutrition	125.75	2098.45
10-1	5520Y	Play-World Online	Toys	Child Development	63.50	2034.95
10-31	4640 Y	Furr's	Groceries for October	Nutrition	55.72	1979.23

- Copies of assessment devices.
- Reports of FCCLA chapter or other youth group activities.
- Records of parent/guardian and/or spouse contacts.

In addition to these items, you will need to manage handouts; homework assignments; resources such as pictures, lab work evaluation sheets, student reports, permission slips, letters to parents, course outlines . . . and the list goes on.

Accurate and detailed records provide data you can use to document accomplishments, present programs to school boards and community groups, and complete annual reports that might affect the future of your program. You can use the information to evaluate student progress and to manage the budget in an objective manner. In addition, you are able to evaluate the curriculum and teaching strategies implemented during the year.

Many of your records and reports can be kept on the computer for ease of use. Attendance, grades, and other administrative tasks may be entered on your computer. Be sure confidentiality is maintained, and you are the only person with access to sensitive files. Always make back-up copies of your computer files and keep these in a separate, secure place. Learning the full capabilities of the computer will help you to reap its fullest benefits.

✳ Filing Systems

Despite the fact that a great deal of information may be stored and managed on the computer, you will still need real files. For example, you will want a file of articles about current events for use in various units. You will have a resource file for interior design projects. You may have pictures of FCCLA events and class projects. You will want to file copies of handouts, exams, and activity materials. You may keep files of sample project ideas and other resources. Then there will be brochures, transparencies, and games you will use in your teaching. You may want hard copies of some computer and Internet documents for easy access. Logs and journals regarding learner and parent conferences should be filed. Each entry can be brief, including the date, the nature of the meeting, and the main points covered.

Although tasks such as record-keeping and filing may be tedious and time consuming, tending to them on an ongoing basis minimizes the overall effort needed. Follow these tips:

- Devote time each week or day to work on the files. Avoid letting papers pile up on your desk.
- Discard out-of-date materials.
- Keep older reports and records that must be retained for several years separate from the current year's business.

Some questions may arise about which materials you are allowed to take with you if you leave your job. Materials that you purchased with your own money or made with personal supplies may be taken, as well as items you acquired in college classes. Materials that were in the files when you arrived, visual media made with program supplies, and items ordered or purchased in the name of the program should remain if you change positions. You may want to mark personal items before you file them.

✳ *Setting Up a Folder System*

Whether revising an existing system or starting a new one, the system should ensure quick location and replacement of materials. Select a filing system to which folders can be added logically without having to rearrange the established sequence. In an alphabetical arrangement, an extra folder can be slipped in place easily or the materials in one folder can be subdivided into additional categories. No two folders should have the same title. When a numerical system is used, folders are initially placed in alphabetical order and numbered accordingly. As additions or subdivisions are made, numbers are either added at the end of each section or decimal points or letters are added to the original designation, such as 12.1, 12.2, or 12A, 12B.

✳ *Labels and Coding*

Labels, highlighter pens, or folders of various colors can be used to designate broad areas included in the file, such as child devel-opment, health, and career education. The labels should be neatly printed or generated on the computer. Just be sure the general subject title stands out and is easy to read.

Coding each document facilitates its return to the correct folder. When all materials are coded in the same easy-to-see place, such as in the upper right corner, filing can be done quickly. The coding may be placed on a small piece of the colored label used to designate that subject. If an alphabetical filing system has been selected, abbreviations such as "CD," "CE," and "H" may be used. If two areas might have the same abbreviation, such as consumer education and career education, carry the abbreviation one letter further—"CoE" and "CaE"—to minimize confusion. Subheadings may be written out or shortened in code, but no other folder should contain the same abbreviation. If a numerical system is used, coding is very simple, because 1.1, 1.2, and 1.3 indicate the exact folder to which an item should be returned. Learners may be able to help with filing.

✳ *Cross-Referencing and Indexing*

Often, an item could be filed logically in one of several folders. A leaflet called *Birthday Cakes for Children* could be filed under child development, foods for special occasions, baking, or several other headings. Once you decide where to file a specific item, reference it in other folders. This cross-reference can be recorded by writing on the folder itself or on some durable material inside. Use "Also see . . . for . . . " Write the actual name of the specific reference so time isn't wasted searching through an entire folder.

Making an index of your files saves time for you and your learners. Prepare one by indicating the color designated for each area and any abbreviations used. Preserve the pages of the index by laminating or putting them in plastic inserts. They can be kept together in a binder. Using an index is more efficient than looking through drawers of file folders.

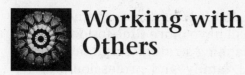

Working with Others

In the process of managing your department or program, you will work with many people. As in all life situations, some will be easier to get along with than others. Communication is the key to establishing good working relationships with other teachers, business owners, administrators, parents, board members, and so on.

✳ Establishing Good Relations Within the Program Setting

Educators have a responsibility to see that the learners and the program aren't exploited, but some requests can be fulfilled while providing enriching experiences. Common requests are to make cookies for a holiday tea, furnish refreshments for meetings, prepare a special dinner for the School Board, make window coverings for another area of the building, repair or launder athletic uniforms, and make robes for the choir or costumes for a play. You will have to use good judgment in deciding when to grant or refuse a request. Certainly, your department shouldn't become a service center to the extent that important learning activities have to be curtailed. Before saying "yes" to a request, be sure you can turn it into a learning experience that will help the participants in your program and meet course objectives.

Learners might take turns serving refreshments at meetings, and a small group can plan and set the table to facilitate quick service. Foods might be prepared earlier in the year during a class when procedures for storage and freezing are taught. Students who complete their laboratory assignments faster than others can be meaningfully involved by working on special service projects. For example, students making costumes for a play may also have an opportunity to do some historical research or to apply knowledge of fabric characteristics or of clothing as an expression of identity. Assembly-line techniques used in commercial clothing construction and other needle trades can be used to produce items in quantity, such as choir robes.

✳ Providing Management Opportunities

If your program doesn't have a system for utilizing assistants, it may be possible to start such a program, perhaps through chapters of FCCLA or Future Educators of America. In some schools, students are assigned as assistants to a teacher. They earn credit in office or business management and are graded for their work. It's advantageous to have an assistant who has computer and management skills. It's also helpful to select a student assistant who has previously been in your program, but who isn't currently enrolled. The individual will be familiar with the procedures used in the department, with the equipment and teaching materials, and with the subject matter. If the student isn't in a class while serving as an assistant, the possibility of confidences being revealed to others is minimized. More work can be accomplished if the student assistant is available during the teacher's planning period than when the teacher is in class.

Teacher's aides are employed in some schools today. Usually they perform tasks that free teachers from routine work. Very often those instructors who come up with ways to use an aide are the ones who receive the most assistance.

The services of both student assistants and teacher's aides can be utilized in keyboarding letters, reports, and assignment sheets; photocopying handouts; creating various types of visual media; and setting up for demonstrations. In some schools, assistants and aides are not allowed to type or grade tests.

In schools without assistants and aides, there are other helpful alternatives available to educators. A community volunteer may be willing to help with your program. Students may be able to prepare materials in other classes, such as in an art or computer course, or in school clubs. By performing some tasks traditionally carried out by the instructor, they help lighten the teacher's workload while gaining valuable experience.

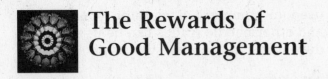

The Rewards of Good Management

Taking advantage of opportunities to implement good management practices in operating a program pays dividends in the long run. Once you have invested the time needed to establish good management practices, you will have more time for developing effective teaching strategies and taking part in personal, family, and professional activities. Learners respond better when their environment is well managed, and administrators appreciate the fact that your program is well run.

Building Your Professional Portfolio

Self-Evaluation. Using the list of characteristics of effective managers, choose five that you feel you need to improve upon. For each, tell why the characteristic is important in your specific educational setting and identify concrete steps for improvement.

Textbook Evaluation. Select at least three textbooks that might be appropriate for a particular course. Each should have a copyright within the last four years. Choose a topic that should be covered in a text of this type. Develop criteria related to the inclusion of this topic in a textbook, then rate the texts on this topic. Complete thorough evaluation of the top one or two books you rated the highest.

Budgeting. Prepare a yearly budget for a situation in which you are employed or hope to be employed in the future.

Space Analysis. Draw floor plans for a remodeled teaching space for your program. Include a rationale for the change and cost estimates for any new equipment.

Chapter 22

Managing Youth Organizations

Youth organizations are affiliated with a variety of educational and service organizations. For years, these organizations have been seen as a source of future leaders in our communities, states, and nation. Leadership skills are honed through a variety of projects and community service efforts unique to each organization. These groups also offer the opportunity for young people to work with their peers and to develop key social skills.

Most youth organizations have adult leadership. You may lead one of these groups in your school or community as you fulfill your role as an educator. The focus of this chapter is on the Family, Career and Community Leaders of America (FCCLA) organization. However, the issues discussed apply to various youth organizations. Some are described in the last section of the chapter.

Family, Career and Community Leaders of America (FCCLA)

Family, Career and Community Leaders of America (FCCLA) is a dynamic, nonprofit national organization that helps young women and men become strong leaders in many settings. FCCLA is affiliated with and functions as an integral part of family and consumer sciences (FCS) classes in middle, secondary, and career-technical schools. It has the distinction of being the only in-school organization with the family as its central focus.

Founded in 1945 as Future Homemakers of America (FHA), FCCLA's original purpose was to prepare young women to be home-makers. In response to changes in society, two name changes have occurred. In the 1970s, FHA became Future Homemakers of America/Home Economics Related Occupations (FHA/HERO) to reflect the growing emphasis on the occupational aspects of vocational education. In 1999, members voted to change the name to Family, Career and Community Leaders of America (FCCLA) to more accurately reflect the group's contemporary mission. Over the years, more than 9 million middle and high school students have participated in the program. Membership is open to any middle or high school student who is or has been enrolled in an FCS course. FCCLA is one of several Career and Technical Student Organizations (CTSO) that are associated with career programs in schools.

The mission of FCCLA is to promote personal growth and leadership development through family and consumer sciences education. Focusing on the multiple roles of family members, wage earners, and community leaders, members develop skills for life through:

- Character development
- Creative and critical thinking
- Interpersonal communication
- Practical knowledge
- Career preparation

See *Figure 22-1* below for FCCLA's current purpose statement.

Figure 22-1

▬ FCCLA PURPOSE STATEMENT ▬

- Provide opportunities for personal development and preparation for adult life.
- Strengthen the function of the family as a basic unit of society.
- Encourage democracy through cooperative action in the home and community.
- Encourage individual and group involvement in helping achieve global cooperation and harmony.
- Promote greater understanding between youth and adults.
- Provide opportunities for making decisions and for assuming responsibilities.
- Prepare for the multiple roles of men and women in today's society.
- Promote Family and Consumer Sciences and related occupations.

Throughout the years, traditions have been a part of FCCLA. There is a national creed; national colors of red and white; a national flower, the rose; and a national emblem. Meetings are conducted with standard opening and closing ceremonies. The National Leadership Meeting is held annually; there are also regional cluster meetings, A+ conferences, and state meetings.

❈ FCCLA Structure

At the national headquarters in Reston, Virginia, a professional staff works with the FCCLA Executive Director to give direction to and carry out programs, communications, membership services, and financial management for advisors and students affiliated with FCCLA. The staff and Executive Director receive direction from two groups: the National Board of Directors and the National Executive Council. The National Board of Directors consists of adult profes-

sionals in the field and student representatives. This board determines policy, oversees financial affairs, evaluates current programs, and assists in long-range planning and organizational management. The National Executive Council is made up of ten students who have been elected as national officers by their peers. Members of this youth decision-making body serve on National Board of Directors committees that shape policies and procedures affecting the national organization.

Each state has an association operating out of its State Department of Education with a designated individual serving as the FCCLA State Adviser. The State Adviser works directly with chapter advisers and students throughout the state. Each state has annual meetings at the regional and/or state level in accordance with their bylaws. Officers, elected by the members, conduct the meetings. Chapter advisers are FCS teachers.

Public and private schools can affiliate as many FCCLA chapters as they want at the state and national levels. At the local level, you and the other teachers in your department will need to decide if you want one chapter per class, one chapter per teacher, or a chapter that combines the classes of two or more teachers. FCCLA chapters may function during class, outside of class, or be a combination of these structures. Integration into classes is promoted as the most efficient means of managing FCCLA. This is known as the co-curricular approach.

National and state dues are required for membership in FCCLA. Dues may also be required at other levels, such as chapter and district/region. Members who pay their state and national dues are known as affiliated members. More detailed information can be acquired online at www.fcclainc.org.

❈ Program Overview

Many resources and opportunities are available for local advisers. The national FCCLA staff works to provide teachers and students with the assistance they need to implement an FCCLA program that emphasizes leadership development. Active participation in FCCLA builds leadership skills, reinforces classroom instruction, recognizes excellence, and provides opportunities for learners to make a positive difference in their schools and communities.

✳ *National Programs*

Curricula are available for a variety of national programs that teachers can use in their classrooms. Programs such as STAR (Students Taking Action with Recognition) Events, Power of One, FACTS (Families Acting for Community Traffic Safety), Career Connection, and Student Body provide FCCLA members with the opportunity to participate in individual or group projects that focus on the purposes of the organization.

STAR Events are a popular component of FCCLA. These competitive events allow learners to share their family and consumer sciences knowledge and skills while competing against peers at the local, state, and national levels. Some of the popular STAR Events include Illustrated Talk, Interpersonal Communication, Job Interview, Entrepreneurship, and Focus on Children. There are helpful handbooks for local advisers focusing on how to carry out various facets of the FCCLA program. New programs are developed and current programs are revised as times change and members' interests dictate.

✳ Link to National Standards

When the *National Standards for Family and Consumer Sciences Education* were released in 1998, leaders in FCCLA crosswalked, or linked, the National Standards with the various curricula and programs in FCCLA. The heart of FCCLA is involvement in projects and activities that learners plan, carry out, and evaluate. These projects create excellent opportunities for learners to demonstrate mastery of the skills identified in the National Standards. On the FCCLA website, you can find an outline of application and assessment activities in FCCLA that parallel each of the National Standards.

✳ The Planning Process

FCCLA members are encouraged to use a five-step planning process to work through individual and group project plans. The process helps members and advisers sort through their thoughts, analyze situations, and plan specific goals. The steps in the planning process are:

1. **Identify Concerns.** Brainstorming concerns, evaluating listed concerns, and narrowing the list to one workable idea.
2. **Set a Goal.** Getting a clear mental picture of what you want to accomplish, writing it down, and evaluating it.
3. **Form a Plan.** Determining the who, what, where, when, and how of your plan.
4. **Act.** Carrying out the project and keeping a record of your progress.
5. **Follow Up.** Evaluating the project, thanking and recognizing the participants.

If members follow this process, they are practicing basic decision-making and problem-solving skills. These steps will assist you in planning for your FCCLA chapter.

✳ *Chapter Projects*

You will be a guiding force in the projects your chapter elects to undertake. These projects can focus on individual, family, career, or community enhancement. FCCLA chapter projects can be considered successful when they have the following characteristics:

- Are developed and directed by the students.
- Balance cooperative, individualized, and competitive approaches.
- Foster leadership, learning, civic and social competence, and cooperation.
- Relate to the curriculum.
- Are feasible in terms of financial, time, and membership constraints.
- Relate to FCCLA purposes and state and national programs and standards.

Some of the projects will be done by individuals, some by subgroups, and some by the entire chapter. The projects your group undertakes will hinge, in part, upon when the FCCLA chapter meets.

In a co-curricular chapter structure, each class has its own FCCLA chapter with its own officers/leaders. Officers from each class may serve on a schoolwide FCCLA executive committee. Chapter meetings, programs, and work sessions occur during class time. Committees meet during class or at other arranged times. Co-curricular projects planned by the learners in class are usually short-term and are directly related to the current course of study. Most of the work occurs in class and may be supplemented with some outside resources. Projects may involve occasional school and community action on weekends or before or after school.

In the past, out-of-class chapters were more common. Now they may be more difficult to arrange due to bus schedules, working students, and other after-school conflicts. You may find, as many FCS teachers do, that the co-curricular, or integrated, approach is the most efficient. After all, you have a captive audience, and the projects really do reinforce your curriculum. Direct application of class concepts takes place through chapter projects.

✳ Benefits of FCCLA

FCCLA chapters support student involvement in worthwhile activities, promote community involvement, and provide volunteer services for those in need. The program provides visibility for the school's FCS program and helps members feel ownership in the program.

✳ *Rewards for Advisers*

The activities of FCCLA can enrich and extend the family and consumer sciences curriculum by providing opportunities to go beyond the physical limitations and time constraints of the classroom. The curriculum can come alive and be perceived as relevant by providing opportunities to show relationships between concepts covered and real-life situations. Authentic assessment opportunities are readily available. In addition, teachers profit by having a chapter in these ways:

• There are additional opportunities to get to know and build rapport with students through positive interaction in nonthreatening situations.
• The organization helps motivate learners and helps to improve attitudes toward school and learning, so teaching is easier and more fun.
• Student leaders emerge who can be helpful in classes and attract new students to the program.
• FCCLA materials can be used to enhance chapter and class activities, thus extending the use of resources.
• It provides a ready-made vehicle for teaching decision-making skills.
• There are additional opportunities to promote FCS careers and implement school-to-career activities.
• There are increased opportunities for teaming with other professionals and demonstrating cooperative working relationships.
• Networking with other advisers provides a support system and cadre of educators who have similar interests and concerns.
• You will be able to witness learners developing self-confidence, poise, hidden talents, and responsibility.
• Recognition will come to your program and school.
• Your preparation time can be shortened as students take on the responsibility for learning.
• FCCLA often helps convince administrators of the value of the family and consumer sciences program. It also helps you gain parental and community support.

✳ *Advantages for Students*

Students profit from involvement in FCCLA in many ways. Some of the advantages for learners are:

• A sense of belonging and purpose.
• Increased opportunities to develop leadership, citizenship, and social skills by serving as officers and committee members, by learning and practicing parliamentary procedure, and by widening their circle of friends.
• Gaining a greater understanding of themselves and their relationships with others.
• Many opportunities for learning to work cooperatively with others, for developing responsibility and commitment, and for exercising decision-making skills.

- Experiences and participation in activities that help build self-confidence and enhance their self-concept.
- Reinforcement and use of academic skills.
- The satisfaction of helping others, performing community service, and working with others toward common goals.
- Opportunities to attend out-of-town meetings and conferences that expand their life experiences.
- Opportunities to learn more about careers in Family and Consumer Sciences; to develop employment skills; and to establish habits of punctuality, dependability, and cooperation.
- Awareness of the many roles they have to play in society as members of families and communities and in employment situations.

✳ Benefits to Administrators

If there isn't an FCCLA chapter where you are teaching, you will need administrative support to start one. Share with administrators that FCCLA:

- Provides a ready-to-use framework for implementing current educational emphases, including school-to-career transition, cooperative learning, authentic assessment, interdisciplinary work, volunteerism, and service learning.
- Reaches into the community through project activities and publicity efforts to demonstrate how academic lessons are applied through the FCS program.
- Makes students excited about learning and enthusiastic ambassadors for the program and school.
- Offers recognition for a diverse population of learners, including many who aren't otherwise involved in school activities.
- Strengthens the public image of the school through recognition students receive at district/regional, state, and national programs.
- Builds community goodwill and support through community service projects.
- Helps students explore careers and prepare for the transition into the work force or higher education.
- Transfers more responsibility to students through supportive teacher-learner rela-

tionships, a key to reducing disciplinary problems, truancy, and dropout rates.

✳ The Adviser

The FCCLA adviser should be just that—an adviser, not a decision maker. As the adviser, your support and guidance can help students develop decision-making and leadership skills.

✳ Role of the Adviser

As the adviser you will be both a facilitator and coach. Students learn by doing. Sometimes they make mistakes, but they grow from these experiences. Your role is to encourage, guide, model, suggest possible resources, redirect, and to assist in leadership development. The latter is particularly important. Here are some ways you can help FCCLA members enhance their leadership skills:

- Assist students in planning and conducting efficient business meetings, including having a written agenda.
- Utilize committees to facilitate programs or conduct the organization's business.
- Offer suggestions, but have learners select their own activities and programs for meetings.
- Help members develop, and later evaluate, a plan of work and a budget for the year.
- Have members take turns leading discussions at chapter meetings.
- Structure activities so group members, over time, experience working with people with varied personalities.
- Delegate organization responsibilities to involve as broad a base of the membership as possible.
- Guide students in planning and implementing a service learning activity.
- Help members plan, carry out, and evaluate fund-raising projects.
- Have members participate in and lead panel discussions for meetings.
- Ask members to introduce guest speakers and panel members at chapter meetings.
- Teach the basics of public relations, including writing news releases. Encourage them to submit releases about chapter activities.

- Encourage chapter members to volunteer their time to worthwhile community activities and organizations.
- Encourage officers and members to make written recommendations to the officers elected for the next year.
- Have students contact, arrange for, and write thank-you notes to guests.

Advisers are the backbone of FCCLA, and they can make or break a chapter. In the early stages, student members will need relatively more help and guidance from you. Remember that if you do most of the work, you are limiting students' potential for developing leadership, organizational, and management skills. Step back and encourage the learners to take the lead.

The best advisers make their chapter's members look good by seeing that they get recognition for work well done. Advisers need to have enough self-confidence to be able to give confidence to students—through member participation in positive and successful experiences and favorable publicity. *Figure 22-2* describes a successful adviser.

```
Figure 22-2
Qualities of a Good Adviser
• Leader
• Motivator
• Facilitator
• Interested in students
• Willing to work hard
• Likes to have fun
• Organizer
• Role model
• Likes variety
• Lets students make decisions
```

✳ *Recognition for Advisers*

Your greatest rewards will come from the students themselves as they sincerely show you how much they appreciate your role in their lives. Sometimes it takes years for them to realize what FCCLA and you meant to them. Don't give up!

At the state level you may be asked to serve as a mentor for new and fledgling advisers. It's an honor to be chosen.

There are other opportunities for FCCLA advisers to be recognized at the state and national levels. These awards yield respect, prestige, and recognition from school administrators, colleagues, parents, and the community. Awards are given annually at the National Leadership Meeting and at state meetings.

✳ *Resources and Support for Advisers*

The staff members at the national FCCLA office work on updating, revising, and developing resources for advisers. Many of these materials are available online at the FCCLA website. Among the types of materials available are:

- **National publications and videos.** Each national program has curriculum materials and/or handbooks that provide step-by-step guidance for implementing the program or event. Various videos are available to assist you with recruitment and program implementation. One of the most valuable pieces is the FCCLA Chapter Handbook.
- **Chapter mailings.** About three times each school year, FCCLA sends out information on the latest developments and materials within the organization.
- **Newsletters.** The Adviser newsletter and Teen Times, a quarterly newsletter for students, provide you with valuable ideas for enhancing your program.
- **Training opportunities.** At cluster meetings, A+ conferences, and the National Leadership Meeting, there are sessions devoted to assisting advisers. In addition, at the state level you will find your State Adviser to be a good source of information and ideas.
- **National and state officers of FCCLA.** These are highly motivated young people. Their enthusiasm and experience with this organization is a resource you will want to tap. They can visit your local chapter and provide more information to your students than you may be able to if you are a novice adviser.
- **State publications and newsletters.** Keep in touch with your State Adviser and be sure you are on the mailing list.
- **Other advisers/mentors.** Advisors with experience with FCCLA have much to offer. Ask for advice and ideas.

❋ Starting an FCCLA Chapter

The most important thing to remember if you are about to start a FCCLA chapter is that "small is okay." You are more likely to feel successful if you have a chapter in just one or two of your classes the first year. Look for classes where there seems to be the most interest. The learners will benefit because you can focus on getting one or two chapters established. If your state doesn't assign you a mentor, find one! Good advisers are always willing to share their learning and expertise with you.

❋ Affiliation and Membership

The first step in forming a new chapter is to obtain an affiliation form and packet from your State Adviser or the national headquarters. You will want to visit the FCCLA home page on the Internet. Contact your State FCCLA Adviser and your state officers. Enlist the support of your administrator. Find an experienced adviser nearby to help you get started. Order a copy of the FCCLA Chapter Handbook. It will assist you with step-by-step guidelines as you begin this exciting process. Schedule an initial chapter meeting and organize a membership drive. Elect chapter officers and develop a calendar of events for the new chapter.

As stated earlier, FCCLA members must be current or former FCS students. Members affiliate by paying local, state, and national dues. There are many affiliation methods at the local level. Some examples of types of affiliations and ways to accomplish them follow:

- All students in class pay their own dues and are affiliated.
- Some students pay dues and are affiliated.
- The chapter pays a portion of dues for each member who affiliates by an early deadline.
- Members earn their dues by participating in a chapter fundraiser.
- The chapter holds a fundraiser to cover dues for all members.
- The financial status of the chapter allows the chapter to pay all students' dues.
- The school budget includes some portion of dues as a course expense.
- Dues are included in a "course fee."
- Adult supporters sponsor individual members and pay their dues.

Affiliation allows students to participate fully in FCCLA programs and leadership experiences at the local, district/region, state, and national levels. It enables students to enjoy the full benefits of FCCLA involvement and builds their commitment to the chapter, while also teaching a valuable lesson in personal ethics.

Once members are affiliated nationally, they begin receiving *Teen Times*. You will also start to receive materials to help you as an adviser.

❋ Gaining Administrative Support

The most effective means of getting and maintaining support from your administrators is to obtain their input in the form of ideas and suggestions and to keep them informed of your progress and activities. Invite administrators to attend meetings, to be honorary members, to participate in panel discussions, and to serve on the advisory council for Family and Consumer Sciences. Administrators are likely to support activities that help build students' self-confidence, enhance and extend classroom learning, and promote good relationships with the community. Remember, too, that your enthusiasm for FCCLA will be contagious.

❋ Building Membership

The co-curricular approach discussed earlier offers membership to a substantial number of students. Tell them how participation in the organization will benefit them personally. Help plan interesting and exciting meetings. Help them develop effective recruitment techniques, such as one-on-one personal invitations to join, telephone calls to prospective members, and the involvement of many members in chapter activities. Here are some additional suggestions for building membership:

- Have a contest to develop effective recruitment materials, awarding the winner free membership or a free trip to a regional meeting.
- Implement a mentoring or buddy program for freshmen and transfer students.

Assign students as big sisters or big brothers to the younger students.

- Publicize meetings by having members deliver "commercials" over the school PA system with the daily announcements.
- Develop a showcase highlighting photos of chapter members during the past school year.
- Show a video or PowerPoint® presentation of chapter members participating in appealing events, such as community service projects and state meetings.

Other Career and Technical Student Organizations (CTSO)

FCCLA is one of ten youth leadership organizations recognized by the U.S. Department of Education and eligible for funds under the 1998 Carl D. Perkins Vocational and Technical Education Act. These student organizations can receive financial support for activities at the state and local levels that help improve learning and assist students in achieving their career goals. Career and Technical Student Organizations (CTSO) may exist at the secondary or post-secondary levels. In your workplace, you may find one or more of the following CTSO. Networking and working with advisers of these organizations may enhance your resource base and provide for interdisciplinary outcomes.

- **Business Professionals of America.** This group's mission is to contribute to the preparation of a world-class workforce through the advancement of leadership, citizenship, academic, and technological skills.
- **DECA—An Association of Marketing Students.** This organization strives to enhance the co-curricular education of students who have an interest in marketing, management, and entrepreneurship. DECA is committed to the advocacy of marketing education and the growth of business and education partnerships.

- **Future Business Leaders of America (FBLA)—Phi Beta Lambda (PBL).** Their mission is to bring business and education together in a positive working relationship through innovative leadership and career development programs. The FBLA division is for grades 5-12. The PBL division serves post-secondary students and alumni.
- **Health Occupations Students of America (HOSA).** The students in this group are focused on enhancing the delivery of compassionate, quality health care by providing opportunities for knowledge, skill, and leadership development to all health occupations education students. In this way, learners help meet the needs of the health care community.
- **National FFA Organization.** This group's mission is to make a positive difference in the lives of students by developing their potential for premier leadership, personal growth, and career success through agricultural education.
- **National Young Farmer Educational Association (NYFEA).** Their goal is to promote the personal and professional growth of people involved in agriculture. The organization aims to inspire personal achievement and strengthen agricultural leadership in the hopes of fostering economic growth.
- **National Postsecondary Agricultural Student Organization (National PAS Organization).** This group has post-secondary chapters that provide opportunities for individual growth, leadership, and career preparation in agriculture.
- **Skills USA-VICA.** The focus is on professional development, business partnerships, community service, public relations, and competitions in occupational and leadership areas.
- **Technology Student Association (TSA).** Their mission is to prepare members for the challenges of a dynamic world by promoting technological literacy, leadership, and problem solving, resulting in personal growth and opportunities.

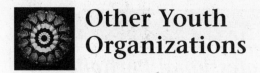

Other Youth Organizations

The youth organizations affiliated with in-school career/technical programs are only the tip of the iceberg when one looks for organizations that promote leadership development in youth. In addition, there are many opportunities for adults of all ages to engage in leadership development in the community through service, civic, and religious organizations.

As an educator, you might be working in a position where you are responsible for the planning, implementation, and evaluation of a youth leadership organization that's affiliated with your employer. Some possibilities are the 4-H program, Boys Scouts of America, and Girls Scouts of the USA.

The 4-H program is the youth leadership organization that is part of the Cooperative Extension System. (You may refer back to page 9 for a brief overview of 4-H.) One of the Extension agents in the Cooperative Extension office usually handles 4-H responsibilities. That could be you! 4-H clubs are frequently organized around common interests of the members, ranging from livestock projects to financial planning to nutrition. Members plan and conduct their local 4-H club meetings. At the national level, there are a variety of curricula developed for various 4-H projects.

Boy Scouts and Girls Scouts are usually administered out of regional council offices. You might be providing leadership in that office. The Boy Scouts and Girl Scouts have comprehensive handbooks and an array of other materials to assist you and the leaders.

✳ Your Leadership Role

With both 4-H and Scouting programs, young people of various ages come together in clubs or troops that are project- and/or age-related. These groups rely on the commitment of volunteer leaders. If you work at a Scout office, your job might include locating individuals who are willing to devote the time to organize and run the clubs and troops. You will sense the need for a new club or troop, or you may work to fit the interested participant into an existing group. If a new club or troop is needed, you may need to secure a new volunteer leader. With today's hectic lifestyles, finding individuals willing to make such a commitment can be challenging. Often, a parent of one of the children or teens will step forward to fulfill the role of group leader. Adults who were active in the organization in their youth are also often willing to serve.

✳ Meeting the Needs of Volunteers

Once you secure volunteer leaders, you may be responsible for providing their training. In addition, you need to make sure that they have or can acquire the resources needed to do an effective job. Visit them to see how they are doing. Use phone calls and e-mail to keep in touch. You will be a constant source of support and ultimately will be judged based on the success of your volunteer leaders.

When enlisting volunteers, be very clear about their responsibilities; be honest about the amount of time you expect them to devote to this job. If you say, "This won't take much time," and it does, they may not be willing to work again.

Remember that volunteers should feel appreciated. Be vigilant in providing them with positive feedback, appreciation, and recognition. Make the community aware of their commitment. Build them into your public relations efforts. Volunteers are usually some of the busiest people in your community, and they deserve recognition.

Help all of your volunteers to see that the focus of community youth organizations is to build future leaders. Be sure that you are providing the volunteer leaders with all the help they need to mold and shape the leaders of tomorrow. It's true that the future really does rest in their hands—and in yours.

Building Your Professional Portfolio

Analyzing a Meeting. Attend a youth organization meeting. Then summarize what you observed and learned from this experience. If you were the adviser, what would you do the same way? Identify what you would do differently and why.

STAR Events. Judge FCCLA STAR Events at a Regional or State meeting. Write a description of how the competition was organized and your experiences judging.

Interviewing an Adviser. Arrange to interview someone with experience advising a youth organization. What rewards and difficulties has the adviser experienced?

Chapter 23

Community Connections and Service Learning

Marilyn Swierk, CFCS, CFLE
President, MS Innovations
AAFCS Chair, Elementary,
   Secondary, and Adult Education

Connecting education with community resources is one of the most effective ways to provide learners with realistic situations and practical applications that will serve them well in the future. There are various ways to prompt community involvement. Community connections can occur through the use of local resources inside and outside of the classroom, educational partnerships, the use of advisory councils, and service learning opportunities. Utilizing the resources of a town or city broadens the horizons for learners in that community.

Why Connect with the Community?

Numerous benefits can be derived from identifying and tapping community resources. First and foremost, the lines of communication between the school and community are opened—often resulting in allies for local educational efforts. In addition, these connections may provide you with guest speakers, field trips, and school-to-career and service learning opportunities. Some entities may provide instructional supplies, incentives, rewards, enrichment activities, student recommendations, and motivation. They may also assist with curriculum development and provide mentors, field placements, human resources, and, of course, their expertise.

Resources in the Community

Community resources are available to all educators, but the quality and quantity vary from one community to the next. Valuable ideas may come from students, coworkers, other staff members, the media, and the business section of the phone book.

✳ Agencies, Businesses, and Groups

Not-for-profit and human service agencies, businesses, and civic, religious, governmental, cultural, or community action groups are good places to start in utilizing community resources. Check with your local chamber of commerce for additional contact possibilities.

Many schools are fortunate to be part of educational partnership programs. If your school already has established educational partnerships, look into ways these programs might benefit your learners. For instance, culinary arts students at a Los Angeles high school recently planned and served a corporate luncheon with the help of their partner, Lawry's®. In a nearby suburb, a local automobile dealer arranged a ceremony congratulating middle school students who completed an anti-gang and anti-drug program.

✳ *Resources for Career Exploration*

A variety of people in diverse professions and occupations can make valuable contributions to a program. It's wise to consider the career exploration benefits that learners will derive if you choose people in careers related to the areas you teach. Their job responsibilities, opportunities for advancement or specialization, satisfactions, and limitations of their positions can be explored. For instance, you might call upon social workers, health-related personnel, interior designers, builders, architects, real estate and insurance representatives, credit bureau employees, counselors, lawyers, and merchandising personnel. Try to determine ahead of time those whose approach might be too commercial for your purposes. Physicians and other health professionals are excellent resource people; however, their schedules frequently rule out speaking engagements. Part-time health professionals, whose schedules may be less demanding, could also provide an authoritative and professional viewpoint.

Be sure to ask your learners for suggestions about career speakers. Their contacts may surprise you. Phillipe's mother might be a registered dietitian and his stepfather a chef. Casey's sister may work as a counselor in an eating disorders program. Jessi's neighbor, a self-defense instructor, might enjoy presenting a demonstration to your class or group.

✳ *Diversity*

Other resources might include senior citizens, first-generation immigrants or people from different ethnic backgrounds, and individuals with disabilities or members of their families. Retirees usually have more flexible schedules than adults who are employed full-time. Inviting seniors to visit your program can provide some memorable intergenerational experiences. It helps to minimize the so-called generation gap. Students gain understanding, respect, and compassion for this age group, and the older adults gain the satisfaction of feeling needed and making a valuable contribution to the community.

Educational Partnerships

If you plan on working with a community resource for an extended period of time, it may be advantageous to form what is known as an educational partnership. This means that a school or educational institution has an agreement to work with a business, agency, or other group to help learners succeed.

The National Association of Partners in Education in Alexandria, VA, provides leadership in the formation and growth of effective partnerships that ensure success for all students. The association connects students and teachers with corporate, higher education, parent, government, and volunteer leaders who can play significant roles in changing the content and delivery of educational services to children and their families.

✳ Assessing Your Needs

To begin a partnership, you first have to determine the needs of your program or subject area. Once you assess your needs, you can better determine whether you need a partnership or a one-time connection. You will need to consider the topic or area on which you will focus. Will it require a guest speaker? Field trip? Field site location for activities, interns, or job shadowing experiences? Resources? It's wise to involve learners in the process of selecting the community resources that best suit the needs of the class or program. Student involvement will yield greater enthusiasm and participation.

✳ Making Connections

Once you have determined the resources and/or partnerships you wish to explore, you can begin making contacts. Keep a record of the information obtained from each resource. It's helpful to create a standard form for recording the basic information. Include the resource name; contact information; directions to the site; hours of operation; and policies governing visitors, workers, and volunteers. Note preferred days and hours for field trips, resources available, and any special notations. This will be helpful for future planning and reference.

It saves time when you can determine the most appropriate person to contact. For queries about guest speakers or field trips, you would probably need to contact the public relations or education department. For job placements, the director of personnel or human resources would be contacted. For service learning, speak to the volunteer coordinator. This may be done through a personal visit, telephone call, or letter.

Don't convey the attitude of "Here I am ... what do you have for us to do?" State your name, position, and the name of your school or organization. Explain the objectives of your program and what its participants are studying. In the case of service learning or school-to-career efforts, let potential partners know that you would like to explore the possibilities of working with them, what you expect your learners to gain from this partnership, and the skills and knowledge your participants will be able to offer in return. Brainstorming ideas with the community resource person may prove helpful.

✳ *Dealing with Resistance*

Not every community resource will be willing or able to participate. Some may be reluctant to be involved. They may not want a long-term commitment, may not be able to fit into your organization's schedule, or have a myriad of other issues. If you meet with resistance, you may instead want to approach a business or agency of someone you know—a friend, neighbor, or relative—for your first partnership. You may subsequently be able to use this partner as a reference for new partnerships.

✳ Sustaining Partnerships

Once a contact or partnership is established, it's important to follow certain guidelines to manage and sustain the relationship.

- Keep the lines of communication open throughout the partnership. Discussion and understanding of each other's terminology, schedules, liability, transportation, and other issues are very important. It's especially important to inform each other if something isn't working out.
- Conduct a needs assessment to determine the needs of both the partner and the school, program, or course. It should be understood from the beginning that the needs of both parties should be aligned.
- Identify the goals of the partnership to be sure that both parties desire the same outcomes. Set a time frame in which you both expect these goals to be achieved.
- Be very specific about what each of you will bring to the partnership. You may have to provide audio-visual equipment, supplies and materials, or space in your facility. In the case of service learning, you will be providing helpers or interns. Partners may provide services or materials, such as guest speakers, training, opportunities for field trips, internships, technical support, funding, supplies, materials, or transportation. It is often an awakening to partners that items they have in surplus, such as unused computers, copy paper, pens, and staplers, are the items that other organizations need.
- Provide adequate training for partners, staff, students, and volunteers. This includes orientation to the rules, regulations, and parameters of each setting.
- Reflect together on the progress of the partnership on a continuous basis. This will help provide positive reinforcement and may elicit new ideas for strengthening or enhancing the partnership.
- Evaluate the partnership during and at the conclusion of the project. This will help you adjust any situations that may need to be corrected or improved. Often, the best times to do this are at the halfway point and again at the conclusion of the experience.

- Recognize the partner through things like celebrations, thank-you notes, and certificates.
- Conduct a dialogue about how you might work together in the future.

Preparing for Guest Speakers and Field Trips

There are times when you will use resource people on an occasional basis, both within and outside of your educational setting. Guest speakers and field trips require careful preparation. The success or failure of these activities depends on how well you lay the groundwork.

✳ Guest Speakers

The use of a guest speaker can add richness and depth to a presentation and provide a stimulating frame of reference for discussion. Possible topics are problems related to sexually transmitted diseases, personal financial crises, unplanned pregnancies, or child abuse.

A panel discussion can also be an excellent way of involving a number of resource people in one presentation. People of different ages and responsibilities might discuss how they manage their time, money, energy, and other resources. A panel of parents representing different family types might discuss the challenges of child rearing; caregivers of patients with dementia might share their stories.

✳ Field Trips

There are opportunities for class field trips in most communities. Trips to businesses, museums, institutions, private residences, recreational facilities, and government offices offer interesting educational possibilities. Many manufacturing plants, research organizations, newspapers, clothing retailers, department stores, and furniture and appliance stores welcome visits. Such field trips can promote a better understanding of merchants' and manufacturers' roles in the national and global economy, as well as in the local community.

Public and private child and adult care centers are interesting and informative places to visit. Some of the following might be observed or noted: special provisions for caring for a specific age group, the type and diversity of activities offered, the approximate cost, and the care and interest shown by personnel.

Concern about community issues can provide a basis for a variety of field trips. Inadequate playgrounds, community facilities that have deteriorated, or poor methods of refuse disposal could serve as focal points for involving young people. One possible result of such field trips is that learners may be motivated to analyze existing problems; collect additional information; propose, and possibly become involved in devising, solutions.

Comparison shopping trips can be enjoyable and informative. Depending on specific product features and services being investigated, learners can be divided into investigating teams. Each team could be responsible for visiting a different type of retailer to check the same or comparable items for certain features. Items might range from home decorating materials to toddlers' toys and from cookware to sergers. For example, in comparison shopping for a particular appliance, the following points could be identified: brand name, model number, special features, directions given for use, warranty, certification or endorsement by various organizations, cost, and finance charges if purchased on credit. When learners return, each team can report its findings. By using a team approach, a considerable amount of information can be gathered and analyzed. Participants could decide which would be the best buy for a variety of given situations.

Making use of community resources offers you a variety of ways to reinforce and expand the content of your program and to motivate young people and help them develop.

✳ *Scheduling Alternatives*

Although it may be desirable to host a guest speaker or to take a field trip, circumstances and scheduling may prohibit it. There are alternatives to consider. If a resource person is available to speak at only one session, tape the talk and play it for other groups. The tape could become part of a library to be used as an additional resource or for individualizing instruction. If a person is unable to come to your learners, or if a field trip can't be scheduled for an entire class, it may work for you and a small group of students to go after school, using a digital camera or camcorder to record the visit. The slides or videotape could then be organized into an interesting PowerPoint® or video presentation.

✳ Guidelines

When working with resource people either out in the community or as visitors to your program, paying attention to details will allow for maximum benefits from your efforts and from theirs. Here are some guidelines to consider:

1. Contact partners and/or resource people well in advance of when you would like to have them work with your group. After you have agreed upon a date, time, place, and directions, send a confirmation letter with the details. File a copy of the letter.

2. Specify exactly the type of material to be covered. It's helpful for a resource person or partner to know the general background of the group with whom they will be working and any particular information that should be emphasized. Let the speaker know if there are topics that shouldn't be discussed.

3. The partner or resource person may request that the learners view a specific videotape; use a CD-ROM or computer program; read a selected story, case study or article; or be introduced to specific information before the presentation. This ensures that the learners and the speaker have a mutual frame of reference.

4. Give the speaker some general tips about speaking to young people, if necessary. Some may feel uncomfortable dealing with this age group or may speak down to them, be too formal, or use language and vocabulary that the learners don't understand. Encourage the contact person to address the group in a conversational manner. Although they have valuable information to share, some people aren't accustomed to public speaking and may direct their comments to the leader rather than the learners. Consequently, if you sit near the back of the room, speakers are more likely to project so everyone can hear. You also have more control over behavior from this point.

5. Prepare your learners adequately for guest speakers, field trips, and site visits. They should know something about the speaker, understand why this connection has been made, and know what the desired outcomes of this experience should be. Initiate a discussion for learners to identify what skills and knowledge they should gain from the experience. Consider combining your group with another class or program if the speaker is of mutual benefit to both groups.

6. It's useful to have a generic sheet or template for learners to fill out about the agency or resource person. You may choose to grade their sheets or make comments on them. This encourages participants to be attentive during the event and to ask questions. Having learners write one or two questions ahead of time that they would like to have answered will also serve to keep them engaged and the discussion moving.

7. Set expectations for behavior and attire. Stress that each individual's demeanor is a reflection of the entire group. Expect learners to be courteous, helpful, refrain from negative comments, exercise confidentiality, and respect the resource person, the surroundings, and any people with whom they come in contact. Confidentiality is especially important in hospital and health care settings. Make students aware that they should never discuss patients they see there.

8. There are times of the year when there will be many requests for field trips. Plan well in advance so that your request isn't denied due to the plans of other instructors. For field trips that are longer than one class period, additional planning may be needed to determine the cost of the trip, set departure and arrival times, obtain chaperones, and possibly to make provisions for a meal. Permission may also be needed from other faculty mem-

bers if students will be missing their classes due to the trip.

9. When resource people come to your department or meeting place, help make their visits pleasant by having someone meet them at the office or main entrance. Share a little of the person's background to help establish rapport with the participants. For example, you or the learner introducing the guest speaker might say, "Mrs. Drury was an FHA member here at Central before the group's name was changed. She remembers working on the first Earth Day and going to convention in St. Louis. Now her catering business handles parties for as few as 10 guests and as many as 500."

10. When a presentation is over or it's time to conclude a field trip, some words of thanks from you and the participants are appropriate. You may want to remind learners beforehand to stop and informally thank a speaker for visiting or a host for allowing you to tour. In fact, you can use such occasions to help your learners practice social behaviors. That includes a thank-you note after the event.

11. At the last minute, plans may change for a guest speaker or a field trip. It's wise to have alternate plans or lessons ready for the group.

 # Establishing an Advisory Council

An advisory council is a group of citizens who serve in an advisory capacity. Their primary tasks are to assist in collecting and interpreting information for use in program planning and evaluation, to make recommendations and offer suggestions to administrators and personnel, to help plan and evaluate your program, and to help showcase the program to the community. Some advisory councils serve only one program, while others are organized to provide input to all the programs in the same content area in a community or district. Advisory councils are not policy-making boards.

Members of an advisory council become important vehicles of communication. They can bring ideas from the community to your program, lend their support, interpret your program to the community, and provide effective networking.

The effectiveness of the advisory council can be directly related to its composition. If it's to communicate advice and the opinions of the community accurately, it must be representative of the entire community, drawing members from different professions, cultural and socioeconomic groups, and from different types of families. However, if the advisory council is to provide effective interpretation of a program to a community, to obtain their support, and to promote projects in the community, it should also include well-known, influential people. You might consider council members from some of the following classifications:

- An administrator (who may prefer to serve as an ex-officio member)
- A member of the faculty outside of your subject area
- Students
- Nonteaching staff
- School vendors, such as those who supply school lunches, class rings, etc.
- School Board members
- A representative of the parent-teacher organization
- Business and professional people
- A Chamber of Commerce representative
- Local employment office personnel
- Representatives from civic and religious groups
- Health and welfare representatives
- An Extension or 4-H agent
- Media representatives, such as editor of the Family Living or Lifestyle section of the local newspaper
- A representative from higher education
- A representative from local government

Once the desired composition of the council is determined, suggestions for prospective members can be made. The advisory council should be large enough to represent appropriate constituencies and organizations within the community, but not so large that it's unwieldy. Eight to twelve members usually constitute a workable size group. The length of members' terms and the number of terms they can serve should be determined and stated.

■ ADVISORY COUNCIL TIPS ■

The American Association of School Administrators, a section of the National Education Association, has recommended these suggestions for developing a successful advisory council:

- The council should be organized during developmental stages, not when a program is in trouble.
- There needs to be a very clear understanding of the functions of the council.
- The cooperation of the parent-teacher group should be secured in organizing an advisory council to prevent duplication of effort.
- The advisory council needs to understand thoroughly its relationship to the School Board.
- The lay advisory council should not be a rubber-stamp organization, serving only to approve policies and issues agreed upon by the superintendent and the Board. Professionals within the organization should be included on the council but not allowed to assume central or domineering roles.
- Time limits need to be set for both short- and long-term committees.
- Lay groups should be treated with sincerity, frankness, and honesty. Council opinions and suggestions need to be received with dignity and respect.

✳ Duties and Responsibilities

Making preliminary preparations will help the advisory council function effectively. A helpful first step is to make arrangements for members to become acquainted with each other. The members of the council need to know the purposes of the council—why it has been organized and what its role and limitations are. In addition, members need to have background information about your program and the guidelines that have been used to plan the current program. It can be effective to have a learner present this information with you. With this preparation, the council members will be able to participate fully and meaningfully.

Some specific duties and responsibilities of your advisory council might be to:

- Set up short-term and long-term goals for the program.
- Help keep curriculum up to date.
- Make plans for growth and expansion of the program.
- Help secure donations and discards of materials and equipment that are needed.
- Give advice, encouragement, and support.
- Act as a public relations liaison.
- Assist in evaluating the program.

In addition, advisory councils for career and technical programs may also assume some of these responsibilities:

- Help determine occupations in the local area for which training is needed.
- Identify and recruit students who are in need of the training (with help from the career and technology preparation guidance counselor, if there is one).
- Help find suitable training positions and/or provide jobs for students.
- Create rapport between industry or business and your program.
- Assist in securing permanent job placements for graduates.
- Make suggestions for other types of programs needed in the community.

✳ Advisory Council Meetings

Most members of advisory councils are busy people who want to feel their input is worthwhile. Council meetings should be thoughtfully planned. They should deal with relevant topics about which the council is knowledgeable. Responsibility for planning the meeting, making the arrangements, and taking care of the follow-up may rest with you, with the chairperson of the advisory council, or with another responsible individual. Regardless of who makes the arrangements, keep the following tips in mind:

- Plan and send a realistic agenda to the members. Try not to waste people's time.
- Follow the agenda as much as possible without cutting anyone off.
- Meet in your department or usual meeting place so council members will see student projects, displays, bulletin boards, and evidence of activities.

- Serve refreshments, perhaps prepared by students or club members, that in some way reflect the study of nutrition and the desire to make healthful choices.
- Photocopy handouts, make transparencies, or develop a computer slide or video program giving background information designed to assist the council in dicussing concerns.
- Send the minutes or a summary of the meeting proceedings to council members.

Follow up on suggestions made by council members. This may involve working with individual council members, talking to administrators, contacting other professionals, working on learning experiences and future plans for the program, and discussing ideas with your learners. It won't be possible to take action on every idea, but it's important that suggestions be explored. You should report the outcomes of members' suggestions to the council, either through a memo or a report during a future advisory council meeting.

 # Service Learning

Service learning is not a modern concept. In fact, it's now more than a century old. Initially part of the Progressive Education Movement in the early days of the 20th century, service learning continues to gather steam. Some states, especially in the East, require that students perform community service in order to graduate from high school. However, not everyone agrees with the concept of service learning. If you would like to implement a service learning program, make sure your administrator knows about and supports your plan.

Rhode Island philanthropist Alan Shawn Feinstein has said, "We spend the first third of our life learning, the next third earning, and the last third returning. Service learning empowers students and teachers by combining all three."

✳ The Connection Between Service Learning and School-to-Career

Service learning is the application of academic skills to address community needs. This provides an opportunity for students to serve the community while learning. Community service, on the other hand, is purely volunteerism with no connection to the curriculum. Service learning provides an opportunity for students to serve the community while learning. School-to-career integrates school-based and work-based learning to combine academics and occupational learning. Service learning shares many similarities with school-to-career efforts. Both rely heavily on connecting with the community and both are based on the experiential philosophy of education of learning by doing.

Service learning and school-to-career impact students and teachers in a number of ways. Students are seen as active learners and providers of service and are viewed as part of the solution, as opposed to being part of the problem. They are better prepared as individuals, family, and community members as a result of their experiences and become productive members of the workforce because they apply their knowledge in practical, real-life situations. Teachers make connections to the community by forming partnerships with outside entities. This often causes them to rethink the way they teach as they become facilitators of learning versus the "sage on stage."

✳ Advantages of Service Learning

Service learning can be done in any subject and at any grade level. It may start as early as preschool and continue as part of lifelong learning. Its benefits are derived from many areas:

- **Academics.** Learning is enriched, hands-on, exciting, interesting, and long-lasting. Service learning is seen as a plus on job, college, and scholarship applications and may lead to job opportunities.

- **Social.** Learners are exposed to settings and situations that help them develop people skills to help them in the future. Teamwork, accountability, and leadership are all enhanced.
- **Personal.** Self-esteem and confidence grow as students learn to plan, implement, and evaluate. They develop career awareness and gain information and other skills they can use throughout life.
- **Emotional.** If you touch their hearts, you will activate their minds! Providing service to others will touch a student and develop a commitment as nothing else can. Skipping a homework assignment is one thing. Disappointing a third grader at a tutoring session is quite a different story.
- **Community.** Community awareness is increased and learners develop a desire to make their hometown a better place. In addition, statistics have shown that crime and dropout rates are reduced, youth are seen in a positive light, and that there is an increase in their desire to volunteer in the future.

❋ Integrating Service Learning into the Curriculum

Much of what educators do depends on the parameters of their program or school. Service can be done during school, after school, in the evening, on weekends, and during school vacations. Assignments might range from helping a Head Start class during the summer to staffing a food pantry at a church to assisting with activities in the children's wing of a hospital. Once learners are "hooked" by the good feelings they derive by helping others, many want to do more.

Service learning can be integrated into any subject area, be required or supplementary, or be a separate class. You may choose to do one project or several less involved activities. These can vary in duration. Perhaps some students in your housing course would devote a Saturday to helping paint the bedrooms of a new Habitat for Humanity house. Other classmates might stain woodwork the following weekend. A hearty, nutritious lunch could be served to the work crew by learners enrolled in a foods class—the same students who planned and prepared the meal. Classmates in a beginning sewing class might construct simple window treatments.

You may customize service learning to an individual as independent study or use it as a group, class, departmental, school, or community project. It is also an effective vehicle for interdisciplinary or club work.

❋ Components of Service Learning

The main steps in service learning are *preparation*, *action*, *reflection*, *assessment*, and *celebration*. Working through these steps is what distinguishes service learning from traditional volunteer activities. Students can use a portfolio format to document these five steps.

Have learners devote a folder or binder to their portfolio, dividing entries into the five sections. Each section should open with a numbered cover sheet to serve as a table of contents. Contents of the respective sections might include guest speaker or field trip sheets, field site brochures, activity records and plans, reflection information, evaluations, photos, copies of thank-you notes, awards, and newspaper clippings.

❋ Preparation

Using this process, the *preparation* component begins by orienting students and staff to the mechanics of service learning and its benefits. Students should complete some type of self-assessment. Any number of self-report tests followed by discussion should suffice, depending upon the nature of the participants. Human relations activities in communication, team building, and forming first impressions are also necessary. This will help them to understand their own needs, feelings, and work styles before they try to relate to the needs of others.

Next, students conduct an assessment of community needs, and then choose an issue or group with which to work. They must study the group or issue. For example, if their intent were to work with senior citizens, they would investigate the social, emotional, physical, mental, ethical, legal, and safety issues, as well as applicable licensing laws and regulations affecting this population. A partnership might be developed between the school and various agencies at this time to provide information on participant rights, advocacy issues, orientation/training, and observation opportunities necessary for work with a particular agency. These partnerships will help to illustrate the power of community networking and collaboration.

During this phase, students should become familiar with their educational partner. It's a good idea to have them fill out an information form for every agency they assist. This should include partner contact information, directions to the site, hours of operation, the major needs of the population to be served, volunteer requirements, scheduling parameters, and career opportunities. This documentation can be kept in numerical order in the first section of the portfolio. The next step is to brainstorm partner needs and the types of activities the participants can do to address these needs. It's essential that learners be a part of the planning process to feel ownership in the projects or activities. *Figure 23-1* on page 323 gives a service learning plan form to assist you in the planning process.

✳ Action

Action is the second step in the service learning process and may be done through direct action, indirect action, or advocacy. Providing *direct action* with a particular population is the ideal situation. Participants develop skills in applied learning situations such as internships, demonstrations for student organization events, or other projects. For example, learners might assist with activities in a nursing home, thereby observing and applying the rules, regulations, policies, and technology affecting the nursing home, its clients, and their families. Students would also learn to work cooperatively and collaboratively with other students, support staff, residents, and their families.

It's particularly important to investigate necessary insurance, liability, and transportation issues when learners work at sites off the school campus. To be safe, have the permission form you use checked by a legal

representative of the school administration. Having the parental signature notarized will also strengthen the document. If students are driving, be sure that you have a photocopy of their license and proof of insurance.

Indirect action may be used when it's not possible to bring the students in contact with those they wish to help. An example would be for students to create educational games or books for children with special needs. This would help educate the learners about the needs and capabilities of the children. In another situation, students might create an informational booklet on health care or social services available in the community. The booklet could be reproduced for distribution. An educational partner may have an in-house printing facility or the financial resources to sponsor the printing.

The third type of action is *advocacy*. In this case, learners might research an issue such as a certain type of substance abuse and prepare a campaign to create awareness of its dangers. Or, after listening to a presentation on the importance of the early years in the formation of the brain, students might also become advocates for the importance of quality nurturing. Child care dos and don'ts might be illustrated through sociodramas or puppet shows. Activity plans, samples, instructions, and photos should be included in the *action* section of the portfolio.

✳ Reflection

The next step, *reflection*, is especially important in service learning. It helps learners think about the work they have done, what it means to them, how it made them feel, how they applied classroom skills, what new skills have been learned, and how the experience might help them in choosing a career. Learners can show their reflection through journals, essays, displays, presentations, or skits. The service experience should also be discussed. Reflection should be required after every activity and should be documented in the *reflection* section of the portfolio.

✳ Assessment

Service learning work needs to be assessed in regard to the program, student learning, and the experience. Assessment of

Figure 23-1

SERVICE LEARNING PLAN

Name: _____ Date: _____ Class Period: _____

Agency, business, or group with whom you will work: _____

Contact person: _____ Phone: _____

E-mail: _____

Group who will be helped by your service: _____

Date: _____ Time: _____ Place: _____

Describe the service you will perform:

Materials needed:

Type of action:

Method of reflection:

Method of evaluation:

Method of celebration:

Subsequent action you will take:

From: Swierk, M. "A Guide to Service Learning" Wickford, RI 1999.

the program can be measured against a national set of standards developed by the Alliance for Service Learning in Educational Reform, referred to as the ASLER Standards. It is a useful tool in measuring program effectiveness. See *Figure 23-2* below.

Teacher, field-site contacts, peer- and self-evaluation can be used to assess student effectiveness in service learning. Attendance, field-site preparation and work, journals, logs, guest speaker reports, and research papers are but a few of the items you may use to assess a student's work. It's also important for students to assess their own work and that of their peers so they can gear toward improving their future performance. An assessment section of a student portfolio should contain evaluation items that are used. The completed portfolio may be used as a final assessment.

Finally, assess the effectiveness of any partnerships in which you have been involved. You will find that some work well and others shouldn't be repeated. Have the students work with you on this process.

✳ *Celebration*

Celebration is the final part of the service learning process. This gives the students and participants the opportunity to recognize each other. Recognition ceremonies, thank-you notes, certificates, awards, T-shirts, and press releases are some examples of what can be used. Take time to explore the various awards that are given for service learning and assist your students in applying for them. You may also have the opportunity to gain recognition and visibility by applying for awards honoring outstanding programs.

Figure 23-2

PROGRAM EVALUATION

The success of any program is determined by evaluation standards. These must be followed and monitored throughout the course of the program (formative) and upon completion of the program (summative). Evaluation must also be quantitative and qualitative to give you a complete assessment.

It is important to develop standards that will not only guide you through this process, but will serve as tangible data to be used for gauging program effectiveness, completing grant proposals, funding applications, program modifications, and program reports. Two main areas that must be assessed are the program and its outcomes.

The ASLER Standards

The Alliance for Service Learning in Educational Reform (ASLER), comprised of a number of various foundations, universities, schools and departments of education, formed a committee to set standards for service learning referred to as the ASLER Standards. They are as follows:

- Effective service learning provides concrete opportunities for youth to learn new skills, to think critically, and to test new roles in an environment that encourages risk taking and that rewards competence.
- Preparation and reflection are essential elements in service learning.
- Youth's efforts are recognized by those served, including their peers, the school, and the community.
- Youth are involved in the planning.
- The service students perform makes a meaningful contribution to the community.
- Effective service learning integrates systematic formative and summative evaluation.
- Service learning connects the school or sponsoring organization and its community in new and positive ways.
- Skilled adult guidance and supervision are essential to the success of service learning.
- Perspective training, orientation, and staff development that include the philosophy and methodology of service learning best ensure that program quality and continuity are maintained.

From: Swierk, M. "A Guide to Service Learning" Wickford, RI 1999.

Having students photograph their activities and write press releases for the school and/or local newspaper is an excellent public relations tool. It also serves as a valuable component of a student portfolio.

✳ *The most important concept to keep in mind in service learning is the real-life connection. Students must be impressed with the fact that their work may impact the lives of others, and therefore confidentiality, accuracy, and timeliness are crucial.* ✳

References

Swierk, M. (1999). A guide to service learning. Available through: MS Innovations, PO Box 813, North Kingston, RI 02852. Phone/Fax 401-294-7804. E-Mail: Msinnovate@aol.com

http://www.PartnersinEducation.org The National Association of Partners in Education, 901 North Pitt St., Suite 320, Alexandria, VA 22314. Phone: 703-836-4880. E Mail: NAPEhq@NAPEhq.org

http//www.umn.edu~serve The National Service Learning Cooperative University of Minnesota, 1954 Buford Avenue, Room R460, St. Paul, MN 55108. Phone: 800-808-SERV (7378). E-Mail: serve@tc.umn.edu

Building Your Professional Portfolio

Analyzing Educational Partnerships. Interview an administrator or educator who has been involved in an educational partnership program. Find out how the partnership was initiated and the benefits for each side, plus any problems that have arisen and how they were addressed. Based on the interview and the information in the chapter, develop guidelines for a partnership program.

Identifying Community Resources. Make a chart for each of the conceptual areas you covered in your program. For each area, list possible resource people and field trips for enriching study in this area.

Forming an Advisory Council. Propose the occupations of individuals you would select for an advisory council for your program. Explain why each individual should be able to make valuable contributions to the goals of the council.

Planning a Service Learning Project. Develop a service learning plan for involving your learners in a worthwhile community service project. Include a description of each of the five components enumerated in this chapter.

Chapter 24

Marketing Your Program

Effective public relations and marketing strategies are essential for most successful education programs. Your top career goal may be to do a great job teaching, but doing that job often extends beyond the work you do with your learners and participants. In order to create a favorable environment in which your program enjoys visibility, acceptance, and respect, you will have to be concerned with public relations.

There are a variety of ways to publicize your efforts. You may write news releases, newsletters, brochures, flyers, and copy for a Web page. You may network with coworkers, give presentations to various groups, and contact legislators. You may plan interesting activities worthy of media coverage. In every effort, let your professionalism shine.

In the beginning, you may feel challenged by these roles, much the way you are challenging your learners. Rest assured, your efforts will be rewarded and your days will not be humdrum.

 ## The Value of Public Relations

How will you respond when someone asks what you do for a living? You will want to be clear about what you are "selling," about the nature of your program. Remember, it's more forceful to say what your program is than to describe what it's not. Develop your own succinct description of your academic area so you can be clear, concise, and positive when asked about it.

It has been said that public relations consists of doing well and getting credit for it. It's important to tell people outside of your field about your successes. Effective public relations and marketing campaigns are developed carefully, not left to chance. They are planned efforts to influence people to your point of view—in this case, to understand the importance, value, and benefits of your program.

Plan your public relations and marketing programs in writing, just as you do your teaching units and lessons. Clearly state your objectives or expected outcomes. Developing a written timetable that includes specific marketing tasks is similar to developing a scope-and-sequence chart for your curriculum. Set a time to evaluate whether your objectives have been met.

Some public relations and marketing objectives will require several months, even several years, to achieve. Few successful campaigns are short-term. They need to be proactive rather than defensive. You need to use a variety of communication strategies.

Enhancing Program Visibility and Image

For your program to grow, you need others to know about and support it. This means boosting the visibility of your program and involving additional people in it.

Decide whom you want to influence. These people will be the target of your marketing plan. Is it the community at large? The sixth-grade or eighth-grade students in feeder schools who will be moving up to your school? Is it parents? School staff, particularly guidance personnel? School Board members? People at nutritional risk? Families in crises? Policymakers? It's important to recognize your target audience because the same approaches won't be equally effective with all groups. What is appealing and humorous to an eighth grader would likely be viewed as ridiculous by a state legislator. Target one audience at a time, but your marketing plan may well include several groups.

There are dozens of interesting projects that would focus positive attention on your program. *Figure 24-1* on page 328 gives examples of worthwhile activities within the community that can help sell your program.

✳ The Community

Get to know local business people, newspaper reporters and editors, and other community leaders, but don't overlook ordinary citizens. Invite people to the department or meetings so they gain a better idea of activities included in your program. Show the importance of what you teach to your learners, now and in the future.

Ask the community members to serve as:
- Guest speakers and panel discussion participants.
- Judges for contests.
- Interviewees.
- Authorities for certain content areas.
- Experts on life experiences; such as parenting triplets or being an organ transplant donor or recipient.
- Advisory council members.

Accept invitations to go to community programs as a resource expert in your subject area. Program visibility also can be gained by having posters, exhibits, displays, brochures, and activities in public places, such as shopping malls, libraries, community centers, town halls, and commercial establishments. Take advantage of opportunities to use free radio and television public service announcements (PSAs); to write articles about department events for the local newspaper, school paper, and parent-teacher newsletter; and to publicize activities on the school's or community's outdoor signs.

✳ Students and Parents

In a school situation, you want to point out the value of your courses to both students and their parents—and also to show what's in it for them. You want to show how the content will benefit learners now and in the future. Course titles and descriptions should be appealing to teens. *Food and Fitness for Life* may garner more interest than *Food and Nutrition*. Similarly, *Life Choices*, or possibly *Choices and Challenges*, sounds more appealing than *Personal and Home Management*.

Develop brochures, leaflets, or flyers capitalizing on how certain courses help students develop skills for a lifetime. Use terms, such as "decision making," "academic content," "essential life skills," "critical thinking," "challenges and choices," and "career connections" that give your courses credibility with both students and parents. Some parents will want to know the specific topics taught in a curriculum, especially those dealing with human development or values. These can be controversial topics, so be prepared to explain how they are treated in your program.

It's helpful for you to be involved in overall school activities so you know learners and they know you. Visibility for you and your program is essential. If your schedule allows, be the adviser for the prom, a judge at a fair, or sponsor of a school-wide service project such as a Career Day or Wellness Day. Attend school plays, concerts, and games.

Figure 24-1

STRATEGIES FOR PROGRAM VISIBILITY

- **Sponsor a monthly "coffeehouse" for area high school students.** With your students or group, plan entertainment and refreshments for the Friday or Saturday evening event. Your learners will earn money and gain valuable experience; students who attend will have a fun and safe place to meet; and you gain exposure for your program, including possible television coverage.

- **Set up a display near the entrance of a supermarket.** Display fresh foods and "Buys of the Season." Have students point out seasonal buys and give out nutritious recipes using these foods.

- **Publish news articles in local papers.** You could write about or report on feature activities in your program. If you teach Family and Consumer Sciences, focus on consumer issues, wellness, parenting, or interior design, rather than just the traditional areas, such as foods. This shows the breadth of your program instead of reinforcing outdated stereotypes.

- **Honor past program participants for their achievements.** Seek endorsements from them for your program to gain greater community support. Alumni might be willing to speak to incoming groups of students, the school board, and/or groups of parents.

- **Form an advisory council.** Refer back to Chapter 23 for more details. Rotate members who can give you fresh ideas and help you gain visibility and credibility.

- **Sponsor a nutrition education poster contest.** Display entries in the library, shopping mall, restaurants, or other appropriate places in the community. Posters might be designed for young children and used in an elementary school. Ask local merchants to donate awards. Submit a press release about the contest and winner.

- **Establish a catering service.** This service might provide simple refreshments for showers, picnics, and birthday parties. If you have a culinary program, additional services might be offered. You could use the profits for learners to dine in a fine restaurant.

- **Plan a party.** Residents of assisted-living facilities and nursing homes enjoy seeing young people, and students gain interpersonal skills.

- **Implement a "phone pal" service.** Participants take turns calling shut-ins' homes daily. If there seems to be a problem, the appropriate authority is contacted. This could be an FCCLA chapter project.

- **Arrange a window display for a business.** You might team with a home furnishing store to develop a room setting with furniture and accessories in a store window. Credit your students and department by placing a sign in the window.

- **Start a business.** Businesses to care for plants and/or pets, to clean homes, or to organize closets are possibilities. The earnings might pay for student organization dues and travel expenses to a convention.

- **Provide a "Parent's Day Out" program.** Publicize the availability of the program one morning or afternoon a week for a month. Plan appropriate activities and refreshments for toddlers and preschoolers.

- **Set up a formal-wear shop.** If there's a nearby college, team up with a sorority in the early spring to sell like-new formal dresses to high school girls. Split the proceeds between your program and the sorority chapter. This project is likely to attract the interest of a television station.

- **Help with a children's group.** Adopt a Cub Scout or Brownie troop and assist at troop meetings. Or, plan and carry out another activity for a children's group. Learners might watch the adult leaders' younger children while they work with the troop.

- **Prepare displays for a fabric or craft store.** Illustrate pattern and fabric selections for sewing projects. Rotate displays until every learner has had a turn. This display could be called "Creating an Original."

- **Conduct a car wash or silent auction.** Use earnings to carry out a community beautification project. Use the decision-making process to select the beautification project and develop it. Evaluate the completed project.

Place exhibits and displays in lobbies, libraries, and hallways. Use them to show administrators, counselors, and students the breadth and relevance of your program.

✳ School Personnel

Get to know your fellow faculty members. Bring them into your department as guest speakers, judges, and panel members. Invite them to attend an FCCLA banquet or 4-H ceremony. Volunteer to go to other departments in the school and organizations in the community as a resource expert on selected topics.

Become well acquainted with the guidance personnel. Work with them all year, not just at course sign-up time. Ask their opinion on coverage of topics, such as human development, relationships, parenting, and wellness, in educational materials you use. Counselors may be available to speak to your learners about topics in their areas of expertise, such as developing interpersonal skills for employment and learning effective communication strategies.

In a school setting, you may be asked to help others in a variety of ways. You will want to be cooperative, but not exploited. If a request for your students' help fits your curriculum objectives, you may be able to accommodate the request and turn it into a learning experience. Your fashion class could research period costumes for the school play. If you are asked to prepare refreshments for an event, use this opportunity to give students experience in comparing homemade, convenience, and ready-to-eat products for taste, texture, and cost. Have them decide when each might be most appropriate. Which has most eye appeal? Which homemade products could be made ahead and stored successfully? Analyze and label the refreshments served for fat, sodium, fiber, calories, and vitamin content.

✳ Board Members

Invite a member of the School Board into your department to observe or take part in a special activity. If you are employed by a nonprofit agency, invite members of its Board of Directors. Prepare a presentation to inform board members about your curriculum. Involve learners in the presentation. Have facts and statistics at your fingertips related to this particular audience and their educational concerns.

As discussed in Chapter 17, work to incorporate dual-credit courses into the curriculum, but do it diplomatically. If a particular department in your school is overloaded, then advocate incorporating a cross-credit course in that area. If you teach Family and Consumer Sciences, work on making it a required subject in your school. Elective courses are being dealt less and less space in the curriculum as graduation requirements are becoming tighter. However, computer science is required in most schools because it's a management skill needed to survive in society today. That is precisely the same reason that FCS skills are needed by all students. Impressing members of the School Board with the value of your program will help accomplish this.

✳ Your Own Image

Always remember that to people in your school and community, you are your program. To sell your program, you must have a strong belief in it. Do you reflect the image you're trying to sell? You need to establish personal and professional credibility. If you think students overlook teachers wearing wrinkled or inappropriate clothes, coming to class unprepared, or smoking as they exit the parking lot, then you are wrong. They notice everything about their role models. To help you enhance your own image as a professional, follow these guidelines:

- Do your job better than well.
- Practice what you preach—or teach.
- Dress professionally.
- Participate in professional organizations.
- Reach out to share your expertise with others.
- Use effective communication skills. Be assertive.
- Emphasize your educational and professional credentials.
- Develop your advocacy and public relations skills.

✳ Learning Environment

Does your classroom or meeting place convey the image you want to portray? An attractive, reasonably uncluttered, and clean room helps say, "I care about you." Changing bulletin boards, having plants and other decorative items, displaying learners' work, and having seating arrangements that foster group interaction all help create a positive attitude toward your program.

Your teaching area should reflect how your curriculum meets your students' and community's current needs. Are computers available or are computer-related projects visible? Do you have appropriate equipment for career-related courses? Are community-based projects highlighted?

Programs that are contemporary, meaningful, relevant, well planned, and effectively taught are the best means of creating a positive image for the profession. Such programs also foster student success. Nothing will enhance your program more than successful learners. They are your most effective ambassadors.

Effective Publicity

When individuals and businesses advertise in various media, they typically spend large sums of money. Advertising is similar to publicity, but the good news is that publicity is free. The bad news is that you often have very little control over the end result. You may submit a three-page news release to the local newspaper and end up with a one-paragraph article. You may get television coverage of a major event but have no control over the "spin" the reporter puts on it.

✳ Skills for Success

While you have no control over the newspaper's space constraints, it's beneficial to submit a well-written news release. Using good journalistic skills also helps ensure the success of newsletters, public service announcements, Web pages, brochures, and flyers that you may develop.

If your goal is to have a segment about your project on the TV news, plan the event for a weekend and notify stations in advance. Sunday is considered a "slow" news day with Saturday ranking next. Stations are more likely to have time for community interest stories.

Good writing skills are essential for successful publicity. To help polish your writing skills, keep these "S-words" in mind:

- Simple, short, specific, and concrete words
- Strong action verbs
- Short sentences, but with some variation
- Short paragraphs
- Spelling, grammar, and punctuation without errors

Don't hesitate to ask others to critique your work.

✳ *News Releases and Articles*

A common writing mistake is to try to impress readers with "big" words. Often, what results is wordiness. Control the urge to use more words than necessary by imagining that every word costs a dollar. If you can say the same thing in fewer words, do so. Consider these sentences: "The Norwood 4-H chapter traveled to Chicago last weekend to be a participant at State Convention, where they were delighted to be named recipients of a new award." A simpler, yet stronger opening sentence would be: "The Norwood 4-H chapter received an award at the state convention in Chicago on March 5."

The most important information in your news release or article should appear first. This is called the *lead*. In the examples above, the newsworthy event was winning the award, not the trip to Chicago. The rest of the news release or article should be constructed in descending order of importance; information is usually cut from the bottom of a news story. Be sure to include *who*, *what*, *where*, *when*, *why*, and *how* early in the story. Use short words and sentences. The narrow columns of a newspaper dictate that paragraphs should also be short.

Proofread the news release before submitting it. Even with a computer's spell-check and grammar-check features, carefully check your work. A word may be misspelled for the context in which you used it, but spelled correctly for another situation. It would reflect poorly on a group to include sentences such as: "Mr. Ricca is there principle." or "Homemade deserts will be severed after the program." Similarly, grammatical errors weaken your message.

Remember that timeliness is a key element of news. Don't delay writing and submitting news releases. They will be discarded if they're late. Always include *contact information* for a person the reporter can call if more information is needed. You may mail your news release or fax it to the newsroom of the newspaper. Unless you are instructed otherwise, don't e-mail news releases. Some editors accept them, but you should follow up with a faxed or mailed copy.

A weekly newspaper is more likely to publish your article than a daily, and a weekly paper is also more likely to run the article just as you send it. A small local paper is typically more receptive to school news than a larger one. If you submit a photograph with an article, it's possible that a weekly newspaper will run it. In most cases, however, newspapers only publish photos taken by a staff photographer. If an editor is interested in running a photo with your news event, she or he will make a photo assignment in advance. *Figure 24-2*, "Basic Bs for Publicity," contains additional tips for working with the news media.

❋ Newsletters

Another technique is to develop a newsletter. This would be sent to a particular audience on a regular basis, perhaps monthly or quarterly. Unlike news stories and features submitted to the media, you control and edit what appears in the newsletter. Newsletters to parents, administrators, and advisory council members are a means of keeping them informed about your program.

Consider what your audience wants to know and provide some of this. Also consider what your audience *needs* to know. Use some of what they want in order to produce what they need.

The guidelines for newspapers and articles also apply to newsletters, however

---

Figure 24-2

━ BASIC BS FOR PUBLICITY ━

- Be the only contact person from your group to approach news media. Two members calling the same newspaper editor or program director are bound to bring conflict or confusion.
- Be quick to establish personal contact with the right persons at each newspaper and radio and television station in your area.
- Be sure to write everything down. Train your memory, but don't trust it.
- Be prompt in meeting deadlines.
- Be legible. Proofread carefully.
- Be accurate. Check over dates, names, places, and other details before you submit your information.
- Be honest and impartial. Give others appropriate credit.
- Be brief. Newspaper space and airtime are costly.
- Be brave. Don't be afraid to suggest something new if you honestly believe you have a workable idea. Media people welcome original ideas when they're practical and logically organized.
- Be businesslike. Don't try to obtain publicity by pressure of friendship or business connections. Don't ask when a story will appear or ask for clippings.
- Be appreciative of all space and time given to publicize your group. The media also have space and time for sale.
- Be professional. Members of the press are always invited guests. Never ask them to buy tickets or pay admission.

---

newsletter content is usually written in a less formal style. Using contractions is one way to create an informal tone. You may also keep the tone conversational and personal by using *you*, *we*, and *us*. Use the present tense and active voice when possible.

A newsletter should be able to pass the "refrigerator test," meaning that the recipient will decide whether to take time to read it before reaching the kitchen. If it's set aside to be read later, it probably won't be read at all.

Computer programs make it easy to design a professional-looking newsletter. The use of headings that break up the page, some variation in type style, and adequate open space help motivate people to read. Two or three columns are easier to read than one wide column. Graphics and clip art can add interest. Of course, any of these techniques can be overused, resulting in a cluttered effect. Aim for a simple, pleasing design.

The newsletter's name may impact its desirability to readers. You may choose an alliteration or a play on words for its name, such as *FCS News to Use* or *Inside Information*. Or, you might appeal to readers' needs and interests with a title like *The Savvy Consumer*.

Plan a balance of news, features, editorials, and promotional columns. Consistency will lend credibility. For example, you might consistently profile a student or member of the month on the first page, run a letter to the editor or thank-you note from a service agency on page two, provide tips for consumers on the third page, and a calendar of events on the back of the newsletter.

✳ *Public Service Announcements*

A public service announcement advocates some change of behavior or attitude. For example, you might want listeners to follow the Dietary Guidelines, to check total interest charges on installment loans, or to enroll in your new adult Extension program for divorcing parents. Your message should clearly convey the course of action you are recommending.

Keep your message simple. About 130 words is average. Use primarily short sentences, but vary sentence length somewhat. Remember that listeners won't be hanging on your every word. They may be working or driving, so repeat essential information. If you give a phone number, try to have one that spells a word associated with your cause.

Read your message aloud to check the timing. Triple-space the copy and use wide margins so it can be edited easily. Use dashes for pauses: "Family and Consumer Sciences—focusing on quality of life—is more important today than ever before."

Do everything you can to make your copy professional. Be sure to include a contact person for more information. *Figure 24-3* on page 333 provides an outline for a sample PSA.

✳ *Web Pages*

You may want your department or program to have its own Web page. You may be able to add your material to the existing website of your school or agency. If you feel you don't have the skills to design a Web page, it's likely that there's a knowledgeable coworker or student who could help. Once the Web page is operational, participants in your program might enjoy helping keep it updated. Your Web page might include:

- Your mission statement.
- Program offerings with descriptions.
- Personnel and their credentials, including areas of expertise and research.
- How to contact program personnel.
- Meeting times and dates.
- Degrees and majors (for college programs).
- Career options and job market information.
- Frequently asked questions with responses.
- Newsletters or selected newsletter articles.
- Links to related websites.
- An alumni network.

✳ *Brochures*

There may be times when you want to get your message to a specific audience at the optimum time and with a special impact. A brochure is meant to have a specific purpose, not to provide complete coverage of a topic. It should be quick and easy to read. With care and imagination, a brochure can be both eye-catching and attractive. Because of its compact size, it can be saved for future reference. You might collect attractive brochures as sources of ideas.

Brochures can be used to highlight program accomplishments such as the placement record or job success of participants. It can describe employment opportunities and encourage people to begin training. A brochure may be used to inform the public about the courses or services available in your program and how to enroll. It may be used to educate the public about a community service that your program offers.

Confine yourself to one subject and one audience at a time. You may be trying to reach taxpayers, parents, students, or your

Figure 24-3

SAMPLE PUBLIC SERVICE ANNOUNCEMENT

Single-space contact information, but triple-space the rest of the announcement.

Your name
Address
E-mail address
Phone number

- Write a summary title, in parentheses, ending with the length in seconds.

    (BEWARE OF HOME IMPROVEMENT SCAMS—60 SECOND PSA)

- If your material will go out of date, add a warning under the title.

    (PLEASE DO NOT USE AFTER APRIL 10)

- Write a lively introductory sentence that will appeal to you audience by linking your message to an audience benefit. Then fill in the details in any logical order while sticking to one main theme.

    WHO is the most common target of scam artists?
    WHAT "services" do they commonly try to sell?
    WHERE are the scams taking place?
    WHEN do most scams occur?
    WHY don't victims report scams?
    HOW can they avoid being victimized?

- Close with an appeal for action. Then indicate that the message is complete by the use of crosshatches or number symbols on a separate line:

    #   #   #

learners' potential employers. Once you determine whom you are targeting, consider how you are going to get their attention, what you want them to learn, and what action you want them to take. Select aspects of your program that should interest them and decide on your approach.

Try to incorporate catchy titles. Convey a simple message by presenting it in a lively style. Illustrations can help tell a story quickly and, sometimes, dramatically. Various computer programs can help you format the brochure and add appealing graphics.

If funds don't permit printing the brochure in color, price having it printed on colored paper instead. If there is a graphic arts or printing program in a local school or technical center, the work often may be done there for less than commercial services. Check about availability.

✳ *Flyers*

Flyers are usually regarded as a one-page, flat sheet that carries a single message with limited information that is clearly aimed at a target audience. It conveys *who*, *what*, *where*, *when*, and *why*. A flyer needs to look clean, uncluttered, and professional. The message should be conveyed in as few words as possible with plenty of free space. Remember that less design is usually better.

As with brochures, your goal is to have the flyer pass the "refrigerator test." An intriguing title, simple graphics, colored paper, and print that's easy to read all increase the likelihood of its success. Make it clear why the reader should want to attend the meeting being publicized, take the course being offered, volunteer to work for a particular organization, or support a specific cause. *Figure 24-4* on page 334 presents a checklist you can use to assess the effectiveness of brochures and flyers.

Figure 24-4

CHECKLIST FOR BROCHURES AND FLYERS

	Yes	No
Audience Appeal		
1. Does the brochure/flyer contain information on advantages and benefits for the audience?		
2. Is it stated from the reader's point of view?		
3. Does it make readers aware of their needs and interests?		
4. Does it appeal to the audience's needs and interests?		
5. Does it present a positive image of the program being promoted?		
Message Guidelines		
6. Is the message brief and simple?		
7. Does the brochure/flyer use short sentences and words that are easy to comprehend?		
8. Is the message conveyed using strong, active verbs?		
9. Is the message stated in the present tense and active voice?		
Content		
10. Is the message clear, specific, and concrete?		
11. Does the message convey convincing facts and data?		
12. Are there illustrative examples appropriate to the audience?		
13. Is contact information included so readers know where and how to get more information?		
14. Is the copy free of errors?		
Layout		
15. Does the brochure/flyer have a pleasing design?		
16. Are photographs, sketches, or other visuals used?		
17. Is the main typestyle easy to read?		
18. Is there some variety in the size and style of lettering, but not too much?		
19. Is there an appropriate amount of free space so the piece doesn't appear cluttered?		

✳ Distribution

The value of a brochure or flyer depends on whether it's read, provokes thought, and encourages action in some way. Therefore, distribution plans are an important component. Proper timing is crucial. Distributed too early, people may forget about the brochure. If it's too late, they don't have time to act.

If your audience is your learners' parents, the easiest method is sending the material home with students. However, with this method not all will reach their intended recipients. Mailing is a more efficient, yet costly, method. To save money, you might be able to mail your information along with students' grades. Another cost-saver is to skip envelopes and fold and staple the pages instead. Strive to have a mailing list that is accurate and current to avoid wasting postage. Depending on quantity, a bulk-mail permit may save money. Your school or agency may already have one. For bulk mail, pieces of mail must be grouped by zip code and all pieces must be identical.

Other ways to distribute brochures and flyers include:

- Placing them on tables at registration sites. This is especially effective for new programs or when existing programs have been revamped.
- Mailing to individuals who inquire about your program.
- Taking them along to banquets, meetings, and conventions.
- Asking a related group to incorporate your piece as part of its bulk mailing.

- Placing them on tables at civic-club meetings.
- Distributing information at exhibits and fairs.
- Hand-delivering them to school counselors and administrators.
- Asking to place them in a brochure holder or on a table in places related to the topic, such as school and community libraries, the public health department, or child care centers.

Effective Presentations

There are many reasons for giving a presentation and often there's much at stake. You may want your area of expertise to be a required subject area in your school or your program to be considered for funding. A presentation is your opportunity to offer your justification and rationale to your administrators, community board, or other influential group. It's absolutely essential to be well prepared for these meetings, as it is for all professional appearances.

✳ Know Your Audience

As you begin to plan a presentation, gear your approach, vocabulary, verbal examples, statistics, arguments, visual materials, and even your attire to your audience. The size of your audience, its composition, the time of day and year, and the seating arrangement are just a few factors to consider. For example, if your audience will be made up of retirees, you might use a reminiscing approach and a microphone. If your presentation takes place with a meal, it's preferable to speak before, rather than after, people eat. Many people tend to be sleepy after a meal.

Present your material from a point of view that will be meaningful to the specific audience. Think about what will get these listeners' attention. Know their positions and attitudes. Find out who the leaders and decision makers are.

Clarify your purpose in speaking to this group. Is it to inform? Persuade? Inspire? Motivate to action? If action is your goal, specify what, when, and how.

✳ *Involve the Audience*

Effective speakers involve their audiences at the beginning of their presentations and throughout, either literally or passively. You might ask a rhetorical question that really doesn't require an answer. You can ask for a show of hands in affirmative response to a question. You can ask the audience to think about some lines of poetry or about a story, song, or play. Listeners can be asked to close their eyes to imagine something you suggest. You might put notes under some chairs so people have to get up to find them. Or, people can be asked to stand up and say something to the person behind them.

✳ Be Prepared

No presentation should be considered ordinary or unimportant. Your image and the image of your program and profession are at stake. Here are some guidelines to follow:

- **Research your topic.** Search for the latest information. Anticipate questions this particular audience might ask. Be able to document your information sources if asked to do so. Don't leave out facts that are detrimental to your cause; it's better for you to bring them up rather than an audience member who might put you on the defensive.
- **Use a conversational tone.** Your spoken vocabulary is different from your written vocabulary. Don't use words that aren't part of your everyday speech.
- **Use effective notes.** Notes help keep you on track, but writing out your presentation word for word isn't the best idea. You are more likely to use long and complex sentences that are hard to follow and to read your speech rather than "talk with" the audience. Writing notes with only key words often works best. They help focus your thoughts and your talk sounds natural. One tip is to write your notes "bifocal style"—using large lettering and extra spacing. This technique helps you to maintain eye contact with your audience because it's easier to find your place when you glance back at your notes.

- **Keep it short.** Few audiences can concentrate on a topic longer than 20 minutes. If you are asked to speak for 45 minutes, try to persuade the meeting's organizer to shorten the time or break the talk up with audience-participation activities.
- **Practice.** Rehearse with the notes you'll use, but know your subject matter so well that you aren't tied to your notes. Time yourself. Be so well prepared that you can deviate from your plan to react to a puzzled look or questioning glance.
- **Check out the location.** Use only equipment you know how to run and make sure everything is working before your presentation begins. A PowerPoint® presentation on "Color Schemes in Kitchen and Bath Designs" will be a real letdown if the equipment malfunctions. Mark the floor with chalk or tape to indicate where the cart holding the equipment needs to be. Focus the slide projector so it can be used immediately. Bring an extra projector bulb. Find out if you will need a microphone and, if so, what kind you will use. Will it allow you to move freely? Note the seating arrangement. Can chairs be moved to form a semicircle or groups? Can refreshments be served?
- **Remove distractions.** Remove clutter, including notes and materials from previous presentations. Don't pass around items while you're talking. It diverts the audience's attention away from your message. Try not to use a podium since it puts a psychological barrier between you and the audience.

❋ Develop a Successful Presentation

Did you know that listeners usually decide if a presentation is going to be worthwhile within the first 10 seconds? That indicates, of course, that your introduction must be strong. The body of your speech, including the visuals you use, and the conclusion are also important components of your presentation.

❋ *The Introduction*

Introducing a presentation is very much like establishing set for a lesson. Using *you*, *we*, and *our* is more effective than using *I*, *me*, and *my*. Limit the use of *I*—unless self-revelation will help establish rapport with the audience or lend credibility to your knowledge of the topic. For example, a recovering drug abuser might share this fact with listeners, if that's the topic. You might tell where you are from if it helps establish a positive atmosphere. Avoid telling a joke unless it's related to the subject and leads into the presentation logically.

"Today we're going to share . . . " or "Today we're going to explore . . . " would create a positive beginning. We like people to share and explore with us. You want to give people reasons to listen. Tell them why they want to listen—what's in it for them. As with lessons, beginning with "I'm going to tell you about . . . " is ineffective because it tends to exclude the audience. A well-chosen question or comment reflecting concern for the audience gives a stronger beginning.

Another technique is to start by arousing curiosity to create interest. The unexpected grabs attention. Make your introduction memorable but not shocking.

❋ *The Body*

The body, or main part, of a presentation conveys your message. It's essential that you make it clear and interesting. You have probably listened to speakers who ramble on and on, making it difficult for listeners to sort out what points are being made.

Organize your information by outlining what you want to say—as you would for a paper. Identify the main points you want to make, then the subpoints within them. Flesh out the outline by noting specific examples you will use.

Many good speakers enhance their listeners' understanding by referring to this structure as they talk. Phrases like "There are three main reasons that . . . and the first is . . . " help listeners take notes or organize their thoughts.

Consequently, more of the speaker's message is likely to be remembered. Sometimes visuals, discussed next, are used for this purpose.

❋ *Using Visuals*

Any element that adds variety, interest, or color can enhance your presentation. You might use computer-generated slides, transparencies, flip charts, posters, or videotapes. Refer to Chapter 10 for more specifics on visual media and follow these general guidelines:

- Use a visual when you think it will enhance your verbal explanation.
- Prepare your audience for viewing the visual before seeing it by giving appropriate guidance such as: "Look at . . ." "After seeing the videotape we will . . ." "You'll notice that. . . ." Verbalize what viewers should learn or understand from the visual.
- Use visual aids that contain only material directly pertinent to your topic. Eliminate whatever might divert the audience's attention to other matters.
- Keep visuals simple. Too much information on any one graphic can be overwhelming. When there's too much reading, the audience tends to read ahead rather than listen to you. A graphic should be like a visual outline with you providing the details.
- Create movement, but not too much. Use fly-ins with computer slides to increase and hold audience attention, but avoid the distraction of too much action.
- Remove a visual from sight when you are ready to move on to the next point.
- Give your attention to the audience, not to the visuals. Maintain eye contact by having a copy of what's being projected; glance at it rather than the screen.

✵ The Conclusion

As you conclude the presentation, it should be abundantly clear what you want the audience to do. It's like a call for action. Do you want the audience to get more exercise, lower their intake of saturated fat, vote in an upcoming election, or promote your curriculum? You might wrap up your presentation by answering a question you posed in the introduction. Regardless of the technique, the conclusion should bring to mind the major points made in the presentation. It should be remembered later as people reflect on the talk. It might be memorable because it's dramatic.

There's no need to say, "Now in conclusion . . ." This tends to send the message,

"You can stop listening." Some presenters say "thank you" to indicate that the speech is finished. If your conclusion is effective, it should be evident that you have finished. Thanking the audience for listening is like apologizing. It lessens your impact. Imagine if Patrick Henry had said, "Give me liberty or give me death! Thank you very much."

✵ Answering Questions

When you are asked a question, look at that questioner until he or she has finished speaking. If you can, take a step toward the individual. Unless the group is very small, repeat the question to the entire audience, then answer it. Address your response to the whole audience, not just to the person who posed the question.

If you don't know an answer, don't try to bluff one. It might be appropriate to say "I'll try to find the answer for you. If you give me your phone number or e-mail address later, I'll get in touch with you." If you're allowed time for your audience to ask questions and no one does, it may be because you did an excellent job of explaining your topic.

You can rate your presentation skills by using *Figure 24-5* on pages 338-339.

✵ Some Don'ts

Besides not using a podium and not thanking the audience, there are several other things you should consciously avoid doing and saying.

- **Don't apologize.** Avoid sentences like these:
  "I'm not as well prepared as I'd hoped, but . . ."
  "I don't know much about . . ."
  "I don't want to offend anyone, but . . ."

  If you don't know the subject, the audience will realize this without you mentioning it. Saying you don't want to offend anyone may do just that.
- **Avoid repetition.** When you are told something repeatedly, you begin to wonder, "Does this speaker think we're stupid?" Summarizing is not considered repetition.
- **Avoid giving too many numbers and statistics in a speech.** Statistics are very difficult to follow unless they're portrayed visually as well as orally.

Figure 24-5

JUDGING PRESENTATIONS

Use the following scale to rate the presenter's effectiveness and the quality of the presentation.
10 = Outstanding,   8 = Very Good,   6 = Average,   4 = Fair,   2 = Poor

	10	8	6	4	2
1. **Introduction/Set:** Gained attention, interest. Stated topic and/or purpose clearly. Established credibility. Related topic to audience, previewed rest of presentation, provided transition into body of presentation. Comments:					
2. **Body of Presentation:** Well organized and effective. Interesting, smooth transitions. Presented at an appropriate rate of speed. Comments:					
3. **Content:** Accurate, appropriate. and narrow enough in scope to be well developed and fully explained in time allowed. Comments:					
4. **Audience Involvement:** Whether active or passive, effective and balanced throughout presentation with minimal self-reference. When feasible, used *you*, *we*, *our*, and *let's* instead of *I*, *me*, *my*, and *mine*. Comments:					
5. **Nonverbal Communication:** Strong eye contact, effective gesturing, minimal distracting mannerisms. Purposeful movement from place to place. Comments:					
6. **Speech:** Conversational and natural with notes used only as a guide. Words well chosen, vivid, articulated clearly, used appropriately. Pauses used effectively. Good voice inflection. Comments:					
7. **Visual(s):** Simple, clear, neat and clean. Only one topic per page. Easily read, attractive, good design, enough free space, effective use of color. Comments:					

Figure 24-5 (cont'd)

JUDGING PRESENTATIONS

	10	8	6	4	2
8. **Media:** Appropriate for audience, situation, content. Relevant. Comments:					
9. **Closure:** Reinforced central idea. Called for clear action. Was vivid, memorable. Comments:					
10. **Overall Presentation:** Involved audience passively or actively. Was well thought out. Held attention and provided growth experience for audience. Used imagination and/or creativity. Completed within time limit. Comments:					
				Total	_____

• **Avoid the word "little."** Saying "I have a little handout" or a "little poster" makes it seem unimportant.

 # Shaping Public Policy

Most elected officials try to represent their constituents. However, their perceptions of their constituents' views often depend on whom they hear from, how often they are contacted, and how persuasive the people's messages are.

❊ Compile Valid Information

Use specific information to add power to your messages about public policy. Collect data showing how your profession is being affected by budget cuts and tax changes or what needs are going unmet. These facts are important, but it's equally important to identify how individuals are being affected personally by cuts in funding. Describe how federal and state money is used to benefit specific groups of citizens, such as pregnant teens, abused children, and at-risk families.

❊ Contact Your Legislators

Contacting state and federal legislators is the most effective way of getting support on legislation. Letters, e-mails, and phone calls from constituents help legislators make up their mind on how to vote. Personal letters addressed to specific legislators are much more effective than form letters. A letter doesn't have to be long to be persuasive.

Here are a few suggestions for writing an effective letter or e-mail:

• **Address the recipient correctly.** For a U.S. representative, send it to: The Honorable (name), U.S. House of Representatives, Washington, D.C. 20515; or if a senator, The Honorable (name), U.S. Senate, Washington, D.C. 20510.

• **Be specific.** When writing about a particular bill, identify the bill by name and number. In the House, bills are listed H.R. (number) and in the Senate, S. (number). If you don't know the number, then give a description.

- **Write or e-mail early.** Messages that arrive at the last minute have less influence.
- **Be brief, but take time to give your own views.** If the topic you are writing about directly affects your life, state this. Give reasons for supporting or opposing legislation.
- **Be polite.** Name-calling, put-downs, and other negative approaches detract from the effectiveness of letters.
- **Ask for assistance.** Members of Congress are happy to answer questions and provide information.

Consider inviting local legislators to a meeting to learn about your programs. Send letters of invitation three to four weeks in advance, and call about a week in advance to confirm that the legislator is coming.

Explain why you are concerned about education in your field. Real-life stories are interesting, but limit them to a few examples that are to the point. If possible, have printed brochures or information to give out. Give legislators your website and e-mail addresses.

If legislators aren't able to visit your program, visit them in your state capital. Present a program with short testimonials from your clientele and/or set up a display focusing on the value of your program. Send thank-you notes to legislators who meet with you. Maintain contact to let the elected officials know that you are interested in the political process and that you will be watching the outcomes of votes.

✳ Develop Public Support

Get all the positive press coverage you can. Keep an eye on the media to determine which reporters are most likely to give you coverage. Let them know who you are, what your program is doing, and any special events planned. Contact them with information and ideas for articles. Here are other ways to communicate your message:

- Letters to the editor are especially appropriate if you are reacting to a recent editorial, news story, or letter to the editor. Perhaps you can point out an irony.
- In less populated areas, radio and TV talk shows often need guests to discuss current issues. You or some of your students or participants might be effective interviewees.
- Radio and TV call-in shows can help you make an impact. Have students, their parents, and other supporters call in and ask questions that give you the opportunity to communicate your message positively. You want to respond to misunderstandings and to predictions you disagree with, but avoid adopting a defensive attitude. Remember that it's much more effective to be proactive than reactive.
- Local community service channels usually welcome programs. Involve students, FCCLA and 4-H club members, athletic trainers, dietitians, or other individuals and groups with whom you work.

 # Sharing Your Story

Not every educator has a natural flair for marketing. In fact, the whole idea of making a concerted effort to sing your program's praises may seem very awkward. Actually, you are just sharing information about an important program that helps others. When you tell groups outside your program about your needs, successes, and dreams, good things happen.

With outside help, you can expand your opportunities to improve your learners' lives. That support may bring higher enrollments, additional funding, more equipment, backing for retaining or expanding your program, or many other positives.

Sharing the story of the work you believe in deeply brings some of the most appealing qualities to your marketing efforts—integrity and commitment.

Building Your Professional Portfolio

Stimulating Interest. For the courses you teach or will teach, develop course descriptions—and new names, if appropriate—to catch the attention and interest of potential students. Make certain your descriptions include the essence of course content.

Getting the Word Out. Design and write a news release, brochure, or flyer aimed at a particular audience on a topic of your choice. Along with the promotional piece, write a rationale for your choice of the marketing vehicle and a distribution plan that fits your audience.

Presentation Skills. Develop a new presentation, or revise one you have given, based on the guidelines in the chapter. Include written versions of your introduction and conclusion, an outline and notes for the body of the presentation, any visuals, and information on the audience for the presentation.

Public Policy. Choose a state or national legislative topic related to education or your course of study. Research pending legislation and write a letter to legislators expressing your viewpoint and giving supportive information. Send your letters and keep copies for your portfolio.

Chapter 25

Managing Your Personal and Professional Lives

Ginny Felstehausen, Ph.D.
Professor, Family & Consumer Sciences Education
Texas Tech University

A master in the art of living draws no sharp distinction between work and play, labor and leisure, mind and body, education and recreation. Masters hardly know which is which. They simply pursue visions of excellence through whatever they are doing and leave others to determine whether they are working or playing. To themselves, they are always doing both.

Author Unknown

At a recent professional meeting of family and consumer sciences educators, new teachers were discussing their first year of teaching. All were excited about their classroom experiences. They genuinely liked their colleagues and appreciated the support from their administrators. They were frustrated with their schedules, however. All commented on their 11-hour workdays. The married teachers lamented that they had very little "quality time" with their spouses. The educators who were stretched the thinnest, however, were those with children who were trying to "do it all."

Their question was, "If I can't manage my personal and family life and my career, how can I teach others how to successfully manage their lives?" This chapter will provide some guidelines for you to follow in organizing your personal life. Remember the words of Golda Meir: "I must govern the clock, not be governed by it."

Focusing on the Connections in Your Life

Everyone agrees that the days of *Ozzie and Harriet* and *Leave It to Beaver* are long gone. Enter the two-income families where both partners are employed full-time and where, according to the latest research, the family they have created is one in which all members are thriving, albeit not without challenges and stress. At the same time, add the single head-of-household families where one parent is attempting to "do it all," often without much outside support and/or help.

There are a number of ways that the family and work connection can be examined. Researchers have based their studies on a number of different theoretical frameworks.

For many years, the two systems—family and work—were viewed as segmented, separate, and distinct. This "separate sphere" theoretical model suggested that the family be the domestic haven for women and the workplace serve as the public arena for men. Basically, the strong connection between the two spheres was largely ignored.

Later, family researchers began to acknowledge that personal and family life couldn't be isolated from the workplace, nor could the workplace be completely segregated from the home and family. Therefore, the spillover model was proposed. This recognizes that either the work system or the personal/family system may have spillover effects on the other, and simultaneous membership in the two systems can bring stress, strain, and overload for individuals, families, and work groups.

Another explanation of the family and work relationship is that women and men use one area to compensate for another area in their lives. As Arlie Hochschild reported in *The Time Bind: When Work Becomes Home & Home Becomes Work (1997)*, it isn't uncommon for workers to have confidence that they can get the job done at work more so than at home. This personal belief, in turn, translates into workers who admit they usually come to work early "just to get away from the house." These workers also may be the first to volunteer to stay late to meet a deadline, again in an attempt to avoid dealing with their home and family. By the same token, the reverse type of compensation can occur. If a job isn't going well, a worker may simply do the minimum or find reasons not to go to work at all. In turn, such an employee spends more time with family and friends to compensate for the negative feelings he or she feels at work.

Today, family and work researchers are most likely to utilize the interactive systems theoretical approach to explain the very complex relationship between family and work. Basically, this theory recognizes the mutual interdependence between what goes on at home and what happens in the workplace, and takes into account the reciprocal influences of the two. It also acknowledges the joint effects of both spheres on the psychological and social conditions of the individual.

Visualize two intersecting circles with you, the individual, in the area common to both. You are part of both circles—the home/family and the workplace. There is independence in each, but, at the same time, there is an interaction between both the family and workplace. In many ways, the relationship between the two is reciprocal. The family and the workplace are subject to change and, as they do, the relationship between the two reflects even more change. In other words, the relationship between the home/family and work is a dynamic one and one that we, as educators, must take into account in our workplaces, as well as in our personal lives. *Figure 25-1* below, the "Mutual Interdependence Model," depicts this theory.

Figure 25-1

Mutual Interdependence Model
Personal, Home/Family, and Work Connections

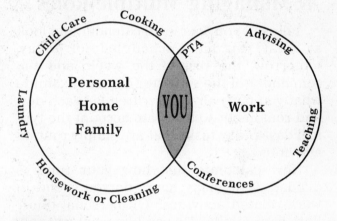

The Roles You Play

No matter what your job is—educator, learner, curriculum specialist, Extension agent, or program coordinator—you are playing many roles. If you make a list of all the roles you currently are handling, the extent of your involvement may surprise you.

Possible examples are: student, sibling, daughter/son, grandchild, niece/nephew, spouse, parent, stepparent, employee, significant other, advisor, caregiver, club member or officer, volunteer, friend, and neighbor. After making your own list, ask yourself the following questions:

- Which of these roles do you consider to be your most important role?
- If you have a significant other, which role do you think he or she would consider to be your most important?
- Which roles will you probably retain throughout your life?
- Which roles might you have in the future that you don't have now?

As you reflect on your responses, keep in mind that "employee" is but one of the many roles you are or will be playing in your life. As you begin a new career, "employee" may well be the most important or demanding role in your life. It isn't uncommon, however, for this role to consume so much of your time that you find yourself neglecting other roles that are extremely important to you. Remember that you do need a life outside of your career!

✳ Managing Multiple Roles

Take out your personal calendar and look at what you have scheduled for today, tomorrow, the rest of the week, and the remainder of the semester or year. Examine what you have already written for each day, and remember to take into account the typical day-to-day tasks that are simply routine activities.

Now calculate just how your time is divided. How many hours do you spend in work-related activities? On personal time? With your family? Do you like what you see, or are you frustrated with the way you spend the 24 hours a day, seven days a week? Try to match up your daily activities to the various roles you identified earlier. Respond to these questions:

- Is it ever difficult to choose which role to assume at a given time?
- If you answered "yes" to the preceding question, which role(s) seem to cause you the most problem(s)? Do you find the problems annoying, troublesome, or really difficult to handle?
- Ask yourself just how important it is that you do everything that's included in your schedule. Are you required to do these tasks or do you really *want* to be involved in the specific activities?

- How would you feel about giving up some of your control over a particular responsibility? Would you be comfortable watching someone else do it, even if it weren't done quite the way you've always done it?
- Could any of your roles be shared cooperatively with others? Perhaps even delegated to someone else?

Be honest with yourself as you reflect on these questions. For some people, dovetailing tasks—doing many things at one time and going in many different directions—may seem perfectly all right. At least it may seem to work most of the time. For others, however, managing these numerous roles may seem overwhelming.

In truth, almost everybody needs help managing time. Diane usually spends about 30 minutes a day complaining to coworkers or the building custodian about how much she has to do that evening. Karen cooks *and* cleans up afterwards because her children do a haphazard job. Chris unwinds by going online after dinner—the "few minutes" often turn into 90 minutes or more. Can you identify any time bandits in your life? How much TV do you watch each day? Each week? How long do you talk on the phone? Does your work always have to be perfect? Or, is procrastination your problem? With all the demands in life, it's important to examine personal management strategies.

 ## The Challenge of Managing Multiple Roles

Balancing personal needs, family, and work isn't easy, and managing multiple roles is a challenge for most people. There are no easy answers. Neither are there any quick fixes for the kinds of situations that most of you face—or will face in the future. Making your life more manageable begins with identifying your goals, setting your priorities, planning for the future, and making a personal commitment to control your time and carry out your plans. Clarifying your own views about what you think is important and what your top priorities are will make it easier to live a balanced life.

✳ Exploring Values and Setting Goals

Ask yourself: What is really important in my life? Your values might include family togetherness, a good education, caring for others, and worthwhile employment. Your parents and other family members, friends and peers, religious beliefs, teachers, mentors, the media, school, and the workplace have influenced your values.

Understanding your values will help you set career and personal goals. For example, if you value spending time with your family, one of your goals will be to make time to be with them. If weekend trips to visit your family aren't possible, keeping in touch with regular phone calls and e-mails helps maintain those bonds. Likewise, if you value helping others, you will find a way to volunteer your time, possibly during the summer when your schedule is lighter.

Your goals enable you to put values into practice. Think of your short-term goals as the more manageable goals that you hope to accomplish in a relatively short time. This may include planning a program for a community group, writing a test for your parenting class, helping a group prepare for 4-H Achievement Days, or entertaining friends on Saturday.

As for long-term goals, look at what you want to be, what you want to do, and what's really important to you. Ask yourself: What are my dreams? Where do I see myself in five years? Ten years? The answers to these questions can be the foundation of your long-term goals.

Another concept that enters into this personal analysis is setting priorities. Priorities help you focus on your most important goals. You are a unique individual, and your priorities are yours alone. They are not your parents', your teacher's, or your best friend's. They are yours. What may be a top priority to you may not be at all important to someone else, and vice versa.

One point to keep in mind is that your priorities reflect your values and personal goals. These priorities also should reflect your relationships with people who are important to you. These people may be your family, close friends, colleagues, and employer.

Setting priorities helps you accomplish specific goals, as well as achieve these goals within specific time frames. And, not surprisingly, achieving your goals is directly linked to effective resource management.

Before you go on to read about time management, take time to explore your values and priorities. List your top five priorities. In other words, identify what you really believe is important in *your* life. Sorting out these priorities is pivotal to overall success in managing your life.

✳ Discovering How You Spend Your Time

Hannah is up by five every morning. She enjoys a brisk walk with her neighbor, followed by a shower and leisurely breakfast. Hannah reads the newspaper from front to back and still arrives at work early. Her time is very well managed, she believes, but evening meetings and commitments are a problem because she's always exhausted by 8:00 p.m. Do you agree that her time is well managed?

How about your own time management practices? *Figure 25-2* on page 346 provides a sample time diary, a follow-up to the activity on managing multiple roles that you completed earlier in the chapter. It involves tracking your activities for one week. Your findings may surprise you and help free you of some of the "clutter" in your life. Follow these steps:

- Estimate how much time you think you spend per week on your regular activities.
- Total the hours.
- If your number is over 168, the total number of hours in a week, rethink your original estimates and recalculate the total so that it equals or is below 168. Subtract that number from 168. Whatever is left is your estimate of hours that you spend in unscheduled activities.
- Now record exactly how you spend your time for the next seven days. In other words, keep a time diary. As you go through the week, write down what you do each hour, indicating when you started and stopped. Don't forget activities that don't seem like "activities," such as sleeping, relaxing, and watching TV or a movie.

Be as honest as possible. Beware of recording how you want to spend your time or how you think you should have spent your time.

- At the end of the week, go through your time diary. Figure how many hours you actually spent on the activities for which you earlier recorded estimates. Total the hours, rounding to half-hours. List the time you spent in each activity category.
- Compare your grand total to your estimated grand total. Then compare your *actual* activity hour totals to your *estimated* activity hour totals. What matches and what doesn't?

Figure 25-2

SAMPLE TIME DIARY

6:00	Up; started laundry; fixed hair and makeup; dressed
7:00	Bagel breakfast; filled car with gas; drove to school
8:00	Class
9:00	Class
10:00	Prep period; called field trip chaperones; graded tests
11:00	Class
12:00	Lunch. 25-minute walk with Tracy. Class at 12:40
1:00	Class
2:00	Class/pep assembly
3:00	FCCLA meeting
4:00	Shopped for groceries; bank; picked up Grandma's Rx
5:00	Microwaved dinner; ate; cleaned up; watered plants
6:00	Watched news; changed clothes; drove back to school
7:00	Back-to-school night with parents
8:00	↓
9:00	Checked e-mail; chatted with Drew and Sue
10:00	Ironed clothes for tomorrow; vacuumed; took bath
11:00	To bed

❋ Examining Your Time Management Skills

What did you learn about yourself as you examined your time diary? Did you actually spend the hours in the week the way you thought you would? What surprised you most about how you spent your time?

Perhaps your personal grooming or household chores consume more of your time than you realized.

Identify at least one change you would like to make in how you spend your time. Reflect on why you would like to make this change by asking these questions:

- What change(s) would you make to help with your daily scheduling?
- Does your schedule reflect your priorities?
- What do you need to change in your daily, weekly, and monthly schedule to improve your ability to achieve your goals?
- How can you use what you have learned about yourself in this activity to be more successful in managing your personal life, family, and career?

❋ Planning Role-Sharing Strategies

In today's fast-paced world, most people feel that there's so much to do and so little time. It's not unusual to feel rushed and that the "To Do" list is crammed with too many entries. For many, the dilemma seems to be a scenario like this: "I really like my job, but it is demanding. My life away from work is extremely important to me, too. If I spend time all the time I want to spend with my family and friends on the weekend, I won't be as well prepared for the coming week at work. Right now I'm simply trying to 'survive.' But I want to do more than that. How can I manage multiple roles so I don't always feel like there's too much to do and not enough time?"

Organization is one key to managing the many roles you play. Remember that you don't have to do everything yourself. It's possible, and often for the best, to delegate some of the tasks at work and at home to others. For some individuals, however, this may be easier said than done.

There are some basic role-sharing strategies that can help you lead a healthier, more satisfying life. Consider the following strategies that are modifications of a list originally developed by Joan Comeau at the Work and Family Institute:

- **You can't do it all yourself.** Recognize that there's no future in martyrdom—at least not a very happy one. Being a martyr can be exhausting and emotionally destructive in the long run. You don't have to do everything all of the time. It's acceptable to say "no." It's also within reason for you to say, "I can't do it now, but if you can wait until ___, I will be able to help you." Several people often can share a particular role very nicely.

- **Let go when others take over.** When giving up a task or activity to someone else, it's important to clarify or negotiate the details of the task or activity. Don't assume the person will know what you have in mind when you say: "Will you do ___ for me today?" Be careful not to make light of the request by saying, "Oh, it's easy to do," or "Anyone can do it." You may think it's a simple task that takes no time at all; it may be easy for you because you have been doing it for a while. It's likely that your replacement will take longer to complete the task the first time and may find it more difficult than he or she had expected. Also keep in mind that the other person may not complete the task exactly the same as you would, but *that is okay.* It may be very hard for you to "let go," and it may be even harder for you to see that the work doesn't quite meet your standards. Practice saying to yourself: "If Sally or John does this, it probably won't be done the same way as I would have done it *and that is okay.*"

- **Clarify roles when sharing responsibilities.** Understand the difference between "helping out" and "taking responsibility." Decide which you want in a role-sharing arrangement. Helping out usually implies that you retain control over the task. The "helper" probably will not assume full responsibility for following through in getting the activity done; he or she probably won't notice that it needs to be accomplished again in the future.

- **Remember the golden rule.** "Do unto others as you would have them do unto you" is a proven adage, though sometimes you may feel as though you are doing it all. That may be your perception, however, rather than reality. In most situations, role-sharing can be a two-way street. Try to reciprocate at some point when someone shares a role with you.

- **Review your priorities and standards.** Thoughtfully reflect on the importance of relationships vs. household or workplace needs. For example, is it essential that everything be completed today and done in a specific manner that meets your expectations? Do you have to be in control? Or, are there family members or colleagues with whom you can share the work and the results? Or, is working late to finish a project according to your standards worth missing a special event that you really wanted to attend? Along with looking at your priorities, it's important for you to step back for a moment and examine your standards. Are they realistic? Does everything need to be perfect? Don't regard perfectionism as a positive trait. Remember the adage: Nature does not demand that we be perfect; it only requires that we grow.

- **Keep an open dialogue with others.** Communicate regularly with your family, significant others, and coworkers. Discuss which tasks are essential to get done; which would be nice to get done, but aren't essential; and which tasks could be put off or eliminated. Look at who might actually like to do a task that you have always done, but now find it difficult to continue. Who would be good at it? Who needs a change and/or a challenge? Consider taking turns with chores no one wants to do all the time.

- **Expect role-sharing to require adjustments.** Role-sharing strategies inevitably lead to some stress and strain. Your family and coworkers may question the need for change. Be open and honest with others, and give the changes a chance to work. You may need to have written schedules at first so everyone involved is clear as to what each has agreed to do.

 # Managing Stress in Your Life

Stress seems to be a part of everyone's life. It doesn't seem to matter if you are a teacher, guidance counselor, teenage high school student, parent, or senior citizen.

Stress has been identified as America's top health problem. Surveys and research reports tell us that:

- About half of all adults suffer adverse health effects due to stress.
- Up to 90% of all visits to primary care physicians are for stress-related complaints or disorders.
- An estimated one million workers are absent on an average workday because of stress-related complaints.

Paul Rosch, a physician and president of the American Institute of Stress in Yonkers, NY, was quoted in an article in *Techniques* magazine, "Of the subgroups of teachers, high school teachers are under the most stress. Jobs themselves are not inherently stressful. But any occupation in which the individual perceives a great deal of responsibility and little decision capacity is going to be stressful." (2000)

How do *you* define stress? What signals does your body send indicating that your stress level is high? The dictionary defines stress as "a physical, chemical, or emotional factor that causes bodily or mental tension and may be a factor in disease causation."

❋ Locating the Stressors in Your Life

Not all stress is bad and some stress is unavoidable. It's part of life. To determine your current stress level, you will want to pinpoint the areas of stress overload in your life. Unless you know what the problem is, you won't be successful in identifying remedies that might be applied. You may already recognize that self-assessment isn't as easy as it first appears. For many, it's too easy to play down sensitive, very personal situations, but at the same time blow other things way out of proportion. For example, you may be going through a difficult time with a family member or close friend, but you don't want to share this information with colleagues. Your personal situation may cause you not to be yourself at work.

To facilitate the task of identifying your stressors, take a look at the "real world" around you. Most important, however, is that you be as honest and as thorough as possible in identifying the stressors in your life.

As you do your self-evaluation, divide situations, activities, or events into two major areas. Ask yourself the following questions:

- What problems go on in my world around me as a result of my interaction with it?
- What problems go on within me as a result of my interaction with my world?

Not surprisingly, each area impacts the other. For example, in your self-analysis you might clearly see that there's a substantial amount of conflict between you and your family, you and your supervisor, you and your students, or you and your friends. This, in turn, could conceivably lead to increased tenseness in your body which could manifest itself in a number of ways, such as frequent tension headaches.

There are more than 50 common signs of stress. Doctors see patients daily with stress-related symptoms. Some warning signs of stress and tension in *your* life may include:

- Working late, more obsessively than usual, or harder than seems appropriate for the situation.
- Having difficulty making decisions, large and small, which normally could be made easily.
- Daydreaming or fantasizing excessively.
- Always wishing to be somewhere else.
- Gaining or losing weight.
- Digestive problems.
- Drinking or smoking more than usual.
- Experiencing depression.
- Sleep problems/nightmares.
- Making more mistakes than usual.
- Feeling "keyed up."
- Back pain and/or shoulder, neck and jaw tension.

If you are feeling overwhelmed by stress or would just like to decrease its impact on your life, there are strategies for helping you do so. The following sections suggest proven approaches. You can look for additional ideas in print and electronic resources.

❋ Relieving Stress

When you are evaluating your current ability to cope with stress, it's important to remember you are a unique individual with a unique situation. *You* can and should be in charge.

An essential ingredient of any stress management program is paying attention to your basic needs. These include nutrition, sleep, exercise and relaxation, and social support.

✳ Nutrition

It's extremely important that you heed the truth in the statement, *"You are what you eat."* As you know, your daily food intake is the energy source that provides replenishment for all your metabolic systems. Inadequate nourishment will contribute toward deficiencies and eventual breakdown. Your pressured lifestyle may prompt you to hurry, eat on the run, miss meals, or skimp on nutritious foods. Eventually, this pattern can lead to a lack of physical energy to cope with stress. Remember to follow the ABCs of the Dietary Guidelines for Americans:

• **A**im for fitness.
• **B**uild a healthy base.
• **C**hoose sensibly.

Every meal doesn't have to be home-cooked. It's possible, even with fast food and deli selections, to make healthful choices. Stock up on frozen meals that can be popped into the microwave. Better yet, when you have some time on a weekend or day off, prepare some favorite dishes that can be frozen for the days you have no time to cook.

✳ Sleep

Sleep is another critical basic that, if abused, can sabotage a stress-management plan. Sleep deprivation can be a serious health threat and is more common than once believed. If you are tempted to sleep less to add some useful time slots to your day, think of another way to save time. Inadequate sleep can lead to irritability, as well as problems with short-term memory and concentration.

While sleep needs vary from person to person, the National Sleep Foundation recommends eight hours of sleep for adults. Their 2001 Sleep in America Poll, however, revealed that only 37 percent of adults sleep eight hours nightly; 31 percent sleep less than seven hours. If you lack energy, and sleep fitfully at night, chances are that you are suffering from a stress overload or, perhaps, a sleep disorder. Check with a health professional if sleep problems don't go away when your stress is decreased.

✳ Exercise and Relaxation Techniques

Participating in moderate exercise is an excellent way to combat unhealthy stress reactions. The Dietary Guidelines for Americans recommend that you spend at least 30 minutes on moderate physical activity most days. To begin or return to an exercise regime, choose one or more forms of exercise that you enjoy and participate in them on a regular basis. Just taking a few minutes at lunch to walk around the block or your building may help reduce your stress level, too.

Recognize what activities you consider relaxing. Be specific when exploring your options. Things such as reading for pleasure, listening to music, and taking a bath may be relaxing for you. Also consider beginning to practice relaxation techniques, such as yoga, meditation, deep-breathing exercise, and muscle relaxation. Decide which relaxation technique works for you and practice it daily.

✳ Social Support

The last of the basic tools in stress management is having a good social support system. A lack of socialization will definitely lower your ability to cope with stress. Consider taking an exercise class or regular walks or bike rides with a friend or family member. This will help fulfill your needs for both social interaction and physical activity.

Talk to others (friends, relatives, or colleagues) about what you are going through. Share your feelings. Having a conversation with someone you trust and care about lets you know that you are not the only one having a bad day or experiencing a very difficult situation. Stay in touch with family and friends. Let them provide love, support, and guidance. Don't try to cope alone.

You also might consider joining (or starting) a support group for others who may be experiencing a similar stressful situation. You will find that it's extremely helpful to find an environment where you can "safely" share your feelings.

On the other hand, if you have friends with negative outlooks on life, minimize the time you spend with them. Don't add to your stress by making it your job to "fix" them.

✳ Putting It All Together

Now that you have looked inwardly at yourself and have examined some of the specific suggestions for stress management, the challenge becomes a personal one for you. It's up to you to put together a program that is tailored for your unique lifestyle. Ask yourself, "How important is an event or situation that's causing stress?" Is it a "must do" activity or is it something you would describe as "nonessential?"

There are a number of stress busters you can try in your quest for improved stress management. Some you might want to consider include:

- Select coping strategies that you are comfortable with and will enjoy. Be creative, even playful, about this selection process. Design your program not so much because you feel compelled to do it or view it as a duty or necessity, but rather as anticipation of something you really will enjoy doing.
- Acknowledge that stress management involves your total lifestyle. At the same time, accept the fact that you can't change everything all at once. It's not only impossible, but thinking you can and should will only create further stress. What and who you are today is the result of developments over your lifetime. You didn't arrive where you are overnight, nor can you change overnight. Implement the desired changes in your life in stages. Set specific manageable and attainable goals, one by one. Remember the saying, "Progress, not perfection."
- Don't think that your overall coping strategy is set in concrete for the rest of your life. Be flexible. Circumstances in your life will change, and so should your stress management responses change to meet those new situations.

A final key in stress management is balance. People's lives tend to become unbalanced because of the many pressures and changes that occur in society. Make a conscious effort to stay aware of this social, cultural, and career imbalance process. Help yourself to restore equilibrium within your personal life. That dramatically increases your chances for health, happiness, and fulfillment. Above all, remember it's essential to be your own best friend.

Working on Balance in Your Life

Balancing your thoughts and attention is difficult when so many needs and demands are experienced every day. It's hard to balance resources and desires. With so many options and opportunities, it's not easy to balance priorities. As you examine your life, ask yourself, "Is the objective to get to a certain destination or to enjoy the journey?" Additional questions you might want to consider:

- Will it matter in ten years?
- What do I need less of?
- How can I make this simpler?

Although many people juggle a number of activities and maintain balance, others struggle with finding that balance because there's so much going on in their lives. The problem with having dozens of priorities is that it's almost impossible to remember them all. During the past decade there's been great interest in "simple living" or "voluntary simplicity." Reference materials on this topic are widely available.

✳ Balancing Tips

Many people want to know: What can a person do to get his or her life in balance? First of all, come to grips with the fact that you're only human. Then work on personal skills to provide you with a strong foundation upon which to balance the multiple roles you have, and will continue to have, in your life. Tips to help balance personal, family, and work include:

- Know that often you have choices over how you feel and react.
- Decide what is and isn't important in your life. Imagine that you'd really like to go to a condominium association meeting, but

you've had commitments every evening for a week. You decide to ask your neighbor who's attending to let you know if any important business comes up.

- Ask yourself: What is best for *me*?
- Don't be too hard on yourself. Stop comparing yourself with others. Remember that everyone is an individual with unique strengths and weaknesses.
- Make a time commitment to yourself. Remind yourself that this is being smart, not selfish. You aren't much use to yourself, your family, or your learners when you are upset, sick, or depressed. Give yourself a gift of some personal time each week. Treat yourself occasionally to something you really like to do. It could be a walk in the park, a massage, or a meal in a favorite restaurant.
- Increase your awareness of how you are living life: how you are eating, sleeping, exercising, and responding to stress. Keep a diary or journal. Get into the habit of jotting down a few thoughts at the end of each day. Reflect on what you have done to take care of yourself.
- Be adaptable. Keeping an accurate, complete schedule in your planner is an excellent way to stay on top of things in your busy life. But remember, things don't always happen as planned. Be versatile when plans change.
- Review your strong points and feel good about what you have going for yourself. Have a "brag" folder in your desk drawer.

When you receive correspondence from students, clients, families with whom you have worked, and administrators who have acknowledged your good work, save them in this folder. Read them when you feel in the need for a morale boost.

- Set realistic goals for improving certain areas in your life. For instance, technology changes so rapidly that it's easy to fall behind in one's knowledge and capabilities in developing presentations, preparing reports, and using the latest graphics. Most people don't need to be an expert in all areas of technology. A helpful approach is to take time to master those new developments that truly will aid your career without feeling as though you need to know it all.
- Seek and accept help. If you don't have time to make treats for the bake sale, perhaps your friend or sister would make them if you bought the ingredients. Ask a staff member to help prepare the visuals for your presentation at the health fair scheduled for Friday.
- Pay attention to your successes. Give yourself small, frequent rewards. It may be as simple as stopping for an ice cream cone or buying a bunch of daisies at the supermarket.
- Be involved with others. This leaves you less time to dwell on your own problems. Build a network of supportive people.
- Enjoy the good times. Plan for fun, laughter, and recreation. Laughter really is great medicine. Use it freely.

References

Hochschild, A.R. (1997). The time bind: When work becomes home and home becomes work. New York: Metropolitan Books.

Lozada, M. (2000). Teachers . . . be revitalized. Techniques, 75, January.

http://www.simpleliving.net The Simple Living Network. (Accessed March 12, 2002)

http://www.sleepfoundation.org The National Sleep Foundation. (Accessed March 21, 2002)

http://www.stress.org The American Institute of Health. "Stress—America's #1 Health Problem." (Accessed March 8, 2002)

Building Your Professional Portfolio

Analyzing Time Usage. Complete a time diary for at least one typical work/school day and one day off, as suggested in the chapter. Use the diaries to determine time-use patterns you would like to change. For two of these, devise specific plans for the change and identify how you would use the time saved.

Sharing a Role. Identify one role you do or might share with another person. Using the suggestions in the chapter, make a plan that would help ensure the collaboration goes smoothly.

Reducing Stress. Choose one significant cause of stress in your life that you want to lessen. Brainstorm ways you could accomplish this, then develop specific strategies for doing so.

Teaching Management Skills. Plan a lesson on some aspect of personal management that would be useful for learners you teach now or those you plan to teach in the future.

Chapter 26

Growing as a Professional

Now that you have prepared to be a professional educator, it's time to find a position where you can put your skills to work. This final chapter lays the foundation for getting a job or changing jobs, for avoiding legal entanglements, and for joining professional organizations. To be an effective educator, you need to continue learning for the rest of your life.

A job search is a learning experience in itself. The sooner you begin the process, the better prepared you will be and the more confident you will feel. Most successful job searches require a lot of thought and effort. The three basic steps in the process are self-awareness, career awareness, and taking action. You have already considered your strengths, skills, interests, values, goals, and areas needing improvement in order to choose your career field. You have at least started the next step by identifying and exploring the career opportunities that are available in that field. The final step involves making decisions about the types of jobs you want to consider and actively working to secure a job.

 ## Initiating a Job Search

Many job seekers play a game of chance in searching for a job. Some wait too long to start the process and miss out on good opportunities. Others depend solely on classified ads, personnel agencies, and mass mailings of their résumés to find a position. You can avoid many job-hunting frustrations by starting early, having a game plan, marketing your skills effectively, and staying organized. All will help get you to the job interview stage.

☀ Focusing Your Search

While you may have planned to be a registered dietitian counseling diabetic patients when you were a sophomore in high school, not everyone has such specific plans. Even if you started out with a clear career goal in mind, it's likely that you've learned about additional opportunities throughout your course of study. It's very helpful to find out as much as you can about the variety of jobs linked to your academic area. You can talk to people working in your field, check out job descriptions on the Internet and in professional publications, and discuss your options with your teachers and advisor. This helps you refine your goals. By the time you are ready to begin a job search, you should have narrowed your options to a few specific positions.

Think about your ideal job. What responsibilities would you have? Do you want to teach in a formal educational setting? If so, what level of students would you prefer? Or, do you want to work for a nonprofit agency, a health provider, the Cooperative Extension system, a trade organization, a small company, or a huge corporation? What geographic area do you prefer? Do you want an urban, suburban, or rural location? How much overtime are you willing to work?

Using your ideal job as a base, consider what other alternatives would be acceptable to you. Would you be willing to work in a different type of educational setting, with learners of another age, or for an employer in another category? Would you work in a different location, if necessary? If you know up-front what your parameters are, you may broaden your search beyond your ideal job. You may consider career opportunities you never imagined.

❋ Finding Job Openings

There are many ways to find out about job openings. Some methods work for all types of jobs, while others work best for certain types. For example, schools may advertise openings in the local paper, through university placement offices or career centers, on websites, and through state, county, or district educational offices. You are unlikely to find a secondary teaching position through an employment agency. However, that's one place you might contact for a job as a health educator for a large business. A company's or district's website may also list openings. If you are unsure where to find out about openings for particular types of jobs, ask your professors or people in similar settings.

Colleges and universities often hold job fairs for students graduating in various disciplines. Potential employers looking for additional staff with background in a particular field send representatives to give out information and make initial contact with students. Keep in mind that most schools' placement or career centers continue to offer services to graduates throughout their careers.

❋ Networking

You have probably heard, "It's not what you know, but who you know." That's not necessarily true, but having contacts, especially in your career area, can open doors for you. When used for a job search, *networking* involves finding and making connections with people who can expand your career understanding and help you find out about jobs that may not be advertised. Learning more about how schools, businesses, or organizations function can help you refine your job objective, find additional places that list job openings, and appear more knowledgeable in interviews. Networking consists of making your career interests known and gathering information from others rather than applying for a specific position. Taking time to do so can pay off. It has been estimated that networking leads to as many as 80 percent of the positions filled each year. During their career, many professionals continue to network with colleagues, often through organizations, in order to learn, grow, and find out about additional career opportunities.

Begin your job search by making a networking plan. Determine what information you are seeking. Set goals. For example, you may decide to contact three people each week for a specified period of time. Consider teaming up with a friend with similar job interests to expand your field of contacts.

Use the following six steps to guide you through the networking process:

1. **Develop your list of people to contact.** Start by listing possible contacts. Using categories such as teachers, advisors, parents, friends, friends' parents, neighbors, religious leaders, and professional acquaintances will help stimulate your thinking. Although most of those on your list may not work in your field of interest, they might know someone who does. Decide which contacts are likely to be of most help.

2. **Research and prepare.** Gather basic information about each of your top potential contacts. Identify how you think each might help you and decide what questions you want to ask.

3. **Write a letter of introduction.** Include who you are and what you would like from the person. This could range from a suggestion on whom to contact in your field to a request for a meeting with the person. Enclose your résumé if it seems appropriate.

4. **Use your contacts respectfully.** If you want to speak with a contact, set up an appointment. Keep to time limits. Listen attentively to what a contact says, adjusting your goals for the meeting based on what you are learning.

5. **Ask for referrals.** Ask a contact for the names of other people who might help you and whether you can use his or her name when contacting these people.

6. **Follow up.** Ask contacts if you can keep them posted. Request that they keep in touch with you. Send thank-you notes, enclosing a résumé if you haven't already provided one.

Develop a list of questions you might ask contacts. Choose those most appropriate for each person. Here are some sample questions you might ask a network contact in your field to learn more about his or her work.

Figure 26-1 on page 356 lists additional networking tips. Keep your networking plan on schedule by remembering your purpose and setting deadlines for yourself.

✳ Whom to Contact About Employment

The traditional job search approach is to send a résumé and cover letter to a specific person, identified by name, who has the authority to hire or to make hiring recommendations. This may be the school superintendent, a department chair, the division manager, or the head of the agency. This person may not only have the power to hire you, but also to create a position for you. Furthermore, the individual may anticipate openings that haven't yet been posted. Research shows that simply sending many non-individualized form letters and résumés is generally ineffective. You also may send your letter and résumé electronically.

Some job seekers try to contact potential employers directly. Calling on the telephone

---

QUESTIONS FOR NETWORKING CONTACTS

Preparation
- What credentials and prior experience are required for entry into this kind of employment?
- How did you prepare for this work?

Present Job
- What do you do during a typical workweek?
- What skills are most important for effective performance in this work?
- What is most rewarding about your job?

Lifestyle
- What obligations does your work place upon your personal time?
- How much flexibility do you have in terms of attire, hours of work, vacation time, place of residence?
- How often do people in your line of work change jobs?

Career Future/Alternatives
- If things develop as you would like, what career changes do you see for yourself in the future?
- How rapidly and in what direction is this career field growing?
- If the work you do were suddenly unavailable, what other types of work could you do?
- What other types of employers hire someone with your background?
- What are some current trends which might shape the future of your field?

Job Search
- How do people find out about jobs in this field? Are they advertised in newspapers? By word of mouth? In trade magazines? By the human resources department?
- Do people normally have to move to another organization to advance or can they move up within this organization?
- If you were to hire someone to work with you today, which of the following factors would be most important in your hiring decision and why?
  Educational credentials
  Past work experience
  Personality traits
  Specific skills
- Do you have any suggestions on how I could improve my résumé?

Figure 26-1

═ NETWORKING TIPS ═

Do	Don't
• Do consider everyone a potential contact.	• Don't approach people with a "What can you do for me?" attitude.
• Do learn something about your contact's organization, company, or school.	• Don't arrive for an appointment without being prepared.
• Do meet in person, if you can, according to the individual's schedule and convenience.	• Don't ask contacts to pass your résumé around. If they are willing to do so, they will offer.
• Do prepare thoughtful questions. Identify what you hope to get from this meeting.	• Don't ask for an interview or a job.
• Do ask open-ended questions so you don't end up with mainly yes and no answers.	• Don't take up more time than was agreed upon.
• Do be as specific as possible about your skills and what you're looking for.	• Don't give the impression you're looking for just any job. Have some focus.
• Do be polite and show appreciation. Ask for names of other people who might be willing to talk with you.	• Don't be discouraged if someone is not helpful or willing to meet with you. Don't take it personally. Move on to your next contact.
• Do ask for a business card before you leave.	• Don't "bad mouth" any past employer.
• Do write thank-you letters. Let contacts know how they have helped you.	• Don't lose patience. It can take time for the seeds planted through networking to grow.
• Do keep the door open and follow up. Consider sending a note to update your contact on your progress or success in securing a job.	

is a timesaving approach, but it may be difficult to reach the decision-making individual. However, if you can reach this person you will find out if there's a position available that is suitable for you.

If you attempt a phone contact, carefully think through what you are going to say. You may want to jot down key points or even practice your message ahead of time. The person you reach is probably busy. Your message will have to "hit home" in a very brief, effective, and positive way if the "phone-an-employer" approach is to be successful.

It is also acceptable to apply for a position or inquire about openings in person. Dress in professional attire and go to the human resources or personnel department or the main receptionist. Be very courteous to receptionists and secretaries; their impres-sions of you can be important. Ask for an application, leave a résumé, and request an interview if it seems appropriate. Of course you should never walk directly into a super-intendent's, director's, or high-level man-ager's office. You can follow up on your personal visit with a phone call.

❋ Creating Your Résumé

A résumé is a concise document that summarizes your education, work experiences, and accomplishments. Its purpose is to give your potential employer a picture of your qualifications and a good idea of how you can contribute to the organizations. A résumé may also be needed if you apply for a scholarship, internship, or to graduate school. Few jobs are offered on the basis of a résumé alone. However, a well-written résumé that highlights solid skills can get you past the initial screening that determines which applications will receive further consideration.

There are two basic formats for a résumé: chronological and functional. In a *chronological résumé*, information is organized in terms of time, the most recent items being placed first. This format is more traditional and showcases work experience and growth. In a *functional résumé*, information is presented in terms of skills. This style works well if you are beginning your career because it emphasizes your skills, rather than your work record. *Figure 26-2* on page 358 shows a chronological résumé. *Figure 26-3* on page 359 shows a functional résumé.

With either format, the layout of a résumé should be concise, uncluttered, and visually pleasing. The content should include experiences that are most relevant to the type of work or academic program you are seeking.

The writing style for résumés is different from that in a letter of application. Phrases, rather than whole sentences, are used. Items in a list, such as your responsibilities on a particular job, are preceded by a bullet, asterisk, or some other symbol. Consistency of style is important.

List the items under each main entry in the same order.

✳ Résumé Sections

A résumé is divided into sections to make the information included easy to find. The names of these sections and their order vary somewhat depending on the style of résumé, the experiences and skills you want to stress, and the type of job you are seeking. Your objective always comes first and references are placed at the end. More specific information on developing common résumé sections follows. Many books and Internet sites also provide good suggestions.

- **Contact Information.** List your name, address, phone number, and e-mail address. Your name should be slightly larger and boldface so it stands out. Make it easy for the reader to find you. For example, you might want to give two addresses—your present address and your permanent address.
- **Professional Objective.** This is a one- or two-sentence statement that concisely

indicates the type of position or scholarship you are seeking. The statement should convey a sense of purpose and direction. Your objective may be fairly broad to apply to a variety of job opportunities, but it shouldn't be vague. Instead of including an objective in your résumé, you can address this point in your cover letter.
- **Education.** List the institution you most recently attended first. Give its location, your major, your degree, graduation date, and any specialized course work related to the position sought. List other colleges and universities attended, but don't give high school information unless the school you attended might have special significance to the reader. Honors and awards can be listed in this section or in a separate section. However, don't make a separate heading if there's only one entry for a category. A one-item entry looks stronger when part of another group of information.
- **Professional Experience/Development or Related Experiences.** Depending upon your background, use the most appropriate of these terms for the title of this section. You may include volunteer work, internship experiences, campus activities, and special academic projects. You can include paid employment here or in a separate section, depending on the number of jobs you have held. Include general skills that are important for most jobs and any specific skills related to your employment objective. Also highlight personal management skills, such as having good judgment, being adaptable, or being reliable. Begin each description with a strong active verb such as these:

achieved	led
administered	participated
began	planned
completed	presented
conducted	produced
coordinated	provided
created	reorganized
demonstrated	revised
developed	scheduled
directed	set up
expanded	supervised
improved	taught
increased	trained

Figure 26-2

SAMPLE CHRONOLOGICAL RÉSUMÉ

<table>
<tr><td colspan="2" align="center">

NAME

Street address
City, State Zip Code
Phone number (work)
Phone number (home)
E-mail address

</td></tr>
<tr>
<td>EDUCATION</td>
<td>

University of _____, City, State
Bachelor of Science, cum laude or other designation
May 20 ___
Major: _____
Minor: _____

Previous Postsecondary Institution, City, State (if applicable)
Dates Attended

</td>
</tr>
<tr>
<td>RELATED EXPERIENCES</td>
<td>

Position Title, Organization, City, State
Description of position responsibilities using action verbs, not complete sentences. (See action verbs on page 357.) Target populations served.
Month/Year to Month/Year
OR
Position Title, Organization, City, State
Descriptive action verb statements
Month/Year to Month/Year

</td>
</tr>
<tr>
<td>GENERAL EMPLOYMENT</td>
<td>

Position Title, Company, City, State
Descriptive action verb statements
Month/Year to Month/Year

</td>
</tr>
<tr>
<td>HONORS</td>
<td>

Name of Award, brief description giving significance of award
Name of Honor Society, qualifications for membership
Dean's List, number of semesters (if three or more)

</td>
</tr>
<tr>
<td>ACTIVITIES</td>
<td>

Position, Organization, Location (Institution or City, State)
Description of involvement or achievements using action verbs
Years involved

</td>
</tr>
<tr>
<td>PROFESSIONAL MEMBERSHIPS</td>
<td>

Current listing of national, regional, and local organizations of which you are a member. Include related committees or leadership positions. Include dates if relevant.

</td>
</tr>
<tr>
<td>INTERESTS</td>
<td>Include personal interests if they are related to your field or are unique.</td>
</tr>
<tr>
<td>REFERENCES</td>
<td>

Available from The Center for Career Services, University of_____, Address, phone number, and e-mail
OR
Available upon request

</td>
</tr>
</table>

Figure 26-3

SAMPLE FUNCTIONAL RÉSUMÉ

NAME
Street address
City, State Zip Code
Phone number (work)
Phone number (home)
E-mail address

OBJECTIVE
Teacher of Family and Consumer Sciences in an urban middle school

QUALIFICATIONS SUMMARY
- Created and taught consumer unit to Grade 7 Life Skills students
- Maintained appropriate discipline while working as an aide with special needs students
- Gained ten years professional experience as a teacher's aide in a city high school
- Planned and created a Teachers' Resource Library

CERTIFICATION
Illinois K-12 Certification in Family and Consumer Sciences, Health

PROFESSIONAL EXPERIENCE

Planning Curriculum
- Developed unit and lesson plans for special needs students
- Wrote and edited modules used by homebound students

Developing Teaching Materials
- Developed Life Skills learning activities, Internet-based modules, and tests for middle school
- Created exhibits, displays, and bulletin boards for Family and Consumer Sciences Department while serving as an aide

Collaborating on a Team
- Conducted assessment of graduates who took courses in all academic areas of the unit
- Designed specialized storage area for quick access to teaching materials
- Revised and upgraded library systems to meet changing information needs of all department programs

EMPLOYMENT HISTORY
Teachers' Aide in Family and Consumer Sciences, High School, City, State, Dates
Assistant Camp Director, Name of Camp, Town, State, Dates

EDUCATION
Associate of Arts,_____Community College, City, State, Graduation Month/Year
Bachelor of Science, Major in Family and Consumer Sciences Education, University of _____, City, State, May 20 ____

REFERENCES
Available upon Request

- **Employment.** If you have considerable work experience, you might call this section *Professional Experience* or *Employment History*. List only paid work, including full-time, part-time, work-study, and summer jobs. List jobs in chronological order, starting with the most recent. Include your position title, name of the business or organization, the address, and dates you worked there. Use action verbs to indicate what you did and what you accomplished there.
- **Professional Memberships.** Do you belong to an organization, such as the Student Dietetic Association, National Education Association, or the American Association of Family and Consumer Sciences? If the professional organization is pertinent to your career objective, list the membership and membership dates. Always provide the full names of organizations rather than acronyms.
- **Campus Activities.** List leadership positions held and dates of involvement. Specify conferences and seminars attended if they relate to your professional goals.
- **Licenses or Certifications.** Give appropriate titles and dates received or anticipated.
- **Publications and/or Presentations.** Use a standard bibliographic style for these entries, listing all coauthors.
- **Interests and Hobbies.** List items that are related to your field or are memorable because they are unusual.
- **References.** Potential employers generally want to contact people who know you and your work. You need three to five references, only one of which can be a personal reference (labeled as that). Other references may be employers, supervisors, professors, and/or coworkers. Before listing individuals as references, ask their permission. Most would appreciate having a copy of your résumé to use as a guide in providing verbal and written recommendations. It's also helpful to inform them of the type of job you are seeking so they may tailor references to that specific position.

You can handle information about references in several ways. You could attach a separate piece of paper to your résumé giving the name, position, and complete contact information for each reference. An alternative is to state "Available upon request" in the *References* section. When requested, supply the paper listing them. Often you can also place letters of recommendation and reference contact information on file at your university's career center.

Additional tips for writing résumés can be found in *Figure 26-4* on page 361.

❋ *Submitting Your Résumé Online*

In addition to sending a paper copy of your résumé with a cover letter to a potential employer, submitting a résumé electronically is often acceptable or preferred. This is especially true of job openings listed on the Internet. To check your transmission, send yourself a copy as well. If you are asked to submit information on an employer's website, you may be able to "cut and paste" from your current résumé to save time and ensure accuracy.

Many large employers keep résumés in a database. When a job opening occurs, possible candidates' résumés can be called up by searching for key words. Make sure your résumé includes terms common to the position you are seeking.

To accommodate this type of search, an employer may require you use a specific format for your résumé. It's important that you read the employer's guidelines carefully. Many large employers require *scannable résumés*—white paper, standard typeface, and crisp black type. Installing a new print cartridge will ensure accurate scanning. Don't use graphics or italic type and don't fold the résumé. If you are asked for an interview, you may give the interviewer a copy of your conventional résumé.

❋ Cover Letter

A cover letter, sometimes called a letter of application, is a business letter sent when you know of an actual job opening. It serves primarily as an introduction and a request for an interview. Without repeating verbatim what's in your résumé, the cover letter highlights your skills and background experiences that relate to the organization or the position you are seeking. A copy of your résumé should accompany your letter of application.

Figure 26-4

RÉSUMÉ WRITING TIPS

DO	DON'T
• Do limit your résumé to one page if possible. Don't exceed two pages. If the second page uses less than one-third of the sheet, try to reformat and rework items to fit on one sheet.	• Don't include personal data such as age, marital status, or number of children unless the information directly relates to job responsibilities. It is illegal for employers to require such information.
• Do use a letter-quality or laser printer and good quality paper. Light buff, gray, pale blue, or other conservative color paper may stand out from other résumés but not look too "flashy."	• Don't use colored paper, pictures, or graphics for a scannable résumé.
• Do devote the most space to your strong areas, whether they be education, professional development, employment experience, or college activities.	• Don't use abbreviations, such as B.S. for a Bachelor of Science degree.
• Do list entries in each category in reverse chronological order with the most recent experience first.	• Don't list an experience more than once.
• Do enter items in each entry in the same order under a category. For instance, if you enter the institution, location, degree and then the date earned in one entry, use the same order in the next entry.	• Don't have any grammatical, punctuation, spelling, or word-processing errors. Your résumé must be perfect.
• Do be consistent in punctuation, such as in using commas at the ends of series and in using two-letter state abbreviations.	• Don't use a small type that's hard to read. Use larger type for headings.
	• Don't have the page so full that there is little "white" or free space. Leave top, bottom, and side margins.

Your cover letter is much more powerful when it's written specifically to target the particular organization or position sought. Whenever possible, address your letter to an individual within the organization rather than "To Whom It May Concern." Resources for researching names of individuals within large and small national and local organizations may be available at your school's career center. The Internet offers some of this information, too. Also research the appropriate title (e.g., Superintendent of Schools, Human Resources Director, or Supervisor of Dietary Services). It's acceptable to call the school, firm, or organization to obtain the name, correct spelling, and title of the contact.

Similar letters, called letters of inquiry, can be sent to potential employers to ask whether any job openings exist. Briefly describe your background for the type of job you are seeking, request an application form, and enclose your résumé.

Remember that the cover letter is the first piece of information about you that a potential employer sees. Be direct about why you are writing and specific about what you can offer, but say it clearly and concisely. As with a résumé, be prepared to substantiate any information you include in the letter. Don't attempt to oversell with exaggerated claims. If possible, have someone knowledgeable about your field read over your letter for its impact, tone, content, and grammar. *Figure 26-5* on page 362 offers a suggested framework for a cover letter. Here are some additional guidelines:

• Follow a standard business format. The most commonly used format is the full-blocked style in which every line begins flush with the left margin.

- Follow the name of the person you are writing to with a colon, not a comma, as in "Dear Mr. Jones:"
- Check your grammar, spelling, and punctuation. An error in your cover letter may disqualify you from consideration.
- Limit your letter to one page.
- Avoid one-sentence paragraphs.
- Make each letter sound individual rather than like a form letter.
- Avoid overusing "I" or any other single word.
- Use high quality paper, preferably the same paper you used for your résumé.
- Close with "Sincerely" followed by a comma. Input your name four lines below this, then sign the letter exactly as you typed your name.

Keep a copy of each letter you send. Make notes on the letter, detailing any additional contacts between you and the recipient. It's confusing to receive a reply from a firm, particularly a request for an interview, and not remember when or if you sent a cover letter and résumé or what you said.

❋ Developing a Professional Portfolio

A professional portfolio is not required for a job search, but a well-prepared one can be a real asset in finding a position. A portfolio includes samples of your work that you have carefully selected and refined to highlight your skills and knowledge. The samples are assembled in a binder, folder, or other device that allows for a simple, attractive, and well-organized presentation.

Portfolios are generally shown to potential employers during the interview process. You may be asked to submit a portfolio to an admissions committee when applying for some educational programs. Some states require completion of a portfolio before you can apply for a teaching license.

Figure 26-5
SUGGESTED FRAMEWORK FOR A COVER LETTER

Your address

Today's date

Ms. ____ ____, Superintendent
Company or School Name
1300 State Street
Any City, XX 00000

Dear Ms. ____:

The opening paragraph should **arouse interest**. Be direct. Be clear about the position or type of position you are seeking. Is this an inquiry or a formal application for a specific job? Indicate how you found out about the position or organization and why you're interested.

Your middle paragraph(s) should **communicate precisely what you have to offer the employer**. As much as possible, select details and skills from past experiences that relate to the organization or position. Avoid vague statements, and back up your claims with specific examples. As a rule, cover letters **do not exceed one page**, so you need to get to the point quickly and state your case concisely. Connect your background as closely as possible to the particular position for which you are applying to demonstrate a good fit. Express your enthusiasm for the position.

In closing, seek to **elicit a response** from the employer. Ask for the opportunity to discuss your qualifications further in an interview. Indicate you will follow up within the next week or two. Tell where you can be reached in the meantime by providing a reliable phone number and/or e-mail address.

Sincerely,

(Sign your name just as typed)

Your full name typed

Like résumés, portfolios can be submitted electronically. If this format is used, you could use a digital camera to take photos of actual products in your portfolio. Using this approach shows your technological skills. However, make certain that the potential employer has equipment that will accept this material from your computer.

If you have kept copies of your best work during your educational and work experiences, you will have many items to choose from for inclusion. This book includes ideas for portfolio materials at the end of each chapter.

Select examples that best demonstrate the knowledge and skills needed for the job you are seeking. Check each item for any potential improvements. Limit the number of samples you include. In final form, your portfolio contents, like your résumé, must be attractive, letter-perfect, and well-organized. A three-ring binder with plastic cover sheets, pocket inserts, and tabbed dividers works well for many types of portfolios. You can vary your portfolio's contents for different types of jobs.

✳ *Portfolio Sections*

A portfolio is as individualized as a résumé. Although some universities, internship sites, school districts, and employers may specify contents to be included in a portfolio, the particular samples you choose to submit are entirely up to you. In many situations the categories of materials submitted are also your choice, though the items at the top of the following list are almost always included:

• Table of contents
• Résumé
• Letter of introduction, statement of purpose, and/or philosophy summary
• Letters of recommendation, if available
• Copies of professional certificates or licenses
• University transcript
• Results from tests, such as PRAXIS, the National Teacher's Exam, the Graduate Record Exam, or the Registration Exam for Dietitians
• Documentation of effective work, paid or volunteer, including letters of appreciation and labeled photographs

• Information on internship, student teaching, and field experiences, including a reflection paper, self-evaluation, labeled pictures, and the cooperating teacher's and supervisor's recommendations and evaluations
• Samples of work, such as unit and lesson plans, educational games, original case studies, and photos of displays, exhibits, and activities
• Evidence of communication skills, such as brochures, newsletters, and professional correspondence
• Extra copies of your résumé
• Videotape of you teaching, giving a professional presentation, or counseling clients. This gives concrete evidence of your teaching style and skills. If privacy issues are involved, as in a counseling session, record from an angle that hides the client's identity.

Your portfolio should present you in the best possible and most professional manner. Take the time to prepare it well. It's also helpful to ask others for feedback on your portfolio before you actually use it.

✳ Interviewing

If you are invited for an interview, you are being considered for a job. However, how well the interview goes will determine whether you are still in the running. Often two or more rounds of interviews are held to narrow the field of applicants down to the final person. The two most common stages are screening interviews and "on-site" or follow-up interviews.

• **Screening Interviews.** Screening interviews determine which candidates will be considered more closely. First impressions are crucial in a screening interview because the employer is trying to determine if you will fit into the organization. Interviewers who visit campuses conduct this type of interview. So do companies or organizations when there are a large number of applicants or the position is especially important. Remember, you are also trying to determine if this organization is right for you. Listen and ask questions so you can make this determination.

- **On-Site Interviews.** An on-site interview is often the second interview. The suggestions given for screening interviews also apply here. In the on-site interview, you may meet with several people, including potential coworkers, advisory council representatives, and board members. Today, it's not uncommon for a job seeker to go through repeated interviews for the same position. Sometimes a committee of people interviews candidates.

✳ *Preparing Well*

Preparation is the key to any successful interview. If you are well prepared, you are more likely to present a professional image and are less likely to get flustered by questions. Based on your résumé, the interviewer has already decided that you meet certain qualifications. The interview provides additional details about your experiences and personality and shows the employer what you can contribute. Some preparation steps can take place well before you start applying for jobs. Others must wait until an interview is scheduled.

Interviewers ask many types of questions, but most have common themes. You will be more at ease and articulate if you have thought through and practiced answers to typical questions. *Figure 26-6* on page 365 gives common interview questions within general categories. What responses would you give to the following situations and questions?

- Describe a situation when you had to think on your feet to get yourself out of a difficult situation.
- Give a specific example of a time when you used good judgment and logic in solving a problem.
- What would you do in this situation . . . ?
- Describe a situation that required a number of things to be done at the same time. How did you handle it? What was the result?
- Give an example of an important goal you set in the past and tell about your success in reaching it.

- Give an example of a time you had to work with someone who was difficult to get along with. Why was this person difficult? How did you handle the situation?
- Describe anonymously the most difficult interpersonal situation you have had with a professor, supervisor, supervisee, or colleague. How did you handle it? Why?
- How would you handle a situation in which your supervisor asked you to do something that wasn't consistent with your professional judgment?

Be prepared to discuss not only why you are the best candidate, but also how your skills, strengths, and abilities are right for this position. Provide examples from previous employment, volunteer work, and/or activities to exemplify your skills. Also be prepared to discuss your weaknesses or lack of experience. Present weaknesses in a positive light and indicate how you are improving. If the question is about an area of inexperience, discuss similar experiences you have had, particularly experiences that required similar skills. Advance preparation will enable you to present yourself favorably in such situations and illustrate how you are working to overcome the weakness.

Once you have an interview scheduled or know that one is likely, research the potential employer. Try to learn as much as possible about the company, school, or organization and the specific job. Discuss the organization and this particular position with anyone you know who might have insights. Also, check the Internet for information from or about the employer. With this knowledge you can target your comments during the interview specifically to the position and the organization. It will show you were interested enough to do your homework. The information will also help you formulate questions to ask the interviewer. Good questions show your enthusiasm for and understanding of the position.

It's advisable not to bring up salary, at least until the latter part of the interview. In most schools, teacher salaries are preset. If you are asked, "What salary are you anticipating?" state a range. If you have prepared well, you will know an appropriate range to give.

Figure 26-6

COMMON INTERVIEW QUESTIONS

Personal Assessment and Career Direction

1. What goals, other than those related to your career, have you set for yourself for the next ten years?
2. What are the most important rewards you anticipate in your career?
3. Why did you choose this career?
4. What are your greatest strengths and weaknesses?
5. How would you describe yourself?
6. How would a friend or professor who knows you well describe you?
7. What motivates you to put forth your greatest effort?
8. Why should I hire you?
9. What qualifications do you have to help you be successful in this career field/position/organization?
10. How do you work under pressure?
11. In what part-time or summer jobs have you been most interested? Why?
12. How would you describe the ideal job for you following graduation?
13. What two or three things are most important to you in your career?
14. How creative are you? What are some examples of your creativity in your field?
15. How do you define success? According to this definition, how successful are you?

Academic Assessment

1. How has your college experience prepared you for this career?
2. Describe your most fulfilling college experience.

3. Did you work while you were going to school? If so, what kind of work?
4. Why did you select your college or university?
5. What college subjects did you like best/least? Why?
6. How would you plan your academic study differently if you could?

Knowledge of the Employer

1. What do you know about this organization? Where did you find this information?
2. What contributions can you make to this organization?
3. If you were hiring a graduate for this position, what qualities would you look for?
4. Why did you decide to seek a position here?
5. How did you get along with your college professors? Classmates?
6. You seem overqualified for this position. Are you?
7. What is the hardest job you have ever performed?
8. Are you opposed to drug testing? Why or why not?

Other Interests and Experiences

1. What two or three accomplishments have given you the most satisfaction? Why?
2. What is a major problem you have encountered and how did you deal with it?
3. What have you learned from your mistakes?

Avoiding Legal Entanglements

Once you have your new job, you will be working with a variety of people in various settings. Not everyone will think and act the way you do. Some will be less tolerant; some less ethical. Their standards may not match yours, and you may even feel that your standards are being compromised by the actions of your colleagues. Professionalism on your part is extremely important.

You will want to be proactive in your interactions with others—whether students, clients, or colleagues—to avoid situations where others might feel you have acted illegally, unethically, or without sufficient care. Even an unfounded accusation can seriously damage your reputation. If you find yourself in a difficult situation or see a potential problem brewing, it's wise to keep careful notes and to document your actions and the actions of others. Within your educational setting, learn the channels that you need to go through to report behaviors that concern you.

✳ Being Proactive

The following list gives examples of potential problems and suggests positive actions you can take as an educator to prevent small problems from mushrooming into big ones or even possible legal action. This list is not inclusive. However, it should prompt you to think about situations you might face and how you can take positive action to prevent problems.

- **Classroom safety.** Whenever an individual is under age 18 and is in your educational environment, you are legally responsible for that learner's well-being and safety. Never leave a group or class of young people alone. Call upon another adult to assist you and watch the group if you must leave the immediate area. See pages 182-184 for additional information on an educator's responsibilities regarding the safety of learners.
- **Content restrictions.** There may be some restrictions on the concepts you can include in your teaching. Check before you plan your curriculum. Your advisory council, administrators, or School Board may have specific stipulations about topics that must and may not be covered. Seek advice on how to handle any potentially controversial topics that you know are included in your curriculum.
- **Diversity.** You will deal with a variety of individuals representing diversity in gender, race, culture, age, background, religion, and ability. All clients, learners, and coworkers must be treated equally under the law. Choose your actions and words so they could never be perceived as discriminatory toward any particular group or individual.
- **Harassment.** Be sure you and others in your educational setting are never perceived as harassing an individual or group. *Harassment* is reoccuring behavior that makes an individual feel uncomfortable. Never put yourself in a position where you might be accused of harassment. Watch what you say and do, especially in terms of physical contact with your learners.
- **Special needs.** You may be working with physically, emotionally, or mentally challenged individuals and involved with the development and implementation of their Individualized Educational Plans (IEPs). As discussed in Chapter 19, it's your legal responsibility to help make certain that the conditions and stipulations of an IEP

are upheld. By law, other accommodations must also be made for those designated as disabled. Find out your responsibilities.
- **Abuse.** Learners may come to your setting from a variety of abusive situations. Some may be abusers themselves. Learn what contributes to physical, mental, and emotional abuse and be alert for possible symptoms. Legally you must report any behavior or symptom you believe is evidence of abuse. A learner could be in a life-threatening situation. Determine to whom you need to make reports. In some cases you may report directly to a community agency or hotline. Follow through immediately.
- **Behavioral changes.** In general, individuals tend to have their own "normal" pattern of behavior. When you notice odd, unusual, or particularly antisocial behaviors by learners, make note of these. If the pattern continues, report what you see. Documenting specific incidents and examples is helpful. If a person's behavior is particularly bizarre or threatening, take immediate action. Don't worry about being overly cautious. Lives can be saved.
- **Confidentiality.** If you really "connect" with your learners, they will start to share and disclose information to you. They will also seek advice and may consult with you on very personal issues. Sometimes the parents of your learners will depend on you for support, advice, and counsel. You must maintain confidentiality. This is a sign of a professional. The only exceptions are if you have the person's permission to speak with others or when you feel the life and/or safety of the individual is at risk. Then you must report the information to the appropriate person or agency. You will want to alert the person you are counseling as to why you find it necessary to share this information with someone else. At the same time, recognize your limitations. Remember that you aren't a trained counselor. It's important to seek input on solving problems. Often this can be done without disclosing the name of the person you are helping. Encourage the person in need to seek additional help. Suggest sources of help and offer to assist the individual in making the connection.

- **Off-site activities.** You may be teaching in a situation where the learners participate in community work experiences or activities such as service learning. In most cases, you need to have written agreements signed by students, their parents, the school or educational agency, and the community organization where your learners' services are being utilized. Work with your school or organization to make certain that issues of liability are covered. Your institution may also have policies and paperwork in place for field trips. Also investigate issues regarding liability if you give students rides. Special insurance requirements may need to be met. Check whether your personal insurance covers you if you transport learners as part of your job.
- **Copyright.** Become familiar with the copyright laws. Know what you can legally copy and reproduce in terms of print and electronic materials.
- **The Internet.** Find out what your institution's policies are regarding the Internet. Be clear to your learners about your personal rules, as well as the institutional guidelines. Clearly explain plagiarism as it relates to reports, visuals, and other assignments. Require learners to document their sources. Pay particular attention to the accuracy of information from the Web.

These are just a few situations and circumstances you might face that could lead to questions of liability. Being aware of these should help prevent problems. One of your first tasks as a new professional will be to ask questions about procedures and potential problems. Know the policies and act in accordance with them.

 Professional Involvement

If there's one word that will describe your life as a professional, it is *change*. The individuals, families, organizations, and communities within society are changing faster than ever before. Information is multiplying at a phenomenal rate and technology is constantly evolving. Since you will be on the front lines helping people solve real problems, you must be aware of the latest developments in various facets of your field.

It will be easier to keep up to date and acquire the resources you need to do your job if you become professionally involved now. You should then continue this involvement throughout your career.

✳ Types of Professional Involvement

There are many different levels and types of professional involvement. Your contributions can be of short- or long-term duration. Your roles can be at the local, state, regional, national, or international levels. You can be a leader or a follower—both are needed. Your involvement may change over the course of your career. The important thing is to get involved. You *do* have a contribution to make. Here are some ways to be professionally involved:

- Read and/or react to professional journal articles, newsletters, and position statements.
- Network formally or informally with other educators in your field and related fields.
- Volunteer to help with projects sponsored by professional organizations.
- Be an officer and serve on committees in state, regional, and/or national professional organizations.
- Contribute articles to professional publications.
- Attend and/or give presentations at state, regional, or national meetings.
- Represent your profession at community, state, or national events of organizations with common interests.
- Lobby for the interests of your organization and your learners with legislators and decision makers.
- Prepare media releases to let others know the work of your profession.
- Distribute literature related to your profession.
- Serve as a peer reviewer or the editor of journals, newsletters, and other publications.

✳ Professional Organizations

As a new professional, you will have to carefully choose which organization(s) to join. Determine which will give you the most information, resources, and support for your career development. You will want to consider the cost of membership dues. Some professional organizations give discounted student rates and offer student members a discount on their first year's dues as a new professional.

Consult with your professors to find out which professional organizations are affiliated with your field. Talk to people who are already members. Visit the organizations' websites and read about their philosophy, mission, and membership requirements.

Some organizations, such as the American Association of Family and Consumer Sciences (AAFCS) and the Association of Career and Technical Education (ACTE), serve as umbrella organizations for a wide variety of professionals in an academic area. AAFCS members represent all facets of the Family and Consumer Sciences field, from nutrition to housing to fashion to gerontology. ACTE is comprised of vocational educators in agriculture, business, and family and consumer sciences, to name a few. Other professional associations, such as the American Dietetic Association (ADA) and the National Council on Family Relations (NCFR) serve professionals in a very specific aspect of their field. You may want to join a broad group, as well as a group serving your specialization. There are professional groups for health, family and consumer sciences, and vocational educators. Find the ones that seem the most appropriate for you.

✳ Benefits of Belonging

There's an array of benefits associated with belonging to professional organizations. Reasons for participating include:

- **Networking.** Through the organization you have opportunities to connect with others in similar situations. You can talk about common challenges and possible solutions. You can share information, techniques, ideas, and support. Your professional network becomes an invaluable resource, both personally and in your work.
- **Current information.** You will receive information about what's going on at the state and national levels in your organization. Many professional organizations provide state and national affiliations as a part of your membership dues. You will receive publications focusing on issues at the state and national levels. In addition, most professional organizations publish journals that focus on the most recent trends and developments in the field. Research findings and success stories are highlighted and give you ideas.
- **Visibility and legislative advocacy.** A portion of your dues goes for increased media visibility for your field and legislative action. There is strength in numbers when representatives of your group lobby for various laws and funding or seek media coverage.
- **Funding opportunities.** Some professional organizations provide members with opportunities for financial help through fellowships for graduate work, money for grant proposals, or funds for special projects.
- **Certification and licensure.** Professional organizations are often responsible for various certifications and licenses needed for professional advancement. In order to access these, you need to be a member of the organization.
- **Insurance discounts.** Some professional organizations offer discounted insurance programs. Professional liability insurance may be one option.
- **Job banks.** Listings of employment opportunities are often maintained by organizations. Access may be limited to members.
- **Meetings and conventions.** Opportunities are available to attend annual meetings, conventions, and special activities. Members usually receive special meeting rates and other advantages unavailable to nonmembers. Annual meetings provide an opportunity to access the latest information and resources.
- **Leadership opportunities.** You can serve on a committee or as a state or national officer. You will be able to choose the opportunities that are right for you to further develop leadership skills.

- **Career development opportunities.** As a member of a professional organization, others get to know you and the skills you have to offer. They may recommend you for opportunities that you may not have otherwise.
- **Collaboration.** As a part of an organization, you are more likely to form collaborative groups to accomplish the mission of your profession or specific goals. You will find yourself working more closely with both those within and those outside your special interest area. More can be accomplished by a group of individuals working together, plus it's more enjoyable working toward goals with others.
- **Honors and awards.** Professional organizations recognize the outstanding achievement of their members. Such awards can be an important addition to your portfolio and boost the visibility of your program.

There are many benefits to joining and participating. Make a commitment to become an active professional association member. You will not regret this decision. Your professional colleagues need you and you need them.

✳ Certifications, Credentials, and Licensures

Throughout your career, there will be certain professional requirements that you will have to meet. Your professional involvement will help you stay abreast of how those requirements change over time.

Depending on your field, you may need a specific certification or licensure to get a job. For example, specific credentials are required of dietitians and public school teachers. To research national or specific state requirements, use the Internet or call the appropriate agency in that state. As a future teacher, you will want to contact the Department of Education in the state or states where you want to teach to determine test requirements. In some cases, such as to become a registered dietitian, there are national criteria to be met and tests to be taken. Your professors, campus career center, and professional organizations can all help you determine requirements for your field.

In addition to required licensures, there may be some optional certifications or credentials that you will want to pursue. These designations may allow you to be considered for career opportunities and advancements. These types of certifications or credentials often require you to accumulate development activities over a certain time period. You need to provide documentation as requested to maintain your status. In some cases, such as that of a Certified Diabetes Educator, you will need to take an exam periodically to exhibit your current knowledge.

 ## Lifelong Learning

To be a top-notch educator, you must find ways to keep up with the changes in your field and in society. Here are some strategies that you will want to incorporate into your lifestyle to become a lifelong learner:

- Read, read, read! Make time to read a daily newspaper, news magazines, professional journals, contemporary magazines, and newsletters published by various organizations.
- Attend meetings, seminars, and public hearings.
- Follow state and national legislation that affects your program and profession. Make your positions known to legislators.
- Take courses. Consider graduate study. It will provide greater depth of understanding and prepare you to "move up the ladder." It may widen your range of skills and abilities for broader applications, again to advance or take your career in a new direction. Distance learning expands the opportunities open to you.
- Talk with others within and outside your field. Converse with your clientele. They will help you to keep up to date on their needs.
- Use the Internet as an information source, but check the accuracy of the information before dispensing it to others.

It's not too early to plan for lifelong learning. To the extent that you make this a part of your life, you will be an effective, creative educator. Your learning has only just begun!

Building Your Professional Portfolio

Finding Job Opportunities. Use at least four different techniques for locating information about job openings. Determine which are most useful for your job objectives. How could you utilize them more fully?

Preparing for an Interview. Prepare answers to the interview questions given in this chapter that you would find most difficult to answer. Also develop some situational questions related to your professional job goal. Decide how you would answer them effectively.

Polishing Your Portfolio. Choose the items that you will include in your professional portfolio for your primary job choice. Make any final changes. Add a table of contents and arrange for a critique of the portfolio. Use the feedback to finalize your portfolio.

Lifelong Learning. Interview professionals in your field to find out how they keep updated. Develop a plan for your continued learning in the next five to ten years.